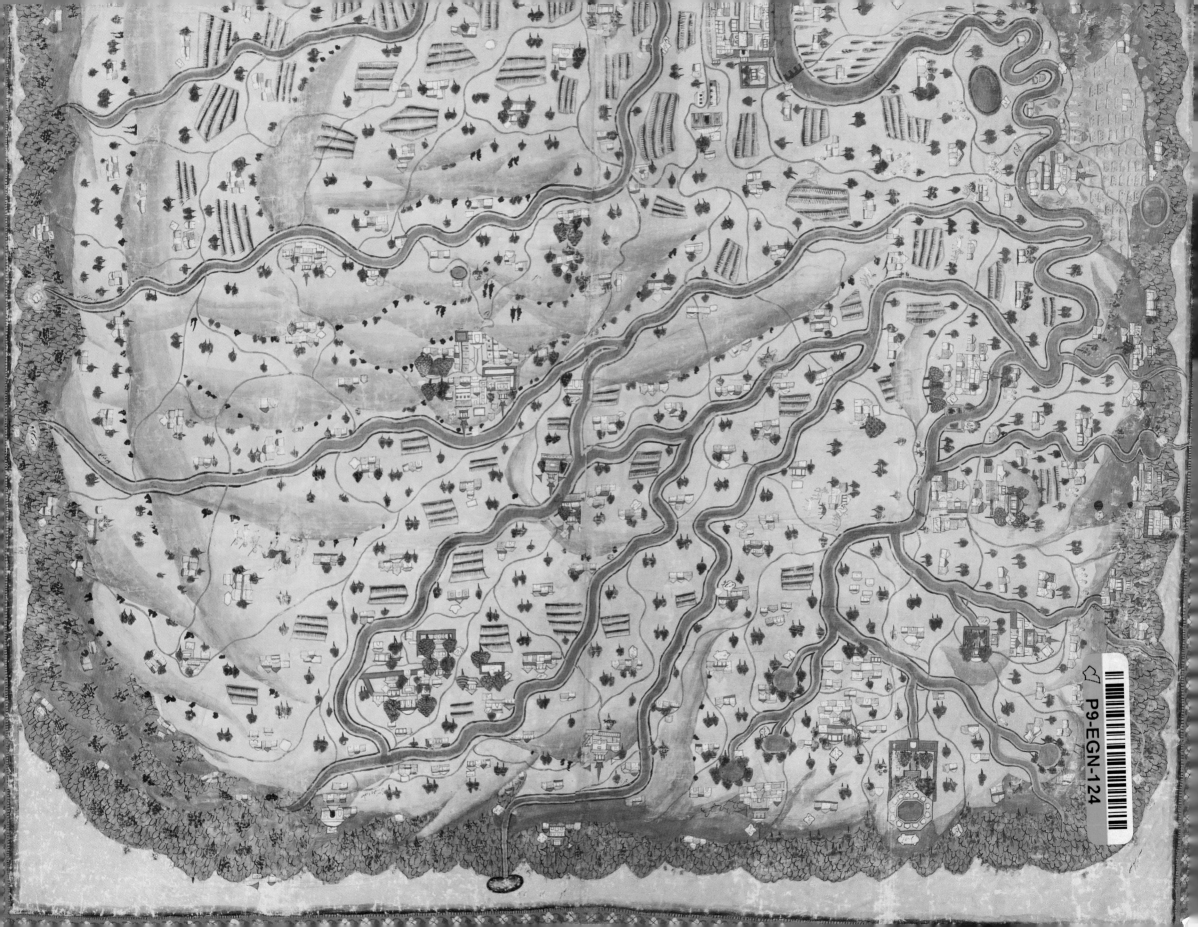

CARTOGRAPHIA

Vincent Virga
and the Library of Congress

Introduction by Ronald E. Grim
Afterword by James H. Billington,
The Librarian of Congress

LITTLE, BROWN AND COMPANY
New York   Boston   London

CARTOGRAPHIA

Mapping Civilizations

To the memory of my dear friends

Susan Sontag and Victoria de los Angeles,

spiritual cartographers,

and to James McCourt, my *carte de tendre*

LITTLE, BROWN AND COMPANY
Hachette Book Group USA
237 Park Avenue, New York, NY 10017
Visit our Web site at www.HachetteBookGroupUSA.com

For the Library of Congress:
W. Ralph Eubanks, Director of Publishing
Margaret E. Wagner, Project Coordinator
Aimee S. Hess and Wilson McBee, Editorial Assistants
Jesse Rhodes, Editorial Intern
Visit our Web site at www.loc.gov

First Edition: October 2007
Second Printing, 2008

CASEWRAP: Detail from Plate 143, *Waldseemüller Map of the World*. ENDPAPERS: Detail from Plate 71, *Pictorial Map on Cloth of the Vale of Kashmir Showing Srinagar in Detail*. PAGE i: Claudius Ptolemy, from a manuscript of the *Cosmography*, 1472. By permission of the Biblioteca Apostolica Vaticana (Codex Urb. lat. 277, fol. 3r). PAGES ii–iii: Detail from Plate 142, *Ruysch Map of the Known World*, 1507. PAGES iv–v: Detail from Plate 119, *A Map of the Arctic Circle*, and spot details from Plates 19, 142, 157.

Library of Congress Cataloging-in-Publication Data
Virga, Vincent.
Cartographia / Vincent Virga and the Library of Congress.
   p.   cm.
Includes bibliographical references.
ISBN 978-0-316-99766-9 (hardcover)
1. Cartography — History. 2. Cartography — Social aspects.
I. Library of Congress. II. Title.
GA203.V57 2006
912 — dc22
                                                2005029047

IMAGO

Design by Laura Lindgren

PRINTED IN SINGAPORE

CONTENTS

Introduction: *Theater of the World* 1

Prologue 5

THE MEDITERRANEAN WORLD

THE THREE-PART WORLD

THE FOURTH PART: THE AMERICAS

THE FIFTH PART: OCEANIA AND ANTARCTICA

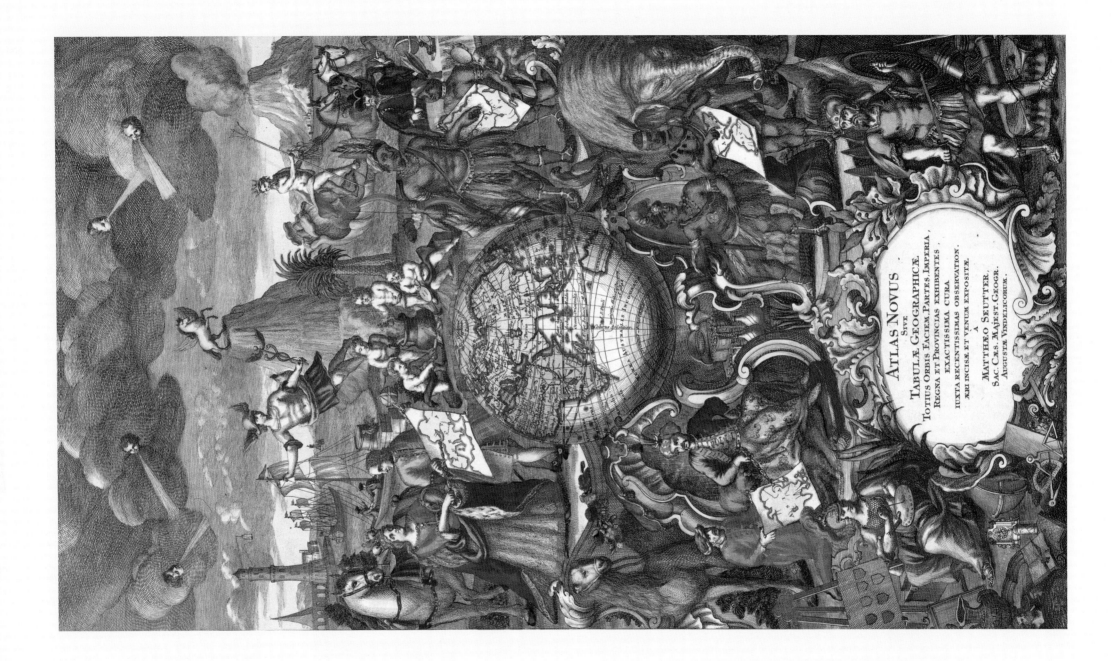

INTRODUCTION

THEATER OF THE WORLD

On the old highway maps of America, the main routes were red and the back roads blue. Now even the colors are changing. But in those brevities just before dawn and a little after dark—times neither day nor night—the old roads return to the sky some of its color. Then, in truth, they cast a mysterious shadow of blue, and it's that time when the pull of the blue highway is strongest, when the open road is a beckoning, a strangeness, a place where a man can lose himself.

—William Least Heat-Moon, *Blue Highways*

❈

He does smile his face into more lines than is in the new map with the augmentation of the Indies.

—Malvolio, in Shakespeare's *Twelfth Night*

A

s William Least Heat-Moon revealed in his travels across America in *Blue Highways: A Journey into America*, a map can be more than a guide to find one's route from one point to another. Through his attraction to the scenic blue highways he found on a road map, Least Heat-Moon discovered an America where he could lose himself. He also learned that a map can be a storyteller, not only about the places documented on the map but also about the people who populate those places.

Like Least Heat-Moon's blue highways, the maps in the pages of *Cartographia* not only tell the story but themselves become the story. Maps, atlases, and related images serve as primary documents on a continent-by-continent exploration of the world. As each chapter traces the broad sweep of human history, the maps center on individual but representative images that illustrate major themes in the development of significant cultures and political empires. The maps are examined not only as a record of a specific place at a particular time but also as documents that have a story to tell, both about how and why the maps were created and about what the maps have to say regarding the culture in which they were created.

Cartographia begins by exploring the remnants of maps that have survived from the ancient civilizations that surrounded the Mediterranean Sea, setting the stage and establishing the base of

geographical knowledge that was available to Abraham Ortelius and his sixteenth-century contemporaries as they entered a new era of gathering and disseminating geographic knowledge. These early geographers made not only Europe but also the other continents—the eastern parts of Asia, the southern parts of Africa, and the newly "discovered" Americas—part of Europeans' geographical consciousness.

Ortelius's *Theatrum Orbis Terrarum* is one of the earliest landmarks in the history of cartography and world geography. First published in Latin in 1570 in Antwerp (when Shakespeare was six years old), Ortelius's map book was subsequently translated into six other languages—German, Dutch, French, Spanish, Italian, and English. Cartographically it is a landmark because it is recognized as the first modern atlas. This was the first time that a set of maps contemporary to the time of publication was designed, drawn, and engraved in a coherent style with the intention of publishing them in a bound book. Geographically it was important because it represents one of the first attempts to compile a composite treatise on the geographical knowledge of the world, incorporating the new geographical data that was becoming available to Europeans during the sixteenth century.

But Ortelius's *Theatrum Orbis Terrarum* also represents a significant cultural development: the merger of two very important

PLATE 1. *Seutter's Atlas Novus*. The extraordinary art of the great atlas makers is exemplified by their frontispieces.

ABOVE: Detail from p. 138.

these icons highlight the theoretical basis of *Cartographia*—that maps are powerful storytellers, providing graphic documentation of human activity as it unfolded on the planet Earth.

Ortelius selected the title *Theatrum Orbis Terrarum*, meaning Theater of the World, possibly reflecting a custom in European Renaissance cities, where the city fathers staged pageants and parades with costumed figures representing the countries of the world. Applying the word "theater" to his book of maps, Ortelius suggests that it too was a microcosm representing the diverse parts of the world in a similar fashion. The decorative elements of the title page use an architectural framework, echoing the proscenium arch of the theater's stage. This massive structure is adorned with four female figures personifying the continents—civilized Europe at the top, ruling over the rest of the world, exotic Asia and Africa on the supporting pillars, and the savage Americas at the base, portrayed as cannibals. There is also a fifth incomplete figure, a truncated bust next to the Americas, representing Magellanica (Tierra del Fuego), or the unknown lands that were not yet explored. Such iconography epitomized the Europeans' worldview at that time, as well as the contents of the atlas. While the atlas included maps of the individual continents, the preponderance of the maps were of European countries and regions.

Applying the image of theater to *Cartographia* implies that the physical earth provides a stage for human action. It also allows the introduction of a concept from human or cultural geography: the cultural landscape. The action of the play's story unfolds amid an array of appropriate props and backdrops that enhance the setting. The action is cumulative, building on previous actions within the confines of the setting, until the play's story is told and the curtain falls. Similarly, human activity unfolds within the confines of a physical setting or landscape. As each new generation and culture enters that setting, there are human modifications to it—the addition of roads, houses, fields, towns, place names, and political boundaries. These changes are cumulative, building on the past, saving some elements and replacing others. These manifestations of culture (the totality of human activity) leave an imprint on the physical landscape. As successive peoples inhabit a particular geographical area, they leave behind layers of their cultural heritage. Fortunately maps become one of the primary sources for reading through the palimpsest created by these cultural landscapes.

Ortelius's personification of the continents implies the need for regionalization, a major device used by modern-day geographers to organize and generalize data. In other words, how will we divide up the earth to talk about it in a coherent and meaningful manner? Region, simply defined, refers to a geographic area that displays common characteristics. Regions can be large or small depending on the generality or specificity of the criteria defining the area. Regions can have precisely defined boundaries, such as a state or country designating a geographic area where inhabitants are governed by the same laws, or may have ill-defined boundaries that fade imperceptibly into a neighboring region. Over the years geographers have developed innumerable regional constructs, many of which have entered into common usage—the South, the West, the Great

historical processes during the Renaissance—the advent of the printing press and the dawn of the European age of discoveries and exploration. Using a technology that was not quite a hundred years old, Ortelius employed movable type and copper-engraved plates and melded text with a uniformly designed set of maps that brought together the known geographic information about Europe and neighboring lands, as well as the Europeans' recently acquired knowledge of the Americas, southern Africa, and southern and eastern Asia. Through this technological development, Ortelius's atlas captured a period of transition and uncertainty as European culture attempted to synthesize and reconcile the information about the discovery of newfound lands. Geographic concepts that had been commonly accepted during the Middle Ages, such as a "flat earth" and "three continents," were suddenly challenged.

This first "atlas" is also important, symbolically, for *Cartographia*, and provides a conceptual framework for its story. Both the title and the title page of Ortelius's compendium use textual and pictorial icons, which were well known to the European audience, to symbolize the contents of the book. Ortelius's atlas, first published in 1570, was reissued in more than thirty editions over the next forty years. The title page's iconography was introduced in the first edition and remained the same throughout all the editions. Likewise,

Plains, the Middle East, or the Far East. Most people have a general concept of what geographic area and what cultural traits help define these particular regions. But on the other hand, it will be almost impossible to get any two people to agree on the specific boundaries or the exact geographic extent of any one of these regions.

One of the regional constructs that geographers and educators have used most successfully over the years is the idea of "continents," particularly as an organizing concept when talking about the earth at its grossest or most general scale. Continents, representing the earth's major landmasses, were a tried-and-true teaching device from the age of European discoveries until the end of the nineteenth century and well into the twentieth century.

In the twentieth century, as geographers became more interested in the human role in shaping the face of the earth, the continental concept of classifying geographical knowledge became less relevant and less useful. The concept of continents, which is based on a physical attribute, namely large, easily identified landmasses surrounded by water, was increasingly questioned. Is Antarctica really a continent, or is it a series of islands joined only by a massive ice shield? Aren't Europe and Asia actually one landmass? Their boundary was an arbitrary convention rather than a line following a recognizable natural feature. Then, from the 1950s to the 1970s, as the detailed mapping of the ocean floors progressed, the theory of plate tectonics was confirmed, providing a more precise definition of continental plates which established the geological basis for our supposed continental landmasses.

Is there a better way of regionalizing geographic data at a global level? Certainly, and geographers have proposed numerous schemes, many of which are based on single themes or topics such as climate, vegetation, or economic activity. Another scheme, which takes into account the totality of human activity, is cultural realms. In this categorization the focus is on identifying large groups of people with similar cultures, as defined by religion, language families, economic activity, and predominant settlement patterns. In this context, the Americas are divided into an Anglo-speaking realm (basically north of the Rio Grande) and a Latin-speaking world to the south. Or an Arabic-Islamic world occupies northern Africa and southwestern Asia, while sub-Saharan Africa forms another unit. Such a conceptualization is not without its problems, however. It was certainly a valid categorization until the middle of the twentieth century; but as society moves into the new millennium and the computer age, and as the world becomes more urbanized, modernized, and homogenized, it is less meaningful.

Despite the limitations of a continental categorization, Cartographia uses a combination of continents and cultural realms as its organizational device. This traditional approach to world history and geography works because the cartographic record from the sixteenth to the twentieth century, which serves as the anchor for our journey through the world of maps, strongly supports it. Whereas the first chapter focuses on the Mediterranean world before the age of European discoveries and the Renaissance, the succeeding chapters deal with the individual continents—Europe, Africa, Asia, and the Americas. A fourth chapter deals with Ortelius's implied

fifth part of the world, the lands that were primarily discovered and explored in the eighteenth and nineteenth centuries—Australia, Antarctica, and the Pacific islands. However, throughout Cartographia, attention is paid to the major cultural realms represented in those areas, because the central point of our discussion is how maps help us read the ever-changing story of world civilization.

Ortelius's placement and portrayal of the continents on his title page, giving them superior and inferior positions on its architectural framework, suggests that there is a perspective or bias to the "story" he is about to present. A map by definition is a selective graphic representation, implying that the cartographer exercises a certain amount of judgment and bias, no matter how scientific the presentation purports to be. As in the case of Ortelius, the examination of this judgment and bias will guide the reader on a journey around the world through the maps presented in Cartographia. This examination will also lead the reader to find a beckoning, sometimes a strangeness, and always a place to lose oneself.

Ronald E. Grim, curator, retired,
Geography and Map Division,
Library of Congress

PLATE 3. Theatrum Orbis Terrarum *Title Page.* The title page from Ortelius's masterpiece.

PROLOGUE

A map is a social document serving many functions. It is a representation of knowledge, an archival device, a concordance of the world and its image. A map is a dream, an idea, an action, an emblem of human endeavor. It instigates adventures. Maps encompass the entirety of what is beheld. They are the result of holistic perception, of the fact that our eyes are constantly traveling. They are also an act of conscious remembering, for there can be no remembering without previous perception that is tied to places and landscapes. Our eyes have evolved into expert observers of landscape, the eyes of hunters and gatherers, of the hunted and the assembled. Careful perceptions of our surroundings have always been matters of life and death.

The subject of maps is fourfold: people, society, culture, and history. Each map is a set of visual clues revealing why it was made and how it was used. Each map expresses a social and political interest, of which there are many. Thus maps are acts of discernment.

Because they organize knowledge visually, maps are rooted in our visual culture. As cartographic historian Christian Jacob explains, "They share a set of codes—geometric, chromatic, figurative, aesthetic—with painting and drawing, book illustration, calligraphy, and architecture." Being works of art, they are uniquely human and reveal the collective values of a community. And as a primary source in the history of the imagination, they are a singular dimension of history. Yet these cultural landscapes have always been expendable: discarded for newer ones, shattered and burned in wars, destroyed for reasons of national security, decimated by time. This makes mapping civilizations an ongoing journey of discovery involving many diverse disciplines.

Mapping represents a spectacular development in human history. The intellectual process of transforming experience *in* space to abstraction *of* space is a revolution in modes of thinking. Humanity's collective history of mapping the whole known world can be paralleled with the child psychologist Jean Piaget's threefold develop-

mental theory of the individual. First, perceptions and representational abilities are not matched; only the simplest topographical relationships are presented, without regard for perspective or distances. Then an intellectual "realism" evolves, one that depicts everything known with burgeoning proportional relationships. And finally, a visual "realism" appears, advocating scientific calculations to achieve it. Mapping is arguably fundamental to humanity's cognitive makeup. It reveals the spiritual bonds between all the people on planet Earth.

The earliest picture maps, or graphic representations, often have text. Writing separates prehistoric, or "primitive," cultures from the historical, or "ancient." It was out of pictographs that Sumerian cuneiform writing developed. Viewing writing as a linear sequence of marks makes its communion with mapping instantly recognizable. (While reading a map, however, there is no starting point and no ending.) "Words," said the anthropologist Claude Lévi-Strauss, "are instruments that people are free to adapt to any use, provided they make clear their intentions." The same can be said of maps. Words make general images specific; the absence of words often leads to interesting speculations.

The cultural historian Fernand Braudel observes that an essential part of a civilization's character depends on "the constraints or advantages" of its geographical situation. He agrees with Napoleon's maxim that geography explains history because of the interaction of history and geography. Interestingly, however, the opportunities offered by geography are not always seized, a fact that helps us understand the social dynamics of particular groups. Our earliest maps, the first compositions in the encoded language of geography, played a leading role in recording the historical dramas of the past. Now they help us *see* in the present the distinctive, collective identities and the dynamics at play in some of the world's great civilizations.

THE MEDITERRANEAN WORLD

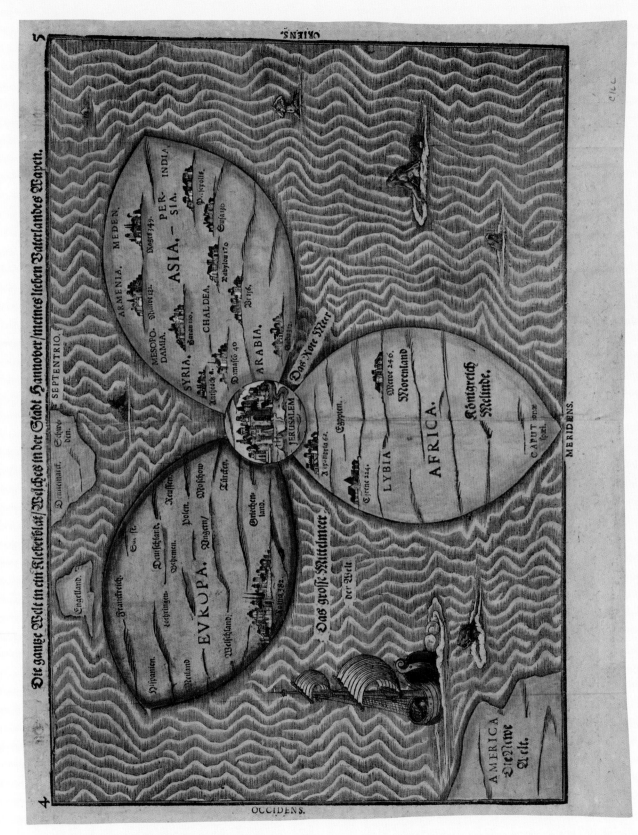

PLATE 5. *The Whole World in a Cloverleaf*. Made to edify Christians, this 1581 map has a cloverleaf representing the Old World continents.

OVERLEAF: Detail from p. 12.

He Mediterranean Sea is 2,200 miles long and 488 miles at its widest. *Medi-Terra-nea* (the sea in the middle of the earth) is the juncture of three landmasses. The Mediterranean world, the sea's known parts of the world, or three continents, overlap and intersect, is very like the shared area of a Venn diagram, which is made up of two or more overlapping circles. At this juncture three broad cultural landscapes intermingle, with many different ways of living and thinking. A fanciful map (Plate 5) from a 1581 book of travels in the Holy Land according to the Scriptures (*Itinerarium Sacrae Scripturae*), by Hanover's Heinrich Bunting, was made to edify Christians. It uses an elliptical cloverleaf, or Venn-like format, and each leaflet actually represents one of the three Old World continents—Europe, Asia, and Africa—to signify the Christian Trinity. (The Johnny-come-lately America is in the southwest corner of the map.) In place of the Mediterranean at the center, or overlap, is the city of Jerusalem, a fundamental symbol of Western culture for Bunting, a Christian theologian, but in reality a fundamental symbol for both Western and Eastern cultures. The historical struggle to dominate the Mediterranean world is neatly visualized by Bunting's religious commentary made in the language of maps. It is Map as Religion Eclipsing Culture.

The Mediterranean world is a multicultural hearth. It is the birthplace of myriad civilizations and many non-Christian religions. Unfortunately for us, there is little surviving map evidence

for the time period in which some of the most famous of these civilizations developed, though each group generally had a good understanding of geographical space as well as of how it fit into the cosmos. No other sea can equal the number of cultures that have emerged and collided on its shores, each with its own methods of seeing and encoding human experience in maps.

During their centuries of dominance in the region, the Romans labeled the Mediterranean *Mare Nostrum*, "our sea." Even this massive empire left us few maps. There was a famous marble one of Rome—the *Forma Urbis Romae*—depicting the entire city in outline ground plan 60 feet across and 45 feet high. Between the years 203 and 211, it was carved on marble slabs several inches thick. Today only 200 identified fragments, 500 unidentified, and 400 blank pieces remain. The fragments range from a few inches to 4 feet across, and some weigh over 150 pounds. Every street and every building's footprint was incised, a cartographic feat that has never been equaled. Every line is a wall; thus parallelograms with gaps in their borders are rooms with doors, small V's are staircases, and rectangles with round holes are porticos supported by columns. This massive masterpiece was displayed on the rear wall of a room in the Templum Pacis. It was an official plan made to facilitate the administration of Rome's fourteen districts, and the plan's architectural exactitude was a boon to the city's fire brigade.

The remains (Plate 6) constitute a heartbreaking metaphor for human frailty, lost knowledge, and our best modern-day attempts to map civilizations from bits and pieces of treasured remnants. We have the unreliable (and falsified) memories of Greek and Roman authors, and the myth-based accounts in the Bible, but little personal experience directly transmitted via early maps. The *Forma Urbis Romae* is Map as Fragmentary Evidence.

THE BABYLONIANS

The most seismic change in the behavior of the Mediterranean world's human population was the merging of isolated groups into large communities circa 5000 BCE and the ingenuity they demonstrated in order to survive. Multifunctional canals were an astounding accomplishment. They facilitated this merging, which is traced to the art of domesticating wild grains on a plain to the east of the Mediterranean known to the ancient Greeks as Mesopotamia

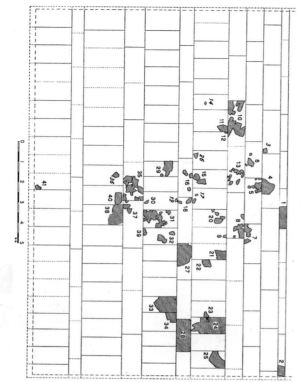

Posizione dei complessi e monumenti localizzati

PLATE 6. *Positioned Remains of the General Plan of the City of Rome*. Here, like pieces of the past, the known marble fragments of the immense *Forma Urbis Romae* have been placed in their proper spatial context.

writing, established banking practices, and had standard weights and measures, written contracts, and complex accounting systems that used the zero—as a placeholder, not the Hindu numerical symbol. Sumerians were the first to codify law, which we can easily understand when we study their canal system as they mapped it. Their legacy also includes the spoked wheel, the rudiments of astronomy, the foundation for astrology as a fortune-telling tool, and our twelve-month year and twenty-four-hour day. Stimulated by commerce with distant lands, this vital creative culture flourished on the life-sustaining water carried by the canals. As the Greek historian Herodotus (c. 484–425 BCE) would later write: "For all the Babylonian country…is cut up with canals. The greatest of these can carry boats." The lack of orientation on the map of Nippur's fields—the word *orient* originally meant "to arrange facing east"—suggests this tablet may be a fragment, since Sumerians recorded directions using the names of the appropriate winds.

Until 1800 BCE Nippur thrived as the center of an agricultural region and as the home of the national cult of Enlil, the chief god of the Mesopotamian pantheon. Nippur was a sacred city built around his temple, and much of the land on the map was royal or religious property. It is reported that Enlil possessed the Tablets of Destiny. They gave him power over the entire cosmos. The only surviving map with a comprehensive description of this cosmos, however, is from the Persian period, c. 600 BCE (Plate 7). It is Map as Belief System. It reveals the relationship between the temporal Babylonian empire and the eternal legendary regions beyond the encircling salt sea.

This map may have been the fabled tablet of destiny, or it may have been a temple priest's teaching tool. Or a scholar's tablet. Or an illustration for a philosophy text in the temple library. (Vast quantities of clay tablets have been discovered; more than half a million remain unread.) As the Islamic scholar Seyyed Hossein Nasr insists, "Ancient cosmologies are not childish attempts to explain the causality of natural phenomena as they may appear to the untrained eye; rather, they are sciences whose central object is to show the unicity of all that exists." The gods of the Sumerian creation myth "merged their waters into a single mass" to create the earth, which is depicted on the map as a flat disk surrounded by a circular "Earthly Ocean," also called the "Bitter River." It resembles a wide city wall.

Beyond this encircling salt sea, the seven legendary realms visited by mythical heroes like Gilgamesh are represented as carefully placed equal triangles. The map's text is a descriptive chart of these "Seven Islands," or regions. (The fifth, in the north, is "where the sun is not seen," a clear indication that the Babylonians knew of the polar night. And, in surviving Sumerian literary texts, the gods are depicted in furs, confirming extensive trade with the far north.) The seven legendary realms were believed to lie between the Earthly Ocean and the "Heavenly Ocean," where distant relatives of Western signs of the zodiac dwelt. In Mesopotamia actions were determined by astrology. For the powerful priests, familiarity with this map's science granted power to make history. Totemically the map reveals the two boundaries of reality, the temporal and the eternal—the things that are seen and those that are invisible. Together they offered "that which is."

PLATE 7. *Babylonian World Map.* This map of the Babylonian cosmos from c. 600 BCE served many purposes.

("between two rivers"—the Tigris and Euphrates). These narrow lowlands, in today's Iraq, are part of an arc, a fertile crescent that is embraced by deserts down to the Persian Gulf. This crescent was ruled by many empires, including the Assyrians (north) and the Babylonians (south). Creators of the first Mesopotamian civilization, the Sumerians established a number of independently ruled and massively walled city-states. Nippur (c. 5000 BCE–c. 800 CE), at the heart of Sumeria, was built on the west bank of the Euphrates.

The Mediterranean climate of wet winters and dry summers often characterized by drought made irrigation canals essential for farming and urban life. Lacking sufficient building stone, Mesopotamia relied on mud for bricks. Similarly, baked clay in the form of tablets became the common stationery. One clay-tablet map from circa 1500 BCE, possibly drawn to scale, is a plan of fields belonging to the great city of Nippur (see Plate 4, page 4). It is dominated by life-giving canals. It is Map as Portrait of Master Builders. It speaks eloquently of the awesome effort expended to create civilizations. This dependence on man-made waterways compelled settlers to live beside and the region's two rivers. The map offers a snapshot of this successful way of life.

Many field plans and estate plans of the region survive. They are among the oldest extant maps and are sometimes inscribed on stone boundary markers. Not surprisingly, the visionary people who drew the elegant plans of Nippur contributed to the invention of

The cosmology preserved on this map was the educated idea of the world and the topography of its mysteries. The Babylonian version places the city of Babylon ("gate of the gods") at the center, reflecting the mapmaker's vision of his city as the hub of the universe. It is represented by a large oblong crossed by the river Euphrates, which is drawn as two parallel lines that run from a mountainous source at the top edge of the flat earth to near its southern coastline, where the river enters a marsh — "Bit Yakin" — on a beaklike Persian Gulf. Several cities, long lost in time's relentless melt, haunt the map with their names or via simple round, unidentified marks, as mysterious to modern cartographers as black holes in space.

THE EGYPTIANS

In contrast to the case in Mesopotamia, very few pictorial maps have been found in Egypt, for unlike their neighbors on the Fertile Crescent, the Egyptians did not make clay tablets. Their stationery of choice was papyrus, a durable material made from marsh plants, from which our word *paper* derives. Papyrus sheets were more portable, more easily stored, and larger than clay tablets. However, Egypt's cartographic archive on papyrus is nearly barren—eroded by time, rotted by humidity, shredded by rough treatment, and eaten by hungry insects. (Many brittle rolls of papyrus rest in museums, awaiting rescue by new scientific techniques; perhaps some commerce.")

contain maps.) In 1822 Jean-François Champollion, the first to read ancient Egyptian in over a thousand years, described his work deciphering hieroglyphs: "I have gathered, while scarcely breathing for fear of reducing them to powder, such little pieces of papyrus, the last and only memory of a king."

Egypt, or Kemet ("the black land" in ancient Egyptian), is the idyllic valley of the river Nile. There, hemmed in by a natural environment of scorching aridity, geography nurtured another Mediterranean civilization contemporaneous to Mesopotamia. It was a long, thin settlement paralleling the Nile River. Every September and October, the Nile rose at a mostly manageable pace (impelled by a southern source that would remain hearsay until the nineteenth century). As the river receded, it deposited a carpet of moist and fertile black silt along the three thousand square miles of the Nile Valley. The river's yearly rise and fall initially caused mayhem for the supremely important Egyptian tax accountants. The solution to the problem transformed cartography and the way mankind recorded space. The Roman historian Strabo (c. 64 BCE–21 CE) told the tale in his book *Geographia:* "There was need of...accurate and minute division on account of the continuous confusion of the boundaries caused by the Nile... And here it was, they say, that the science of geometry originated, just as accounting and mathematics originated with the Phoenicians, because of their commerce."

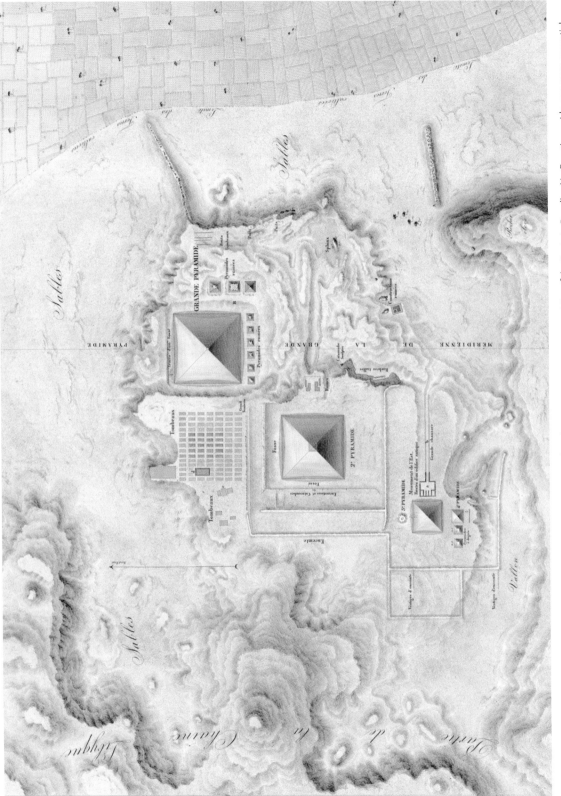

ABOVE: PLATE 9. *Pyramids at Memphis*. Napoleon's failed expedition to Egypt produced many cartographic triumphs.

BELOW: PLATE 10. *Map of the Route to Paradise*. No Egyptian guide was more essential than this funereal gift.

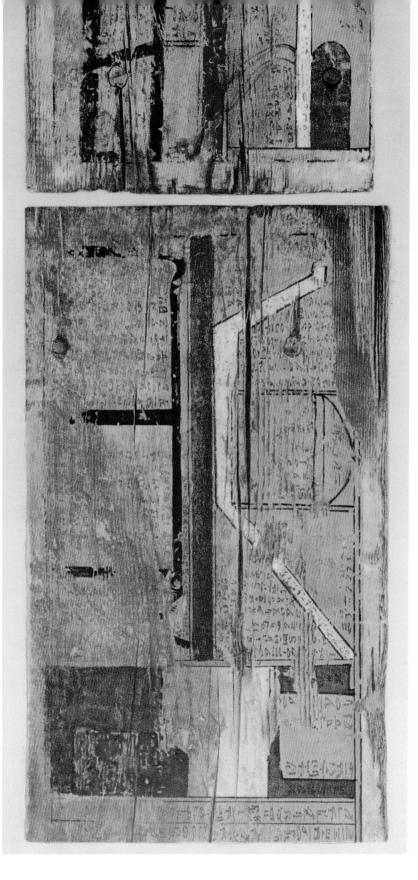

Egypt—alone in the ancient world—could predict tax revenue, which was paid in crops, because the Nile's yearly deposit of fertile silt was consistently nurturing. Thus geometric triangulation, the basis of surveying, charted perfectly delineated individual holdings using the horizon or a simple leveling device. One of Egypt's gods was Thoth, the inventor of surveying, who helped humanity keep an orderly—taxable—Earth.

An ancient survey drawing of a garden, done in red and black ink on a wooden tablet surfaced with plaster, reveals the perfection of geometric form that epitomizes the Egyptian civilization (see Plate 8). Found in a tomb at Thebes, the plan may be an idealization of an earthly garden, but it signifies the newly departed's reluctance to leave his refashioned landscape, his microclimate created in desert and marshlands by canals distributing the Nile water. The plan records his life's consolations: beauty and harmony in all things. It is Map as the Aesthetics of Geometry. It was made in a period when royal exploits were executed in relief on the walls of temples as chronological narratives, like today's graphic novels, with buildings and landscapes drawn in a cartographic manner. The garden plan reveals a culture enchanted by visual beauty. But while they used the Nile to create formal gardens for wealthy aristocrats, the Egyptians webbed the valley with canals to increase the economic vitality of the community as well.

The history of Egypt is the chronology of its despotic pharaohs. The great tombs of the pharaohs, for whom death was the most important event in life, were the major projects of their reigns, and harbored dwellings furnished for a life beyond death. These pyramids were the ultimate expression of the Egyptian obsession with geometric form. Fragments of plans incised on flakes of limestone certify an architect's hand. These tombs became museums and libraries preserving Egyptian culture for modern archeologists. A new

generation of Egyptology began after Napoleon unsuccessfully invaded the country in 1798. The tremendous architectural and artistic achievements of ancient Egypt inspired the French. Their savants in Paris produced the most magnificent engraved studies and diagrammatic maps of the pharaohs' imperialistic careers in twenty oversized volumes called *Description de l'Égypt*, a work that took two decades to complete.

One map from this work (Plate 9) displays the geometric perfection of the pyramids. It is Map as Homage to Greatness. It is an expression of wonder at the Egyptians' audacity, for no other culture of the time had produced anything comparable in magnitude and finish. Encased in polished, shiny limestone under a gilded or polished capstone, the pyramids were designed to mimic the rays of the adored sun while reflecting them, making the king buried within shine like a god, the indestructible lord of eternity. If Napoleon's expedition was a military fiasco, it was a cartographic triumph.

Nearly one hundred pyramid-tombs were built over a period of a thousand years. The grandest are the mountainous ensemble of three on a desert plain at Giza (near modern Cairo). These pyramids were erected to enclose the burial chambers of pharaohs primarily of the IV Dynasty (2613–2494 BCE). By using astronomical observations, the Egyptians oriented the four sides to the four cardinal points of the compass, and some believe they aligned them to the constellation Orion. Built by 100,000 men working twenty years to glorify their kings, the pyramids are masterpieces of still-unfathomable engineering and architecture. The French map embodies the monumental calm, grandeur, and spiritual essence of Egypt's singular genius.

The Egyptians had no word for religion. Life was part of a cosmic order permeated by the gods. The earth was contained within their realm. As historians Elias Bickerman and Morton Smith explain: "In Egypt, and only in Egypt, the living, the dead, and the

THE GREEKS

The Greek peninsula and archipelago are an extension of the Balkan Mountains, and the soil is rocky though suitable for farming, which developed there about 6000 BCE. The isolated and independent Greek communities were always fractious with one another—the eventual cause of their decline. Explorers sailed both eastward to the Anatolian (Turkish) coast and westward to Spain, colonizing more hospitable places along the shores of the Mediterranean and the Black Sea, "like ants and frogs around a pool," in Plato's words. "Greece" became all lands inhabited by those who spoke Greek.

Though the Greeks supposedly lacked the cornerstone of modern mapping—detailed surveying—their scientific investigations for engineering projects always ignored Plato's criticism of experimentation and inspired them to depict the world on a map. This is evident in the earliest surviving Hellenic image: a Minoan fresco fragment from circa 1500 BCE, executed in plan, in elevation, and from an oblique perspective (Plate 11). It is one of three fragments found in the house of an admiral, part of an excavation in Akrotiri, on the Greek island of Santorini (formerly Thera) in 1971. The Minoans (c. 2800–1000 BCE) created the first major civilization on European soil and ruled the Mediterranean—their sea. The longest of the three fragments tells the story of a fleet leaving and returning home, a suitable decorative motif for a naval officer. Another depicts a stretch of river. The third has segments of warriors, flocks, and women. These detailed picture maps from the dawn of Greek civilization, together with the major role geographical descriptions play in Greek literature, raise expectations. Enthralled by the beauty of the earth, how could the Greeks not try to pin it down on papyrus, as they pinned it down in frescoes? Yet the only known Greek map on papyrus is a sketch of Spain circa 100 CE.

There are no surviving Greek way-finding artifacts. If there were sea charts based on the stars, they got wet, torn, and were blown overboard—or were discarded when updated, or destroyed to protect trading routes. Greeks wrote of maps drawn on *pinax*, which might mean either wooden panels—a good fuel to keep sailors warm—or portable bronze tablets, easily melted down for war tools. *Pinax* were often covered with impressionable wax, not a sturdy surface. As late as 401 BCE, the Greek general and historian Xenophon reported that he relied on capturing locals "so that they

---

gods were three species of the same substance." This is verified by their maps.

Originally, only the sun-god pharaohs melded with Osiris, king of the underworld, after surviving their underworld journey. During the early Middle Kingdom (2050–1652 BCE), however, maps of the country of the dead, originally painted on the walls of lesser Pyramids' secret chambers, began to be placed in the tombs of less-exalted people who could afford mummification and a sarcophagus, because it was believed that life continued in the afterworld as long as the corpse, or an image of the self, existed. The journey in the underworld being hazardous, the deceased required extensive knowledge of its topography and of its inhabitants—both gods and spirits, good and evil. The underworld map in Plate 10 was painted on the lid of the sarcophagus. Writing in ancient Egypt with pen and ink on papyrus bestowed a kind of immortality, and the art was located in the House of Life (Per-Ankh). This may be why cursive hieratic writing was used on the map instead of hieroglyphs. It is the underworld map as Spiritual Way-Finding Tool. A knowledge of magic spells and intricately coded ritual dialogues was also essential to pass unharmed the monkeys who cut off the heads of unwary travelers, the bulls with four horns, and the door of the Watery Abyss.

Thus the underworld map was accompanied by *The Book of Two Ways*, which detailed the two roads leading to Rosetau, a necropolis west of Memphis, the home of Osiris. Both roads are in the domain of the sky, yet one is on water and one on land. There are channels and watercourses and islands with roads that lead nowhere. *The Book of Two Ways* became the first essential travel book. If the Egyptians attained a geographical visualization of the distant communities they conquered as far north as Syria equal to the one they had of the underworld, the maps await discovery. For now, they are lost, gone as completely as the majestic buildings of Egypt's last imperial ruler, Ramses II (1295–25 BCE), who in Shelley's "Ozymándias" boasts on his vast temple walls: "Look on my works, ye Mighty, and despair!" Today a fallen collossus of Ramses rests at Luxor. Shelley paraphrased the inscription on the face of the statue. Ozymandias was part of Ramses' throne name.

PLATE 11. *The Thera Fresco from the West Room.* This fresco adorned an admiral's house when the Minoans ruled the Mediterranean world.

might act as guides," though his army of 10,000 Greek mercenaries straggling home from the distant banks of the Euphrates might have been an exceptional military expedition. Yet the sophistication of the Thera frescoes indicates that early Greek culture was one of cartographic accomplishment. When the Minoan civilization was destroyed circa 1000 BCE by the barbaric, illiterate Dorians, a dark age descended throughout the Greek world. Farming techniques, writing—mapping?—and all traces of surviving human achievement vanished for three centuries as cities turned to dust.

Following the dark age, the ancient Greeks—those after 600 BCE—mysteriously detached from the common view that the gods had all the answers. They created a singular relationship with the natural world, one that imagined a humanistic universe manifested on earth by free city-states—poleis—dotted throughout the Mediterranean world, poleis inhabited by men who identified themselves not as the subjects of a pharaoh or a king but as independent citizens with freedoms clearly distinguishing them from slaves to man or god. The wonder and beauty of mankind and of the earth became paramount. As the Greek philosopher Socrates (469–399 BCE) said, "Wisdom begins in wonder." Their gods acquired human form, lived in an actual place—Mount Olympus—and slept at

night. Besides using all known practical science and math to mechanize artillery and invent the steam engine, metal gear trains, accurate clocks, and animated images, the Greeks ventured into theoretical and speculative science to create cartographic images, endorsing the distinction between faith and reason.

Geminus (c. 10 BCE–c. 60 CE), a Greek writer and astronomer, tells us: "Homer and nearly all the ancient poets conceived the earth to be a plane; they likewise supposed the Ocean to encircle it as a horizon, and the stars to arise from and set in the ocean." The belief in the earth as a circular disk logically arose from observing the horizon from a height or from a point at sea. Upon this premise, the earliest Greek maps were built. Those maps first appeared in the sixth century BCE in Miletus, a Greek colony and a major seaport in the area of Asia Minor called Ionia, on the Anatolian coast (Turkey).

In Miletus an epoch-making circle of men formed an Ionian school of science known as the Seven Sages. Their word for cosmos means "order." They considered creation myths a starting point: What exactly had the gods wrought? Wonder supplanted the fear of offending the gods and their priests. In effect, these visionary men concluded that a reason for humanity's existence was to comprehend and map the earth. One of them, Hecataeus of Miletus (fl. 500 BCE),

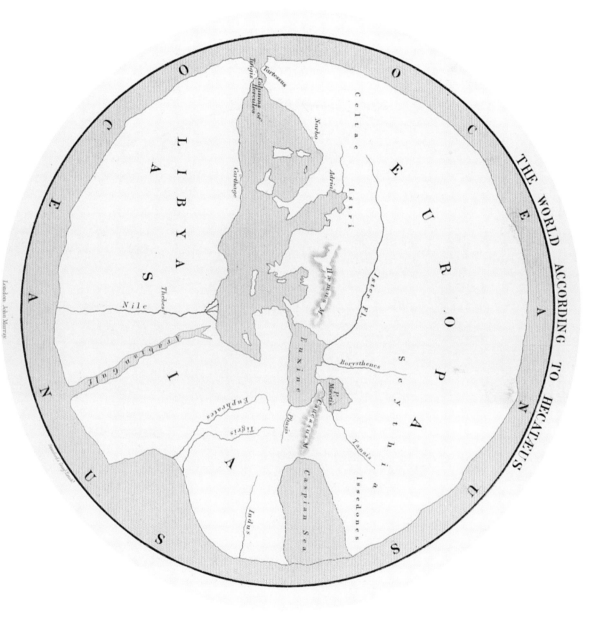

PLATE 12. *The World According to Hecataeus.* A reconstruction of the c. 500 BCE lost map by the indomitable Hecataeus of Miletus.

based his map (now lost but often re-created over the centuries by scholars; see Plate 12) on the work of another sage, Anaximander of Miletus (c. 610–546 BCE), who conceived the idea of a detailed map of the known, or habitable, world, from which our word "ecumenical" is derived. His map was of a flat, circular upper surface on the earth, which was imagined cylindrical in shape, the form of a stone pillar. Though this *oikoumene* was considered theoretically possible, the concept raised questions: If the balance imagined to exist in the cosmos required a matching geographical order — a southern hemisphere — how would it rain upside down? How would people not drop off? Believed to be the first Westerner to map the *oikoumene*, Anaximander had to devise the graphic form needed to convey his idea. As the biographer Diogenes Laertius wrote in the first half of the third century, Anaximander "first had the hardihood to depict the inhabited earth on a tablet."

How did he do it? First he converted the gnomon, a primitive sundial developed by the Babylonians, into a tool to calculate latitudes. Living in a major seaport and in an oral culture, Anaximander gathered geographical information from sailors, soldiers, traders, travelers, bards. He compared their narratives (mental maps) and reconciled their differences, assembling the pieces of an immense geographical puzzle. His map is oriented north, perhaps out of deference to the North Star, the guiding light. At its center is Greece's sacred Delphic temple of Apollo, designated by tradition as the navel (*omphalos*) of the *oikoumene*. The map signals the birth of geopiety — reverence and attachment to the earth and the homeland. The recognizable outline of the Mediterranean coast is a testament to the power of Greek observation, Greek collaboration, and the scientific, visionary genius of Anaximander. It is Map as Heroic Collective Effort. It is a product of the democratic process being spawned at the time in the poleis. Appropriately, it looks like a human brain nestled in its skull.

There were two symmetrical continents for the Greeks: Europe and Asia, which included Libya (Africa). This concept was not changed by Hecataeus of Miletus, the scholar of the orient, on his update of Anaximander's map. It differed little in its geometrical pattern. Hecataeus's map, however, marks the debut in the *West* of the Indus River, indicating either that news spread quickly in his era — India was newly annexed by the neighboring Persian empire — or that Hecataeus's Persian friends were talkative. Some information that he added to Anaximander's map he observed during his *periplus* (a description of a journey), which he called *Periodos*. It included a formulation of world history in chronological order. Hecataeus made it clear that writing history without measures of time was like mapping without measures of space. What geography he did not know for certain was deduced with Greek ingenuity, which the classicist W. S. Landor describes this way: "The Greeks soar but keep their feet on the ground." Theirs was a language of clarity and directness of statement. "We are lovers of beauty and economy," Pericles said. Poetic symbolism is rare in Greek art. Theirs was the scientific language of maps.

However speculative Hecataeus may appear in later Roman texts, to bolster the myth of their superiority, the reverse side of many Ionian silver tetradrachm coins dating from circa 330 BCE shows the practical effects, as opposed to the theoretical, of Greek cartography, and the wide understanding of maps in Greece. The image on the coin shown in Plate 13 depicts an area near Ephesus. It is Map as Common Currency. As the classicist A.E.M. Johnson reasons: "If such an accurate and detailed map could be conceived of as a coin type, the maps for ordinary use must have been the products of highly developed technique."

Jokes about maps made by crowd-pleasing playwrights are as potent a piece of evidence for the popular use of maps as is a fresco or a coin. The most famous Greek map joke is in *The Clouds* (423 BCE) by the Athenian comic playwright Aristophanes (c. 450–386 BCE). His work was performed before as many as 30,000 average citizens, who would not have appreciated obscure references. The map scene was written during the Athenian war with Sparta that demolished the world of the classical Greeks. In the play, an uneducated farmer goes to the "Think-shop" of Socrates to learn the science of subtle speech. A student shows him a map of the known world, and he asks to see Sparta. He recoils at its proximity to Athens: "That's much too close! You'd better move it further away." Aghast, the student explains that such a thing is impossible and is presciently warned: "You'll be sorry!"

While the notion of the inhabited earth as a flat disk in the center of the universe equally balanced in every direction prevailed with Anaximander and Hecataeus, the mathematician and philosopher Pythagoras (fl. 530 BCE) first proposed the theory of a spherical earth. He based his belief on the geometrical perfection of the circle, as well as on other abstract theoretical speculations and actual observations. Didn't observed ships "tilt" downward at the horizon? And didn't the earth's shadow appear curved on the surface of the moon during a lunar eclipse? The spherical earth became a fact of Greek life. And, the cartographic historian Chris-

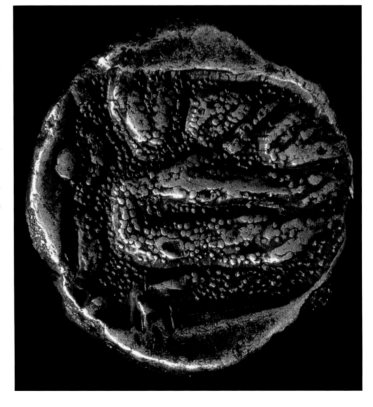

PLATE 13. *Ionian Coin.* This coin shows how familiar the Greeks were with maps.

tian Jacob suggests, globes (and maps) became tools of spiritual enlightenment from the moment the spherical earth was conceived by Pythagoras. They were used by the Greeks to trigger the meditative process and to initiate the flight of the soul. The globe-viewer's gaze became the cosmic gaze of the liberated soul with the vantage point of the sun god Apollo, who directed the Muses. Thus, studying globes and maps helped the Greeks attain their cultural vision, one that united religion, science, and philosophy. *What is the plan of the world?* they asked. *What part do I play in it?*

It was a contemporary of Plato (427–347 BCE), Eudoxus (c. 390–c. 340 BCE), who invented the general theory of proportion and ascribed a geometrical model to the heavens in order to fathom why the night sky behaved as it did. Living in an age before telescopes, he worked with the naked eye and a simple T-shaped instrument (*dioptra*) that had nails partially driven in at regular intervals across the top of the T. By lining up a nail with a given star, he measured

distances and angles between stars to make the first fairly accurate maps of the heavens. Along with calculating the main celestial circles—the equator, the tropics, the polar circles, the ecliptic, and the zodiac—he helped conventionalize the figures of the constellations with calendric tables of their risings and settings. He established a model for mathematical astronomy, as reiterated on a 1742 atlas page (Plate 14). It is Map as Stellar Ingenuity. The constellations were serious business for all navigators of the Mediterranean world.

Drawing the stars on a globe, Eudoxus replicated the night sky as seen from behind it, as if he were looking in at the encased earth. For him the celestial sphere with the stars affixed to it was the outermost boundary of the universe. He conceived nothing beyond. The stars revolved east to west. Also revolving around the enclosed earth were five planets, points of light like stars, but with erratic motions—"wanderings...of wondrous complexity" (Plato)—and

PLATE 14. *The Comet of 1742.* The Greek Eudoxus recorded the various celestial circles and helped conventionalize the constellations depicted on this atlas page.

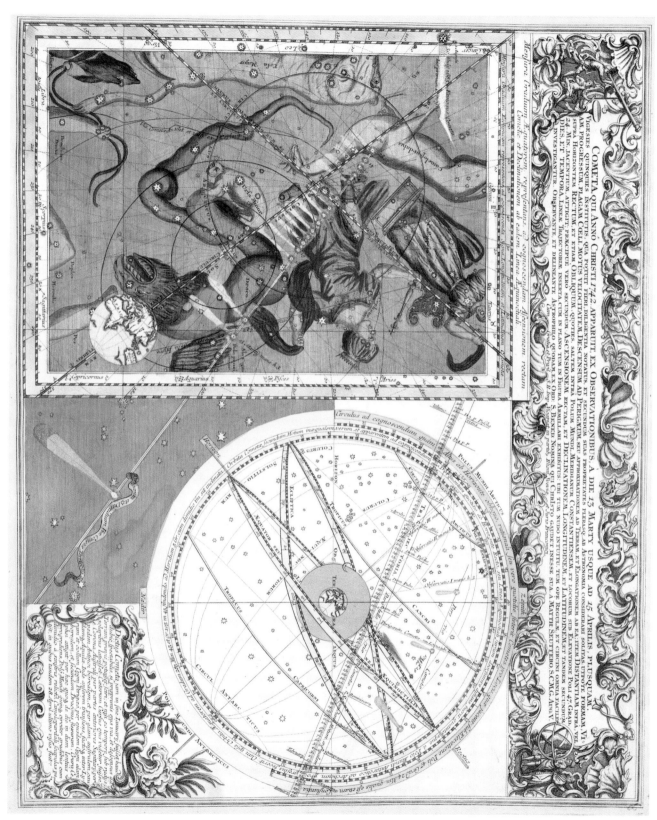

the moon with its visible features, and a unique sun, which was not just another star among billions. It was Plato's pupil Aristotle (384–322 BCE) who laid the foundation for ordering the knowledge of the sages: *Where do the various subjects fit in the scheme of things? How does everything relate?* These essential philosophical questions are also the basic cartographic mysteries. It was Aristotle who imagined a ship sailing due west and arriving in India, since nothing but water filled the other side of the sphere, a notion still prevalent in 1492. The fall of Greece and the ascension of destructive, philistine Rome and the power-driven Roman Catholic Church were a disaster for Western civilization.

THE ETRUSCANS

The Etruscans emerged in Italy from obscurity about 950 BCE. With origins unknown — indigenous? Greek? Asian? — and language still undeciphered, they and their nation of Etruria became the first civilization on the Italian peninsula and one of the founders of Western civilization. The center of their world was the modern region of Tuscany. Modern maps testify to their power: the Adriatic Sea is named for their trading port Adria, and the Tyrrhenian Sea bears the Greek name for them (Tyrrhenoi).

Hellenization of Etruscan culture brought the Greek gods into their pantheon, but the Etruscan relationship with their gods was unique in the Mediterranean world. It produced extraordinary cartography. Though heavily influenced by the Greeks and the Egyptians via trade of their unrivaled gold work, the Etruscans eschewed the Greek mathematical ideals of beauty, endowing their exquisite portraiture with the feeling and essence of the person being por-

trayed. This sense of their own individualism was specifically located in geographic space. Classicist Larissa Bonfante explains: "The Etruscans were distinguished by the importance of boundaries in their life and in their religion; boundaries between properties, boundaries between life and death, and between gods and men."

Knowing humanity's covetousness and greed, Jupiter (Zeus), legendary founder of Etruria, wanted the boundaries of everything to be calculated. Accordingly, all space was divided into "dwellings," each inhabited by a divinity, and every sacral and secular undertaking on earth had to be coordinated with the signs emanating from them in their realms. The orientation and division of space were of equal importance in divination as in surveying land, or marking out a garden and field. It was the Etruscans who created the system of centuriation, surveying land in rectangular parcels, each with an internal division of hundreds, and each separated by paths or roads. (Two millennia later, in 1784, a centuriation plan was submitted by Thomas Jefferson to Congress for land division initially described as "hundreds" but quickly relabeled "townships." This rectilinear survey system, historically miscredited to the enveloping Romans, had a profound influence on the cultural landscape of the United States, especially evident in rural field and road patterns as well as in urban grid street patterns.)

Early Christianity absorbed many aspects of the Etruscan civilization, then denied their "pagan" origins. In the fourth century, after Christian Trinitarianism (known as Catholicism) defeated the Arian Christians and became the official form of Christianity, the Catholics systematically destroyed Etruscan literature, which may have included books with maps — "Etruria is the originator and mother of all superstitions," wrote the Christian apologist Arnobius (fl. c. 300). Adding to this aggressive, intolerant destruction was the Etruscan stationery of choice, linen, more vulnerable to time than papyrus. Thus Etruscan mystical beliefs survived not as revealed in their three books of fate but as discussed by Roman historians, most notably Marcus Terentius Varro (116–27 BCE). One of the three lost books, the *Libri haruspicini*, dealt with divining the will of the gods from the livers of sacrificed sheep.

Every natural phenomenon, such as lightning, the structure of internal organs of sacrificial animals, or the flight patterns of birds, was an expression of the divine will. A small bronze religious relic discovered near Piacenza, Italy (Plates 15 and 16) — a replica of a liver roughly five by three inches — is marked and molded like a teaching tool from one of the institutions that prepared the priesthood to read the complex signs (*ostenda*) discovered on the sheep's liver. It is a startlingly innovative cartographic entryway into the magical realm where humans could intervene in the harmonies between celestial and elemental worlds. It is Map as Will of the Gods. It offers a vision of a spiritually complicated people whose sacred geometry is comparable to that of the founders of modern cartography. (The moderns also marked globes and maps with metaphysical references.) Since the Etruscans reckoned east and west by

PLATES 15 AND 16. *The Bronze Liver of Piacenza* (viewed from above and from the side). The Etruscans used this religious relic to change people's lives.

means of the traveling sun and moon, the convex underside of the bronze is divided into two regions inscribed "sun" and "moon." Its three-dimensional top side—roughly two and a half inches high—is divided by lines into surveyed parcels, each with its resident deity's name inscribed. Knowing the auspicious and inauspicious powers lodged in the four quarters of the sky, rigorously trained augurs in the *disciplina etrusca* would read the pleasure or displeasure of these gods in the corresponding portions of the sheep's liver, then prescribe the correct rituals, either for thanksgiving or appeasement.

Varro also noted that Etruscan soothsayers divided the earth into two parts: north (right) and south (left). By displaying the symbol of Egypt, the pyramid, on the left (south), the bronze piece becomes an Etruscan world map, with a teardrop-shaped Mediterranean, a three-quarter-moon Black Sea, and, on the right, the centuriated Etruscan empire complete with its umbilicus. The decorated rim is the enclosing Ocean River of the Greeks, with whom the Etruscans had a long, profitable, and contentious relationship. Greek influence is discernible in every different age and style of Etruscan art from before the period of Hecataeus. Inspired as they were by the Greek imagination, their conceiving a world map seems inevitable; and their being celebrated from a very early period for their skills in metallurgy, especially bronze, makes reasonable their capturing the terrestrial realm of their gods in that medium.

When the city of Rome was laid out using Etruscan ritual, the cosmic conceptions associated with directions were in accordance with the bronze liver of Piacenza. It influenced the significance of the city's gates: the auspicious eastern-facing gate was the lucky one through which Roman armies eventually marched to eradicate their ancestors the Etruscans, who once dominated and ruled Rome.

THE ROMANS

Just as Alexander the Great expanded knowledge of the *oikoumene*, so did Rome's career of aggression with the world's first professional army. According to myth-making tradition, on April 21, 753 BCE, a Latin prince named Romulus founded the city-state of Rome on seven hills beside the Tiber River, where it had begun life as a tiny village. In fact the Etruscans transformed what had been a collection of tribal sheep herders into a city with sacred boundaries laid out according to their geometric ritual, then ruled it with a dynasty of their own. In 390 BCE, the Celts (Keltoi/Gauls) sacked Rome and created the Roman mindset to expand to infinity as a form of self-protection. By the third century BCE, the ruthless Romans had decimated the mentoring Etruscans and controlled Italy. In 267 they added the Greek states to the Roman Confederation and they quickly unified the entire Mediterranean world politically. Then they began to move eastward. The resulting empire, comprising more than twenty-five modern countries, was one of the greatest the world has ever known. It was dominant for 830 years—from 190 BCE to 640 CE. Even after the Roman Empire's defeat in the Mediterranean world, its partner state in the east continued as the Byzantine Empire for 800 years more.

The Romans' psychologically astute policy extended a form of citizenship to the vanquished, binding them in a partnership that included an allotment of land to farm, employment in the army, and a share in all future booty. Though the Romans obliterated the language, literature, art, philosophy, and science of the vanquished, they utilized the stolen practical aspects for self-enrichment. They used mathematics for accounting and surveying their empire, not as an abstract system of logic. Roman cartography became a pragmatic discipline: *How does what we have today fit with what we had yesterday? How can we best use what we now have?* Their own innovations were principally in law and architecture: they created concrete, which made their wondrous aqueducts possible. Their political and legal thought, cobbled together from Celtic and Byzantine law codes, shaped every subsequent European state.

No topographical surveys of Rome have survived. But Roman literature accords land management inside and outside city limits a primary focus of the empire. It accomplished the two principal aims of imperial Rome: maintaining internal order and extracting

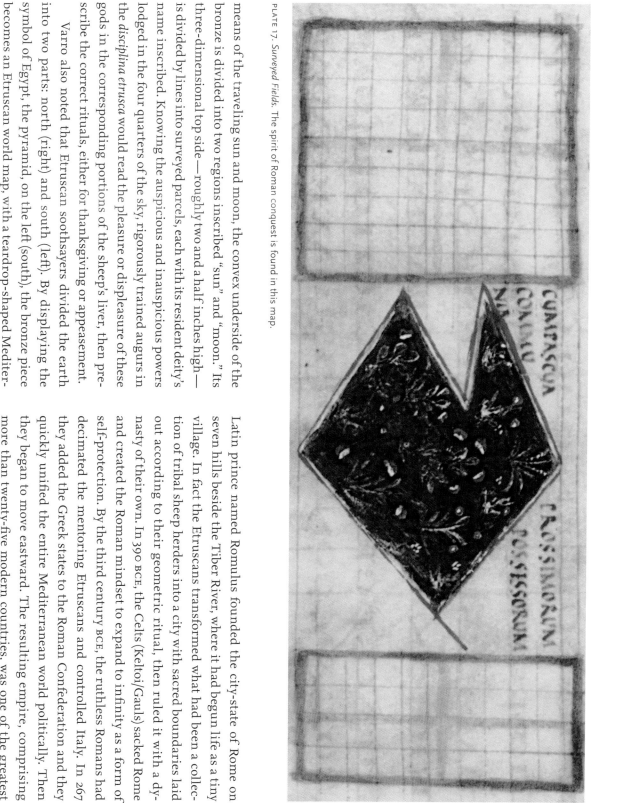

PLATE 17. *Surveyed Fields.* The spirit of Roman conquest is found in this map.

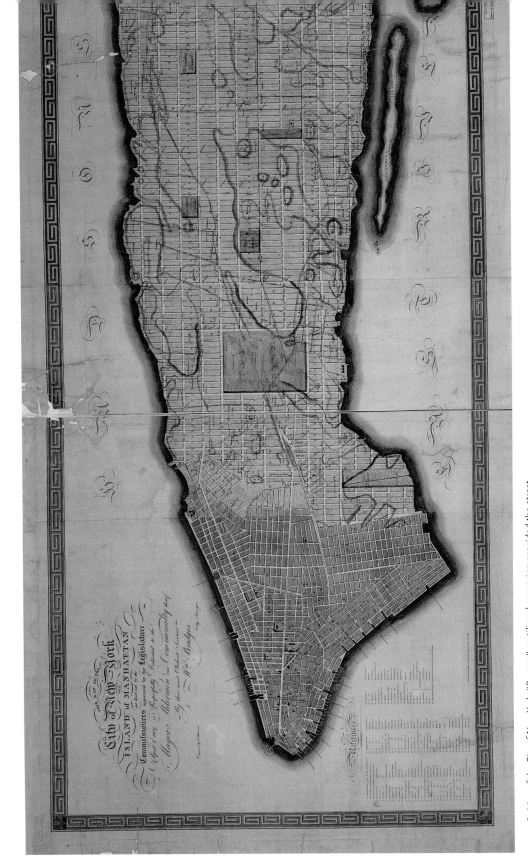

PLATE 18. *Map of the City of New York.* "Roman" rectilineal surveying provided the street pattern grid for Manhattan Island.

resources, via taxation. The soldiers who maintained order were rewarded with land, and property rentals were taxable. Legal occupancy was a major social issue. The Latin word *cadastre* embraces all aspects of their system of surveying, including centuriation.

Fragments of several survey manuals from about 100 BCE were copied by monks during the Middle Ages into the *Corpus Agrimensorum.* The illustration from this work (see Plate 17) dramatizes the importance of social interaction in the Roman concept of empire. It is expressed poetically by a flowering pasture rented for communal use by occupants of the two adjoining, neatly surveyed areas. The pasture reflects both the eradication of defeated civilizations and the cooperation expected of the different nationalities being melded into one empire, while the surveyed fields reflect the steady, disciplined, "civilizing" hand of Rome. In the words of the Latin poet Horace (65–8 BCE): "The peasant loves to scratch his bit of earth / And no amount of money could convert / Him to a sailor, trembling as he ploughs / across the ocean." The newly centuriated land was expected, by dint of hard labor, to become the fecund farmland needed to feed the Roman multitudes. It is Map as Roman Mastery of Human Psychology. Hyginus, an author of one of the manuals, commented on Roman meticulousness when he wrote of a man assigning land in Pannonia (western Hungary), who "was not satisfied to merely note on the bronze tablet the area assigned to each man, but drew in the outline of

each lot." The Romans inscribed their presence on the surface of the earth.

Though invented by the Etruscans, the rectilineal survey became Roman by dint of its employment throughout the vast empire. The oldest surviving form of land surveying, "Roman" rectilineal surveys with numbering systems remain in use today. The practical value of this imposed grid can be seen in places as diverse as Lugo (in the Italian province of Ravenna) and, most famously, on Manhattan Island, New York City, the emblematic metropolis of the twentieth century. The 1811 Randel Survey, or Commissioners' Plan, introduced Manhattan's gridiron street pattern on an eight-foot-long manuscript map. It is Map as Grand Vision. That same year, William Bridges adapted and published the map shown in Plate 18 with no credit to John Randel, who was the first to completely survey Manhattan, an island of hills, streams, and small lakes. Poet Clement Moore, a Manhattan real estate owner, observed: "The great principle which governs these plans is to reduce the surface of the earth as nearly as possible to dead level. These are men…who would have cut down the seven hills of Rome."

The most famous Greco-Roman cartographer, Claudius Ptolemaeus, known as Ptolemy (90–168 CE), was also one of antiquity's great astronomers. He worked in the tradition of his Greek predecessor Hipparchus (fl. c. 150 BCE), who had built upon Babylonian astronomy and arithmetical methods to found trigonometry, which he then used to convert to set positions on the globe the parallels of latitude and meridians of longitude randomly deployed by Eratosthenes (275–194 BCE), who had synthesized all before him to create a mathematically calculated grid system in order to specify the positions of places on earth.

Ptolemy was an Alexandrian Greek in the Roman Empire, which embraced the whole of the known civilized world. As a true Roman, he criticized the ancient Greeks for neglecting perceptual evidence, though his access to the great library at Alexandria, the second city of the Roman Empire, kept him in touch with their legacy. (Circa 391, the library was decreed a form of pagan worship and burned by fundamentalist Catholics.) The city was also the main port of the eastern Mediterranean, directly linking it with India and Rome, which expanded his access to news of the entire known world. His book *Geographia* is the first atlas of the world, and the only surviving book on cartography from the classical period. Written in the second century, it is one of the most influential scientific works of all time. Modern cartography developed from it.

Like Eratosthenes, Ptolemy compiled a how-to book on mapmaking—"We propose to describe our habitable earth." It was he who probably first employed systematically the grid of latitude and longitude lines to pinpoint exact locations. He included over eight thousand sets of coordinates, though most of them were not de-

duced mathematically or astrologically but from travel itineraries in a period when the reliable prototypical mechanical clocks of the Greeks were lost by the militaristic Romans, and when calculations were based on "a few days' voyage," or "an overland march of four months." His elongated Mediterranean shows the modern viewer the results of mathematical calculations using such unreliable data: he produced a 50 percent error in longitude.

Since zero degrees latitude, the equator, was based on the location of the midpoint between the poles and the relation of the earth to the sun and stars, distance north or south of the equator was easily calculated from the position of the sun or several known stars. Zero degrees longitude, however, had no natural or astronomical equivalent. The beginning point for measuring longitude could be totally arbitrary. Ptolemy located his zero-degree longitude line off the northwest coast of Africa—the end of the known world. But to fix another place's longitude relative to the starting point requires knowledge of the exact time difference between the two locations; the hour difference can then be converted into a geographical separation calculated on the 360-degree circumference of a circle. The problem of precisely calculating longitude bedeviled mariners and cartographers until the invention of the modern chronometer in the mid-to-late eighteenth century.

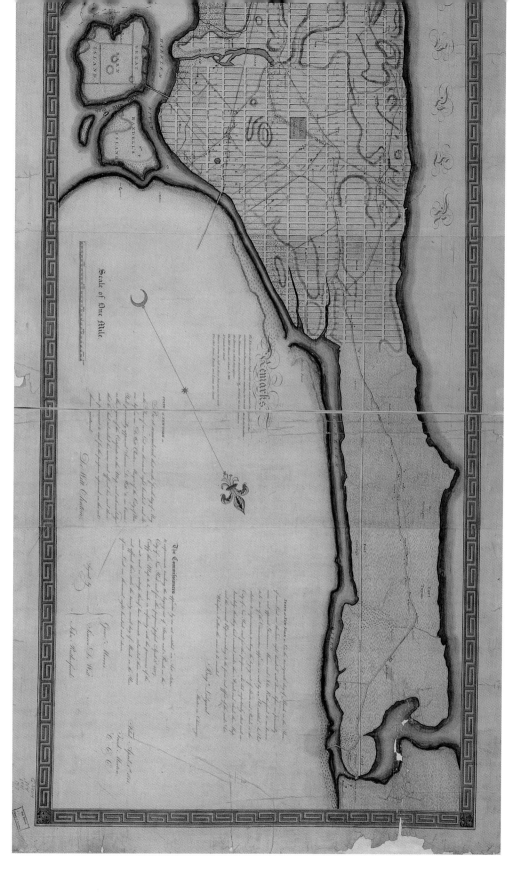

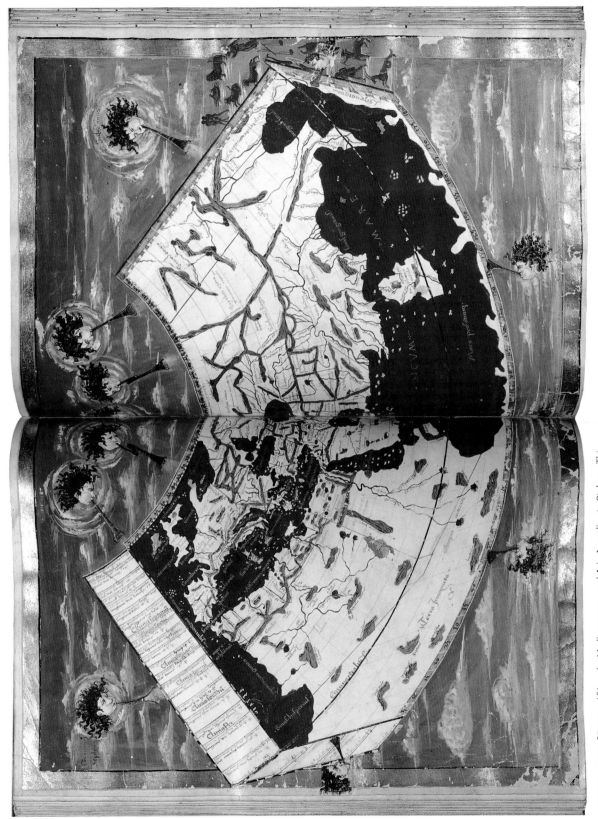

PLATE 19. *Map of Europe, Africa, the Mediterranean, and Asia According to Ptolemy.* This 1460 drawing of the known world used a newly discovered Ptolemaic projection.

Nevertheless his work remained the standard cartographic reference until the sixteenth century. Thought lost after the fall of the Western Roman Empire, it resurfaced via Islamic Asia in the twelfth century. Ptolemy's methods for devising two different projections in order to represent a portion of a globe on a plane, or flat, surface are mathematical formulations fairly close to those in use today. A fifteenth-century Latin manuscript of *Geographia* includes a map of the known world drawn using his "conic" projection with 36 straight meridians 5 degrees apart at the equator and converging at the North Pole (Plate 19.) It is based on a hollow cone's being placed over a sphere and unrolled. In the tradition of the great Greek dramatists, he transformed ritual into art. (Greek theater was rigidly conventional in form and diction, and not "realistic.") The map is a masterpiece of drama and perspective. It is Map as Greek Theater.

The known, inhabited world floating suspended in space communicates directly the wonder of Ptolemy's undertaking to depict "all things having regard to our earthly habitation." His method of representing those imaginary converging meridian lines at a van-

ishing point is very like the linear perspective devised by Florentine Renaissance painters in the 1400s, right after *Geographia* resurfaced in Italy. For the Italians, according to the historian Jacob Burckhardt, the ancient Greeks "were held in the most absolute sense to be the wellspring of all knowledge." The stunning visual audacity of the projection combines the Greek love of beauty with the Roman desire for vastness. The map's theatrical flair may have inspired the manuscript copyist to add the signs of the zodiac on the right, like a stellar company of actors waiting in the wings of the world's stage. Without those constellations, there would have been no scientific play, no constructed stage, no latitude, no longitude. And without the accompanying winds, there would have been no sea trade, a major supplier of data. Trade, of course, was not conducted only by sea, and the absence of a Chinese seacoast on the map implies that the overland "silk route" supplied the primary links between imperial Rome and imperial China (Sinae).

Those land-link traders—as well as Herodotus, recorder of Alexander's geographical exploits—provided the news of an apparently endless "unknown land" to the east. Thus the *oikoumene*

were only different customs at work. In fact, the puritanical and peaceful Christian (Arian) Vandals never "sacked" Rome and had nothing but contempt for its blood sports and debaucheries. When the Vandals entered North Africa, they did so on invitation from the Roman leader there, who was seeking allies against tyrannizing Rome, and when the Vandals took Carthage, they were seen as liberators from Roman economic and Catholic religious oppression. Thus the Mediterranean Sea became Mare Barbicum despite Ptolemy's heeding of Augustus Caesar's warning to his successor Tiberius to keep the empire within the boundaries of the Rhine, the Danube, and the Euphrates rivers.

During Ptolemy's lifetime there was a Roman frontier settlement in Egypt named Hierasycaminus (20 BCE–298 CE). The presence of this settlement on a map of the cosmos (Plate 20) helps determine when the map was created. Originally found in both Greek and Arabic copies of commentary on Ptolemy's astronomical opus, *Almagest*, the map could have been a mnemonic device or a teaching tool. On one plane, it locates the known inhabited world, the celestial sphere, and the underworld. It is Map as Greco-Roman Psyche. Produced in the vocabulary of geometry that would come to dominate the upcoming Islamic world's maps, the various elements generate the same mystical quality as the Babylonian world map (Plate 7) with its cosmic overview. A searching gaze reveals a representation of the place these ancient people believed they inhabited physically, mentally, and spiritually, both in their lifetimes

was no longer a world island. There was now an open frontier waiting for Roman expansion. The global circumference posited by Eratosthenes, which Ptolemy incorrectly reduced by a quarter, has the door open to the east *and* the west. (Ptolemy's downsizing of the earth helped convince Christopher Columbus that a westbound voyage to India was feasible.) Even though Africa was surrounded by water on the map of Eratosthenes, Ptolemy refused to make Africa a singular continent. The results have a contorted Africa enclosing the Indian Ocean, and Ptolemy insists that, like the Mediterranean, the Indian Ocean is one of "the seas surrounded by land." His belief in this landmass knitting southern Africa into eastern Asia was possibly generated by sailors' tales of a massive sighting "down under"—Australia?—that needed to be affixed to the northern hemisphere's known world because a southern hemisphere was unimaginable. The enclosed Indian Ocean remained rooted in the Western imagination until fifteenth-century Venetian mapmakers challenged it.

The map's projection gives the distinct impression that only a small piece of the globe is represented, and that more will be revealed by those to come. Here the practical Roman mind outweighs the Greek observant one, though much has been imagined by Ptolemy. Even on his other map projections, this sense of incompleteness is part of Ptolemy's plan. We are offered the "known habitable world," and never has this been made more obvious cartographically. His maps espouse through numbers and geometry the inspiring myths of heroic travel to the horizon line of a curving earth. Like the classic Greek dramas structured on the armature of heroic myth, the maps deliver the rewards offered by the dramatists: both a painful series of recognitions—"we have only begun the journey"—and an initiation into more enlightened states of consciousness.

Ptolemy's maps advertise the Roman takeover. The conquerors have successfully realized the general outlines of their empire and of the immediately surrounding areas, such as the closed Caspian Sea, and the profile of western Europe. Their diligence has accurately widened Libya (northern Africa) and found its southern Lunae Montes (Mountains of the Moon), "from which," Ptolemy writes, "the lakes of the Nile receive snow water." (The Greek playwright Aristophanes' joke about the importance of geographical realities in *The Clouds* is made poignant by the way maps gradually reveal the intrepid human spirit's success in solving the mystery of the Nile.)

Even more telling is Ptolemy's professed ignorance of the Rhine River's true course in what was Rome's Germania Magna—the northern region from the Danube to the Netherlands and western Russia—until the year 9, when the Germanic tribes (Goths) defeated and ejected the Romans after having been conquered and trained as Roman soldiers. By the second century only 2 percent of the Roman army was of Italian origin; the rest was comprised of Goths, Huns, Celts (Gauls), Visigoths, Shereans, and Vandals. The late Latin word for soldier was *barbarus*, and Ptolemy is promulgating the fantasy of the "barbarians" as mindless rampaging hordes, while there

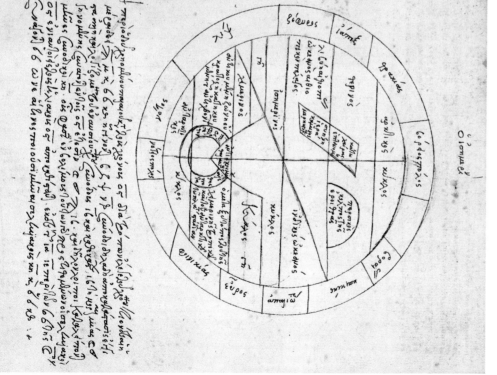

PLATE 20. *Map from Anonymous Astrological Miscellany.* The Greco-Roman map mindscape is revealed here.

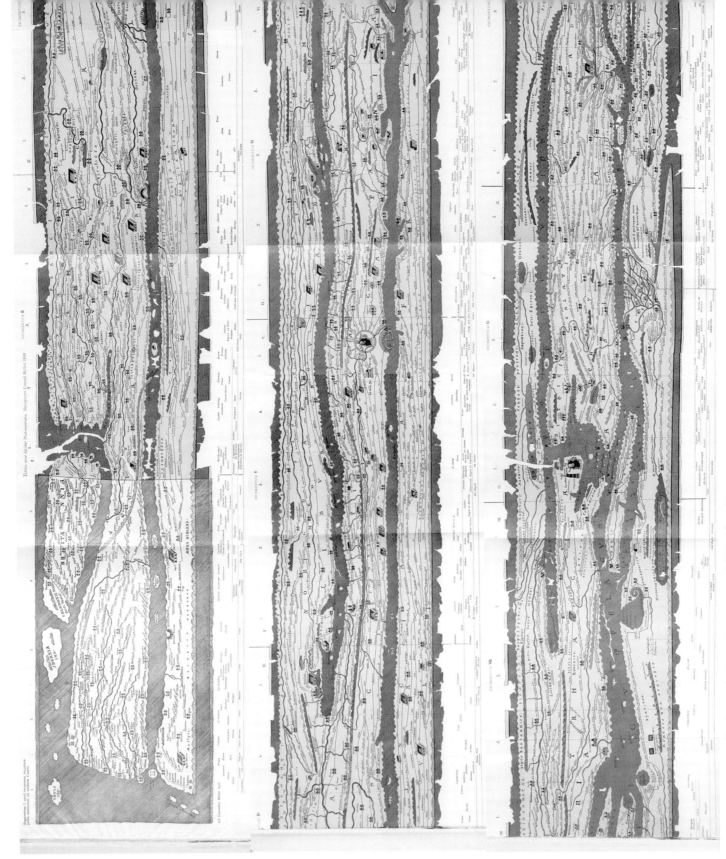

PLATE 21. *The Peutinger Table.* The way the Roman Empire rose and fell is reflected in this quintessential road map.

and after their deaths. Locating the underworld on the map makes geography exhibit the common ground between the natural and the cultural, which is the genius of cartography.

Among the identified localities is Egypt, a prominent rhomboid floating on the map's upper half. The Persian Gulf is a semicircle on its right. The Indian Ocean is a closed triangle below the Gulf. Connected by a vertical line, the North (top) and South Pole are identified in the outer rim—reminiscent of encircling Oceanus—along with the ten encircling winds. The terrestrial equator halves the main circle of earth, and the rest is divided into zones: two frigid, two temperate, and two torrid.

The places identified—Persia, Libya, and five spots in Egypt—are all found in Ptolemy's *Geographia.* The celestial ecliptic's path—

the oblique zodiac—traverses the equator. Earth and its Heavens coexist as they do in life. The River of Oblivion and the River of Fire, two curving tributaries of the River of the Dead (Acheron), are artfully arranged as a small circle to create the sense of a hole, or a descent to the underworld, another dimension of existence. The rivers flow "under" a reversed arc, an open triangle resembling the tip of Africa without its Ptolemaic extension; it is marked on the commentary copies of the map as "a fiery unnavigable sea," a common notion of the earth's torrid zone. As the medievalist scholars Evelyn Edson and Emile Savage-Smith conclude, the purpose of the map was "to orient users to their place in the world, both geographically and cosmologically. Such orientation was the goal of astrology, which linked events on earth to the movements of the heavens."

Traveling the Roman world in many of its particulars is still possible through the dazzling example of Roman cartography that has become known as the Peutinger Map, or Peutinger Table (Plate 21), in honor of its sixteenth-century owner, Konrad Peutinger. Faithfully copied in the eleventh or twelfth century from a fourth-century map (with first-century antecedents), it is a stunning graphic solution to the problem of fitting the roads, harbors, rivers, altars (places of pilgrimage), settlements, spas, granaries, and staging points for travel throughout the entire Roman Empire on a single strip of parchment—a foot high and roughly twenty feet long. The original was probably a papyrus roll carried by hand in a *capsa*, or roll box. The Peutinger Map is the sole surviving Roman pictorial itinerary map. It is Map as The Way That They Went. It is the

hands-on measured vision of about 70,000 miles of Roman roads, built on Celtic models, from Britain to Sri Lanka, and it neatly aligns scientific and commercial with geopolitical concerns. The sheer expanse of it becomes a metaphor for the reach of the Roman Empire. At a glance it shows roads to be both the spine of rising civilizations and, with historical hindsight, the means of breaking an empire's back during its decline.

Distances are recorded mostly in Roman miles, though misshapen Gaul's acreage is covered in leagues, Persian lands in parasangs, and India's expanse in Indian miles, which would have made asking directions from the locals—and fellow Roman citizens—easier. The scroll map's diagrammatic style is without a constant scale, yet it displays the equivalent of the empire's interstate

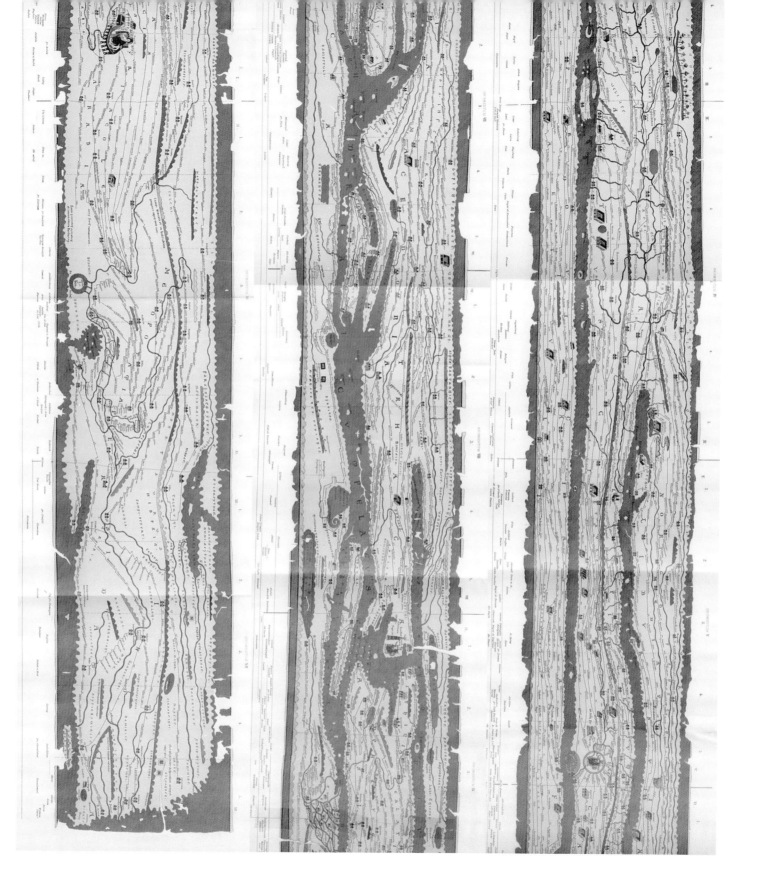

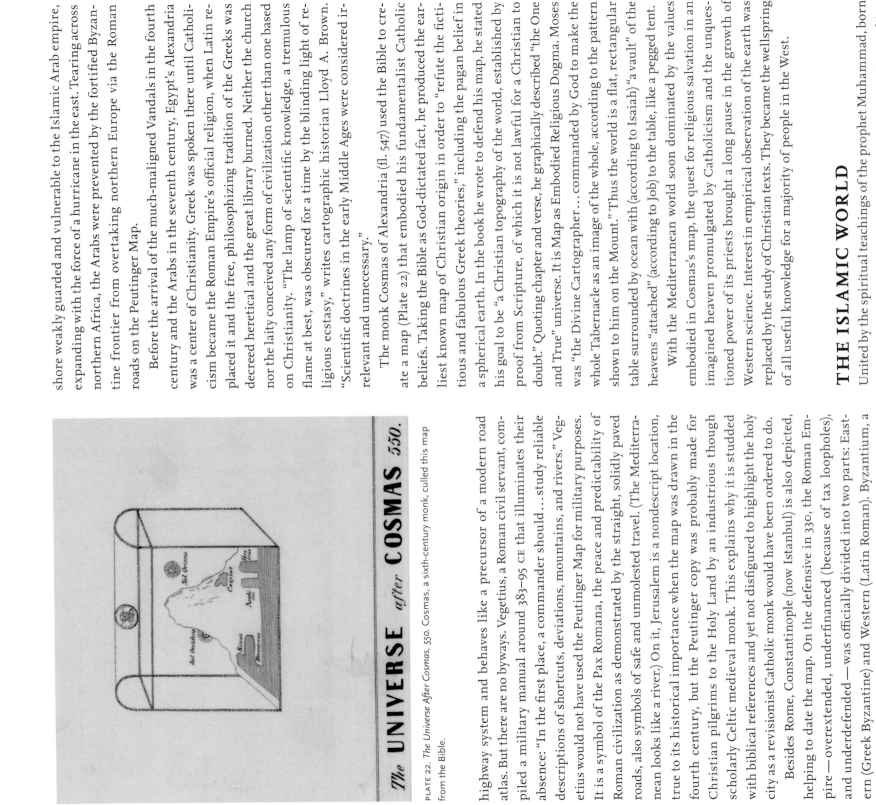

PLATE 22. *The Universe After Cosmas, 550.* Cosmas, a sixth-century monk, culled this map from the Bible.

highway system and behaves like a precursor of a modern road atlas. But there are no byways. Vegetius, a Roman civil servant, compiled a military manual around 383–95 CE that illuminates their absence: "In the first place, a commander should…study reliable descriptions of shortcuts, deviations, mountains, and rivers." Vegetius would not have used the Peutinger Map for military purposes. It is a symbol of the Pax Romana, the peace and predictability of Roman civilization as demonstrated by the straight, solidly paved roads, also symbols of safe and unmolested travel. (The Mediterranean looks like a river.) On it, Jerusalem is a nondescript location, true to its historical importance when the map was drawn in the fourth century, but the Peutinger copy was probably made for Christian pilgrims to the Holy Land by an industrious though scholarly Celtic medieval monk. This explains why it is studded with biblical references and yet not disfigured to highlight the holy city as a revisionist Catholic monk would have been ordered to do.

Besides Rome, Constantinople (now Istanbul) is also depicted, helping to date the map. On the defensive in 330, the Roman Empire—overextended, underfinanced (because of tax loopholes), and underdefended—was officially divided into two parts: Eastern (Greek Byzantine) and Western (Latin Roman). Byzantium, a natural citadel, was rechristened Constantinople and became the capital of the Eastern Roman Empire. It is easy to see the map's roads as huge red staples holding the two portions together in the imperial imagination. It is just as easy to see them as blood-soaked pathways of oppression under the new Pope-kings soon to come after bankrupt Rome was abandoned by the rich and by its unpaid soldiers, and looted by starving Romans during civil war in the early 470s. Constantinople, however, continued to reign over the Eastern Roman Empire after the Byzantines reclaimed Carthage in 533. The effort left Byzantium's southern Mediterranean shore weakly guarded and vulnerable to the Islamic Arab empire, expanding with the force of a hurricane in the east. Tearing across northern Africa, the Arabs were prevented by the fortified Byzantine frontier from overtaking northern Europe via the Roman roads on the Peutinger Map.

Before the arrival of the much-maligned Vandals in the fourth century and the Arabs in the seventh century, Egypt's Alexandria was a center of Christianity. Greek was spoken there until Catholicism became the Roman Empire's official religion, when Latin replaced it and the free, philosophizing tradition of the Greeks was decreed heretical and the great library burned. Neither the church nor the laity conceived any form of civilization other than one based on Christianity. "The lamp of scientific knowledge, a tremulous flame at best, was obscured for a time by the blinding light of religious ecstasy," writes cartographic historian Lloyd A. Brown. "Scientific doctrines in the early Middle Ages were considered irrelevant and unnecessary."

The monk Cosmas of Alexandria (fl. 547) used the Bible to create a map (Plate 22) that embodied his fundamentalist Catholic beliefs. Taking the Bible as God-dictated fact, he produced the earliest known map of Christian origin in order to "refute the fictitious and fabulous Greek theories," including the pagan belief in a spherical earth. In the book he wrote to defend his map, he stated his goal to be "a Christian topography of the world, established by proof from Scripture, of which it is not lawful for a Christian to doubt." Quoting chapter and verse, he graphically described "the One and True" universe. It is Map as Embodied Religious Dogma. Moses was "the Divine Cartographer…commanded by God to make the whole Tabernacle as an image of the whole, according to the pattern shown to him on the Mount." Thus the world is a flat, rectangular table surrounded by ocean with (according to Isaiah) "a vault" of the heavens "attached" (according to Job) to the table, like a pegged tent.

With the Mediterranean world soon dominated by the values embodied in Cosmas's map, the quest for religious salvation in an imagined heaven promulgated by Catholicism and the unquestioned power of its priests brought a long pause in the growth of Western science. Interest in empirical observation of the earth was replaced by the study of Christian texts. They became the wellspring of all useful knowledge for a majority of people in the West.

THE ISLAMIC WORLD

United by the spiritual teachings of the prophet Muhammad, born in Mecca in 570, the once clannish and fractious Semitic-speaking peoples inhabiting the desert of the Arabian Peninsula built powerful armies. They conquered the Fertile Crescent and neighboring areas of Persia and Egypt before moving into North Africa and the Iberian Peninsula, Sicily, Asia Minor, and parts of western China. Within a century of their ascension, these pre-medieval Muslims controlled an empire greater than Rome's, developed Arabic as a written language, and made the Mediterranean primarily a Muslim lake. Islam—literally, "submission to God's will"—was the dominant faith along the great lines of trade, which helped accelerate the religion's growth and spread the cartographic systems created by its believers. These conquerors played a pivotal role in the history of Western mapping. As the scholar Edward J. Jurji explains, their science "reflected the light of the Hellenic sun, when its day had fled, and...shone like a moon illuminating the darkest night of medieval Europe."

The Arabs originally had only one art form: poetry. Along with this gift for using symbolism and for expressing the essence of experience—both Eratosthenes and Ptolemy also wrote poems—the Muslims became enthralled by India's mathematics, its "Arabic" numerals with zero as a number (not as the Babylonian place-holder), and its astrological tables. They absorbed Egyptian geometry and Pythagorean theories of mathematical structure as the form of things. And while developing their own singular astrology, they founded algebra. Since geography instigated the study of celestial regions, and geometry helped measure the earth, the Islamic cartographers expressed their belief in the sacred order of nature and in the intellectual and spiritual wonder that arose from bridging the gap between the earth and the sky, each a metaphysical truth. As Charles Seife explains in his book *Zero*: "Number-shapes inspired a different way of thinking. Geometric constructions and shapes were the same thing."

Everything in Islam, the youngest of the three Middle Eastern religions after Judaism and Christianity, arises from its holy book, Muhammad's Quran. He placed his book with the Jewish Old Testament and the four Christian Gospels, believing it was the third message from God. Copying the Quran made calligraphy the highest visual art form. Like Judaism, Islam decried imagery. However, by employing their poetic traditions, calligraphic sophistication, and fascination with mathematics, Islamic cartographers invented a visual language able to interpret the complete and holy law revealed to Muhammad. In Islam, mathematics was not bound to the world of "matter." It was related more to the world of life forms, and beyond them to the archetypal world. Thus Muslim cartographers described the sacredness of space with qualitative geometry. Their mapmaking—a form of writing—reflected the wisdom of the "Grand Architect of the Universe." Working in two languages, Arabic and geometry, they proved their adage: "Writing is spiritual geometry."

The world map attributed to Ibn al-Wardī (Plate 23), written in Arabic and geometry, represents the many exponents of the school

PLATE 23: *Medieval Islamic Map of the World*. Ibn al-Wardī expresses an Islamic cosmic reality in two languages—Arabic and geometry.

of Balkhi (d. 934). Found in a 1481 Turkish manuscript of al-Wardī's *Enumeration of Wonders*, the map could be five hundred years older. Oriented south, it shows the known world as a sphere surrounded by the Encircling Sea, which is enclosed by mountains. They may represent the Islamic creation myth's mountains intended as a rampart against the Demonic Powers, and the means to unify earth with heaven. Mecca, the focal point of all spatial references, is near the center of the Arabian Peninsula, which is embraced by the Persian Gulf and the Red Sea in the shape of a crescent moon to signify the unity of the celestial and terrestrial worlds, a unity of conjoined sacredness. It posits a middle reality between sensory perception and divine perception. Like a prayer, it is an expression of a mode of being. The earth is an event lived by the soul. It is Map as Prayer.

Little of northern Europe is shown on the lower right, but Turkish Constantinople is a red crescent "wall" or barrier against the "people of the cross." The scar left on the Islamic psyche by the Byzantine Empire's defeat of the Arabs at Constantinople in 717 seems to pulsate on the imaginal earth's surface; for had the Arabs not been stopped there, they probably would have gone on to conquer the weaker West and to end the dominance of Christianity. At the top, Africa is extended the length of the Indian Ocean, but unlike on Ptolemy's map, here the continent does not enclose the ocean. The Arabs revered Ptolemy, but their own observations led them to discard many errors in his *Geographia*.

Arab sailors also had close contact with China. Hugging the southern coast of Asia, these navigators knew there was a water route there, and it may have been they or the Chinese who had sighted the landmass "down there," which Ptolemy converted into Africa's extension. The Nile, drawn in red on *The Enumeration of Wonders*, takes a right-angle turn, possibly reflecting the river's great bend.

When the various Arabic geographers referred to their maps, they always made them subordinate to an accompanying detailed text with precise coordinate tables. The text mediated between the scientific and the archetypal.

Al-Wardī's map gives the essence of place without any indication of distances. It shows that the things of this world belong to the realm of forms, which are but a mirror image of their celestial origins. Believing every form possessed an inner meaning, al-Wardī and the other Islamic cartographers reimagined outward dimensions to express the symbolic nature of the world. As the Persian philosopher Nāsir-i Khusraw wrote a thousand years ago: "Gaze upon the inner dimension of the world / with the eye of inwardness. / For with the outward eye, / thou shalt not see the inward."

Yet even with the initial influence of Ptolemy, the individuality of Islamic mapping affirms the words of the Arabic scholar A. I. Sabra: "Greek science was not thrust upon Muslim society any more than it was later upon Renaissance Europe. What the Muslims of the eighth and ninth centuries did was to seek out, take hold of, and finally make their own a legacy which appeared to them laden with a variety of practical *and* spiritual benefits." From the eighth to the twelfth centuries, they held the intellectual supremacy throughout the Mediterranean world. In an enormously creative act, the Islamic people absorbed the rudiments of philosophy, medicine, and other scientific lore, including cartography, from Hellenized Persia, as well as from Syria, Egypt, and Asia Minor. With Islam, Persian art forms acquired new fields of operation in a realm accustomed to poetic symbolism. By the late seventh century, the known world was conceived by Arabs in the shape of a bird. The head was China, the right wing India, the left wing North Caucasus, and the tail North Africa. A tenth-century ceramic from eastern Persia (Plate 24) has refocused matters by making Arabia the bird's head—Mecca its eye?—with Asia and Africa its wings and Europe its tail. It is Map as Environmentalism.

For Islamic cartographers, nature displayed the wisdom of God, and all creatures were governed by divine law. There was no dichotomy between laws governing the moral character of human society and those governing nature. "Wheresoever ye turn, there is the face of God" (Quran, II:115). The known world symbolically portrayed as a bird tells of the Islamic relationship between man and the natural environment: the destiny of the human and natural orders were believed intertwined. One could not exist without the other. Thus Islamic sciences of nature had roots in religious ethics, and the Persian bowl image restates visually the spiritual significance of balance (*al-mīzān*) in the Islamic community of life. Balance is a requirement of Islamic cartography.

Aside from a few literary references to military maps, there is no evidence of mapping in the pre-Islamic Arabic world. After the rise of Islam, there were itineraries or route maps for diplomatic missions, military operations, and trade. Then, in 830, when the scholarly Caliph al-Ma'mūn (786–833) was convinced by Aristotle in a dream that there was no difference between reason and religion, he established in Baghdad his Bayt al-Hikmah (House of Wisdom), for which Syrian translators acquired Greek manuscripts, including Ptolemy, from Byzantium. (Until the Mongols sacked Baghdad in 1258, the House of Wisdom was the successor to the Alexandrian Library.) Since the Quran teaches that "there shall be no compulsion in religion," the warrior Arabs did not impose their faith upon the surviving vanquished. All were encouraged to make contributions to science. The first translation into Arabic of a treatise on the astrolabe is credited to a Jewish astrologer working near Baghdad about 809. The astrolabe, forerunner of the sextant, was attributed to the Greek astronomer Hipparchus (fl. 150 BCE). It was used by Islamic scientists to calculate the position of

celestial bodies in order to make astrological predictions, and to determine the *qibla*, direction of Mecca, for the performance of the five daily prayers and for other ritual acts.

Practical religious need made astronomy a main concern of Muslim scientists. They produced a massive corpus on the subject of mathematically locating longitude, a feat they learned from Indian astronomical texts. One of two surviving brass Arabic maps complete with sundial and compass from the seventeenth century (Plate 25) has the majesty of a space station yet is based on medieval Islamic maps, the only ones known with localities exactly placed

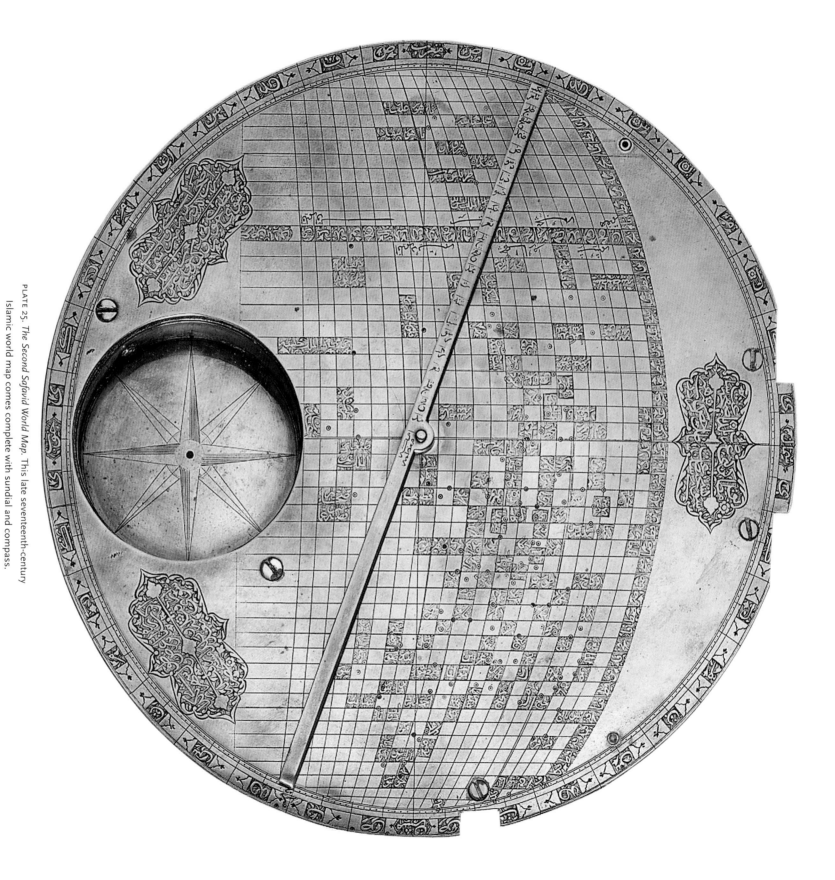

PLATE 25. *The Second Safavid World Map.* This late seventeenth-century Islamic world map comes complete with sundial and compass.

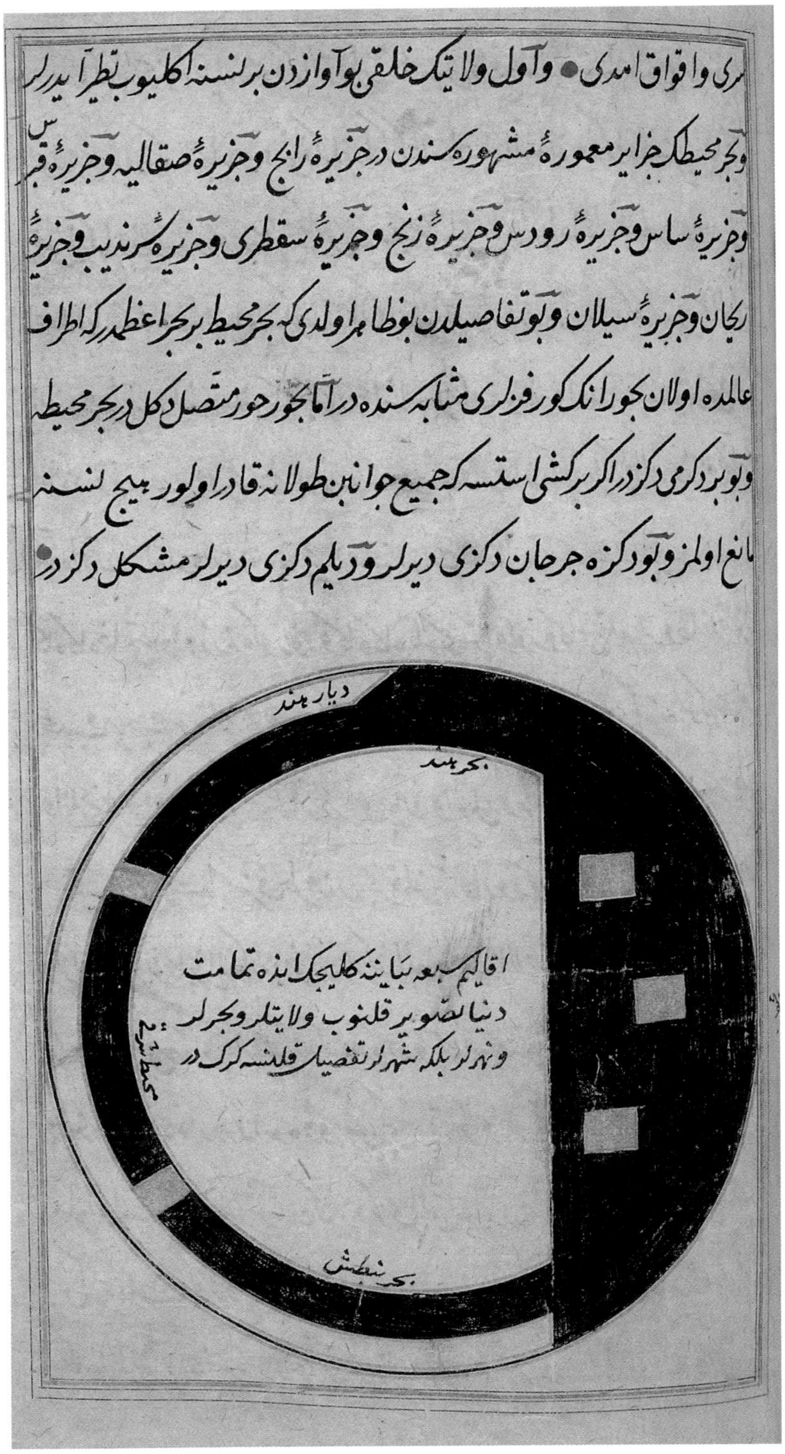

Whereas the Mediterranean world's cartographic tradition has north at the top, Islamic maps have south at the top. The later medieval European Christian map tradition oriented east to identify with the world of the spiritual; the Garden of Eden was believed to be in the east. Why did Islamic cartographers orient south? There are many theories. For the Arabs, Mecca—which lay in the southernmost portion of the Islamic empire—was the center of the Islamic world and the point where the heavenly axis touched the terrestrial plane. However, even though the words *light* and *illumination* in the Arabic language share the same root (*shrq*) as the words *east* or *oriented*, the Arabic symbolism associated with the cardinal directions posits south as positive perfection, which is inclusive, whereas north is negative perfection, which is exclusive. And possibly there was decisive influence from the all-pervasive genius of imperial China, where maps were oriented south, for as Muhammad said: "Seek knowledge, even until China. That is the duty of every Muslim."

Like Pythagoras, who believed the soul to be a numerical principle, Islam rejected lush folkloric traditions, myth, or legends. In the Commentaries on the Quran, only the rational was acceptable. Geometry negated suggestions of illusion, for as Euclid demonstrated, it could be used to reveal, not merely to describe. It was al-Ghazzāli (b. 1072), the greatest Muslim religious figure after Muhammad, who proved the value of human reason in demonstrating the truth about divine things, and about the divine simplicity, "the clear and complete knowledge of things, such knowledge as leaves no room for doubt nor possibility of error and conjecture." The Islamic concept of knowledge is based upon the two fundamental axes of unity and hierarchy. They lead ultimately to the knowledge of the One, the supreme Substance. A manuscript map in *Acaib-ül Mahlokat* by Zakariya (born Muhammad al-Qazwini; 1208–84), from a circa 1553 Turkish translation (Plate 26), shows "The Sundering Sea of the East," or the sea sundering the habitable part of the world from the uninhabitable. The map demonstrates the bare essentials of the habitable world—sea (black) and earth (white)—discarding all topographical features as accidentals to the substance of the world of Nature, our complement, companion, abode. Oriented south, the map has scripted names: India and Indian Ocean are at the top and Nubia/Africa at the bottom; on the left of the central known world is the Eastern Ocean—the sundering or surrounding sea. The five squares in this encircling ocean indicate the "islands beyond India," or Indonesia; these eastern islands are depicted on both the eastern and western sides of the map to show the spherical nature of the earth. There is no Pacific Ocean. There is no sign of America. At the time the map was originally created, the Atlantic was presumed to wrap around the globe, with no major landmass impeding its currents.

Muhammad taught the interrelatedness of all things, a unity of nature (*al-tawhīd*). The map offers a classic scheme of things where the spiritual takes body, and the body becomes spiritual. It is Map as Divine Simplicity.

PLATE 26. *The Sundering Sea of the East. The essence of the world is revealed in this c. 1553 Islamic map.*

on a coordinate grid, as described by Ptolemy and tabulated by astrolabe. The map displays a monumental job of tabulation. Not only are longitudes and latitudes of some 250 places engraved on it, but also the accurate distance of each from Mecca. The Muslim scholar and scientist al-Baruni (973–c. 1051) did the foremost Islamic work on mathematical geography, synthesizing Greek, Persian, and Indian geography and his own observations and studies. The grid pattern, as a cartographic tool, is affixed to his reputation. The brass map is a testament to his genius. Its coordinate grid ignores topography entirely. It is Map as Spatial Emblem of Empire. Mecca is placed at the center of what is essentially the Ptolemaic world. Here is Allah's spiritual empire expressed in its purest essentials.

THE HOLY LAND

At the crossroads of Africa, Asia, and Europe lies the birthplace of Judaism, Christianity, and Islam. For centuries, the Holy Land has been what modern scholars call a site of contestation. A beacon for pilgrims, historians, and, simply the curious, this small area has also been a prime target of aggression by expanding empires for millennia. It is, therefore, possibly the most mapped section of the earth.

Some of the earliest itinerary maps of the Holy Land may be found in the Bible. The Old Testament is rich in boundary descriptions and historical geography. Just as Cosmas of Alexandria based a map on biblical passages, so did the greatest rabbi of the Ottoman Empire, Elijah Mizrahi (1450–1526). His commentary on Rashi (1040–1105), the most favored of Bible commentators by Hebrew scholars, includes a map of Israel suggestive of Arab/Islamic influence. In 1574 it became the first printed Hebrew map (Plate 27).

Every year, at the conclusion of Passover and the Day of Atonement prayer service, Jews pledge to return to their ancestral soil of Jerusalem. Its location is of paramount importance. The maps attributed to Ptolemy first transformed this legendary symbolic landscape into a topographical reality like any other place on earth, one with scientific coordinates. Discarding all forms of scientific exactitude, Mizrahi used a spare, allusory visual language to match the poetic and geographically vague biblical narrative from which he drew his inspiration. By suggesting place, he focused the mind's eye on the *idea* of the Holy Land. By rigidly disciplining space, he taught his students to be stoic and wise, neither passion's slave nor slave of any nation. Like a commentary, the map stimulated discussion and thought. It is Map as Mentor. Don't just look, *see*. Don't just read, *think*.

At the center of an oblong desert region oriented east is the Land of Israel bordered on the right by the Land of Edon and the River of Egypt (Nile), which empties into the Mediterranean (The Great Sea) at the bottom, creating an angular Egypt. Situated on the Mediterranean is the Land of the Philistines—the supposed derivation of "Palestine." At the top, the Lands of Moab and of Sihon and Og are above the River Jordan. The river descends at a forty-five-degree angle into a semicircular Sea of Galilee and an elongated Dead Sea that flows into the extreme right border of the Red Sea (Sea of Reeds). The stops made by the Hebrews during their exodus from Egypt are shown as rectangles (Encampments). This is the Holy Land abstracted geometrically into the Islamic realm of sacred geography.

Undertaken by the Christians of western Europe for the recovery of the Holy Land from Islam, the ongoing series of campaigns known as the Crusades (1096–1291) shattered the bond between the Roman and Greek Orthodox Christians. Matthew Paris's circa 1252 interpretive map of the Holy Land (Plate 28, page 32) can be read as a history of all the Crusades. Paris (1195–1259) was living in England's foremost Benedictine abbey at St. Albans. Pilgrims, bishops, princes, knights, and Crusaders visited; all were interviewed for his maps, forged in two languages: the visual and the verbal. "What the ear hears," he wrote, "the eyes may see."

The Crusades were born in 1095 with the threat of a Turkish western thrust and a request for help from the Byzantine emperor Alexius I. Pope Urban II had urged the faithful to "enter upon the road to the Holy Sepulcher and deliver it from the wicked race." Greatly assisted by general anarchy among Muslim rulers, Urban II's First Crusade created what was known as the Crusader Kingdom of Outremer (beyond the sea)—four Latin states in Palestine, three of them narrow strips along the Mediterranean. Thus a tiny Latin Christian presence was established in the vast Islamic world. Paris's map makes the correspondence between economic realities and religious sentiment.

Outremer originally comprised the Latin Kingdom of Jerusalem (including Acre, the key to Palestine, and dominant on the map), the Latin city of Antioch (a fleur-de-lis gateway to Syria above the map's circular cemetery in Acre), and the Latin Counties of Edessa and Tripoli (not on the map). The majority of conquered Crusader sites are present, but the magnified crenellated walled city of Acre—most of the map's lower half—dwarfs everything else. It articulates Acre's immense value to the Crusaders, a value also symbolized by the huge camel striding at the end of a major trade route from the interior of Asia to the shores of the Mediterranean. The inscription in front of the camel reports that the neighboring gate leads "to the mill at Doc (Da'uq)," which was a city two miles north on the Acre River. Mills were at the heart of the European agrarian system. A modified and fortified mill was transplanted to the Holy Land by the Crusaders as a working symbol of their supposedly transformative presence.

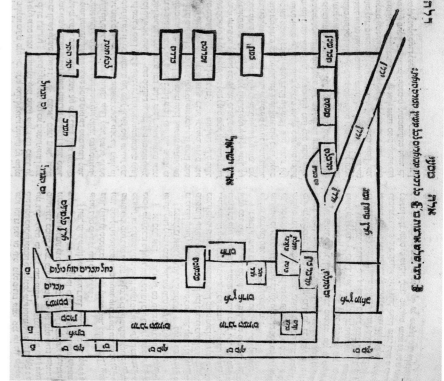

PLATE 27. *Schematic Map of the Land of Israel.* Rabbi Elijah Mizrahi based his Holy Land map on the Bible's historical geography.

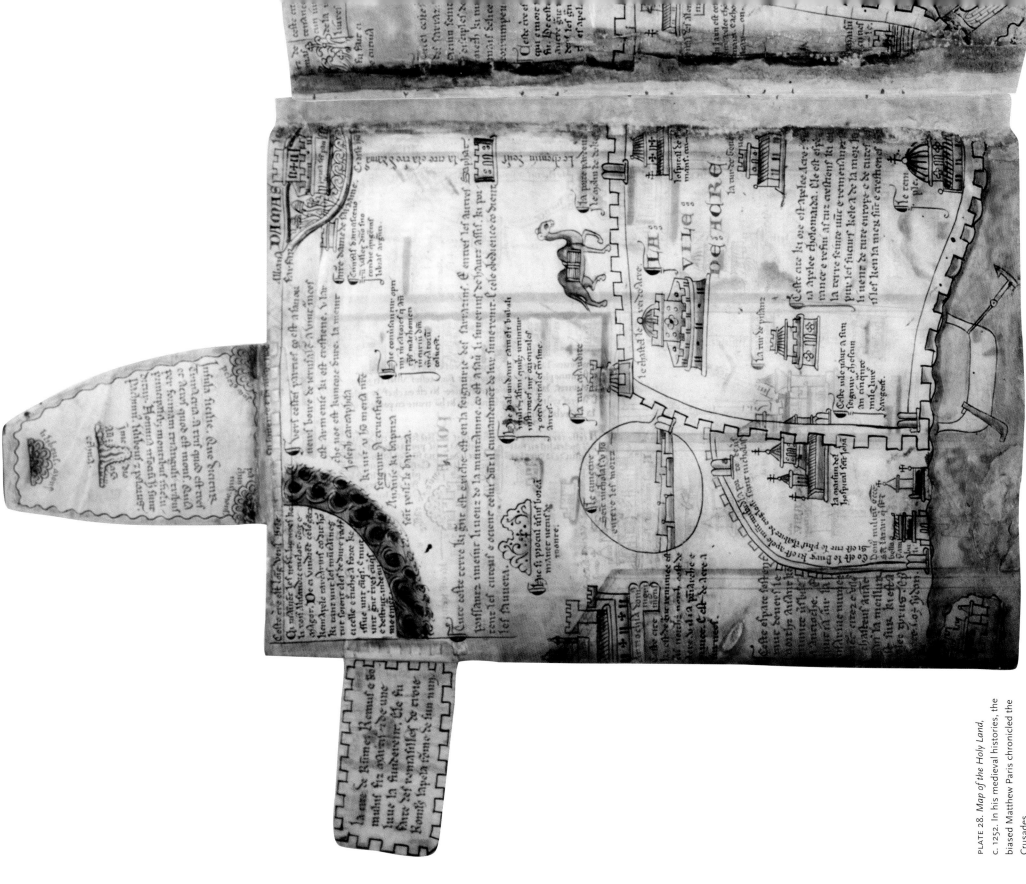

PLATE 28. *Map of the Holy Land*,
c. 1252. In his medieval histories, the
biased Matthew Paris chronicled the
Crusades.

At the upper center of Paris's map is the great Syrian city of Damascus, ruled by the Seljuk Turks, who had retaken Jerusalem in 1244. Its enveloping walls look impregnable. They are a haunting reminder of the fiasco that was the Second Crusade (1147–49), which began with a massacre of Jews by the journeying Crusaders in the Rhineland and climaxed with the most shaming Christian defeat of the era: the French Crusaders' foolhardy attack on Damascus. Adding a sense of futility to the Crusaders' cause is the lone oared warship headed for the last city on the map, the Nile port of Damietta, which was Saracen headquarters in Egypt. It was the site of an ephemeral Crusader victory in 1219, which nearly won back Jerusalem from the sultan of Egypt in a trade, until the Crusaders refused to negotiate. Then the rising Nile cut them off from their bases, leaving them stranded like that single oared ship. They were forced to surrender and were ransomed by an exorbitant sum—100,000 pounds of gold!

In 1191, the Third Crusade made Acre the capital of a Latin kingdom reduced by Saladin in 1187 to a thin chain of Crusader forts running from Tyre (a jutting on the map's lower left), to Jaffa (four cities from the end on the right), with Jerusalem still under a crescent flag. The tiny earthly realm of Acre is reconfigured by Paris into a boast of Latin Christian power. The biased chronicler commits the specific sin of the warrior—Pride, which was publicly condemned by James of Vitry, who became Bishop of Acre in 1216. Paris's map fostered pride in future Knight Crusaders everywhere, and in the stay-at-homes too. It is Map as Occasion of Sin.

His heavily fortified Acre is the actuality of the Holy Land Crusades. Agreeing with James of Vitry was the Arab-Syrian gentleman-warrior Usāmah ibn Munqidh (1095–1188), to whom all Europeans were Franks. "The Franks (may Allah render them helpless!) possess none of the virtues of men, except courage, consider no precedence or high rank except that of knights, and have nobody that counts except knights." Yet these East-West clashes did lead to an increase in geographical knowledge for Westerners, along with their rediscovery of Ptolemy, which during the coming Italian Renaissance unsettled the popes as mightily as any Islamic incursion. The Venetians financed the Fourth Crusade; it demolished Constantinople in 1204 and established a Latin Christian power base there. When Acre fell to the Saracens in 1291, the historian Philip K. Hitti concludes, "the curtain fell on the last act of the East-West medieval drama."

Though relatively few medieval Europeans went to the Holy Land, the fifteenth-century travel books focused on pilgrimages to Jerusalem. With detailed itinerary and visual maps, the Holy Land was the ultimate in long-distance travel, until Columbus's astounding discovery in 1492 changed the way the Mediterranean world viewed the earth. (The primary purpose of his heroic navigation—stated in a letter of March 4, 1493—was to finance a new Crusade to Jerusalem.) In 1486 Bernhard von Breydenbach published the first Holy Land guidebook to include a printed map (see Plate 29). This large foldout map was based on firsthand sketches by his traveling companion, the Utrecht painter Erhard Reuwich. For the travel writer after the invention of the printing press in 1454, the

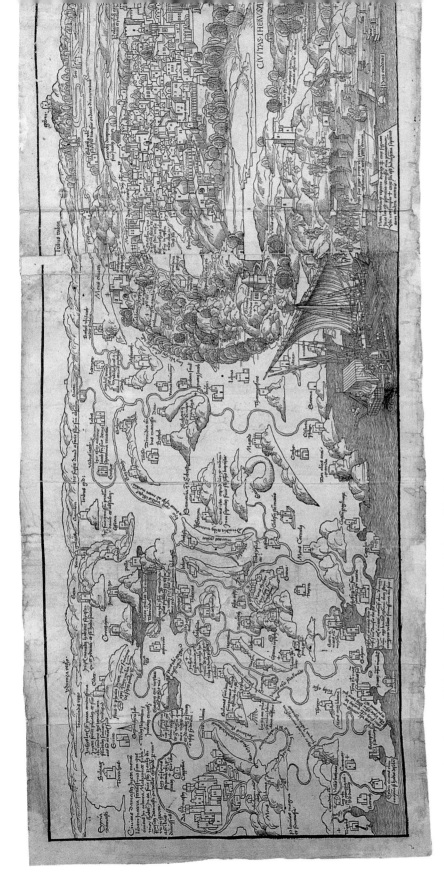

PLATE 29. *The City of Jerusalem.* In 1486 the first guidebook with a printed map of the Holy Land appeared.

medieval pilgrimage to the theater of sacred history was a devotional act of intrepid travel, a literary act of writing books, and a social act of satisfying the curiosity of readers. The map in Breydenbach's book satisfied everyone. With this lavishly printed book in hand, it is easy to comprehend the triumph of pictorial maps over the ancient itinerary lists of places, and to appreciate the way printing increased the functions performed by images.

Unlike a medieval map in a church viewed communally and then remembered, Reuwich's map, purchased in a book, was a private affair studied at leisure by members of a burgeoning commonwealth of learning. It is Map as Voyeur. Similar maps soon helped transform the nature of collective memory. The depiction of pilgrims, with whom the reader could identify, cunningly made the excitement of the journey part of the map experience; they are caught, as if by a camera, disembarking from their transporting ship. Jerusalem, the goal of the adventure, looks superimposed at the center of a generalized geographical area covering Damascus to Alexandria. The city is the reason for the map's existence; and, as if under a magnifying glass, it is immensely out of scale with the rest of the world. Unlike the devotional impulse at the heart of most medieval Christian maps, Reuwich's panoramic response to the Holy Land is that of a documentarian. In addition to cities along the route, he depicts religious sites for the three religions that make the place sacred, indigenous wildlife, and the ethnic life of Palestine. He even includes the pyramids. His is not a proselytizing eye, and his unbiased map is the last depiction of Jerusalem before the Turks destroyed much of it in 1517. The two travelers relied upon trusted sources to fill in the blanks on their visual travel itinerary.

The elaborate, bestselling book—and its famous map—was originally published in German and Latin, then translated and dispersed across Europe. Religious woodcuts were added to the Spanish edition (1498) produced at the time of the infamous Inquisition, a Roman Catholic tribunal for the discovery and punishment of heresy. The holy pictures transformed a travel book into a prayer book. Battling with the belief of loyalty to the church was the new idea of loyalty to the state. Devoid of religious symbolism, Reuwich's map is the essence of the struggle between the religious and the secular worlds at this formative period of Western thought, when the Middle Ages ended and the modern age of Western cartography began with the reappearance of Ptolemy's *Geographia.*

The appearance of the printing press in Europe in the 1450s was a demarcation line in the history of cartography. According to Elizabeth Eisenstein, "The invention and development of printing with movable type brought about the most radical transformation in the condition of intellectual life in the history of Western civilization." It was a communication revolution underpinning the political revolutions of modern times. The functions performed by maps increased as science went to press and as Hellenic knowledge emerged from obscurity. Multiple copies of printed maps helped assure their survival. National boundaries were unequivocally delineated, place names became fixed, and political consciousness rose with the general dissemination of maps as a support for humanistic philosophy.

Abraham Ortelius (1527–98) also included a map of the Holy Land in the 1590 Latin edition of his hugely successful atlas *Theatrum Orbis Terrarum*, the first modern printed atlas. The enterprise was a cooperative, international event, and Ortelius's map of the Holy Land (see Plate 30) expressed a further transition into modern consciousness. The map appeared in the Parergon section of his atlas, a supplement of historical maps in which the ancient tribal names were restored to the region. This was done to satisfy the sixteenth century's fascination with classical geography. However, in a momentous departure from cartographic tradition, the map is decorated with scenes from the life of Abraham. For the first time, human beings inhabit the space traditionally reserved for depictions of the winds. The humans also enclose the earth, as if they are in charge of it, and up until the Industrial Revolution human beings would see themselves as the earth's caretakers. This radical change in map decoration epitomizes the ascent of European humanism. It is Map as the Triumph of Humanism.

Thanks to Copernicus (1473–1543), who removed the earth from the center of the universe, educated people no longer thought of themselves as more significant than *all* creation. Ortelius depicts mankind as a complement to the world of nature. Even the rectangular shape of the map is what was deemed visually pleasing to the human sense of form by the age's mathematicians, who had learned about the golden mean, or golden measure, by studying the texts of the ancient Greeks. It was originally discovered in Arabic intermediary texts.

This masterful, hand-colored Holy Land map also raises visually for the first time the question of humanity's physical and emo-

tional relationship with the landscape. At the time, scholars in Rome were eagerly collecting and studying plant life, inspired by the rediscovery of Greek texts on the subject. The Accademia dei Lincei (Academy of the Lynx, so named because lynx were known for their keen eyesight) was founded in 1603 with botany as its primary concern and controlled observation of the natural world its goal. On the map, the resonant Holy Land becomes a stage for the recorded scenes from a specific human historical drama: the saga of Abraham. Ortelius graphically demonstrates cultural geography. Although illustrating the origination story of Judaism, dated circa 1800 BCE, the costumes in the insets are contemporary to Ortelius, and the settings are wholly imaginary. There is no attempt at period accuracy, in the same way—and at the same time—that Shakespeare created his history plays and tragedies set in earlier times, yet written in Elizabethan English. Both Ortelius and Shakespeare took part in the invention of the modern human sensibility. Abraham's achievement during his limited time on earth is honored, but the dominating cartographic image is that of the timeless landscape. It triggers in the mind of the beholder other biblical and historical stories. Yet taken as a whole, Ortelius's map induces intimations of mortality. Every viewer, like Abraham, becomes "a poor player that struts and frets his hour upon the stage." This map is the product of a complex culture, visually literate, historically informed, and receptive to maps as a form of narrative art.

One of the earliest printed cartographic expressions of Jewish devotion to Israel is the 1695 Amsterdam *Seder Haggadah shel Pesah* (Passover Haggadah) by Abraham ben Jacob. Related during Passover, the haggadah story—the word means "to tell"—describes

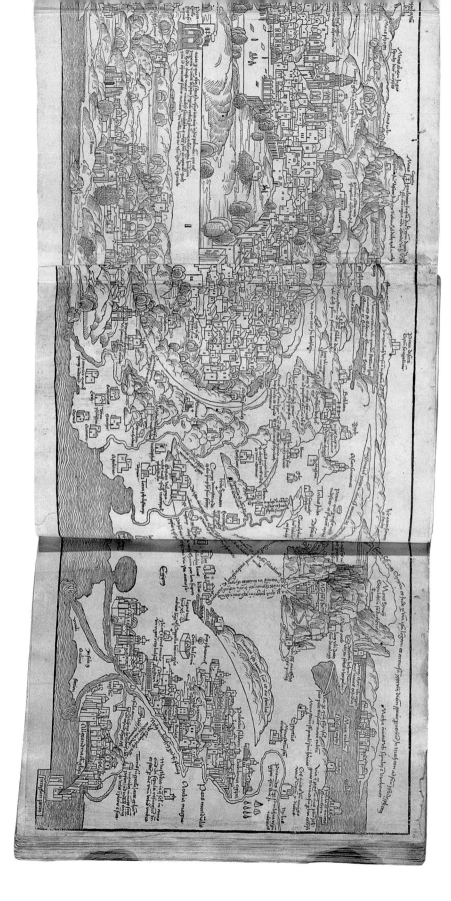

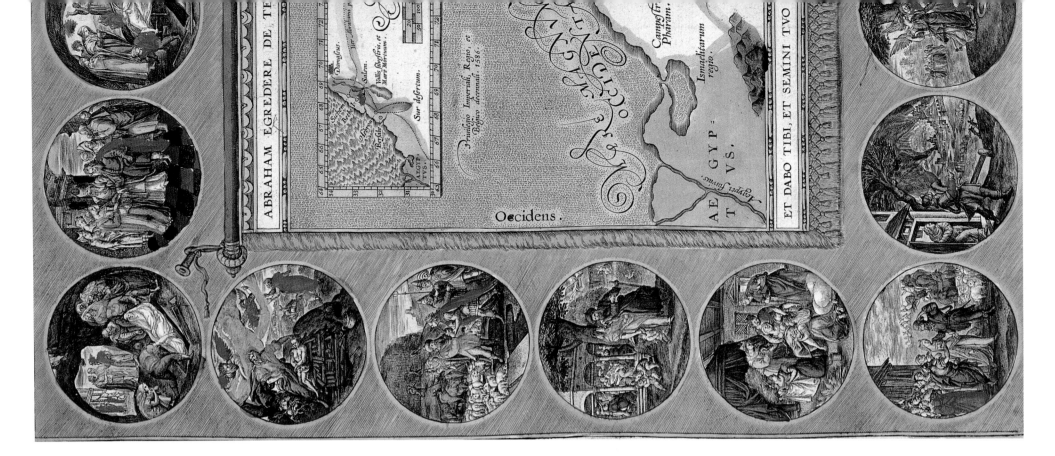

Within the map image: ABRAHAM EGREDERE DE TE... | Campefri... Pharan. | Ismaelitarum regio. | ET DABO TIBI, ET SEMINI TVO | Damafcus. Salem. Vallis fyluefiris, et Mare Mortuum. Sur defertum. | Principatus Imperiali Regio, et Belgico decennali. 1586. | AEGYP= TVS. | Occidens.

the exodus of the Israelites from Egypt. Ben Jacob's map (see Plate 31) is one of the first to use Hebrew letters exclusively, and it became famous throughout Europe, though his original purpose was lost for three hundred years. His hidden agenda to entertain while educating by making his unique map masquerade as an ordinary one either went unnoticed, or his purposeful "adjustments" were thought of as mistakes. The history lesson in a traditional haggadah is, first of all, usually without a map depicting the exodus and early history of what is now the state of Israel. Ben Jacob transformed his rarity into a test by means of selective misspellings, symbolic numbers, cabalistic symbols, cryptic visuals, and deleted place names. It is Map as Puzzle.

Geography professor Harold Brodsky, modern discoverer of this inventive cartographic teaching tool, said, "I can visualize a father or grandfather opening the map and saying, 'Come here, young man, and explain what that loop is there for.'" Or he might ask why there are four ships for Jaffa pulling thirteen rafts loaded with cedars of Lebanon. (Four represents the four blessings of God and the four sons in the story of the four questions; thirteen symbolizes the thirteen attributes of mercy mentioned in the Book of Exodus; cedars were used to build Solomon's temple.) Or why are there three beehives on the house porch? Or what is the zigzag maneuver going on in the Red Sea (far right)? Everything is waiting to be decoded. The exercise was to test knowledge and instill gratitude for the gift of freedom in a group of people who prized learning as part of their cultural heritage. First and foremost, learning was a mitzvah, a commandment or law, but learning was never to be made a chore.

To further complicate matters, Ben Jacob, a pastor in the Rhineland before converting to Judaism, used as his template a sixteenth-century map of the Holy Land by a Catholic theologian. So King David is shown in a Christian praying position, kneeling with hands joined. And most unusual in a book intended for family seders is the depiction lower right of Egypt as a bare-breasted woman on a crocodile (Nile). Possibly she is tempting those wandering Israelites tired of desert life to go home (and back to bondage); but most probably she is a borrowing by Ben Jacob from the Christian-dominated cartographic realm's use of women to represent the continents.

THE MEDITERRANEAN SEA

It is function that differentiates charts from maps. A chart is a map intended for navigators, and it usually shows only coastlines. Among the Western cartographic wonders are the surviving medieval portolan charts made with ink on vellum. (*Portolano* is Italian for a pilot book of sailing directions to various ports.) Navigation emerged into the light of Western recorded history with portolan charts. They are the purest form of spatial writing, and they communicate directly the social implications of maps. Originally

PLATE 30. *The Life and Wanderings of Patriarch Abraham.* The ascension of humanism is celebrated in this elaborate map of the Holy Land from Ortelius's 1590 atlas.

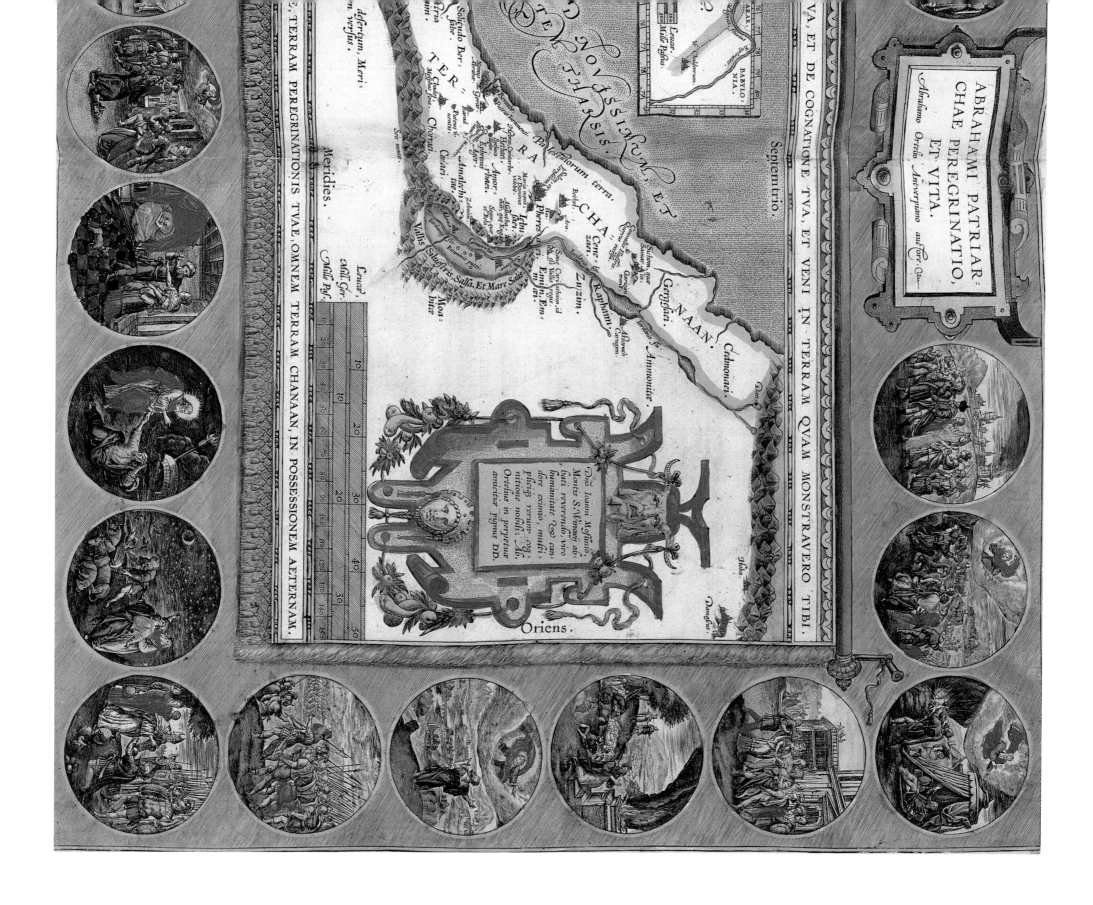

ABRAHAMI PATRIAR=
CHAE PEREGRINATIO,
ET VITA.
Abrahamo Ortelio Antverpiano auctore.

Septemtrio.

Oriens.

Meridies.

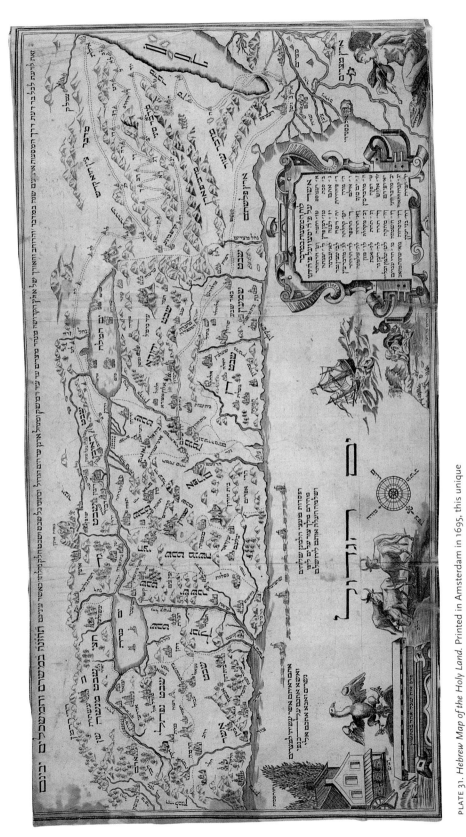

PLATE 31. *Hebrew Map of the Holy Land.* Printed in Amsterdam in 1695, this unique Passover Haggadah map has a hidden agenda.

limited to the Mediterranean, the Black Sea, the North African coast, the European coast south of Scandinavia, England, Ireland, and some islands in the Atlantic, they show all the trading stops a Mediterranean sailor might have made on the job. As cartographic historians Armando Cortesão and Avelino Teixeira da Mota conclude, portolans "are indeed the first true charts in which medieval speculation and fantasy gave place to scientific cartography based on experiment and observation, in accord with the spirit of the times."

The portolans display early navigational wisdom. Sailing along a constant bearing, in a straight line, rather than calculating the myriad changes in direction necessary to sail on a curving earth, extended the journey but made it more practical. Mathematically driven in the Arabic tradition, the charts are dominated by a complex weave of radiating multicolored rhumb lines, dense as a spider's web, straight as Rome's paved roads. The word *rhumb* comes from the name of angle measurement representing the "point" on old-fashioned compass cards; there are thirty-two rhumbs in 360 degrees. Thus thirty-two rhumbs emanate like extended spokes from each of the compass rose circles arranged on the map. The eye rides each rhumb line like a sailing vessel from point of embarkation to port of call. It is Chart as Web of Human Ingenuity. Portolans chronicled a geographic revolution. They illustrated international ties developed in the Mediterranean world. The earliest surviving portolan charts the course between Acre and Venice during the Crusades.

The source of portolan charts is unknown. They appeared at the time the compass debuted in the West, and the earliest Italian

charts, from Genoa about 1270, are devoid of all embellishment. Along with the purists of the northern Italian school centered on the cities of Genoa, Venice, and Ancona, there were those in Spain who used an elaborately embellished portolan style—the direct result of centuries of Arab domination—known as the Catalan school. It flourished in Majorca and Barcelona, major centers of the rich and worldly Catalan empire. Typical of portolans, names of ports are given "on land," perpendicular to the shoreline, making it necessary to rotate the chart as the journey required. Cities and dangerous shoals are stippled in red, reflecting the influence of the copyist monks who used red to mark important liturgical events, hence "red-letter days."

A surviving 1559 Catalan masterpiece on vellum signed by Mateo Prunes (fl. 1533–94), a member of a family of Majorcan cartographers, is in such perfect condition that it may have been prepared to decorate a wall or to enrich the library of a prince or a wealthy merchant, rather than to be manhandled at sea (see Plate 32). While the Italians focused on the Mediterranean, Catalan cartographers embraced the Atlantic coasts of Europe and Africa, and subsequently encompassed journeys across the ocean, once people learned the Atlantic was not only a border but a highway offering many different destinations. The Prunes chart, oriented west, concentrates on the Mediterranean world, with the Black Sea, part of the Red Sea, the Atlantic African coast down to Senegal, and the European coast up to northern Scandinavia; there are also some real islands (Iceland

PLATE 32. *Chart of the Mediterranean and Western Europe.* This 1559 embellished *portolano* is from the Catalan school.

and Greenland) and some imaginary ones in the northwest. A crescent flag dominating Africa announces the power of the Islamic Turks in the Mediterranean world. In fact, one flies over a fortress on the European continent, where the Ottomans had reached the gates of Vienna. With those flags, the Prunes chart depicts what compelled Spain to sail west to the Indies and Portugal to sail south around Africa, a region Prunes imagines as still inhabited by legendary freakish humans and unicorns. Rhumb lines emboldened the Age of Exploration.

Christian piety thrones at the top, on the neck of the animal's skin (vellum), with pictures of a bishop, the Virgin and Child, cherubs, and an angel. But, directly below, an ornate scientific compass rose has the initials of the eight winds named according to a newly translated essay by Aristotle; each wind is personified around the edges of the map. Much of Aristotle's lost work was transmitted to the West via Muslim Spain in the eleventh and twelfth centuries. It was the first decisive impetus to a more sophisticated intellectual tradition in Europe. In the name of commerce, religious and secular worlds were thrown together, another sign of change in Catholic Spain instigated by the unstoppable European late Renaissance. Three obligatory colors—gold was a luxurious extra—marked the network of rhumb lines: black or brown for the eight cardinal winds, green for the eight half winds, and red for the sixteen quarter winds. Taken together they form the thirty-two points of the mariner's compass.

These portolan charts provided a unified image of the Mediterranean world. They were distilled from seafaring experience into sailing directions. Soon these instructions would have explorers crossing the Atlantic Ocean and circumnavigating Africa for the first time by traversing speculative rhumb lines that were often highly misleading but nevertheless successful enough to have Shakespeare's Maria say of Malvolio in *Twelfth Night* (1601): "He does smile his face into more lines than is in the new map with the augmentation of the Indies."

Using the new gunpowder weapons, the Ottoman Turks took the city of Constantinople in 1453: it became popularly known as Istanbul. Already strong in the Black Sea, Turkish naval power soon spearheaded one of the greatest imperial expansions in the history of the Mediterranean world. The Ottoman Empire became the most powerful state on earth. Istanbul was its mapmaking center. A miniature in a sixteenth-century manuscript by Alaaddin Mansur (Plate 33) depicts the famous astronomer and cartographer Taki al-Din—"He has drawn to scale all the angles of space." It portrays him in his busy observatory. The globe shown at the bottom of the miniature features the newly discovered eastern seaboard of South America and the South Pole.

It was Muhiddin Piri Reis (c. 1465–1554)—Reis means admiral or captain—who wrote, "If a man who understands nothing of compasses and charts sets out to sea his affairs will suffer loss.... It is necessary to know the science of this business." One of the sources on his 1513 world map was "the map of the western lands drawn by Columbus." All of the maps made by Columbus on his four voyages to America between 1492 and 1504 have been lost. Whether by spying or piracy, Reis saw those lost maps, and some of their precious information appears on this Turkish miniature. In the Western imagination, the Ottoman Empire seems removed from the Age of Discovery. Yet when Europeans crisscrossed the globe traversing all the angles of space on imaginary rhumb lines, the Mediterranean Sea was again a Muslim lake.

THE THREE-PART WORLD

PLATE 34. *Han Cosmic Mirror.* A Han dynasty (206 BCE–220 CE) cosmos has a square earth and a round heaven.

OVERLEAF: Detail from p. 76.

t was the ancient Greek mariners who gave the names Europe and Asia to the lands on either side of their home in the Aegean Sea. The early Greek philosophers, the Ionians of Miletus, were first to identify the Aegean as part of a larger sea, the Mediterranean, which they came to view as a divider of the surrounding landmasses: Europe to the west and north of them, Asia to the east, and Libya (Africa) to the south. The Greeks inhabited a three-part world, a notion inherited by the Romans and passed on to early Christendom, and one which found perhaps its purest cartographic expression in the so-called T&O (*orbis terrarum*) map of medieval Europe (see Plate 103). Maps both record the evolution of our understanding of this three-part world and open a window into the many cultures that have flourished there.

ASIA

Written after Marco Polo spent twenty-four years in China, his geography book, *Description of the World*, brought wondrous news to the insulated Mediterranean world of the rich and wholly unknown civilized empire of the khans, its vast area inhabited by millions of people right next door, though a universe apart. Observing as a cultural geographer, Polo pioneered ethnographical science. In 1271 he had traveled to Beijing with his merchant father and uncle bearing full diplomatic credentials from Pope Gregory X and from the Great Khan himself, a complex man with tremendous interest in the Western world, who had been visited by Marco's father and uncle in 1266. As a court member of the conquering Mongols, however, Marco lived detached from the most glorious and awesome Asian reality: the influential Chinese mindscape, infused with a genius distinctly dissimilar from that of his own culture, a genius that expresses itself beautifully in the language of mapping.

Essentially out of reach to Western travelers after the meteoric rise of Islam in the seventh century, Asia, or the Orient, was a place of myths and legends. The Crusades brought Europeans a little nearer to comprehending something of Central Asia, but then the Orient quickly became a terrifying reality. By 1259 the Mongols, united under Genghis Khan (1155–1227), had created the largest empire in recorded history by savagely conquering most of Eurasia, failing to win only the four major peninsulas: western Europe (bordered by Mongol-occupied Russia, Poland, and Hungary), Arabia, India, and Indochina. After the death of Genghis, his empire was divided into three main lordships, with Kublai Khan (1215–94), now the Great Khan, residing in the eastern part. The Mongol Empire unified many eastern countries, and the various branches of the

trade route from the Mediterranean world to China known as the Silk Road (or Silk Route) became safe and important again to both Western and Eastern merchants. Each branch passed through oasis settlements where cities grew and thrived. Though many precious commodities traveled by caravans east to west, exotic silks were the most desirable and gave their name to the entire enterprise.

Satisfied by fables of a heathen East—the lucrative exchange of goods along the Silk Road did not engender cultural exchange—Polo and his Western contemporaries still referred to the exploits of Alexander the Great. Polo's geography book was neither the first authentic account of Asia nor the best, but it was the only one to trace a route across the entire continent, and the most encouraging to geographical studies because of its immense popularity. Thus his journey from the Mediterranean world serves as a convenient organizing principle for a look at the mapping of Asian civilizations.

The heaviest baggage seventeen-year-old Marco Polo carried from his native Venice was the intellectual imprint of Christianity on the Mediterranean world. For him, everything fell under its shadow. The Mongols, and in particular Kublai Khan, were more open to new ideas. The complex Chinese concepts of the universe were initially alien, but the Mongols eventually made many of them their own.

A mirror from the Han dynasty (206 BCE–220 CE) is believed to be a symbolic representation of a square earth (frame) in a round heaven (Plate 34). Modern eyes can imagine that square earth in thrall to the central, jewel-like "sun" dominating the round heaven. Or that square island of the known world may contain jewel-like China, the source of all civilization, at its center amid the encircling sea. There are many possibilities. The options capture exquisitely the multifaceted sensibility and imagination of the Chinese.

Like Xenophon, Polo traveled without maps. He relied upon the kindness of strangers and followed prescribed routes. (The only maps he refers to are sea charts.) Nor did he draw maps, perhaps because—as the Greek philosopher Heraclitus (fl. c. 500 BCE) observed—to reach the truth from appearances, it is necessary to interpret, to guess the riddle, and though this is within mankind's capacity, it is something most people never attempt. Instead of visual diagrams, Polo worked in the age-old verbal and written tradition of lists known as itinerary mapping.

Because Polo wrote of places "he has not seen but has heard from men of credit and veracity," his book did not transform Western topographical concepts, in part because his path could not be mapped from the text even when the trade routes were known. But he did indicate bearings and distances, which introduced to the

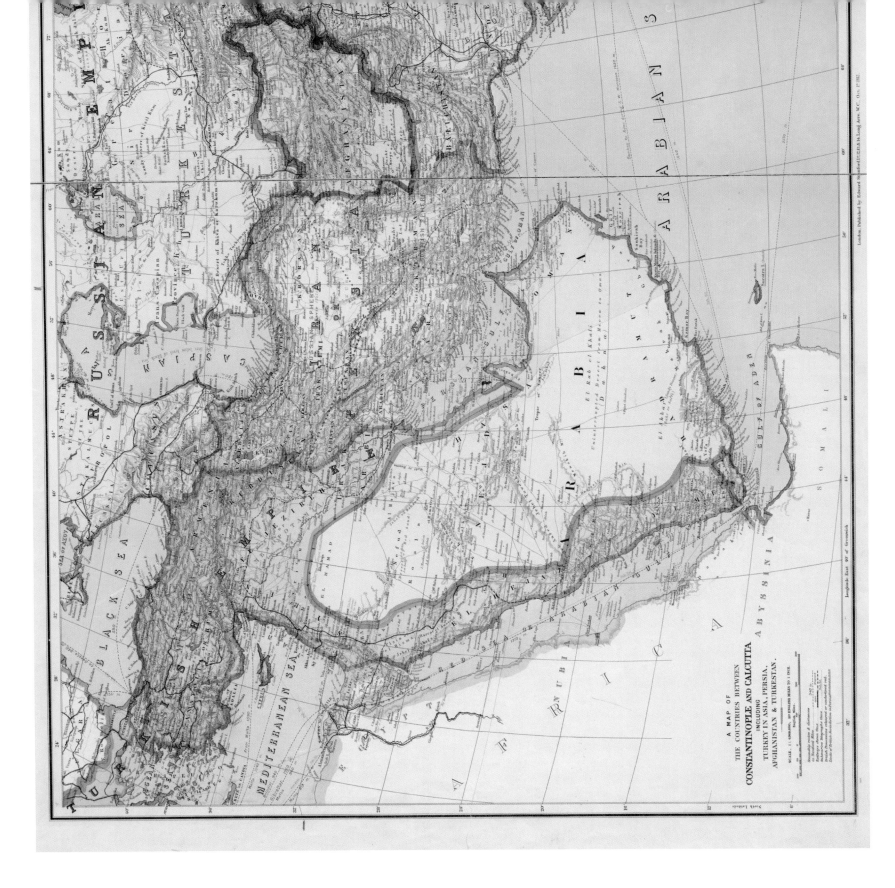

Western medieval imagination a geographical rather than a theological approach to the world. Most important, he disabused his readers of Jerusalem's being at the center of the known world, equidistant from the Atlantic and the Sea of Japan. The interest he aroused begot research, and research produced sound knowledge. Until the Age of Discovery and the invention in the West of the printing press, the manuscripts of his book were read primarily as literary entertainment, a book of a million marvels.

Armenia

"Let me begin with Armenia," Marco Polo writes. "The truth is there are actually two Armenias, a Greater and a Lesser." The truth is, the history of Armenia is long, complicated, and further proof that geography influences destiny. Polo began his journey at the terminus of the Silk Route in Lesser Armenia, a Mediterranean coastal strip subject to the Mongols, where the Christian Armenian kingdom of Cilicia was located (1198–1375). The Armenian

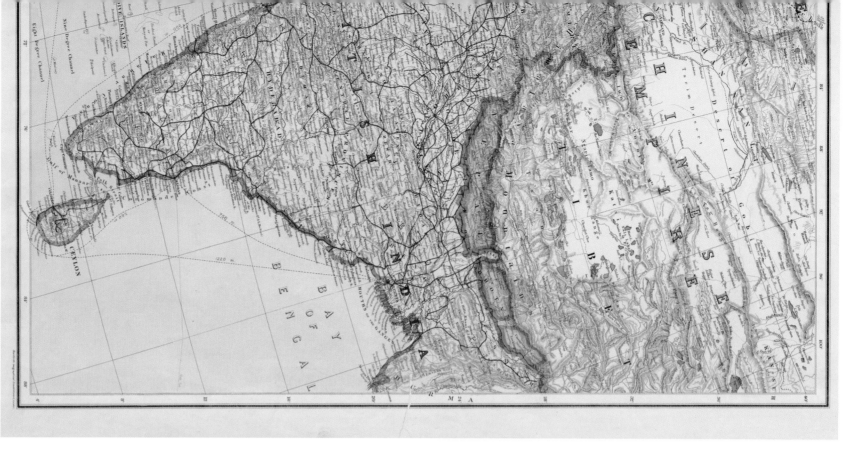

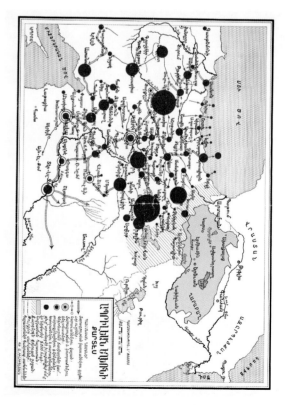

Though the classical Armenian mathematician and astronomer Ananias of Shirak (c. 595–670) based his *Ashkharhatsoyts,* or Geography Text, on Greek sources, his description of Armenia codified the Armenian cultural realm for all time, even when Armenians were stateless from 375 to 1918. Technically without a country of their own, these highlanders prospered as one of the most important ethnic groups in the heterogeneous populations of the various conquering empires. Many an Armenian ascended an imperial throne. For centuries their acknowledged presence as a unified community haunted foreign maps, such as a British one from 1912 (Plate 35). This map documents Armenia as a nation of people, a recognized cultural realm spanning both the Turkish (green) and Persian (yellow) empires. It is Map as Agent Provocateur. The English mapmakers were, in fact, raising the querulous question of land rights. The map boldly states that Turkish and Persian boundaries were imposed on the resident Armenians. This helped foster the political agendas of the British and their allies, which resulted in a cataclysmic disaster for the Armenian people.

The conquering Mongols had no need for maps in 1236. As Polo explains, "They made up their minds to conquer the whole world." For the most part, the religions they encountered were left untouched. Armenia, the first state to adopt Christianity as its official religion, in 301—the traditional date—was no exception. Throughout Armenia's stateless centuries, the church was the guardian and repository of Armenian culture, education, art, and society. During World War 1, the Islamic Turkish Ottoman Empire, aligned with Germany, grew fearful that its enemies, the Christian Russians, would use religion as an excuse to repeat their successful 1828 invasion of the region usually identified on European maps (similar to the one in Plate 35) as "Armenia." Russian Armenia is colored pink on a 1965 Armenian map (Plate 36) that re-creates—in shockingly graphic terms—the Ottoman Empire's 1915 final solution to the "Armenian question": ethnically cleanse

nation is perhaps the oldest of the civilized races in Western Asia. In 95 BCE, Armenians ruled the three mountainous plateaus rising above the Fertile Crescent to form the northern sector of the Middle East. This land bridge links the easternmost part of Europe with the westernmost part of Asia—from the Mediterranean to the Caspian Sea. (Today, Armenians hold a fifth of the area.) Every power struggle in the region involved Armenia, and probably eradicated any examples of indigenous mapping.

the region via genocide and prevent the Russians from expanding their pink property again under the guise of unifying Christian people.

To prevent this second Russian expansion, the Turks uprooted the Armenians and sent them on a forced march to wilderness tracts in the directions shown by arrows on the map. In the course of the journey, more than 1 million were slaughtered by Turk and Kurd citizens of the Ottoman Empire. The code of conventional signs is transformed by the Armenian mapmaker's use of the color red. It translates this "Map of the April Tragedy" into a visual portrait of a nation's bloody anguish. It is Map as Rhetoric of Rage. By engaging the viewer's emotions, it exemplifies the tension between science and art in the language of cartography.

Afghanistan

Polo followed the Mongol-controlled and safeguarded Silk Route — the most famous east–west trading trail — across the deserts of Persia (Iran) onto the naturally fertile plateaus of northern Afghanistan. About the size of Texas, with two-thirds of its 250,000 square miles 5,000 feet above sea level, Afghanistan is mostly mountain

PLATE 37. *Letts's Bird's Eye View of the Approaches to India.* The British colonial attitude toward Afghanistan is not kept secret on this map.

and desert or semidesert, though there are many fertile valleys and plains. "Armies are prone to loiter here because of the abundance of supplies," Polo wrote. But armies serviced by the merchants on the Silk Route were *always* present there because geography made it a meeting ground for migratory hordes and conquering soldiers bringing the abundance of divergent cultures that produced the eminent arts and letters of Afghanistan.

In the face of much resistance, the Mongols and their descendants remained in control of part or all of the country from 1220 to 1500. After the country's economic collapse, when the Silk Route's usefulness was destroyed in 1498 by Vasco da Gama's circumnavigation of Africa and his opening of a water route to the East, the tribes fought to maintain their integrity during a power struggle between the Moguls of northern India and the Safavids of Persia. Then, in the last decade of the eighteenth century, two new imperialistic powers — the British Empire and Czarist Russia — laid siege to the entire country. The British were looking to protect their colonial holdings in India from invasion via neighboring Afghanistan; the Russians were expanding their empire south and east. With its attendant disregard for Afghan life and the overthrowing of all indigenous administrations in the path of both contending powers for supremacy in Central Asia, the ensuing power struggle became known as the Great Game.

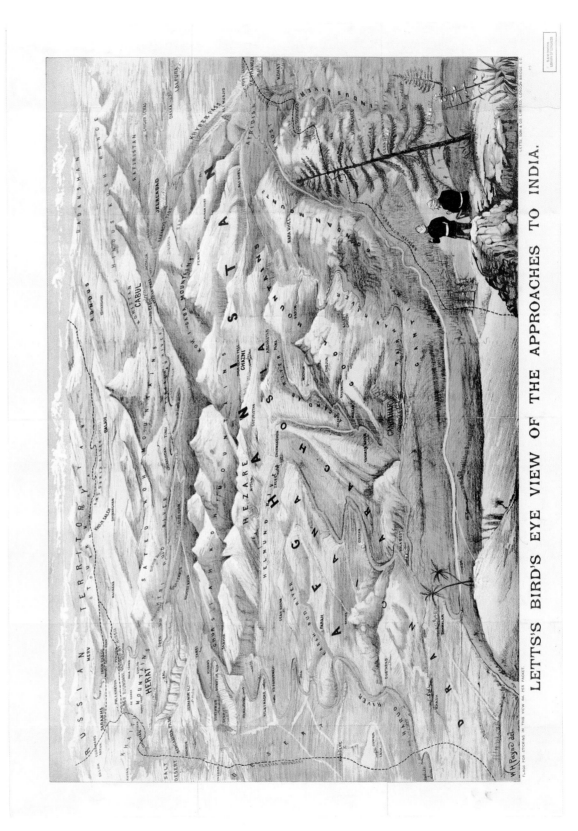

LETTS'S BIRD'S EYE VIEW OF THE APPROACHES TO INDIA.

At its start, there were more than 2,000 miles separating British India from Russia, most of them unmapped. By 1868, the Russians were in control of the northern bank of the Amu Darya River, which, by Anglo-Russian treaty, eventually became the northern border of Afghanistan. Though no direct conflict ever erupted between the two alien aggressors, Afghanistan was the center of activity. The British launched two wars (1838, 1878) in the country, set up a national puppet government in 1881, and gained full control of Afghanistan's foreign policy, which unified the country under one law and one ruler while breaking up the tribal system—giving birth to Afghanistan as a single political entity. A British map from 1907 (Plate 37) dramatizes the country's fate. It is the year the Great Game ended with Russia accepting Afghanistan's place within Britain's "sphere of influence." It is Map as Managed Real Estate.

On this map, two unarmed, relaxed British soldiers—symbolically bigger than any mountain—are admiring their country's latest appropriation. One is pointing out "approaches to India," as if they are paths in his garden. Or he could be lecturing the earth on what's what. The British public is being assured by this image of conquest that everything "out there" is under control, and all troublesome human elements have been erased. This map is a not-so-subtle manifesto for British imperialism. It literally projects British values into the world.

Afghanistan remained a British protectorate until 1919. Later in the century, Russia pounced again.

Mongolia

Genghis Khan's clan belonged to an obscure Mongol tribe from the outskirts of the Gobi River in what is now Outer Mongolia. As with the Romans, the cultures conquered by the Mongols transformed these invaders themselves. Nowhere is this more evident than in cartography. In thirteenth-century China, the Mongols founded the Yuan dynasty (1279–1368), never accepted by the Chinese as a legitimate dynasty but always regarded as blow-in bandits. Nevertheless, the outside world has inaccurately labeled an astoundingly modern-looking form of Chinese cartography from the Yuan period, when Polo visited there, as "the Mongolian style." Oriented with north in the bottom right-hand corner, a map from the *History of Institutions of the Yuan Dynasty* (1329) in this style uses a schematic grid upon which mathematically expressed geographical information appears in lieu of pictorial representation of the northwestern part of China (Plate 38). Places are located on the featureless grid, as on a piece of graph paper, allowing positions, distances, and itineraries to be studied as mathematical abstractions. It is Map as Genius of China. Had it been seen by Polo's Western contemporaries, it would have confounded most but enthralled those familiar with compass-driven portolan charts, while calling into question for many the received notions of a barbaric, medieval Orient in dire need of Western Christian civilization.

The grid and its resulting quantitative cartography are credited to China's Chang Heng, who lived in the second century. According to the official history of the Han dynasty, he laid the groundwork for the mathematical use of grids with maps when he "cast a network of co-ordinates about heaven and earth, and reckoned on the basis of it." (He also invented the seismograph.) The map is the forerunner of later Arabic astrolabes. It visualizes the cultural exchange that eventually did occur via the Silk Route as a result of the Chinese-inspired Mongols. After the fall of the Yuan dynasty, the Mongolians retired to their original steppe homelands and came under Chinese rule until 1921, when Mongolia won its independence with Soviet assistance. In 2000 a democratic coalition was elected to office.

China

When Marco Polo arrived at the imperial court of Kublai Khan in Cathay (China), the conquered Chinese existed in a world apart from the barbaric and tyrannical Mongolians. A gifted linguist, Polo held various jobs in the Great Khan's administration for over seventeen years, but he never learned Chinese or anything about China's indigenous culture, which was the lodestar for much of Kublai Khan's east Asian empire. The adaptable Mongols with nothing of their own had adopted Chinese institutions mostly based upon the teachings of Confucius (c. 550–479 BCE), who taught that government service was a proper concern of the scholar and literary scholarship a proper concern of government. These beliefs had created an administration that was, theoretically, a democratic meritocracy in China and encouraged the khan to welcome competent foreigners, such as Polo, into his realm.

Two of the oldest extant comprehensive maps of China are engraved on opposite sides of a stone tablet (see Plates 39 and 40). In 1136 they were made as teaching aids, enabling students in the Song period (960–1279) preparing for government civil-servant examinations to understand the geographical history and idealized political hopes of China, where reasoning and historical analogy were inseparable, where the emperor ruled "all under Heaven" (*tian xia*), and where all foreign peoples were "barbarians." China was the Middle Kingdom (*zhongguo*), the terrestrial focal point of *tian xia*, and the source of all civilization, the way Jerusalem and Mecca were focal points for Europeans and Arabs.

Each of these maps is upside down to the other because the tablet was not for reading but for printing. The maps represent the

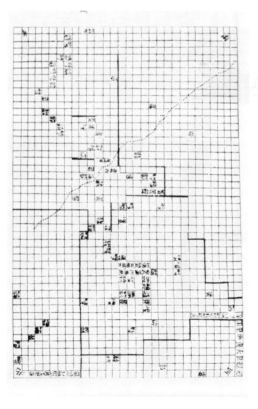

PLATE 38. *Mongolian Style of Cartography.* This abstract form of cartography was practiced in China during Marco Polo's time.

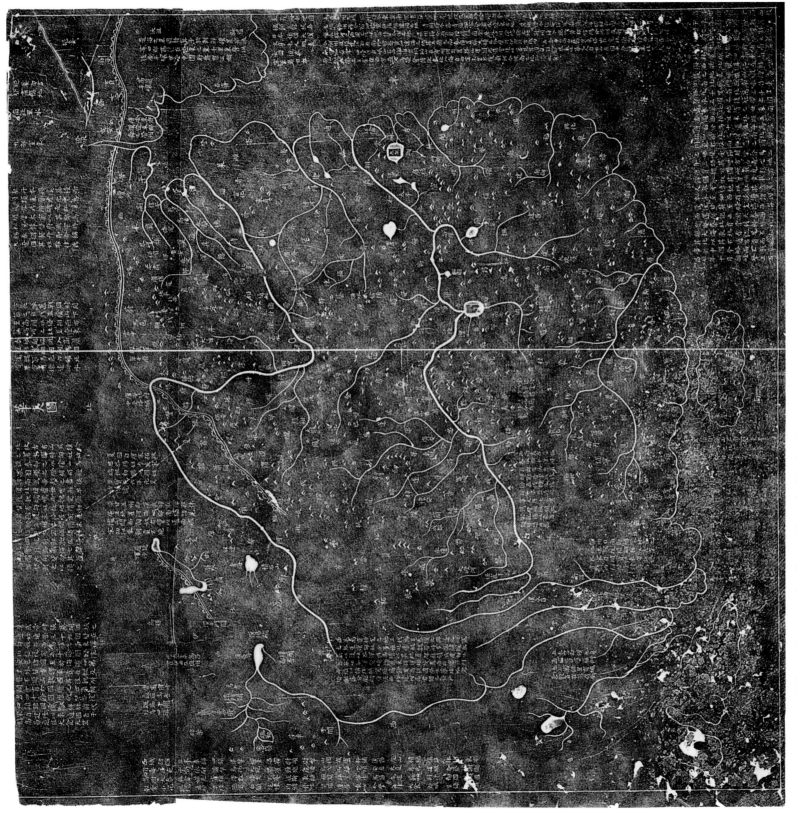

PLATES 39 AND 40. *Map of China and Foreign Lands* and *Map of the Tracks of Yu.* The oldest extant Chinese maps of China are the two forms of their cartographic traditions.

two classical styles of Chinese mapping. One of them, *Hua yi tu* (Map of China and Foreign Lands) is in the multilayered traditional or indigenous style, drawn by the cartographically untrained court administrator assigned to the task. (Until the nineteenth century there were no professional or specialist cartographers in China.) With its ninth-century names of administrative divisions, this is reckoned the oldest Chinese map extant. On it the coast, a feature of only minor concern to the government, is represented metaphorically as being far from the capital. *Hua yi tu* is Map as

Concept of Place. Lacking scale, heavily annotated, it reveals an introspective preoccupation with local administrative concerns by emphasizing the heartland (west and northwest China), and by a topographical laxness, which includes misplacing unimportant rivers and poorly realizing the undervalued, though generally well-known, coastline. Surveying instruments adequate for greater accuracy were nevertheless common in the third century. The magnetic compass, for instance, which became a tool in the Mediterranean world by 1190, had appeared in China a century before.

The map lists seventy western countries on one side, bespeaking a country far from isolated.

Since the Han period, each dynasty had its own history compiled from its court's "daily chronicles" (*Jih-li*), and these histories contained special chapters on foreign places—"geographical chapters"—in which each visiting trader described his home. Regular traffic by sea with Syria began early, and the military traveler Pan Ch'ao visited the Mediterranean world's city of Ta-ts'in, believed to be Antioch, in the first century. He was discouraged from

going to Rome by local traders who feared their own loss of China's business if Pan Ch'ao took word home of the great capital city.

Meanwhile the stone's reverse map—*Yu ji tu* (Map of the Tracks of Yu)—uses a grid system to indicate a scale noted on the map in the "modern," or mathematical, international style devised contemporaneously in the West by Ptolemy. Each side of each square represents approximately thirty-three miles. Here, the coastline is impressively close to present-day representations. It is Map as Contours of Place. The date the map was drawn is inferred by the

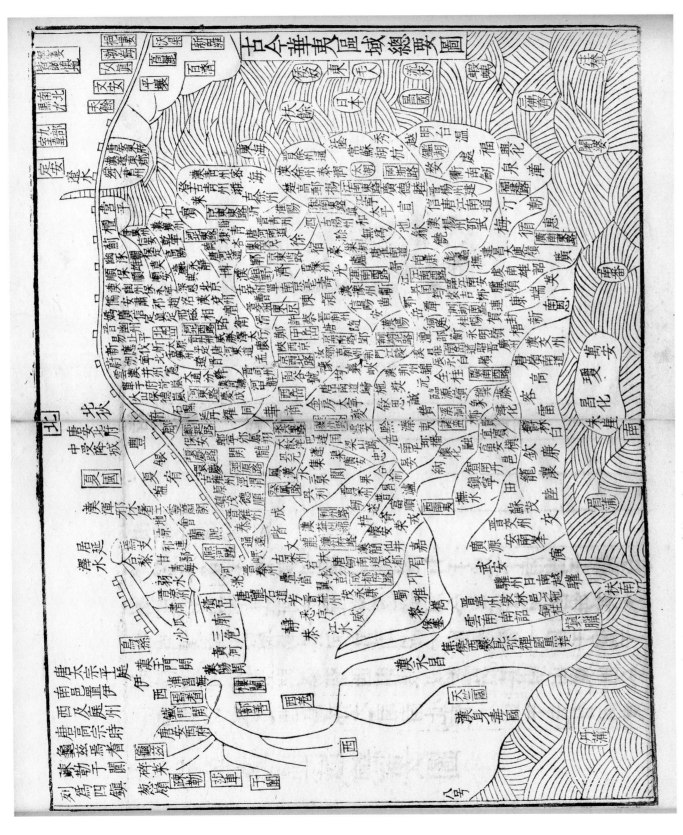

PLATE 41. *General Map of Territories from the Ancient to Present, of China and Foreign Countries.* This image of power and security is from the earliest Chinese atlas extant.

absence of any administrative districts established after 1080, and by the ancient course of the Yellow River, which changed during 1080–81. The grid was not used to locate longitude or latitude but for maintaining scale. *Yu ji tu* is most likely based on earlier imperial regional maps and geographical writings. Though the text of the map honors Confucian ideas of the fanciful sources for the major rivers, the rivers are depicted in their geographical reality. The obstacle that prevented the mapmaker from erasing the disparity was his unwillingness to challenge the established "fact" in Confucian classics. Thus the two truths exist side by side, for what was once believed true was honored as always true—a concept that would have baffled the Western consciousness of Marco Polo had he come upon it. The map demonstrates technical facility far in advance of comparable European terrestrial cartography at the time and is on a par with portolan charts of the Mediterranean

world—a place not unfamiliar to the Chinese. On this one stone are the twin spirits of Chinese cartography: subjective and objective mapmaking.

Since the Chinese valued literary training above technical knowledge, mathematicians and astronomers were usually not part of the ruling bureaucratic class responsible for producing maps. Official Chinese mapping was not antimathematical; it was *more than mathematical.* The knowledge of history and literature required of the scholarly administrators fostered a strong sense of social unity—"Do unto others as you would have them do unto you" (Confucius). The Chinese visually expressed in many forms their unique society, in which the way of the ancients was the pattern for the present. *Lidai dili zhichang* (Geographical Maps of Successive Dynasties) is the oldest extant atlas. It would have been in use when Polo arrived in China. From the Song period, just before the Mongols' Yuan period, it bears a strong resemblance to *Hua yi tu*, the subjective gridless stone map from that same period.

Comprising several volumes, the atlas contains forty-eight traditional maps showing the administrative units of twenty-eight different political periods, beginning in the era of legendary kings (twenty-first century BCE). Unsurprising in a literary culture, and as with Islamic maps, text predominates. The first map in the atlas, *Gujin hua yi quyu zongyao tu* (General Map of Territories from the Ancient to Present, of China and Foreign Countries; Plate 41) shows the provinces (*lu*) established during the Song period and still in place when Kublai Khan arrived. The topography is less than accurate because it is the boundary changes during the preceding centuries that are the map's concern. It is Map as Narrative of a Shared Past. On it, the eye is drawn to China's frontiers. The seemingly unbreachable Great Wall barricades the north from invading barbarians — such as their Mongol conquerors — and while some neighboring borders and western countries are placed fairly accurately, others, like Japan, Vietnam, and India, are approximately placed to locate economic activities. The expressed self-image is one of power and security, bolstered by the imperial continuity detailed in the atlas's other maps. The Chinese people's admiration for their own culture is dramatized by the dominant Chinese characters. These ideograms were the civilizing instrument for many neighboring countries, and they seem to be on the march westward, carrying the message of Chinese superiority to the rest of the known world.

Dating from 210 BCE, the tomb of the unifier of China, Emperor Ch'in Shih Huang Ti, contained a famous representation of the country's rivers and the sea in mercury; mechanical devices made the liquid flow and circulate around a huge map of the earth in the most grandiose expression known of an ancient tradition of including maps in tombs. The earliest bits and pieces of maps or plans (*tu*) — from the Zhanguo (Warring States) period (403–221 BCE) — are from ancient tombs of administrators. In life, they needed maps to define the boundaries of their power and to assess taxes; in death, the maps of their regions defined their roles on earth to command respect from their descendants. Tombs from the Han dynasty hold three-dimensional clay models of fields and ponds.

Kublai Khan's rejection of the Chinese language, script, and rituals, and Polo's subsequent ignorance of them, blinded the Venetian to the depth of Chinese cultural and historical unity made manifest in many artful ways, particularly with maps. His detachment was due not only to the language barrier — he spoke the Mongols' preferred Persian — but also to the reality of conquest: the Chinese were banished from Mongol court life. Thus, this most curious of men never came to comprehend the many functions served by mapping (*di tu*) in China. For example, the spiritual relationship experienced by the Chinese with the earth led to its contours' being represented in models (relief maps) for the first time in the fourth or third century BCE (1510 dates the earliest relief map in Europe). Incense burners were made in the shape of P'eng Lai, a

PLATE 42. *Bronze Incense Burner of P'eng Lai.* A legendary mountain is the subject of this fourth- or third-century BCE Chinese incense burner and relief map.

legendary mountain paradise believed to exist on the far side of the Pacific (Plate 42). There were also wooden jigsaw-puzzle relief maps, and Polo might have seen children using them as toys.

Cartography seems always to have played a leading role in China's political life. A centralized bureaucracy was established in China during the Qin period (221–207 BCE), and its political philosopher Han Feizi (d. 223 BCE) wrote: "The laws are codified in maps (or charts) and books, kept in government offices, and promulgated among the people." Maps were visual records of political history. Since culture is also spatially constituted, maps made manifest China's cultural inheritance. They documented treaties, confirmed subservience by exposing territory to scrutiny, and formalized foreign visits by including ethnographic sketches of the guests. Maps revealed conceptions of "the other." Geography was a subdivision of history, which is a logical development when the highest officials are literary scholars. Knowledge of maps and its attendant command over space was an all-pervasive source of social power for the ruling elite. None proved more effective than *Jiankang zhi* (The Gazetteer of the Jiankang [Nanking] Prefecture), first printed in 1261. Over eight thousand ancient gazetteers — comprehensive records of

believed a dynasty fell as a result of weakness and failings in its dealings with heaven, and new ones rose with the blessings of history. Thus Chinese gazetteers chronicle the rise and fall of dynasties.

When Marco Polo arrived in China, the legendary cartographer Zhu Siben (1273–1333) was two years old. As a grown man, Zhu created a world map, now lost. While European-Arabic mapmakers had the southern tip of Africa pointing eastward, even enclosing the Indian Ocean, Zhu Siben drew its correct triangular shape. This fact further refutes the popular theory that China was isolated from the West until the Jesuit missionary Matteo Ricci (1552–1610) arrived, bringing "modern" mathematical or international mapping to the scientifically naive Far East. In general, Ricci's use of mathematical statistics became yet another genre of mapping for the Chinese, one relegated by the mapmaking bureaucrats to a position below visualizing cultural data, which was more relevant to their lives. In China it was understood that cartographers constructed a world, they did not reproduce it.

For example, three years after Ricci presented the global earth in 1604, a Chinese encyclopedia honored tradition by depicting the heavens as round and the earth as square in accordance with classical geographical poems (fu, or rhapsody) and philosophical tomes, regardless of recorded empirical evidence to the contrary. Again, the ancient way was respected as the pattern for the present. In China the natural separation in any society of scientists and literati was heightened by the social disparity the two groups experienced, with the literati in the upper echelons of government and society and the scientists the equivalent of blue-collar workers. Modern astronomical discoveries and mathematically dominated cartography were not disseminated among the scholar-administrators. The provincial mapmaker drew heartfelt pictures of his region, then added text to describe it more precisely. To the emperor, who believed he could read a person's character from his map as easily as from his handwriting, this method avoided a soulless, mathematical proficiency.

The key to understanding this collusion between art and science can be found in the fact that Chinese writing is drawing symbols instead of forming letters, and, as such, is directly related to mapmaking. Each character, being pictographic, is the image of an idea, as a map is the image of an idea of the earth. Chinese characters, like maps, evolved by simplifying observed objects. Thus, the ideogram for map (Plate 44) contains a schematic map. Calligraphy and cartography are delineations of the mind. "Those looking to develop principles for other forms of graphic expression, such as

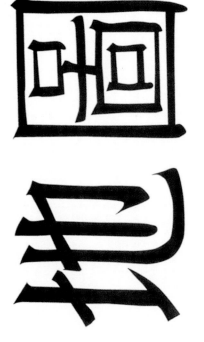

PLATE 44. Chinese Characters di tu (Map of the Land). The Chinese ideogram for "map" contains a schematic map.

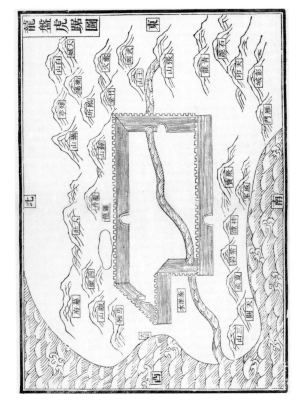

PLATE 43. The Map of a Place Coiled by a Dragon and Crouched by a Tiger. Symbolism enchants on this map from a Chinese gazetteer first printed in 1261.

particular regions—are still in existence, and Jiankang zhi served as a model for many. According to the renowned sinologist Joseph Needham, "In other literatures there is little comparable to this forest of monuments which the industry of provincial scholars erected over the centuries."

The contents of these gazetteers are arranged by order of importance. The first map in Jiankang zhi (Plate 43) is dominated by the walls of the populous (250,000) Jiankang city—now Nanking—presented in a three-dimensional manner from two points of view: looking down and head-on at the same time. There are also the Jiankang Mountains, the bordering sea, and a canal dissecting Jiankang, symbolized by its walls. The poetic title, however, is Long pan hu ju tu (The Map of a Place Coiled by a Dragon and Crouched by a Tiger). Dragons, considered just, benevolent, and the bearers of good fortune, were a symbol for the emperor, who in fact lived in Jiankang. A crouching tiger was a protector, a preserver of family, and a symbol of strength. The political meaning of this map outweighs its geographical content. It is Map as Symbolic Conceit.

The emperor bore responsibility for the running of the entire universe as well as for his earthly kingdom. The seasonal cycles depended upon his performing the proper sacrifices. If all went well, he lived removed from sight behind the towering walls of his palace. On the map, his awesome power transforms his consecrated city walls into earth's imperial crown. The fact of his presence is Jiankang, the still center of all under heaven. His strength is represented by those walls and their attendant mountains. Political power informs everything, just as it controlled the way the gazetteer's major author, Zhou Yinghe, proceeded as noted in his text: he received orders from the local governor to assist in administration and to be "helpful to society." The book reinforced the values and beliefs of the people to whom it was offered. It was reproduced under the auspices of the khan in 1342 because it fostered his legitimacy in a society that

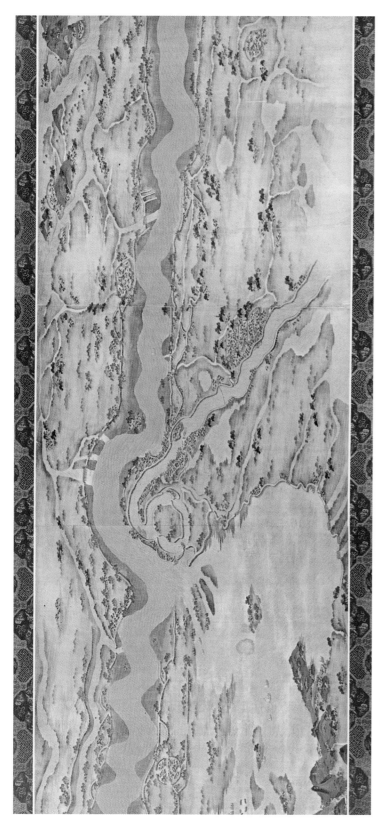

PLATE 45. *Measuring the Yellow River.* The aesthetic elements found in both calligraphy and cartography were employed for this Ming (1368–1644) scroll map.

maps, would turn to writing for guidance," concludes the cartographic historian Cordell Yee. Chinese characters not only convey thought, they also express the beauty of the thought and the artist's emotions, as well as his moral character. Organically vital, fine calligraphy encompasses *qiyun* (breath-resonance) and is an essential element in the artistic life of the Chinese people. While Western alphabets severely limit the forms of words and produce consistency, Chinese characters have a variety of shapes and thicknesses to stimulate the eye, and each is constructed in an imaginary grid that imposes boundaries, a technique similar to mapmaking. Written text dominated the map image because the written word remained the primary source of representational authority in China.

This multiplicity of form, the heart of the Chinese sensibility, is a fundamental difference between Eastern and Western cartography. Asians strove to *experience* rather than to *understand* the world. The West searched for a single, objective truth—a unified cosmos. The Chinese held to the "ten thousand things," a phrase found in Taoist and Buddhist writings to connote the material diversity of the universe, or endless creativity. Their totality does not equal an ordered world, but expresses the Earth in its process of change. In the words of the poet Li Po (701–762): "No one could whip the changing seasons along so fast;/ the ten thousand things rise and fall of themselves." Each Chinese map is different. Each resonates with these values and doctrines. Personal aesthetics ruled Chinese mapmaking. Maps, however, were never considered true art because they lacked the qualities of "life force" (*qi*) and "kinesthetic power" (*shi*) that distinguished artistic creativity from craftsmanship.

As Confucius taught: "A noble person does not act like an instrument." Most scientists and mathematicians were technicians striving for exactitude. Thus Cordell Yee writes of the Chinese mapmaking tradition: "A map, like a painting, is not just a record,

but is a product of the mapmaker's intuitive sense of underlying form—mapmaking involves abstraction of external details into something internal, a 'mindscape.'" Yet during the Tang period (618–907), maps were a genre of painting. Chinese landscape painting displays all the aesthetic elements found in calligraphy and cartography, and has similar representative powers for the Chinese. (There was no landscape painting as a genre in the West until the seventeenth century.) This is exemplified in a scroll picture map with variable perspectives and a movable focus—as in life—painted in the Ming period (1368–1644) under orders from its first emperor. *Measuring the Yellow River* (Plate 45) combined the work of ten famous painters representing both northern and southern schools of fine art. It is Map as Summation of Statements. It offers spatial understanding of an actual place. Though it lacks the abstractions associated with maps, it is a map and not a landscape painting, because it was not commissioned to capture natural beauty for the emperor but to document the area for strategic purposes in order to perpetuate the dynasty's power. It makes apparent the magical, dreamlike quality achieved when psychological and physical worlds fuse.

Always, the individual observer's values are implicated in observation. This is something the Chinese recognized from their earliest history by establishing *five* directions: north, south, east, west, and center or middle. This acknowledgment of our all being at the center of our own landscapes exercised the Chinese tendency toward introspection. Classical Chinese philosophy teaches that each phenomenon is embedded in a context, a welter of associations. Since each person is a focal point, a social center of relevant roles and ritually constituted relationships with the world, a map contains both the physical world and the mapmaker's memories and reflections. For example, when *Yi Jiang,* a scholar-administrator in Guangdong

PLATE 46. *Atlas of Guangdong Province.* A Chinese scholar-administrator aimed to deliver his sense of place with this map in 1685.

Province, made his provincial atlas in 1685 (Plate 46), he attempted to capture the emotional experience of the province by embuing his work with his own sense of place, as did each of the others with similar assignments, none of them having been trained as cartographers. There is no attempt at naturalism. Scale is of no importance to Yi Jiang; neither is exact placement of named hills or rivers, only their relationships with one another. His intent was to express his intuitive sense of underlying form, to abstract external forms into something internal—Yee's "mindscape." Understanding the full range of his subjects' perceptions, each personal history, each unique particular, was as essential to the emperor's understanding of China's reality as were recorded histories of the provinces.

This humanistic approach to cartography may explain the presence of multiple viewpoints and abstract geography in Chinese traditional mapping. One hand-colored manuscript map of the Yunnan Province (Plate 47) can be revolved, allowing the viewer to experience the mountains from four different points of view, as if occupying the fifth direction of center, where the Hsin-Hsi fortress is placed. The absence of a fixed scale requires that distances be listed on all four sides. Being near the southern border of China and vulnerable to invasion, the province was heavily fortified with circular garrisons. River dikes are labeled, as are embankments.

During the Qing period (1644–1911), *kaozheng* (evidential learning), or the use of empirical evidence, such as longitude and latitude, was stressed by the Jesuit-inspired Manchu rulers for purposes of political and military control. Cultural data and personal expression were not discarded. When the Western world attempted unsuccessfully to make contact government-to-government, the

Manchus had no concept of separate-but-equal nations. However, a China made national boundaries a paramount security issue as the Westerners encroached. The mathematical forms of mapping that gave more precise geographical information were merged with the more traditional forms. This is clearly the case on a scroll of the coast of China painted at the end of the eighteenth century for maritime defense (see Plate 48). Ricci's influence is evident. The cartographer has absorbed the "foreign" template to a great degree. Unrolling the scroll reveals little stylization. Then the island of Macau appears, and traditional cartographic symbolism comes into play.

Macau was leased from China by the Portuguese in 1557. A parched and desolate spot easily supervised by the Chinese, it became an integral part of Portugal's Asian trading programs. Situated at the mouth of the Zhu Jiang (Pearl River), Macau grew to have tremendous strategic importance to the Chinese as conflicts with other Western powers escalated. In order to express this fact visually, the mapmaker has moved Macau to completely dominate the river entrance and enlarged it dramatically. It is Map as Alert. Full of foreigners or "barbarians," albeit peaceful and useful ones, Macau still required special attention from the military map users. It became on the map as large as it was in the life of the Chinese administrators.

There is a traditional Chinese science devoted to the importance of siting, or geomancy. Called feng shui (wind and water), it is

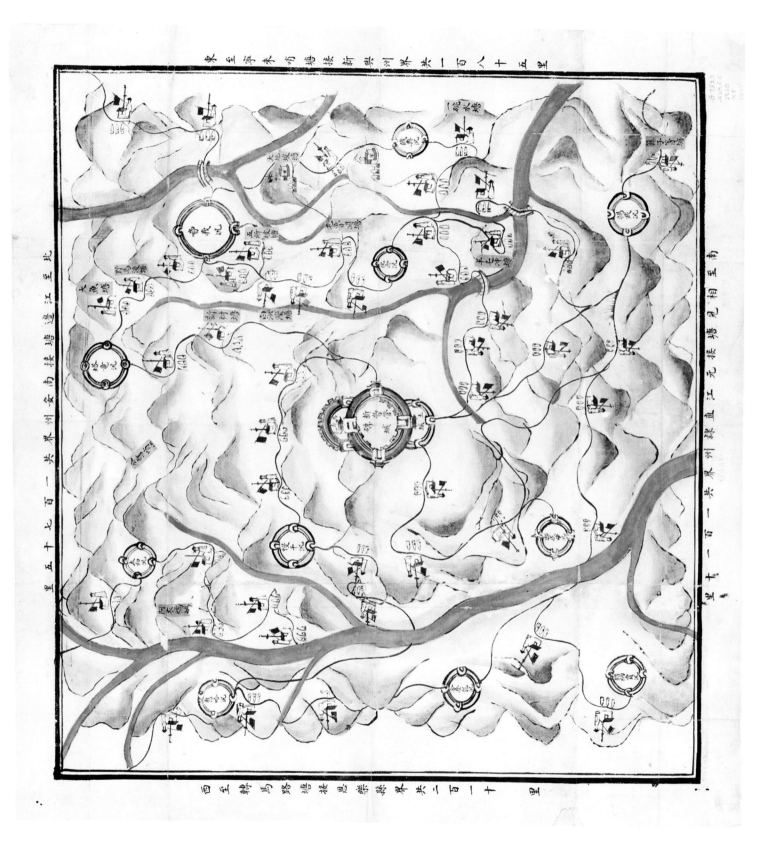

PLATE 47. *Military Map of Xinping County*. The five Chinese cartographic orientations are made manifest by this nineteenth-century map.

THE THREE-PART WORLD

{57}

the art of harmonizing residences of the living and tombs for the dead with the local currents of the cosmic breath. Teardrop-shaped in life, Hainan Island is transformed on a nineteenth-century map by having the blackest object on the map be the coal smoke into a rectangular shape (Plate 49), one more auspicious according to the principles of feng shui because its four sides correspond to the four cardinal directions. The key port towns of Haikou and Yaizhou are shifted to occupy the bottom (north) and top (south) central points on the island, in order to form the north-south axis of the map; the other towns are placed symmetrically in relation to them, creating an auspicious interior configuration. Tiny rectangular boxes of text give place names and useful information to Hainan officials about the native Li people, who are depicted in various economical and social activities: fishing with arrows, farming, gathering forest products, participating in religious rituals. Tall and robust, the Li are characterized as illiterates, fierce-natured but honest, with no tolerance for cheats. Slightly below center: "Each Spring in an open field deep in the mountains, males and females gather together to sing and express their feelings. They pair up, man and woman, and know no restraint." It is Map as Auspicious Report on Hainan.

Even a standard bird's-eye-viewpoint map of a city, which was probably introduced to China by 1608 from Europe, became a means of personal expression in the hands of Chinese cartographers. One 1899 example by Feng Qihuang depicts the walled city of Tianjin and its environs (see Plate 50). It is basically a study of the community's self-defense system: the army encampments are compounds with red flags. Created forty-one years after the city was opened to foreign trade following the 1858 Treaties of Tianjin with Great Britain ending the Second Opium War, the map reflects Western influences in the ships at the bottom, the structure of the British buildings to the far right, the factory occupying the temple grounds just outside the old city's blue walls, and, most notably, the railroad station and the trains. However, instead of sticking to the Western style of representation in bird's-eye city views, the artist eschewed a singular or a convergent perspective and shifted ground planes in the traditional Chinese manner of depicting a nonflat earth.

Most dramatically, he makes his opinion of westernization's effects on China brazenly clear to the visually literate reader of the map by having the blackest object on the map be the coal smoke emanating from the factories and train locomotives introduced by Western entrepreneurs. (There was a widespread fear that sparks from the trains would set the wooden houses beside the tracks on fire.) And the oversized trains (upper right) are set on a collision course! As if going along with the mapmaker's political position, the local official for whom the map was made chose the *zhuan* form of Chinese script, an ancient form used before the standardization of Chinese writing in the third century BCE. Originally carved in bronze or stone and used for official seals, the *zhuan* form gave the map an authoritative aura and acted as a reminder of China's greatness before Europe or America existed on any map.

The year the map of Tianjin was created, 1899, saw a resurgence of Chinese isolationism. It is Map as Warning of Disaster. Feng Qihuang seems to be questioning the "self-strengthening" philosophy of Chang Chih-tung (1837–1909), a regional governor, who wrote, "Chinese learning for principles, Western learning for instruments."

After the British actually gained entry in 1860, treaties had been signed with the United States, France, Russia, and others, in the hope that the ambitious "barbarians" could be used to control each other. Nevertheless, in 1900 Tianjin became a focal point of the Boxer Rebellion. It was the Boxers who sought to oust the alien, or "foreign devil," and his ways, arguing that foreign railroad builders would want to own the territory under their rails as they did in the United States, thus partitioning China and making the vast country easier to conquer. The trains on the map of Tianjin symbolized the colonizing West, and warned of what lay in store for China if the railroad magnates and their ilk were not ejected.

Maps (plans), such as the one of Tianjin, instigate action. Landscape painting provokes contemplation. The tension between the

PLATE 49. *Hainan Island.* Feng shui is the driving force behind this nineteenth-century Chinese map.

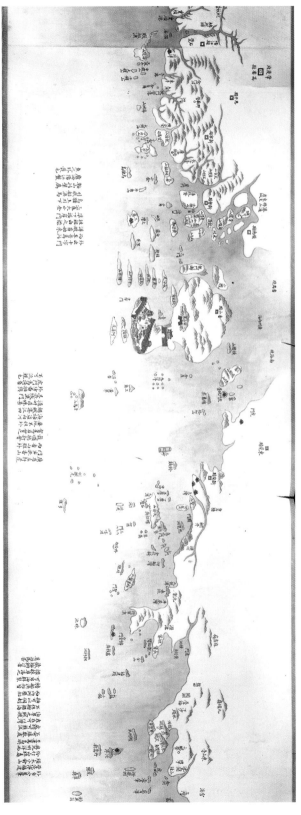

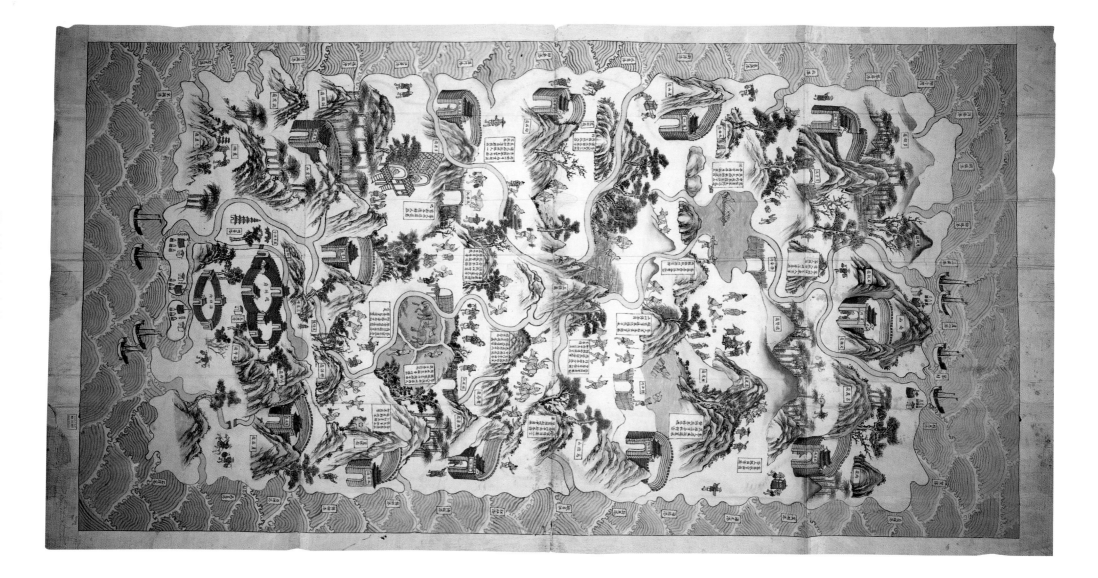

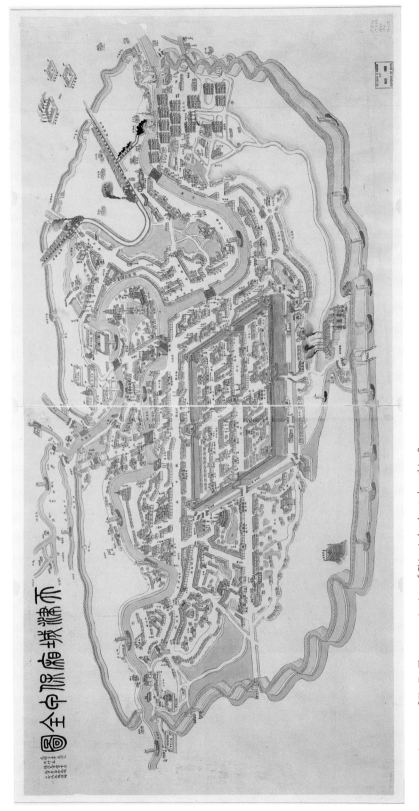

PLATE 50. *Urban Map of Tianjin.* The westernization of China is lambasted on this 1899 Chinese map.

plan and landscape elements is palpable and might be compared with the Chinese philosophical tenet of yin and yang, which rests on the tension of two opposite principles. This tension is at the heart of Asian cartography.

Korea

Unlike the Roman Empire, the Far East through which Marco Polo traveled had no unifying construct beyond Mongol domination. The Mongol province of China, like the city of Rome, was a cultural force field, and its institutions, ideologies, and methods of cartographic expression had inspired many diverse peoples throughout central and southeast Asia. Of all China's neighbors, Korea, Japan, and Vietnam were the most influenced by the Chinese ethos. Together they formed one of civilization's great cultural communities.

Until the tenth century, when the southern kingdom of Silla united all the people, there were various kingdoms on the Korean Peninsula. This eastern neighbor of China's, a geographical position from which the word Korea evolved, is a mountainous peninsula, 135 miles wide and 600 long, extending southward from Manchuria between Japan and China. The Koryŏ kings (918–1392) of Silla were held in thrall by Chinese ways, and after the Mongols conquered the Far East, the Koryŏ princes were made to reside in the khan's Beijing until the death or abdication of their predecessors. Korean administrators, however, were left to their own devices.

Long before the Silla unification wars, maps with Chinese pictorial aspects of landscape painting were used by local administrative tions—"maps and registers" (*tojŏk*). A distinctly Korean cartographic statement, however, was made by the rulers' minting large ceremonial silver money (*ŭnbyŏng*) in the shape of the country. The form

expressed reverence for country, and the silver evinced economic pride in its mountains. After the Ming dynasty (1368–1644) ousted the Mongols from China, the Chinese moved on Koryŏ. General Yi was selected to fight them. After his success, he founded his own Korean dynasty, the Chosŏn (1392–1910).

The 1402 *Kangnido* map of the world (Plate 51) was drawn by Liu Hui and Chŭan Chin, Korean ministers, to demonstrate the new dynasty's cosmic legitimacy. The two strove to make an integrated map including everything known of the world in order to show that Korea was not only an East Asian country but also a part of a larger world. The map's ambition and its success in imagining that larger world were intended to validate their position in it. It represents the last phase of Chinese traditional cartography, which was based on the idea of a single terrestrial continent, with Africa a southern extension. It expresses the influences of China while placing Koreans in the front rank of cartographic accomplishment as undeniably as it magnifies Korea—larger than all of Europe—on the world's stage.

No contemporary European map comes close to its all-encompassing vision of the world. Like the profoundly brilliant Korean alphabet, invented by King Sejong and introduced in 1446, the map's structure contains nothing formulaic or mandated. Both map and alphabet created a new Korean reality. Unlike the tradition-bound Chinese maps, with everywhere not China considered "other"—an ill-defined outlying zone of barbarian settlements— the *Kangnido* offered a different picture. An expression of the Confucian revolution that was reshaping the nation under the Chosŏn dynasty, it displays the Confucian verities of discipline, a well-trained mind, and mental labor, all inscribed in the canonical au-

PLATE 51. *Kangnido: Map of Historical Emperors and Kings of Integrated Borders and Terrain.* There is no contemporary European equivalent for this 1402 Korean map.

thority of Confucius, where the extension of knowledge lay in the investigation of things. It is Map as Visualization of "Heaven-Loosed Wisdom." In addition to verified Chinese sources, Arabic and Persian maps introduced into China under Mongol rule almost certainly provided its striking details. It shows Africa with its characteristic triangle shape pointing southward, and includes the Mountains of the Moon as sources of the Nile. Europe has about a hundred identified localities. The image of Japan, though too far to the south in the open sea, was based on a Japanese map from 1401 brought home to Korea by a diplomat.

The shock from Mongol conquest had induced a long-standing mood of political isolation and cultural introspection in China.

The *Kangnido* indicates that Korea experienced no such trauma. Korea projects itself as a major Asian state and demonstrates with the map extraordinary intellectual resources, while refurbishing its traditional view of China as the major center of civilization and playing its eternal game of keeping Japan as far away as possible. Diplomatic attempts were under way to end the constant torment imposed on Korean coasts by marauding Japanese pirates.

The Chosŏn instigated a renaissance of Korean culture. Matteo Ricci's scientific and mathematical teachings in China had filtered into Korea, but the intolerant proselytizing of his fellow Roman Catholics and its social repercussions forced Chosŏn rulers to condemn anything Western. Then Japan in quest of empire attacked

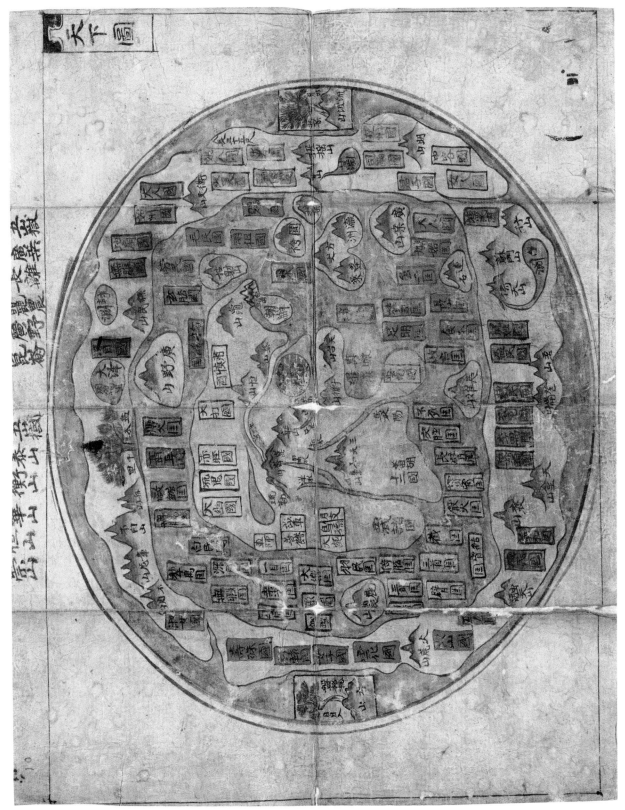

PLATE 52. *Korean Traditional World Map.* There is no date of origin for this revered traditional Korean map of "all under heaven."

in 1592. Somewhere during this period of great turmoil, the *Ch'onhado*, or wheel map, translated as "all under heaven," appeared (Plate 52). Mysterious in its origins and tenacious in its grip on the Korean collective imagination, it is a relic bearing very early Chinese mental organization of the world. It is Map as Comforting Symbol. It is believed to have "evolved" from the *Kangnido*, though the integrated known world has been "exploded," like a myth, and China returned to center stage as the Middle Kingdom, with all the other countries, excepting Korea and India, arranged around it like islands. Unique to Korea, the *Ch'onhado* was usually the first map in every Korean atlas, and existed into the late nineteenth century, offering familiarity in a rapidly changing world.

On the map, the rivers unifying Korea are extended to become the major rivers of the known world, symbols of Korea's involvement and equality with the intellectual and economic community of mankind. And Korea remains close to China — as in life — close to the matrix of civilization. Being the only peninsula on the face of the map's flat earth seems to make Korea venerable enough to remain

attached to China. Surrounding the known world is a sea ring, like Homer's Oceanus, which is encased by a land ring, an unknown continent. The trees on the east and west sides mark the places where the sun and moon rise and set, and near the eastern tree is the land of "Pusang," which may be America. Along with actual places are fictional ones from the classics and histories. The source of the major place names is a mapless classic from Han China, *Shanhai jing* (Classic of Mountains and Seas). Because many Chinese maps survived in Korea owing to their durable paper, it is possible that the *Ch'onhado* is an embodiment of an early one raised to the level of mythology.

Japan

Although Marco Polo never visited Japan, his book contained a fantastical description of "the island" of Cipangu (*Jin-pon-kuo* in Chinese: Land of the Rising Sun), "some 1,500 miles" from the mainland. "They have gold in great abundance," he wrote, "because it is found there in measureless quantities." Two centuries later Columbus, going "to seek gold and precious stones," headed for Cipangu, and

decided Cuba had to be Cipangu off Cathay (China), which he had visualized "in this region" from world maps devoid of the as yet unencountered America.

Polo's "island" of Cipangu is, in fact, an archipelago comprising four main and many smaller islands, and separated from the southern tip of the Korean Peninsula by the Tsushima Strait (115 miles). Running eastward for 700 miles, Japan then turns abruptly northward for about the same distance, approaching the coast of Russia. Only 143 percent of mountainous Japan is arable land, including the land suitable for homes and industry; there is less available for use than in Illinois.

Twice, Polo's Kublai Khan unsuccessfully tried to conquer Japan—in 1274 and in 1281. Twice his expeditions encountered typhoons, which the Japanese call *kamikaze* (divine wind). The invasion the Mongols attempted to achieve by force the Chinese had achieved centuries before via a more civilized route, that of the mind. However, by Kublai Khan's time, the Japanese had developed a mind and spirit of their own, albeit with a long lineage of continental Asia's culture. Their geographic location determined their history. Japan was a cul de sac, a terminus of successive waves of influence that washed into it over the millennia. Its culture incorporated traditions developed elsewhere in highly diverse times and places. Isolated for long periods from the source of all it contains, Japan was a place where accommodation, transformation, and amalgamation proceeded uninterrupted until the next tidal sweep irrevocably altered its composition. These infusions provided the essential elements for the vigor and scope, the means and methods of expression, in Japanese cartography.

The equitable division of land and labor first aroused social reformers in Japan's central government during the seventh century. A series of edicts known collectively as the Taika Confucian Reforms (646) were responsible for the earliest portable extant maps of Japan, which were diagrams of estates (*shōen*) required of the rich warrior aristocracy to stake claims with the emperor. Japanese historical periods are named for the city from which the ruling power governed, be it the emperor (*tennō*) or a warrior shogun (*bakufu*). The ruler's order to map the estates is preserved in the *Shoku Nihongi* (Chronicles of Japan) from the Nara period (710–84). The main purpose of the decree, and of all the other reforms, was to strengthen the centralized government, thus uniting Japan. However, in 743 this reclaimed land became immune to taxation for Buddhist establishments, then for other religious institutions, and then for secular landlords, often part of the imperial household; in 745 the exemption was made hereditary. By the tenth century, more land was under control of religious and military leaders than was taxed and controlled by the imperial government—a dangerous political and economic situation for the emperor.

As a pictorial map on cloth from 756 (Plate 53) makes clear, the *shōen* economies became largely self-contained economic worlds. Oriented east, the map shows the Minase Manor in Settsu Province ringed by forbidding mountains painted boldly in ink. They create an unapproachable private domain with fields, storehouses, houses, and a village. (The peasant farmers working the land they owned were heavily taxed by the estate holder to add to his wealth.) It is Map as Contours of Feudalism. New rice terraces rise on several levels up the slopes on the western perimeter. Rivers complete the sense of a barricaded fortress. Communication with outsiders was rigidly controlled, and such estates had their own militias (*samurai*) of primarily former farmers. If written, messages were in Chinese. Soon these smaller *shōen* consolidated under a powerful military

leader and evolved into semi-independent states. As a patriarch of the Taira clan declared: "If one is not a Taira, then one is not even considered human."

This map sets the scene for the wresting of control of the imperial house by the Minamoto clan, and the transformation of a private military administration into the national government — the shogunate, or *bakufu* (literally, "tent government," or warrior shogun's regime). It occurred during the Heian period (794–1185), the age of court aristocracy, when the emperor moved the capital city from Nara to Kyoto (Heiankyo), where the seat of the imperial court remained until 1868. There the minuscule, ancient, and completely urbanized society of aristocratic civilians lived mostly on incomes from royal appointments or patronage, while the emperor's military deputy (shogun) actually ruled Japan. He, with his own social hierarchy, established a hegemony over the Kyoto court by assuming control of landholding rights, tax payments, and the legal affairs of the entire society.

Just as Japan imported Chinese culture and failed to reproduce its administration's classless meritocracy, preferring management by the aristocracy, so it took in Buddhism and failed to condemn personal desire, though physical pleasures, however worthy of cultivation, were never to interfere with duty. The Japanese have long celebrated the delights of the five senses, and sight is well serviced by their ravishing maps, which by necessity neatly combine pleasure and duty.

PLATE 54. *Evening Faces.* The scope of an established cartographic convention was broadened by this 1634 wood-block print from *The Tale of Genji.*

The oblique, bird's-eye point of view had been used in China to map both interior and exterior spaces, showing them from above. This overhead plan became a convention in illustrating romantic novels of the Heian period, and this concept of interior space was broadened by the Japanese to include the interior life. Emotional states were revealed by the placement of the novel's characters in separate levels or zones of experience within a one-story room by picturing a sharply tilted ground plane, the way maps placed monasteries on a hill. This technique was called *fukinuki-yatai* (blown-off roof). It is Map as Tool of Psychology.

Written by women, the novels were the rage of the court, and their images had a profound influence on mapmaking. *The Tale of Genji,* written circa 1000 by Murasaki Shikibu, is one of the earliest and finest examples of romantic literature in the world. Derived from the lyric tradition, this majestic novel — laced with poetry — is centered upon the love life of its protagonist, Prince Genji. Through the interactions of the various other characters, the very long and complex tale captures the aesthetics of a time when the Japanese were becoming conscious and proud of their unique characteristics. The book is hailed as Japan's coming-of-age in the literary sphere, and it is honeycombed with allusions and references to Chinese poetry, literature, and history. Exquisite wood-block prints from a rare 1634 edition offer perfect examples of *fukinuki-yatai* (Plate 54). The illustrations in *Genji* inspired intense discussions among the book's aristocratic readers, all of whom, like

It was in the period known as Yayoi (c. 250 BCE–250 CE) that the first outside cultural forces swept over Japan. With surveying tools came Korean Confucian texts. These texts introduced influential ethical concepts of community and the Chinese written language. Then from China came the structure of imperial government, dynastic histories, art education, literature, and (in 552) Buddhism. To consolidate political and social power, everything depended upon the social nature of maps —*zu* in Japanese. In isolated Japan, each person's identity and actions evolved in human relationships, never autonomously, and were always located in experience, not in the abstract. If the American archetype cultivates a self that knows it is unique in the cosmos, the Japanese archetype defined a self that can feel human only in the company of others.

For the most part, the Japanese isolated themselves after 838. Unlike the isolation imposed by law during the later Tokugawa period, this initial withdrawal from outside contacts began when official missions to the Chinese court ended because of Korean piracy, sea storms, and the unsettled political scene at the end of the Tang dynasty (618–907) in China. There followed a semiconscious process of evolving indigenous Japanese forms, and the "Japanization" of previous cultural imports. It was a time of deep introspection. Japanese self-expression emerged from Chinese tutelage during this, the Heian period. With the rise of court culture, pedigree and birth determined everything. A new form of map appeared in Japan.

Genji, held the illiterate "country rustics" in contempt, the very rustics whose rough feudal warrior society would soon overpower their effete, overrefined court. This court's art and poetry inspired a sensual pleasure in the visual organization of space. It is an art made manifest in calligraphy and cartography.

The ascension of the "female" lyrical and spiritual sensibility in the Heian court produced a full-blown fulfillment of feminine aesthetics unlike anything in China. Breaking from paternal authority, the Japanese submitted to the authority of their own genius and transformed forever the way they represented space in their evocative and poetic maps. Chinese learning, including the written language, like Latin in Europe, became the property of educated aristocratic men and was deemed inappropriate for women.

Spoken Chinese is tonal and monosyllabic; Japanese is highly inflected and polysyllabic. Written Chinese had to be adapted to fit Japanese language structure, which was done by modifying Chinese ideograms into a phonetic alphabet called *kana*, its elements chosen for sound regardless of meaning and reconfigured into Japanese words. Women mastered the simple *kana* system, and a "feminine hand" calligraphy (*onnade*) evolved as the property of educated court women. From these women's brushes, slender and elegant characters flowed and rippled down the page, reminiscent of the *yamato-e* (Japanese-style) landscape paintings of the Nara region, their topography more softly rounded than the spiking Chinese-style hills of earlier days. The maps created in this era do not

simply delineate the topography, they celebrate the inherent beauty and sublimity of the land. The powerful, formal rhetoric of mapping was perpetually unsettled in the East by this quest to balance science and art.

Except to go on pilgrimage, an arduous and perilous communal adventure, Heian aristocrats rarely left Kyoto's straight, broad streets and avenues for the twisting, dangerous paths of a country suffering from constant warfare and atrocity among the warlords. Only the two imperial cities of Japan, Nara and Kyoto, mirrored imperial Beijing's checkerboard pattern for the layout of their streets, albeit on a more intimate and modest scale. A nineteenth-century map of Yamashiro Province, which included Kyoto, displays the small royal city as gilded boxes, a rectangular jewel nestled in a baroque natural setting that is its environs (Plate 55). Like Genji, the "Shining Prince," the gilded imperial boxes shine with the reflected glory of the emperor, descendant of the sun. They are a metaphor for the rigidly observed aristocratic hierarchy. It is Map as Aesthetics Made Visible. Its exquisite order symbolizes both a well-structured government and the city's self-proclaimed prominence as arbiter of taste, values, and intellectual achievement. Kyoto's society defined the Heian period, which obliterated the cultural and economic accomplishments of the remainder of the population, though the aristocratic attitudes and taste did largely determine the course of the contemporary civilization, especially in religion.

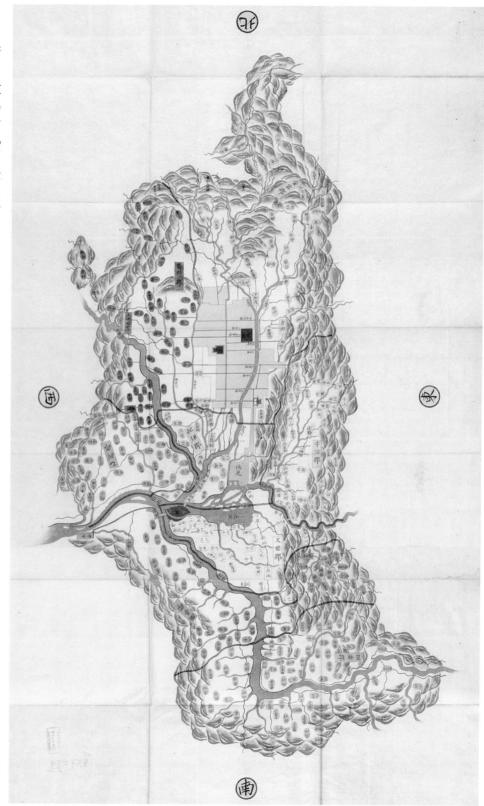

PLATE 55. *Kyoto and the Region of Yamashiro.* Only Japan's two imperial cities relied upon urban planning.

strongly associated in Japan with concrete benefits. He also made maps. His most famous map elongates the archipelago and runs it east to west. This is the Cipangu of Columbus's imagination. As reproduced on a porcelain plate in 1839 (Plate 56), the Gyōki-type map places Japan's three major islands at the center; the northern island of Hokkaido is conspicuously absent, presenting a visual picture that survived a millennium in the minds of the Japanese themselves, with serious consequences.

Of the four other "countries" depicted at the edges of the plate, two are real places (Korea and the Ryukyus) and two (the Country of the Dwarfs and the Women Protected Country) represent ancient Japanese myths. There are practical marginal notes giving the number of days it takes to carry tribute to Nara, the capital city during Gyōki's lifetime. Mirroring the way the Japanese divided life into "circles" — e.g., the circle of "human feelings" and so on — the individual provinces of a Gyōki map are generally oval in shape, as is the whole, which calls to mind the legs of the Buddha in the lotus position. Thus the map promulgates the "truth" and "the way" of the ancient Buddhist mapmaker.

PLATE 56. *Porcelain Plate with Gyōki-type Map.* The decoration on this plate is the first map of Japan.

Heian's Buddha Amida offered instant rebirth at death into the Pure Land of the Western Paradise without a lifelong arduous religious practice. Hence, pilgrimages became pious works. Lady Sarashina (born c. 1008) wrote the classic *As I Crossed the Bridge of Dreams,* one of the first extant examples of typically Japanese travel writing. Ivan Morris, Japanese scholar and translator, explains: "It is clear that for Lady Sarashina, as for most of her Courtly contemporaries, the long journeys to the temples were not primarily religious — unless of course we accept the worship of nature as a form of religion." Her joy arises from the ever-changing beauties of the countryside, which she describes in poetry and lyrical prose tailored after adored tales such as *Genji.* In terms of her traveling time, Japan was about five hundred times larger than it is today, and for all her travels, she is ignorant of the geography beyond her walled garden. She typifies her class both in her general indifference to the goings-on in the far-flung world and in her prevalent Buddhist sense of impermanence, the belief in life as a flimsy, dreamlike structure, a bridge we cross in our movement from one state of existence to another. She never mentions maps or directions, though place names — towns, rivers, mountains, valleys — are savored in the tradition of itinerary maps, and actual maps have been drawn from the precise descriptions of place in her autobiographical narrative. It is Map as Poetic Memoir.

The first person to draw a map of Japan was a Buddhist monk, Gyōki (668–749). Buddhism first reached the Japanese masses through the activities of this itinerant holy man, who combined his teachings with his civil engineering skills to create public works such as roads, bridges, irrigation systems, and wells. Buddhism is not a belief system offering divine revelation but a discipline for attaining heightened insight, and thanks to Gyōki it became

It wasn't until 1605, at the dawn of the Edo period (1603–1867) and the Tokugawa shogunate, that the next systematic surveying occurred. This was soon after the reunification of Japan by the Tokugawa family, a clan powerful enough to end civil war and unite the 250 baronial domains that had evolved between the tenth and sixteenth centuries. As shoguns, the Tokugawas moved their capital to Edo (Tokyo), closed Japan to the dangerously disruptive West (1636–1854), and banned all Western books. Nevertheless the mapping instructions, given when the economically astute Tokugawa shogunate was newly settled in Edo, included a prescribed scale and reveals the influence of the Mediterranean world.

The ban on Western books obviously did not pertain to the government. One regional land ownership watercolor map from 1786 (Plate 57) is in the traditional style inherited from China and lacks scale. It is Map as Spirit of the Age. While subtly evoking nature's splendor in the Japanese manner during a unique period when Japan was a world unto itself, it tells a complex story of Western-influenced technological development and land management.

A beautifully evocative sandy beach on the Pacific, irregularly dotted with a pine forest, borders the property around Numazu. At any other time, without Western knowledge of fertilizers, the soil could not have been forced into fecundity; nor would it have been desirable to do so, sitting as it does on the main road (pink) between Edo and Kyoto (the imperial city) behind a thriving tourist town represented emotively on the map by thatched roofs. (Unable to travel abroad, the Japanese were madly keen travelers at home.) The new rice fields are painted gray, the color of wet earth, and yellow is used for crops like wheat or sweet potatoes. Each plot is named for its owners, members of a corporation, who do not live in the illustrated town but in an adjoining one not necessary to the map's narrative. The township information is given as written text along the boundary lines (roads) in red.

This is an image of rural social harmony, when taxable land could be created by a town government for a needy community. By this time the technology traveled in legally translated, European agricultural textbooks. (The 1636 ban on Western books was lifted for scholars by the shogun in 1720—only excepting books relating to Christianity, which had proven a divisive influence for his government.) Maps and scientific information were top secret, but the search for practical improvements to increase revenues was a hallmark of the Tokugawa clan.

A hallmark of the Japanese people is encapsulated in a detailed field map from the mid-nineteenth century (see Plate 58). For hundreds of years the Japanese had been devoted to self-management. Crops were assigned by the shogunate to various regions, with instructions to develop stronger, hardier varieties. This legally binding map carefully identifies landowners and crops. It can be viewed as a microcosm of insular Japan elegantly arranged and draped on the page like a silk kimono. Mirroring the prescribed silence about the outside world, the map supplies no news about the white areas surrounding the fields. Obedience is a great virtue in Japan, and the mapmaker has fulfilled his specific task to the letter. It is Map as Respect for Authority. Like a snapshot of a mindscape, it captures a deep commitment to order and a profound understanding of cartography's link with economic policy. Lines

on the map impose space discipline, as hands on a clock induce time discipline. The social classes were as rigidly demarcated as these fields, and while the outside world was experiencing great change and turmoil, Japan remained at relative peace in a state of stasis.

Thus, also in this map can be read the unraveling of the Tokugawa shogunate in 1867. The entire society was structured on imposed social ideas of neo-Confucianism, which were based upon a twelfth-century Chinese rural, self-sufficient, agricultural society. Time had been stopped by Tokugawa Ieyasu, the founder of the dynasty in 1603. His new breed of warlord (daimyō) knew that power depended on the productivity of the land. Social barriers were reinstated, and peasants could no longer become samurai, much less warlords, as some great heroes of the past had done. Artisans, merchants, and samurai, who regulated them all, were forever locked in their narrow roles. The revisionist system worked for 268 years, the Japanese scholar Louis Perez concludes, "because all segments of society really believed that what they did in their lives was honorable and valuable." This feudal mentality could not survive the inevitable confrontation with the "modern" West.

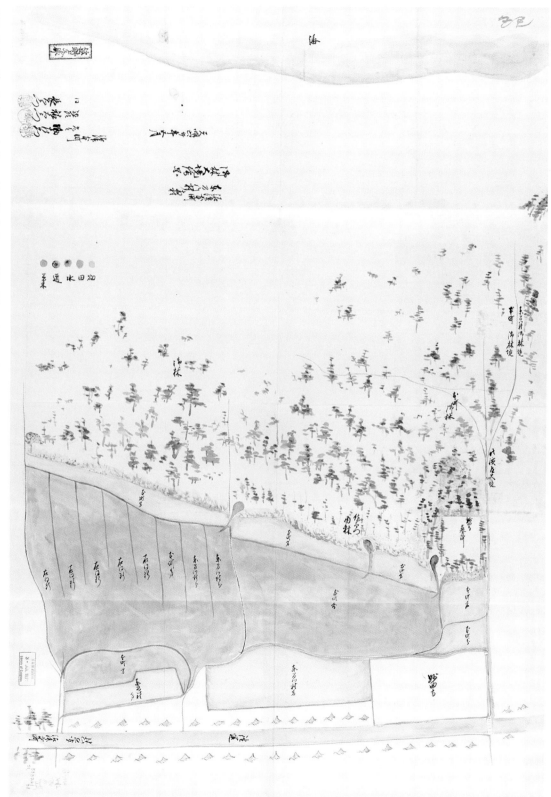

PLATE 57: *Map Showing Corporate Ownership of Agriculture and Forest Property Around Numazu.* An image of Japanese rural social harmony is offered by this 1786 regional map of land ownership.

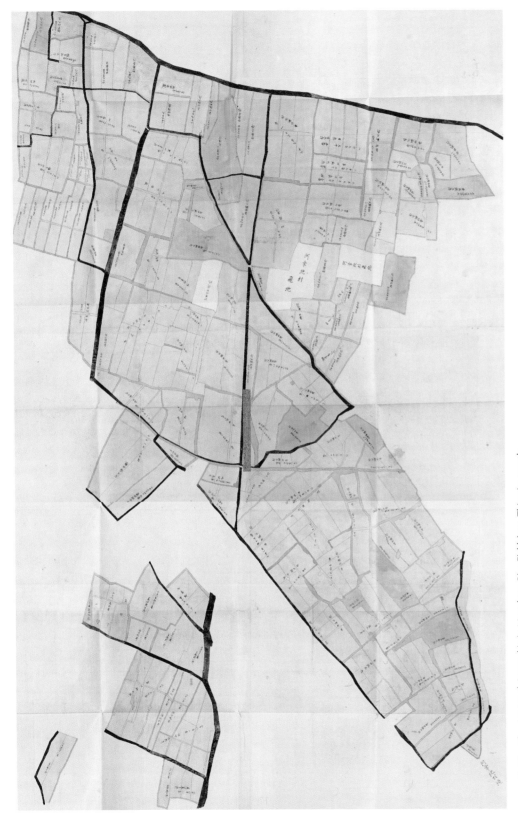

PLATE 58. *Map Showing Land Ownership in Manohara Rice Field Area.* This nineteenth-century field map was a legally binding document in Japan.

The Tokugawas' use of Gyōki's cartographic image of a tubular Japan fostered seclusion; the shogunate banned all the cartographic evidence gleaned from Western gun-toting traders and divisive Christocentric missionaries, who threatened the society's Buddhist harmony. The tenacity of Japan's shape according to Gyōki in the nation's collective unconscious helps explain its confusion in the eighteenth century about the northern frontier, while eloquently demonstrating the unbroken continuity of Japanese culture, especially the culture's immense indebtedness to the past and what it had bestowed.

Japanese ships had regularly sailed "up north" on the Pacific to the southern tip of Hokkaido (Ezo), the uppermost of the four major islands in the archipelago. Though it was inhabited by Japanese, everyone in Japan believed Hokkaido to be mainland Asia, until the seventeenth century, when the island was finally circumnavigated by the Japanese. Since ancient times, "up north" had been home to unconquered and unassimilated peoples, direct descendants of the original inhabitants of Japan—the Caucasian Ainu. This geographical ignorance about Hokkaido illustrates the time-honored concentration of Japan's power in the south. The ruling elite never ventured into the primitive hinterlands where no anarchic politicians lurked. In response to requests for maps, Hokkaido's daimyos sent drawings of their particular domains. There is no clearer sign of the shogunate's belief in Japan's invis-

ibility with its drawbridge up. A self-sustaining universe, Japan officially promulgated a vagueness of place, one where Japan's native ideas, institutions, and customs were superior to all things foreign. Then, in 1771, a rumor of Russia's imminent invasion of Hokkaido spread horror among Japanese officials and instigated calls for national defense. Maps were needed to represent topographical reality.

Russian-occupied Sakhalin was discovered to be an island, not an Asian peninsula, separated from Hokkaido by the narrow Soya Strait, which made Japan as accessible to Russia as the Bering Sea made North America via Alaska. After the shogun saw this stark reality delineated on maps, he ordered unemployed samurai relocated to the north. Accumulated knowledge of the north is revealed on Fujita Tonsai's large-scale 1854 map of great ornamental beauty, which displays the artful elements in Japanese mapping technique and the geographic sensibility of the period (Plate 59). The lack of visual distinction between Japanese and Russian territory indicates that an ongoing dispute with Russia (1853–75) over the ownership of nearly contiguous Sakhalin and the northern extension of the Kuril Islands is settled in the cartographer's mind—in Japan's favor. Both are depicted as part of Japan. It is Map as Dawning of Modern Empire.

PLATE 59. *Hokkaido (Ezo).* Hokkaido was generally unknown to the Japanese before this 1854 traveler's guide.

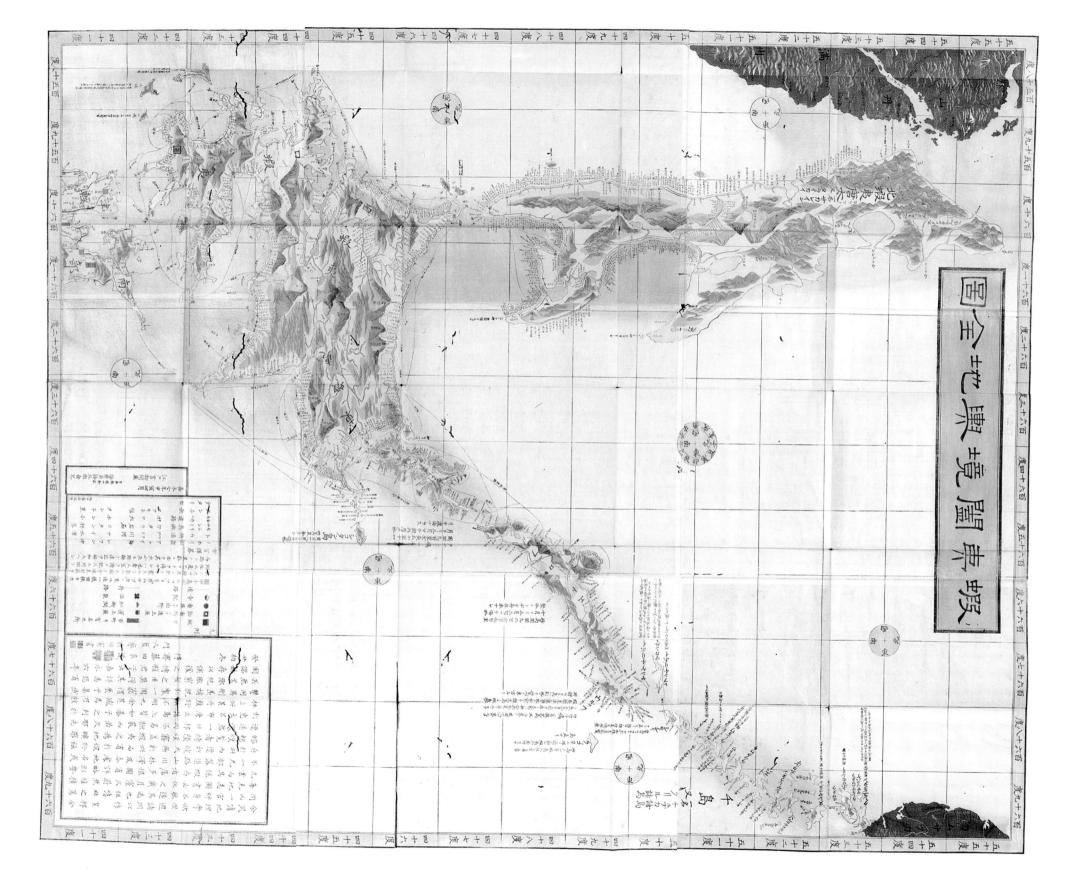

PLATE 60. *Scenes of Life in and Around the Capital.* Forbidden maps were transformed into elaborate city scenes on Japanese screens.

Like a Japanese flower arrangement in a vase, the islands appear as a single unit poetically balanced in a square projection with grid lines one degree apart. Besides the unstated boundary issue between Russia and Japan, there are considerable pictorial geographic inaccuracies, but the detailed information given as text—the sea routes for mariners, coastal roads, villages, and towns—made this map a useful traveler's guide for many years. (Between 1700 and 1850, Japan was more peaceful, generally more equitably fed, and more secure than any other country in the world.) The relationship between text and illustration, between word and image, always becomes complex wherever there is an undeclared process of domination through maps, such as of the islands on this particu-

lar one. The weight of the image swamps the text, often left unread by the viewer using it as a wayfinding tool.

Unlike most major cities, Edo, like Washington, DC, was created as an administrative center. At the time of the city's founding, Japan was rigidly divided into four classes of descending importance: samurai (defenders of the realm), peasants (food providers of the realm), artisans (maintainers of the realm), and merchants (transporters of the realm). All were neatly segregated in the bustling city. Tokugawa's Confucian contempt for commerce, however, made government income dependent on agrarian policies, which came to depend on bank loans from the merchants. With no tax on their commerce, merchant bankers gained control of the

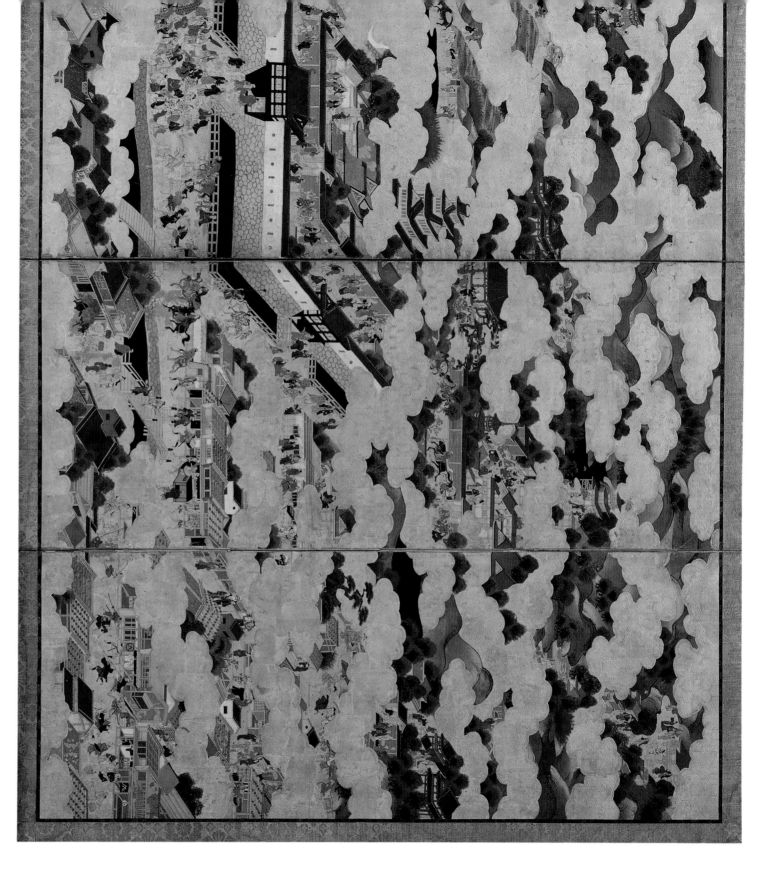

empire's purse strings and the heart of the city. Soon the lowly merchants amassed huge political power.

Cut off from the outside world in a period of unprecedented growth, the people of Edo reached new levels of skill and sophistication to fill the void. Wealthy merchants hid their assets lest they be confiscated or forcibly "loaned" to the shogunate or to the debt-ridden regional daimyo. Prohibited from wearing embroidered silk or cloth woven with gold thread, the merchant class found an ingenious cartographic way to display its wealth and urban pride at a time when the Japanese did not make a distinction between the fine and the applied arts. Patterns of disciplined social conformity were publicly honored. In theory, the city was compartmen-

talized. However, the forbidden art of mapping—disguised as decor—provided ways of revealing the truth of Edo society by exposing the diversity and social interaction in the city dweller's daily life. Basically, the merchant class encouraged and financed a visual display of the exciting, beautiful, and vibrant urban life it had helped created. The luxurious novelty of gilded, multipaneled screens with bird's-eye views of city life flourished (Plate 60). It is Map as Emblem of Self-Esteem. As with kimonos, the simplicity of screen construction is precisely what favored the complexity of design. Peace and prosperity reign in the views' stylized action. People from every social stratum are given equal weight mingling in the streets. Their temples, gardens, mansions, humble dwellings,

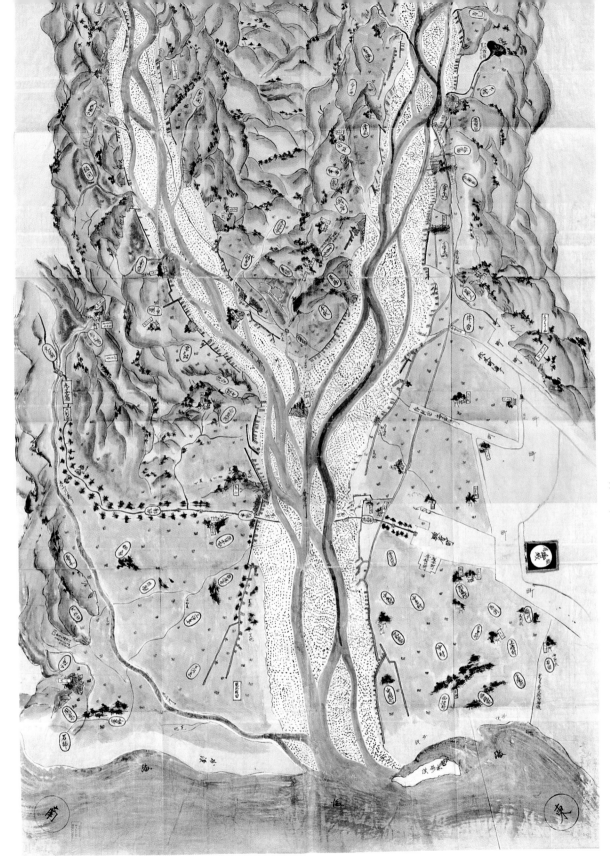

PLATE 61. *Abe River Region*. The collapse of the Tokugawa regime in Japan is explained by this 1862 map.

storehouses, theaters, fairs, markets, and shops are presented as a unified community's common experience.

The bird's-eye view, an ancient Chinese tradition of mapping, connected the nouveau riche merchants to a classical past and to the aristocrats of the Heian period, who employed the device to illustrate their much-read literary masterpieces, the delight of this literate society. The gorgeous gilding and embossed cloud forms linked the metropolitan screens to the poetic and literary-based screen paintings enjoyed by the elite clergy and by the daimyos, whom many of the merchants now represented as commercial agents and commodity speculators in Osaka. Cunningly, the choice of subject (cities), and the cartographic method of representation that allowed the homes and streets of the merchants to be featured on the screens, legitimized their influence. If theirs was a control of space that went unacknowledged by the shogunate, their screens confirm the observation of the cartographic historian J. P. Harley: "Maps are preeminently a language of power, not of protest."

The successful functioning of Edo made it the model for the other cities and for the castle towns of the various daimyo domains in the provinces. One watercolor manuscript map of the Shizuoka Prefecture from 1862 tells a detailed story with political, economic, and social ramifications (Plate 61). Just as the map of the *shōen* set the scene for the birth of the *bakufu*, so this prefecture map sets the scene for its demise. It is Map as Beginning of the End.

In the Tokugawa era, the village (*mura*) emerged when the *shōen* system folded. The shogun and the daimyo's agents controlled the villages (marked with yellow on the map) and from there managed the affairs of the peasants, who represented more than 80 percent of the population. "Sesame seeds and peasants are much alike," an eighteenth-century senior councillor said. "The more you squeeze them, the more you can extract from them." No arable land was left idle, and in most places the peasants had their own plots of land to farm. Every foot of ground was accounted for and documented by the daimyo for taxation purposes. The fields on the map are colored brown and show a very industrious people. Flood walls control the river Abe.

As Japan was transformed from a consolidated fief supporting a military dictatorship into a sprawling estate sustaining a civil bureaucracy, the shogunate's concern with national wealth and with the rational balance between central and local power made maps of every area critical. Tokugawa rulings had all military forts torn down that were not the central domain (*han*) of the vassal daimyo, and the presence of only one castle town on this regional map makes the transition visible. Here is the agrarian base that proved unworkable when the social order changed. It led to the eventual collapse of the Tokugawa shogunate.

When the single castle towns on the map went from military to economic centers in early modern Japan, they became supremely important. In fact the opening salvo in the Tokugawa's' final battle for survival came from the provinces. There, men in the larger domains were province oriented until the reentry of the West in 1854 brought a national consciousness. Early on, the shogunate initiated programs for local maps to be compiled from field surveys undertaken by the most powerful clans in the provinces. It is obvious that painters as well as calligraphers were employed on some, like a manuscript map from the 1820s (see Plate 62) shown with its peripheral mountains drawn pictorially, as if seen from

inside the province, in the Chinese manner. This cartographic device was repeated throughout the centuries, and it is used to great effect to show four feudal domains in the region of Mount Fuji in the province of Suruga (today Shizuoka Prefecture), the birthplace of Tokugawa Ieyasu. Fuji dominates the map, as it does the Japanese consciousness, just as the first legendary Tokugawa shogun, officially divine, looms in history. It is Map as a Nation's Psyche.

The text gives geographical characteristics, acreage in rice fields, and yield. Four poems written about the popular region are included to signify how the scene inspires poets, as well as to link the map with the great masterpieces of the past, such as the poem-bejeweled *Tale of Genji*. From the nineteenth century, painting and poetry were inseparable in Japan, possibly because paintings served as a form of memory bank in the days when narratives were transmitted orally. The map summarizes the unrivaled devotion to nature's beauty in all her forms that is Japan. It combines delicacy of decoration with refinement and sureness of taste, characteristics of Japan's culture that have become keystones of its cartographic identity.

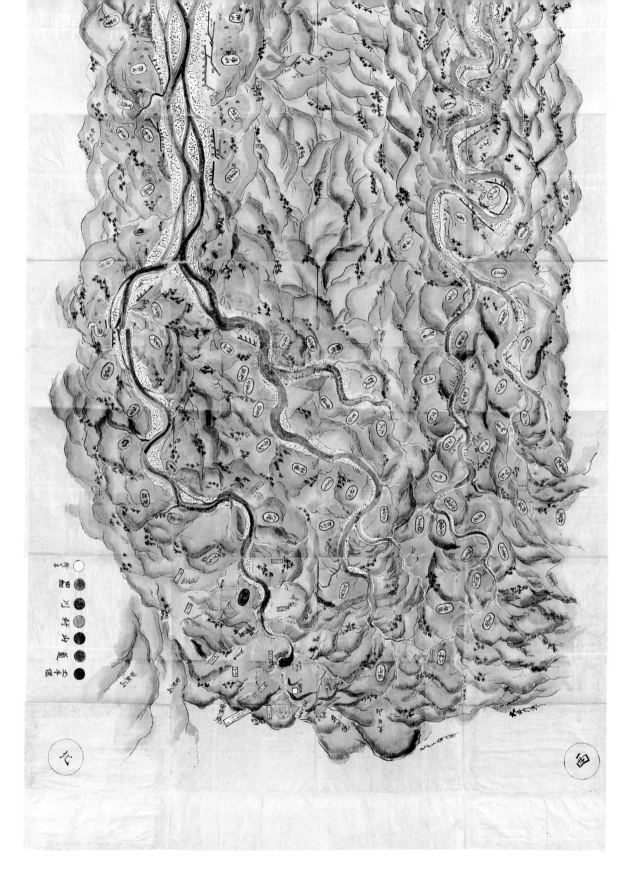

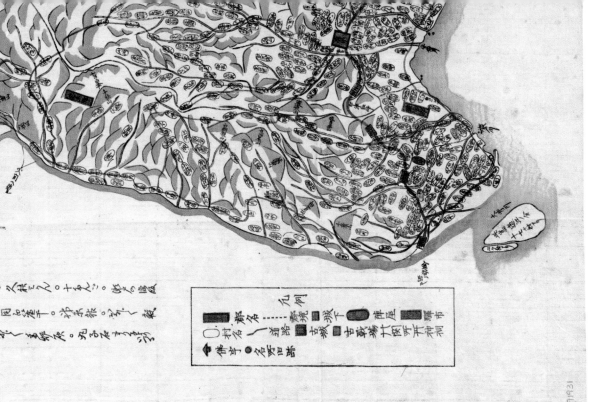

PLATE 62. *Suruga Province / Shizuoka Prefecture.* The four feudal domains graced by Mount Fuji's presence were poeticized by this 1820s map.

Ironically, Japan's relationship with the civilization of the Mediterranean world began when the isolationist Tokugawa Ieyasu was an infant. In 1542 Spanish and Portuguese navigators arrived in Marco Polo's Cipangu. In Japan, unlike in America, however, the conquistadores and missionaries met a people superior in military matters and more sophisticated in much else as well. The Europeans were called—"southern barbarians," *nanbanjin,* as the Europeans were called—because they arrived from a southerly direction—brought technical information about making marine charts and national and world maps in the Ptolemaic manner. Maps in this Western tradition were *nanban.* This European method of mapping was not disseminated widely in Japan. Europeans with their firearms—for sale to feuding, ambitious feudal lords—and their boastful tales of conquering ancient civilizations in America, and their Christianity, with its militant, intolerant priests, profoundly upset the shogunate. Thus the Japanese closed their ports to foreigners, except Koreans, Chinese, and the pragmatic Dutch, who never mixed business with religion. From 1641 to 1853 the Dutch were the only Westerners trading with and educating the Japanese in Western ways. The term *rangaku* referred to Dutch learning or studies.

During Sakoku, the Age of National Isolation (1636–1854), the Dutch, or "red-haired barbarians," were licensed to use only the port of Nagasaki. Each year the Dutch paid annual tribute to the shogun and presented a detailed account of world affairs. By the nineteenth century, the reports of Western imperialism in Asia, and Russia's expansion in northeast Asia, deeply unsettled the shogunate and engendered a deep fear of the West. However, these reports did not spur an increase in military preparedness among administrators immersed in peace for generations. In 1852, when the Dutch government warned the shogun that the United States intended to open Japan by force, the fear deepened. An 1852 Japanese map of Edo Bay (see Plate 63) was made the year before Commodore Matthew C. Perry first sailed into the bay, forcing Japan's closed doors open and instigating panic.

Edo (Tokyo) is on the sea at the headland of a bay. The map's text is a list of military equipment, while the land is dotted with the names of samurai and small daimyo domains guarding the entrance to Edo. In fact by 1852 the majority of samurai were no longer warriors; they were honor-conscious, ritualized figureheads, irrelevant in the operation of a peaceful society. The shogunate was well aware of its inability to defend itself against any major assault, and had done nothing to change that fact as foreigners encroached—not only Russians, but also the English, who defeated the Chinese in the first Opium War (1839–42), and became a firm presence in the neighborhood. And then there were the Americans, from the United States. They first appeared in 1837 on a merchant ship, aiming to establish contact. Driven away, they reappeared with two warships in 1846—again they were refused access. The fanciful map of 1852 shows Edo Bay in full military regalia with a cluster of warships and imaginary island fortifications (*odaiba*) placed at its head, where they would best protect the shogun. To confuse any attacker who might win this military map in battle,

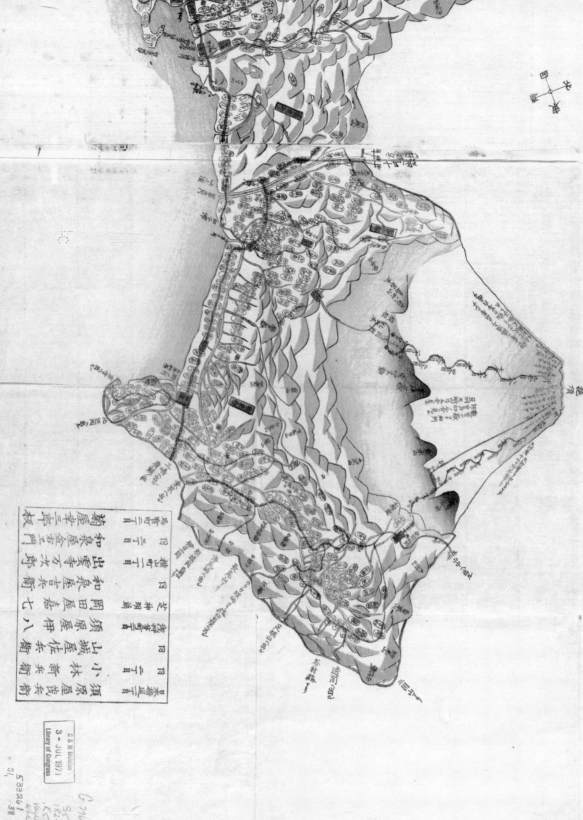

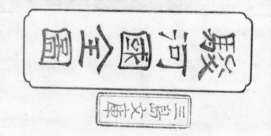

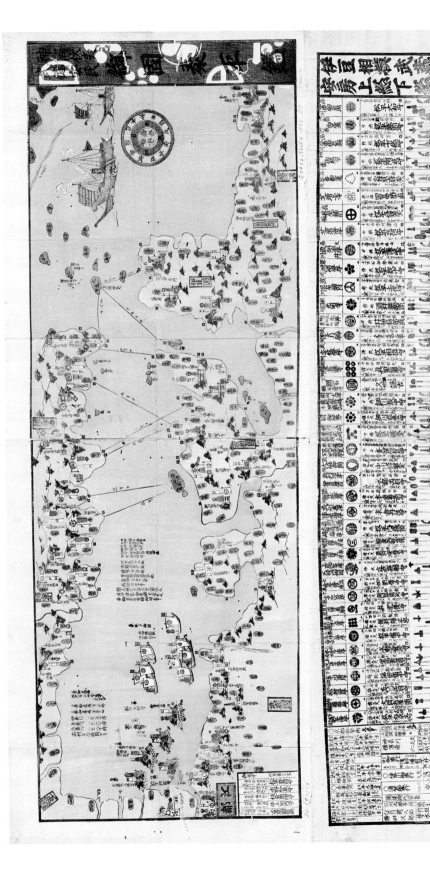

PLATE 63. *Tokyo Bay Coast Defenses.* This 1852 Japanese map of Edo (Tokyo) Bay unsuccessfully relied upon camouflage and lies.

the prefectures are shuffled around and geographical formations are altered to imply impregnability. It is Map as Ruse.

Cartography did not come to Japan's rescue. On July 8, 1853, Perry appeared in the lower reaches of Edo Bay with a squadron of four large warships. (The following year he actually presented a map of "Yedo" Bay's western shore to Congress with its inlets renamed "Mississippi Bay," "Susquehanna Bay," and "Goldborough Inlet.") Pandemonium ensued in Edo. Even with dangerous-looking Japanese maps, the seclusionist policy seemed doomed, and a Tokugawa warlord lamented: "In these feeble days, men tend to cling to peace; they are not fond of defending their country by war." Concessions to the foreigners by the shogun, who knew resistance was futile, induced fighting among the daimyos. A new form of nationalism appeared focused on the emperor, Komei, who denied imperial consent to the treaties with the United States of America. No longer effete courtiers from the Heian era, the aristocracy of Kyoto took active roles in restoring the emperor to power and destroying the shogunate. In January 1868 the Tokugawa regime proclaimed the restoration of imperial rule; and for the first time in over five hundred years, an emperor— Meiji, fifteen-year-old son of Komei— ruled without a shogun. The Meiji era (1868–1912) was born.

By 1877 Emperor Meiji transferred his throne from Kyoto to Edo, which was renamed Tokyo (Eastern Capital). It became functionally the capital of Japan, the political center of the country, and the symbol of feudalism's end. Led by Meiji, the Japanese em-

braced a belief in their own racial and spiritual superiority and obsessively strove for equality with the major Western powers, with whom they were soon competing for Asian colonies. The enthronement of Meiji's son, Hirohito, in 1926 brought the "imperial way" (*kodo*), which has been compared to the rhetoric of America's Manifest Destiny. The emperor, a theocratic monarch with near absolute political and military powers, was a prime mover in his brief empire's military decisions, including the attack on Pearl Harbor in 1941 and the management of Japanese strategy during World War II, actions in the Pacific that killed about 3.1 million Japanese and more than 60,000 Westerners.

When militarism did not work for the Japanese, the "peaceful arts" were eagerly embraced by the shattered populace, even if imposed by the victors. A Japanese proverb teaches that the mighty oak can be toppled by a storm, but the resilient bamboo can bend to the ground and spring back when the storm has passed. The unleashed aggressions required for war were rechanneled to create the most distinctive non-Western democracy on earth. As the social historian Eric Z. Vogel explains, "If any single factor explains Japanese success, it is the group-directed quest for knowledge." A 1987 bird's-eye-view tourist map of Tokyo's Ginza district (Plate 64) encapsulates the fastest, most astonishing economic recovery in modern history, achieved with more than a little help from Japan's former enemies. It visualizes the accommodation, transformation, and amalgamation that have defined Japanese culture forever. It is Map as Ethic of Alternatives.

To most Westerners, the skyscrapers depicted in the 1987 map look familiar yet the map's detailed axonometric projection is disorienting. A closer look reveals a different set of cultural premises at play. They are predicated on the ancient Asian notion of multiple points of view adopted by the Japanese. The tension created in the viewer provokes a vivid sense of place. Revolving the map merges the physical sensation of looking up at tall buildings with the emotional response of moving around in a dense, modern city and pausing to check a map. Snapshot objectivity is of interest to the cartographer. Thus the experience of being in Tokyo is folded into the information expected of a tourist's map. And the traditional Asian map coexists with the modern, scientific Western diagram. Japan's genius for transforming foreign influences into its own unique way of examining its world is again made evident. (The Japanese alone among the writers of Asia have succeeded in creating a truly modern literature; they took to European literature as if Japan were an island off Europe rather than off Asia.)

PLATE 64. *Isometric Map of the Ginza in Detailed Axonometric Projection.* Tokyo's Ginza district is visualized on this 1987 tourist map in a uniquely Asian manner.

This marriage of East and West elevates the bird's-eye city view into a series of suspended moments on the Bridge of Dreams each of us crosses during our brief stay on earth.

Tibet

Marco Polo's first mission as personal ambassador for Kublai Khan was to inspect the distant area on the borders between Tibet and Yunnan Province. Before his visit and subsequent book, European merchants located all exotic Eastern spices and gems in "India," and it was he who localized them, including ascribing cinnamon to Tibet, which was well to the south of the Silk Route. Before recorded history, Tibetans lived as nomads on their formidably mountainous plateau, the highest region on earth. An agricultural revolution in the fifth century birthed the Tibetan civilization, and by the seventh century a monarchy was in place, one that created an empire and spread India's Buddhism throughout Tibet. But like Japan's creative civilization, Tibet absorbed and transformed the world's output into its own highland culture. Tibetan Buddhism, however, was unique. It metamorphosed the entire course of Tibet's history and culture. Not merely a belief system

for Tibetans, Buddhism encompasses the entirety of their culture and civilization. It constitutes the very essence of their lives. It forms the social fabric connecting them to the land, and it is the strongest bond defining them as a nation.

The aggressive Tibetan empire's collapse in the early ninth century brought on a dark age that ended in the eleventh century through the unifying force of Buddhism. The later Mongol invasion did not interfere with Tibet's native imperial tradition. Rather, from the time of Genghis Khan, Tibetan Buddhism infiltrated the Mongol aristocracy, and by Polo's time it was the preferred religion of Kublai Khan, though he treated all religions as political tools. After the decline of Mongol power in the fourteenth century, a new Buddhist religious order emerged whose lamas, known as Dalai Lamas, were believed to be reincarnations of their predecessors. In 1652 an era of "harmonious blend of religion and politics" was established, and the Dalai Lama became the spiritual and temporal ruler of Tibet. Some three hundred years later (1959), the ruling Dalai Lama fled to India after ten years of Chinese autocratic rule in Tibet. In exile, he wrote: "Wherever I am, accompanied by my government, the Tibetan people recognize us as the Government of Tibet."

A particular form of Tibetan Buddhist mandala, attributed to the Buddha himself, represents humanity's mundane cravings and earthly misapprehensions, and it maps our endlessly repeating pasts, presents, and futures according to the pure Buddhist dogma that would have dominated the realm of Kublai Khan. Although popularly known as the Wheel of Life, the original Tibetan title, Sipay Korlo, can be translated as Circle of Delusion (Plate 65). It encodes sentient existence as a delusion, a veil of ignorance that prevents us from understanding nobler truths. The mandala uses the substantive body of earth itself to discuss how easily we are misled by the substantive.

The mandala map represents *samsara* (the cycle of life and death) and why we are in *samsara*. Human nature is seen as an embodiment of the world. Shenje, ruler of the dead, holds the wheel in his embrace, showing that life is about impermanence. Outside the wheel is the figure of Lord Buddha, who is free from the moral and mental obstructions that can prevent all living beings from achieving enlightenment. The wheel is divided into three parts: axle, spokes, and rim. The axle depicts the three root poisons in the form of Pig (ignorance), Cock (lust), and Snake (anger). To relieve all living beings from suffering, Tibetan Buddhists must be aware of these three evils. Spokes are composed of elaborate allegorical images representing the six sensual realms, or realms of existence, into which we can be reborn. Rim is divided into a dozen sections symbolizing the twelve conditions or worldly attachments that ultimately cause us to be continually reborn, to endlessly transmigrate. The mandala is a symbolic meditative device to foster reflection, specifically on the doctrines of causation and reincarnation, in order to be freed from these cycles. It is Map as Permutations of Desire.

Vietnam

In 1285, on his diplomatic mission for Kublai Khan, and in 1292, on his way home to Venice, Marco Polo visited the rich kingdom of Cianba (Champa), which corresponds to the central portion of modern Vietnam. To the north of Champa lived the Viets in Dai Viet, or Annam (Chinese for "the pacified south"), where a difficult climate, lethal jungles, and popular resistance accomplished by brilliantly strategic guerrilla warfare had forced Kublai to settle for tribute and supremacy over the Viets in name only.

Having control of the China Sea, the Viets were visited by many foreign merchants, and this cultural influx helped them maintain their individuation from China. In 1545 a civil war divided the country between two families. The wider northern portion on the Chinese border became Tonkin, under the Trinh family; the narrow central portion became Annam, under the Nguyen family, who took the broad southernmost piece of today's Vietnam—the Mekong Delta—from neighboring Cambodia, and made it their principality of Cochin-China, which the French invaded through the southern city of Saigon in 1859. By 1887 France had established its Indochinese Union (Indochine), comprising the colony of Cochin-China and the protectorates of Annam, Tonkin, and Cambodia.

After World War I a nationalist movement arose in Vietnam. In 1946 France recognized Tonkin and Annam as the Free State of Vietnam under the control of the Viet Minh party—a coalition of nationalist and communist groups led by Ho Chi Minh—within the federation of Indochina, with Cochin-China an autonomous state. The Viet Minh wanted all three parts of their country. When they took up arms against France, the French invaded Tonkin. In 1949, after China became a communist state, France united the three parts of Vietnam in the French Union, with its own leader, who governed from France, ignoring the Viet Minh and their 1946 agreements. Thus two Vietnams existed: one in the head of the French and their allies—including the United States—and one in the consciousness of the Vietnamese majority, supported by the Chinese and the Soviets.

War erupted in the north. The French were defeated, and the ensuing agreement brokered by the Geneva Convention in 1954 effectively divided Vietnam at the seventeenth parallel into a northern part governed by the Viet Minh and a southern part governed by France's puppet, Ngo Dinh Diem. Nationwide elections were to be held within two years. Immediately after the agreement was signed, both Diem and the United States refused to abide by the upcoming election results because the Viet Minh were the national favorites and, for the United States, Cold War anxieties overshadowed issues of democratic procedures.

Civil war broke out in the south. Opposition to Diem's southern government was led by local northern supporters known collectively as Viet Cong. A 1966 U.S. map (see Plate 66) certifies the unified political identity of the Vietnamese. Made from captured Viet Cong documents by low-ranking Political Order of Battle (OB) analysts working in the Combined Intelligence Center, Vietnam (CICV), it shows the coexisting administrative and military divisions created by the two contending forces. Along with Diem's

PLATE 65. *Wheel of Life.* The Tibetan Buddhist worldview is expressed in this mandala map.

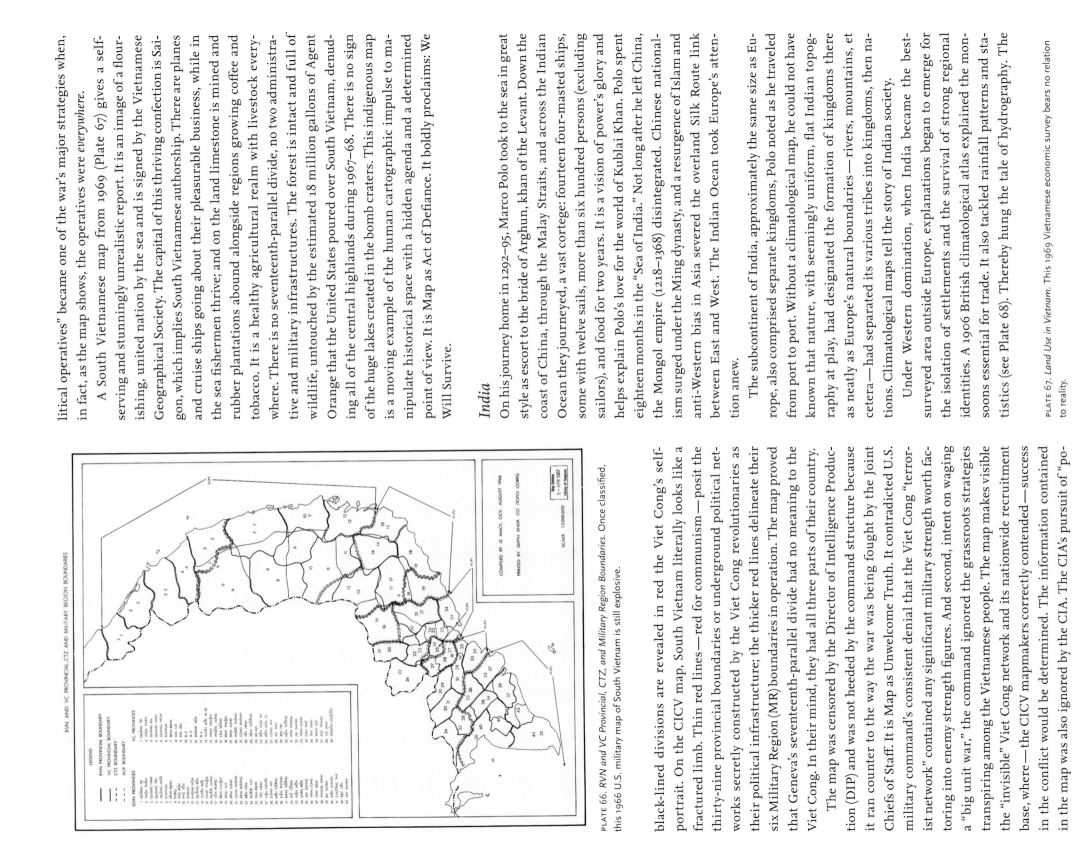

PLATE 66. *RVN and VC Provincial, CTZ, and Military Region Boundaries.* Once classified, this 1966 U.S. military map of South Vietnam is still explosive.

litical operatives" became one of the war's major strategies when, in fact, as the map shows, the operatives were *everywhere*.

A South Vietnamese map from 1969 (Plate 67) gives a self-serving and stunningly unrealistic report. It is an image of a flourishing, united nation by the sea and is signed by the Vietnamese Geographical Society. The capital of this thriving confection is Saigon, which implies South Vietnamese authorship. There are planes and cruise ships going about their pleasurable business, while in the sea fishermen thrive; and on the land limestone is mined and rubber plantations abound alongside regions growing coffee and tobacco. It is a healthy agricultural realm with livestock everywhere. There is no seventeenth-parallel divide, no two administrative and military infrastructures. The forest is intact and full of wildlife, untouched by the estimated 18 million gallons of Agent Orange that the United States poured over South Vietnam, denuding all of the central highlands during 1967–68. There is no sign of the huge lakes created in the bomb craters. This indigenous map is a moving example of the human cartographic impulse to manipulate historical space with a hidden agenda and a determined point of view. It is Map as Act of Defiance. It boldly proclaims: We Will Survive.

India

On his journey home in 1292–95, Marco Polo took to the sea in great style as escort to the bride of Arghun, khan of the Levant. Down the coast of China, through the Malay Straits, and across the Indian Ocean they journeyed, a vast cortege: fourteen four-masted ships, some with twelve sails, more than six hundred persons (excluding sailors), and food for two years. It is a vision of power's glory and helps explain Polo's love for the world of Kublai Khan. Polo spent eighteen months in the "Sea of India." Not long after he left China, the Mongol empire (1218–1368) disintegrated. Chinese nationalism surged under the Ming dynasty, and a resurgence of Islam and anti-Western bias in Asia severed the overland Silk Route link between East and West. The Indian Ocean took Europe's attention anew.

The subcontinent of India, approximately the same size as Europe, also comprised separate kingdoms, Polo noted as he traveled from port to port. Without a climatological map, he could not have known that nature, with seemingly uniform, flat Indian topography at play, had designated the formation of kingdoms there as neatly as Europe's natural boundaries—rivers, mountains, et cetera—had separated its various tribes into kingdoms, then nations. Climatological maps tell the story of Indian society.

Under Western domination, when India became the best-surveyed area outside Europe, explanations began to emerge for the isolation of settlements and the survival of strong regional identities. A 1906 British climatological atlas explained the monsoons essential for trade. It also tackled rainfall patterns and statistics (see Plate 68). Thereby hung the tale of hydrography. The

PLATE 67. *Land Use in Vietnam.* This 1969 Vietnamese economic survey bears no relation to reality.

black-lined divisions are revealed in red the Viet Cong's self-portrait. On the CICV map, South Vietnam literally looks like a fractured limb. Thin red lines—red for communism—posit the thirty-nine provincial boundaries or underground political networks secretly constructed by the Viet Cong revolutionaries as their political infrastructure; the thicker red lines delineate their six Military Region (MR) boundaries in operation. The map proved that Geneva's seventeenth-parallel divide had no meaning to the Viet Cong. In their mind, they had all three parts of their country.

The map was censored by the Director of Intelligence Production (DIP) and was not heeded by the command structure because it ran counter to the way the war was being fought by the Joint Chiefs of Staff. It is Map as Unwelcome Truth. It contradicted U.S. military command's consistent denial that the Viet Cong "terrorist network" contained any significant military strength worth factoring into enemy strength figures. And second, intent on waging a "big unit war," the command ignored the grassroots strategies transpiring among the Vietnamese people. The map makes visible the "invisible" Viet Cong network and its nationwide recruitment base, where—the CICV mapmakers correctly contended—success in the conflict would be determined. The information contained in the map was also ignored by the CIA. The CIA's pursuit of "po-

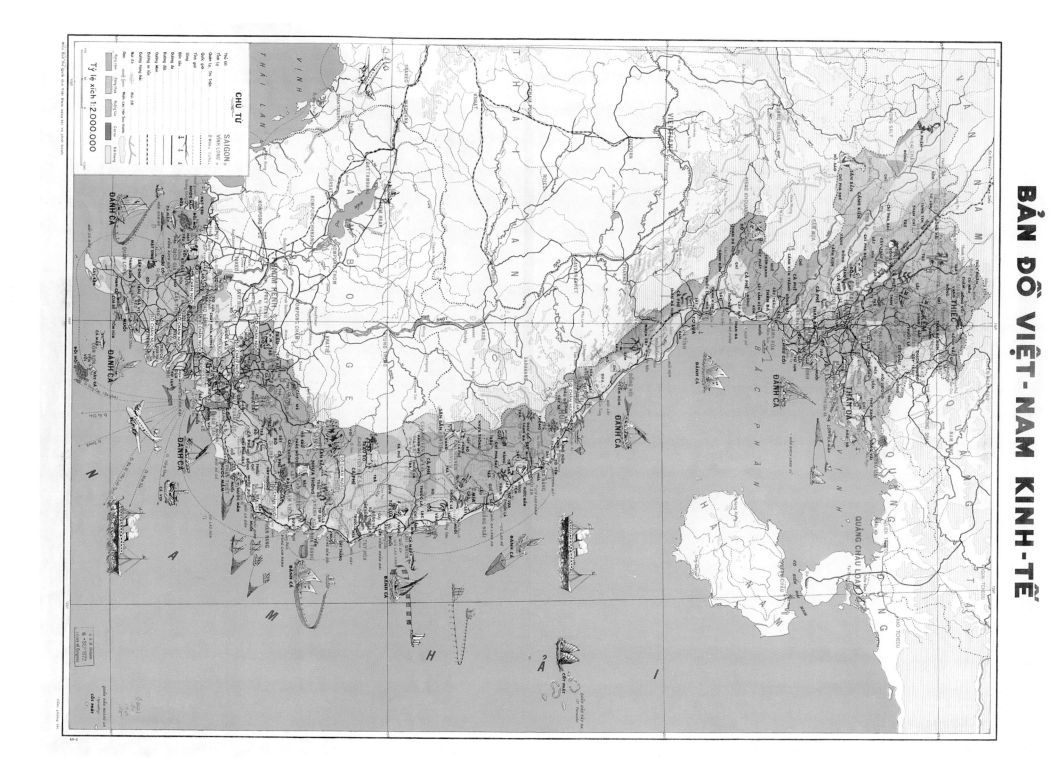

BẢN ĐỒ VIỆT-NAM KINH-TẾ

Many post-twelfth-century maps that have survived, and many produced in India today, are religious in origin, made for use in temples or for pilgrimages, a major part of modern Indian life. This has fostered the widely held misconception that the diverse Indian peoples en masse have no interest in the terrestrial affairs assigned to maps. One pilgrimage map from about 1760 is for Jainism, an important sect of dissenters from Hinduism (Plate 69). The Jain code was formulated in the fifth and sixth centuries BCE at the same time that Siddhartha Gautama (Buddha) was preaching his Middle Way. Jainism's central tenet is *ahimsa* (nonviolence). Its goal is liberation from the transmigration of the soul, which the founding sage taught was available to all castes. (Saints who have attained nirvana are called Jinas—hence "Jain.")

By virtue of their religion, the Jains, like the European Jews, were barred from certain professions. They became merchants, jewelers, or bankers, amassed fabulous wealth, and built huge temples of unsurpassed beauty between the ninth and fifteenth centuries. These bedazzling shrines of translucent, carved white marble are located mostly on holy mountaintops and number among the astonishing architectural wonders in the world, comparable to Europe's most transcendent Gothic cathedrals. Paradoxically, they bear testimony to a religion which, to an extent seen in no other, upholds the ideals of renunciation and of withdrawal from the world.

Common to Hinduism and Jainism is the belief that pilgrimages wash away sins. For many they are also festive occasions, the preferred form of tourism. Created in Jodhpur Rajasthan, the Jain pilgrimage map of Plate 69 is made with opaque watercolor and gold on easily rolled or folded cotton. It combines the two aspects of the physical, mental, and spiritual journey known as pilgrimage: The right side shows the exciting, bustling path to the holy site, while the left depicts the holy site's iconography. This map reveals both a practical and a sublimely visual culture. It delivers the sense of communal adventure experienced by the pilgrims, for whom ideas are as energizing as actions. It is Map as Action Plan. The energy of long processionals winding along mountainous terrain is very present, as is the reality of crowds and long lines toiling up steep steps to glimpse a sacred image. Priests who specialized in pilgrimage trade planned, for a fee, the pilgrim's schedule and ritual activity. This professional guidance ensured that maximum spiritual benefit would be gained in the days allotted, and the inclusion on the map of walking or riding time between the primary *tirthas* was probably invaluable. For the Jain, it is just as meritorious to finance the pilgrimage of another as to go oneself. However, if possible, it is best to personally escort the pilgrim and to temporarily lead the life of a monk—restricting meals to one a day, practicing chastity, and sleeping on the ground.

Influenced by the Chinese style, there is no set perspective on the map, only relative positions with scale used to demonstrate the site's significance. Geographical features are stylized convention-

All ancient Indian literature mentions maps, though the concern is the poetical vortex of inspirational mythology—again, time's relentless melt—not mundane realities such as historical chronology and cartographic representation. A century before Christ, India's geography was intertwined with its folklore and myths, and dozens of *tirthas* (pilgrim sites) were visited by thousands annually. This literary heritage, including the sacred Sanskrit hymns called Vedas and the two great Sanskrit epics, the *Mahabharata* and the *Ramayana*, is Indian history before about 500 BCE. Not until the twelfth century, when northern India fell under Islamic rule, are there chronological historical texts of any kind. If some of them included maps, none survive. The Indian worldview of life's impermanence, the climate, the rise and fall of empires—all these were simply not conducive to preserving the cartographic treasures referred to in texts.

historian and South Asia expert John Keay explains: "The pattern of rainfall, and the extent to which particular landscapes can benefit from it by slowing and conserving its runoff, were the decisive factors in determining patterns of settlement." By isolating regions, rainfall also produced a diversity as complex as those that evolved in Europe and Africa, a fact supported by the many different languages that developed in India.

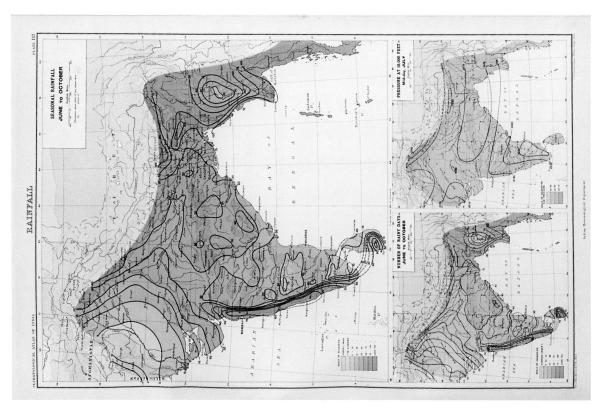

PLATE 68. *Seasonal Rainfall June to October.* The evolution of India's complex society can be explained by this 1906 climatological map.

ally to convey the essence of place. As with Chinese and Arabic maps, guidebooks supplied the accurate physical details. The gods abound to encourage meditation. Their dominating presence makes paramount the gravity and grandeur of this particular pilgrimage destination. The map may have been made to hang in a temple near the idol, or to be hung at home as a tool for meditating on the site, which produced its own spiritual merits. Or it may have been painted for a rich tourist as a souvenir.

Marco Polo's movements from Indian coastal port to coastal port was later replicated by the aggressive Europeans taking control. Until the Dutch East India Company (1602–1798) became scandalously corrupt and nearly insolvent, the powerful Dutch had mastered sufficient trade in the Indian Ocean to convince the English, as embodied in their East India Company—"the Company" (1600–1858)—to stick to mainland India. By 1750 British support of

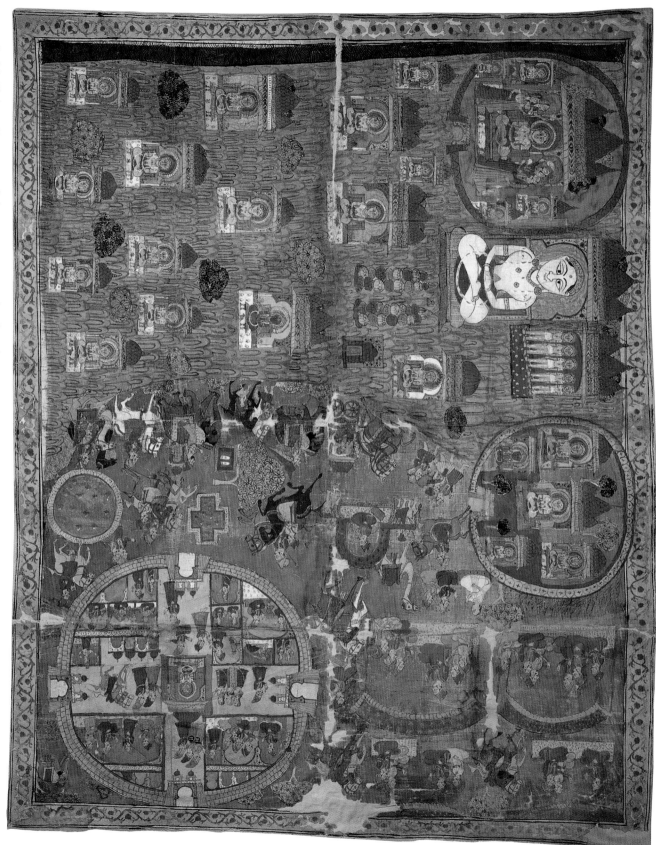

vasions by Persia and Afghanistan and rebellions in regional states, had taken their toll on the dominant Mogul empire. This empire, which by the seventeenth century had ruled nearly 90 percent of India (all but the southern region) from its seat in the northern plains, was disintegrating, and the rebelling regional states were ripe for controlling. In exchange for support, the local potentates gave the English vast land grants with immense tax revenues: the substance, if not the name, of territorial power. The Company became the true political force behind the thrones at a time when the subjugation to European colonial rule—begun in India—was occurring in other parts of Asia.

So, when the nawab (governor) of Bengal took on the Company and was defeated in 1757, the English gained full control of the rich Mogul province of Bengal. As Matthew Edney explains: "The triumph of the British Empire, from the imperialist perspective, was its replacement of the multitude of political and cultural

Hindu revolts, civil wars, and succession struggles, along with in-

components of India with a single all-India state coincident with the cartographically defined geographical whole." In his influential 1782 map *Hindoostan* (Plate 70), the Bengal surveyor general, J. R. Rennell, presented the modern geographical conception of India as a single entity (land of the Hindus) by visually equating all of "India" with the Mogul empire, and not just the portions traditionally under Mogul control. By extension, India became sole inhabitant of the subcontinent, divorced from the Hellenistic concept of the Indies, which included everything east of the Indus River. Rennell's authority made his map a template for maps of the region. It is Map as Political Geography. Its geographical rhetoric literally changed the face of the earth in the human imagination.

Rennell openly informed the public: "It must be observed, that since the empire has been dismembered a new division of its provinces has also taken place." To differentiate between the original Mogul provinces (*suba*) and the contemporary political divisions, he used two typefaces. He neglected, however, to identify the East India Company as the true ruler of Bengal, implying that the British takeover had been a legitimate delegation of Mogul authority. But his elaborate cartouche tells the story of glorious conquest in the manner of ancient Rome by using very explicit words and symbols, similar in boldness to the scale bar for Roman miles he includes on the map itself. Britannia stands on a stone pedestal on which the British victories in India are inscribed, "victories," Rennell wrote in his memoirs, "by means of which the British Nation obtained, and has hitherto upheld, its influence in India." Meanwhile the learned Brahmins humbly present the sacred Books of the "Hindoos" to Britannia for "protection," while she rests her spear on cotton, one of the Company's major exports from India.

Brilliant manipulations led to the Company's "splendid territorial aggrandizement," in Rennell's British imperialistic lingo. For example, Kashmir. Ranjit Singh (1780–1839), a Sikh maharaja, conquered most of the Punjab hill states and occupied Kashmir. He had unified the Punjab—a community of Sikh, Hindu, and Muslim people—by the time the British reached the northern region. In 1809 he signed a treaty with them agreeing not to expand his domain beyond the Sutlej River. After his death, the regent sent troops across the river, met defeat, and in 1846 was forced to cede Kashmir to the British. They made it a protectorate until a second war with the Sikhs erupted and the territory was annexed by Great Britain in 1849. In turn the British sold Kashmir and the title of maharaja to Gulab Singh for three-quarters of a million pounds. Gulab had won power in Kashmir by forming an alliance with the British to defeat the other Sikhs vying for Ranjit's throne, and the British needed a friendly power to defend India's northwest frontier against the Afghans.

A large nineteenth-century pictorial map on cloth of the Kashmir Valley was done after the British entered the scene, though the map (see Plate 71) demonstrates no Western cartographic influences. It does, however, depict beardless soldiers, a clear sign that it was painted after Sikh military rule ended, because Sikhs—as

part of their identity—left their hair uncut, along with taking the epithet Singh (lion). The map is painted in gouache and metallic silver, and its aesthetics identify the mapmaker as an Indian master in the Pahari school of miniature painting, which developed in the Himalayan foothills, with origins traceable to the Jain merchants in Gujarat at the time of Marco Polo's visit there. It exemplifies the refined stylization, the realism, and the Mogul craftsmanship that defines the Pahari movement in Indian art—as opposed to symbolism and poetic metaphor. It is, in fact, the last vital miniature art form before the impact of British colonialism made itself felt in the nineteenth century.

The map's Pahari style also displays the influence of delicate Islamic Persian miniatures, crossed with Indian painted plans of religious centers of pilgrimage. (Pilgrims abound on the map.) The script is Persian with inscriptions in Urdu. The soft colors—borders excluded—capture the cool, temperate climate of Kashmir, which has been described as a country where the sun shines mildly. A tantric influence (Hindu) is evident in the way the rivers "snake," as opposed to an Islamic geometric order. This blend of cultures is not surprising in the diverse Punjab. "This is nature's lovely face," the multicultural map offers, displaying spring (blossoming fruit trees), summer (expansive foliage in the legendary gardens), and fall (autumn leaves and crocus plants laden with saffron).

The images on the map—elaborate gardens, saffron, different religious shrines, diverse architecture—denote prosperity and declare economic soundness. There is also a reflection of the rich heritage in what was once a royal playground for all of India. Lake Dal is crowded with houseboats, both domiciles and pleasure boats—a tradition still alive today. With the mountains oriented to the outside world, Kashmir becomes a private wonderland. Like the map shawls of Kashmir from the same period, the map may have been a rich tourist's souvenir. Different points of view reveal the influence of neighboring China, as does the shifting scale, and the soft colors impart the "feel" of the region, the spiritual essence of the beautiful valley, a crossroads of the Asian world.

India's spiritual essence was not of much interest to the Company. In the tradition of Rome, what it wanted was an inch-perfect survey of the entire subcontinent it called India, a term not yet in common usage by the peoples of south Asia, and vague throughout Europe, where the subcontinent was still a set of Mogul empires, city-states, and wild areas, many under British influence. The British survey and its resulting map were to confirm India's geography and confer a practical mastery over it, one far surpassing that of the country's own military commanders, while notifying the world that all of India was a British property. The survey also aimed to solve one of the great mysteries of the age: the exact shape or curvature of the earth, which is the science of geodesy, inaugurated by Eratosthenes about 250 BCE.

In order to measure the length of India, a clear vision of the horizon was required. To England's chagrin, the survey substantiated the native belief that the British were autocratic and unresponsive imperialists, as they traipsed over the countryside for

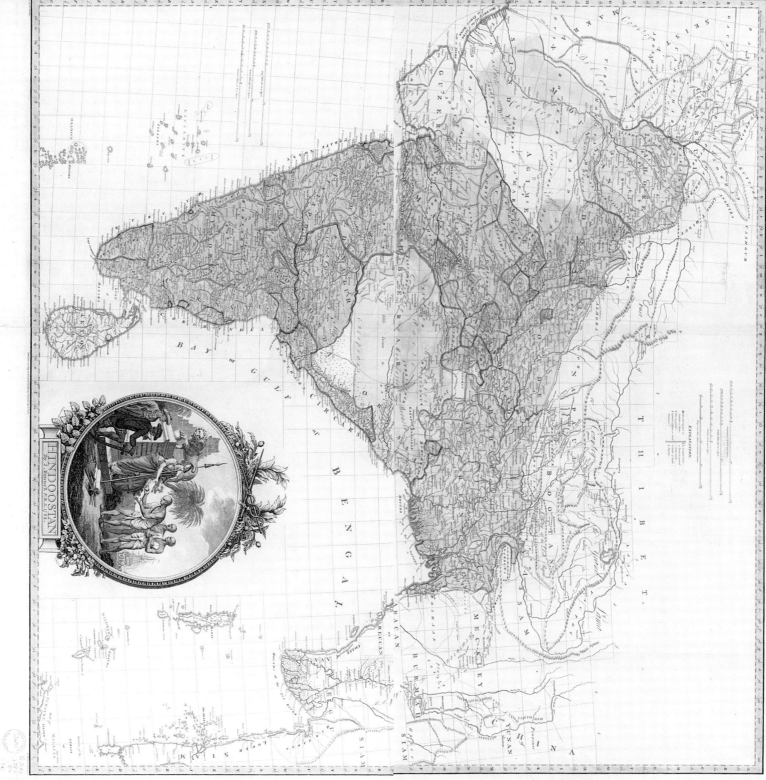

PLATE 70. *Map of Hindoostan*. This 1782 map of "British India" is a consummate example of political geography.

nearly fifty years in groups of sometimes as many as a thousand people (most of them Indians), cutting gaps thirty feet wide in forests and villages, evicting families, trampling and leveling sacred hills, eating everything in sight like fire ants, and making maps to be used for exact land assessment taxes. Touted as a British achievement, the survey relied entirely upon Indian precision engineering—the senior instrument designer and engineer was Syed Hussain Mohsin—and most of the mathematical work, the fun-

damental aspect of the expedition, was done by Indians. (The geometric measuring instrument used was a great theodolite that weighed more than half a ton and required twelve Indian men to carry it.) And when, according to legend, the Bengali mathematical genius Radhanath Sickdhar, chief computer, exclaims to the superintendent general, Sir Andrew Waugh, in 1850, "Sir, I have discovered the highest mountain in the world!" he is referring to "Peak XV" in the Himalayas, the northern boundary of the survey, but

PLATE 71. *Pictorial Map on Cloth of the Vale of Kashmir Showing Srinagar in Detail.* The blend
of cultures in the diverse Punjab are revealed by this map of the Kashmir Valley.

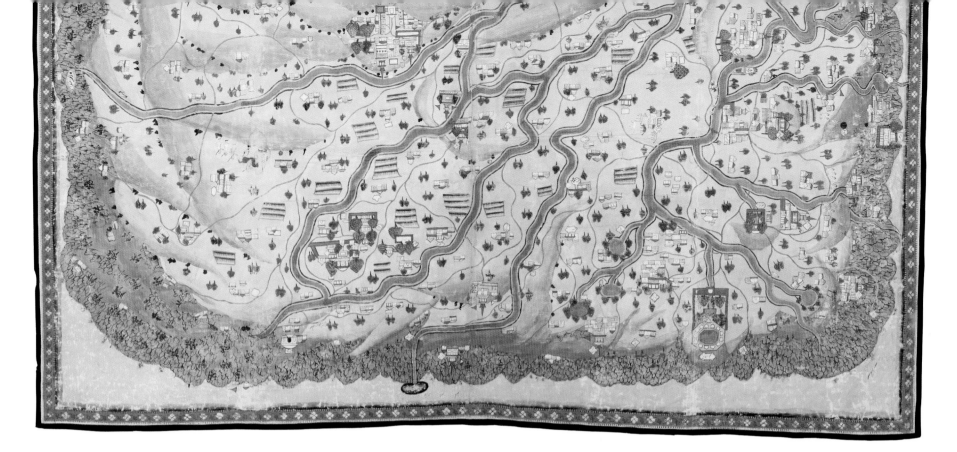

more important, he is expressing his own and his Indian colleagues' sense of participation in their great work.

The Great Trigonometric Survey of India (GTS), begun in 1800, completed its primary task in 1843, but the task was extended to survey northern India, the heartland of British rule. It cast a net of surveying triangles over India and has been hailed as one of the most stupendous works in the history of science. According to historian John Keay, "No scientific undertaking on such a massive scale had previously been attempted." In 1814 William Lambton was appointed surveyor general of India. Using trigonometry to measure the subcontinent, he created a network of small triangles whose sides and interior angles helped calculate distance along a straight, central line, or Great Arc—"the Great Indian Arc of the Meridian"—with inch-perfect accuracy. After Lambton's death in 1823, his successor, George Everest, for whom the tallest mountain, Peak XV, was named, completed the survey from central India to the Himalayas. The arc eventually dissected the entire 1,600-mile length of the country at the 78-degree meridian (or north-south line of longitude), and a systematized "grid-iron" of triangles was spun off it to cover all of India. The index chart to the Great Trigonometrical Survey of India (see Plate 72) lists the network of primary triangles. Unable to escape the Company's hold, heart-shaped India can be seen as symbolically chained and bound. It is Map as Definitive Metaphor of Imperialism. Though the survey team did not make any contributions to the theory of geodesy as a science, they did introduce important innovations in practical procedures in the field, such as spacing of triangulation into a definite chain and deducing astronomical arcs by simultaneous observation of identical stars from either end of the triangle to confirm accurate positions of fixed points with reference to longitude and latitude.

In 1858 the East India Company was dissolved and India's Raj period began, with Queen Victoria acknowledged as empress of India—the jewel in her imperial crown. Major reforms were initiated by the British. Yet their military presence was increased to discourage any further uprisings of native Indian nationalism, which was far from extinguished in spite of the might and seductive power of the Raj. The European Age of Enlightenment had had a direct effect upon India in the eighteenth century. The resulting Indian renaissance focused on the education of all Indians in order to break free of the caste system and of the Vedas and Sastras, which were worshipped as sacred words, and to encourage a contemporary interpretation of life. Eventually the renascent nationalism grew into a successful attempt to rescue India from British bondage.

Queen Victoria's 1858 proclamation promised equality in the Indian civil service. Nearly thirty years later, this still had not been achieved, and a large group of India's newly educated middle class formed the Indian National Congress (INC), an Indian political party, with its core of activism in Bengal. They met for the first time in 1885 and proposed economic reforms, since tariff policies favored British imports, for example, and demanded a larger role in the making of British policy for India. Suddenly, in 1905, without consulting any Indians, Viceroy George Curzon (1898–1905)

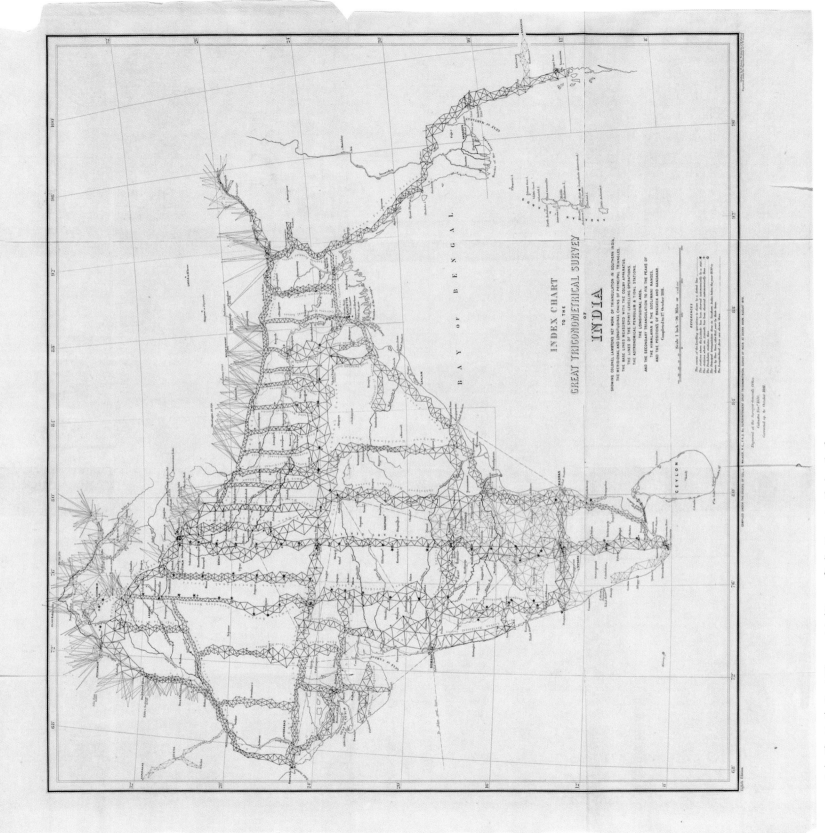

PLATE 72. *Index Chart to the Great Trigonometrical Survey of India.* Measuring the length of India involved several British hidden agendas.

partitioned troublesome Bengal, uniting all Bengalis and the rest of India in protest. Lord Minto, Curzon's successor, placated the INC—now fractured by the formation of the All India Muslim League (1907)—with *possible* transitions of power, until the outbreak of terrible violence, most notably when British soldiers fired upon a protest rally in 1919. The next year, Mohandas K. Gandhi, a national symbol of nonviolent, anticolonial protest, became president of the INC. He transformed its agenda to focus on the Jain teaching of nonviolence and successfully proposed simple noncooperation with the corrupt state.

Gandhi understood the importance of a union between the two largest communities in India, Hindu and Muslim, in the fight for liberation. In time they worked together, but never as one. In December 1929, presided over by Jawaharlal Nehru, the INC declared independence its goal. January 26, 1930, was proclaimed independence day. In 1932 an Indian map showed India's two major languages—Hindi and Urdu—sharing the same geographical space (Plate 73). Only a language of its own can speak to the heart of a nation truly. The elegant scripts' enchanting shapes seem to float

above the surface of the map like the Trigonometrical Survey's binding triangles unloosed and liberated. The map is a call for full nationhood. It is Map as Song of Liberation. The need had compelled Indians to celebrate their independence day on January 26, 1930, a full seventeen years before independence actually came. At the time, Western empires were withdrawing from Asia. The world order was changing forever.

The Persian/Arabian Gulf

After journeying up the coast of India in the Arabian Sea, Marco Polo sailed into the Gulf of Kalhat (the Persian Gulf to Westerners). Its northern coast—which today belongs to Iran and Iraq—was in the hands of the Mongols; its southern coast was controlled by Arabic Muslim tribes. After the Mongol empire disintegrated, two major powers influenced the history of the gulf: the northern Ottomans (in Anatolia/Turkey), and the northeastern Persians (in Iran). The Turkish Ottomans, who had begun expanding south through Mesopotamia/Iraq toward the Persian Gulf region in 1530, took Basra on the gulf coast from its Arab chief in 1546.

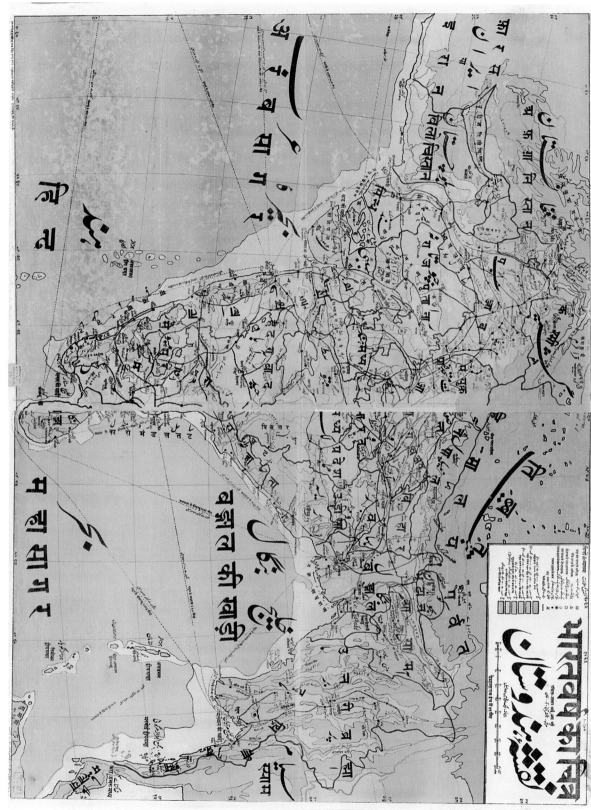

PLATE 73. *Map of India in Urdu and Hindi.* Written in two languages, this 1932 map of India speaks of a critical union of people.

was discovered in commercial quantities 125 miles north of the Persian Gulf in Persia/Iran in 1902. In 1914 the British bought a majority interest in the Anglo-Persian Oil Company to fuel their naval fleet.

After World War I, Iraq was created by the League of Nations from three Ottoman provinces—Basra, Baghdad, and Mosul—before being placed under British mandate in preparation for independence. Except for holdings by Ibn Saud, the Persian Gulf was totally under British control. In 1932 Saudi Arabia was officially established. A year later, Standard Oil was awarded an oil concession by the Saudis; in 1938 they began oil production. Then in 1941, as World War II raged, a military coup occurred in Iraq and an anti-British, pro-German government came into power. This the British defeated, reclaiming control over Iraq, while joining forces with the Soviets to invade Iraq's neighbor Iran (known as Persia until 1935), in order to prevent another pro-German coup there. One-quarter of American war aid for the USSR passed through Iran, which brought a large number of American soldiers—more than 30,000 served in the gulf region. An Allied Forces World War II propaganda map (1942; Plate 74) was printed in Alexandria as a poster with a quote in Arabic from U.S. major general B. M. Giles, chief of air staff and deputy commander of the U.S. Army Air Corps, praising all Islamic allies in the Middle East as "a living link between East and West" and touting a "shining future" for all the Allies. The map shows a sword, symbol of the Islamic people, guarding the Indian Ocean once traversed by Marco Polo and making it a safe route for Allied ships and planes to wage war with the Axis Japanese, transformed into a coiled reptile ready to strike.

Resource-poor Japan, completely dependent on oil and rubber from Indonesia, Borneo, and other possessions of European colonial powers, had attacked Pearl Harbor in 1941 after a U.S. trade embargo was initiated. Franklin D. Roosevelt's carefully measured policies of trade sanctions devised to hamper Japanese aggression, mistakenly perceived at home as appeasement, were misapplied by, in historian David M. Kennedy's words, "poorly instructed and temperamentally aggressive government officials" who refused to approve any Japanese purchases while Roosevelt was attending the Argentina Conference. This installed a total embargo, including the oil desperately needed to fuel Japan's Imperial Navy. "Roosevelt," Kennedy continues, "was only unsheathing that ultimate economic weapon, not yet plunging it into the vitals of his foe." As the president himself explained, "I simply have not got enough Navy to go round," and "the control of the Atlantic" was his primary concern at the time. But to resume any trade with Japan was impossible once the embargo was in place.

Having conquered Muslim southeast Asia, Japan is depicted on the poster as the Islamic world's sole enemy. (Germany, having gone into Russia for oil, does not appear on this map.) Allied ships pass into the Indian Ocean on the way to the Pacific from the Allied-

PLATE 74. *World War II Poster in Arabic.* Our Middle Eastern Islamic allies are the object of this military propaganda poster.

Meanwhile, European access to the Persian Gulf's trading wealth began in 1515, when the Portuguese took the island of Hormuz, at the mouth of the gulf, from the ruling Safavids in Persia/Iran. From their stronghold in neighboring India, the British helped the shah of Iran defeat the Portuguese in 1622 and became the dominant military power in the gulf. The southern gulf's remaining quasi-independent sheiks, in Bahrain and the nine sheikdoms composing the Trucial Coast—derived from "truce"—were nominally under the control of the geographically distant Ottomans. But their various treaty entanglements with Great Britain, dating from 1820, explain how the small emirates (now the United Arab Emirates) maintained their individual identities in the region.

Marco Polo's contemporaries did not know that the gulf's environs were what historian Philip Hitti calls "a desert floating on a sea of oil." However, Polo does make the first mention in Western literature of Iraqi petroleum: "There is a spring from which gushes a stream of oil, in such abundance that a hundred ships may load there at once. This oil is not good to eat; but it is good for burning and as a salve for men and camels affected with itch or scab. Men come from a long distance to fetch this oil." Oil, or "liquid gold,"

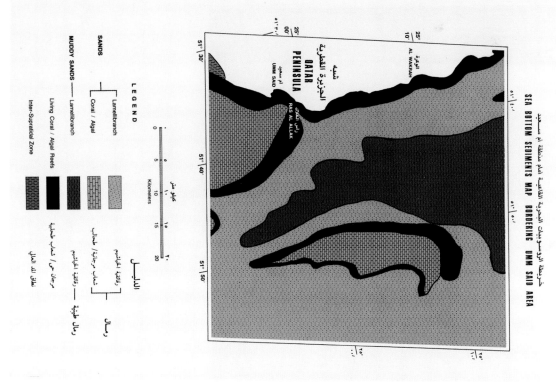

controlled Mediterranean world via the Suez Canal. The war in the Pacific was from the very beginning a naval war with marines on the ground, though Major General Giles eventually helped direct the B-29 raids on Japan and formulated plans for dropping the atomic bomb. Arabs and the Allies are projected on the 1942 map as a united front, securely in command of their extensive portion of the globe. In truth, however, until the Allied forces defeated the Axis powers in the Mediterranean, many Arabs took the side of the Axis, either overtly (like Iraq) or indirectly by withholding support for the Allies, as a reaction to centuries of British domination and the Christian-Allied invasion of Islamic Iran. Because it was increasingly focused on exploiting the oil in the region, the American presence throughout the gulf also was resented. Oil was a source of wealth and foreign investment but did little to help the independence of the people. (In 1960 the Organization of Petroleum Exporting Countries—OPEC—was formed; it created an intergovernmental organization to bring a fair return on capital to those investing in the industry.)

Besides petroleum, pearls—their places of origin and their principal markets—were a treasure that fascinated Polo. Pearls were prized in his medieval world for their ornamental and medicinal qualities. Pearls were traded at Hormuz for centuries. For tiny, pearl-rich Qatar (pronounced "cutter"), geography largely determined all aspects of its history. Qatar, a thumb-shaped peninsula, juts out into the Persian Gulf across from Hormuz, about 160 miles from Saudi Arabia. Trading pearls led to treaty relations with Britain (1868), a strategy that helped confirm Qatar's boundaries and, despite Ottoman soldiers garrisoned there, helped ensure its survival. Pearls remained Qatar's main export until oil was discovered there in 1939, at the same moment that the world's pearl market collapsed. Qatar gained independence in 1971, the year its natural gas deposit was discovered, the single largest gas reservoir of its type in the world, enough to heat every U.S. home for sixty years. The gas deposits lie in shallow waters beneath the sea's sediments.

The 1983 *Scientific Atlas of Qatar* contains maps of those sea bottom sediments off the peninsula (Plate 75). It interprets NASA's Landsat space satellite images of Qatar. The atlas was ordered by Sheikh Hamad bin Khalifa al-Thani. While set firmly in the Islamic cartographic tradition of producing uniquely beautiful and visually entrancing maps graced by abstraction, the atlas places the sheik among the new generation of royal Arab leaders, along with those in Jordan, Morocco, and Bahrain, rulers educated in the West and sponsors of scientific, economic, and bureaucratic reforms that challenge the conservative religious majority. The atlas is a link to the work of Muhammad Abduh (1849–1905), the first modern Arab Muslim intellectual to stress the spiritual and intellectual rejuvenation of Islam by accepting the products of scientific research, a challenge presented to all ancient faiths by modern societies.

In 1990 Iraq invaded its oil-rich neighbor Kuwait. Qatar, Kuwait's southern neighbor, sent troops and allowed the United States, as part of a coalition force, to set up a staging base for an air assault on

Iraq. Independent since 1961, Kuwait existed as a recognized political entity before Iraq was carved out of the defeated Ottoman Empire. However, Iraq's dream of a deep-water port on the Persian Gulf necessitated Kuwait's becoming Iraq's nineteenth province, like it or not. A 1995 *Atlas of Iraqi War Crimes in the State of Kuwait* graphically details the individual "atrocities" Iraq committed throughout the country during the 1990 invasion (see Plates 76 and 77). Large gray numbers coordinate with photographs of each destroyed locale. When studied with an accompanying Symbols of Events chart, the map conveys the barbarism and the megalomania of Iraq's leader, Saddam Hussein, whose portrait was installed in choice locations on immense screens—see bottom of map—to make his presence known to all involved. It is Map as Story Board of War. Presenting the intersection of all pertinent information—news, art, and politics—it serves as a contemporary depiction of war and horrific disaster for a modern world steeped in the universal availability of imagery intended to shock.

The world's media has made the Symbols of Events chart a live-action, you-are-there actuality in the mind's eye. This map could be a mock-up for a segment of the U.S. evening television news. Unfortunately history has proven that atlases of war crimes are not

PLATE 75. *Sea Bottom Sediments Map Bordering Umm Said Area.* Looking to the future, this 1983 map was created in Qatar from NASA satellite images.

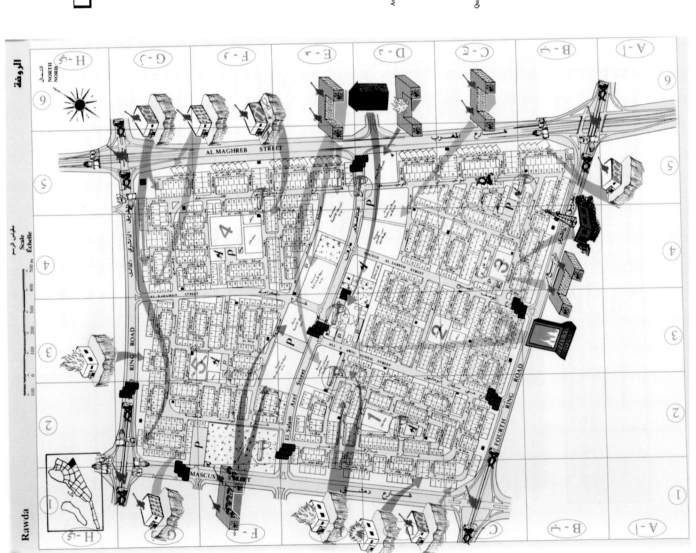

PLATES 76 AND 77. *The Rawda District of Kuwait City.* This modern mapping of warfare has an accompanying Key to Symbols.

successful deterrents to making war, while seemingly neutral boundary maps expressing their maker's point of view can be prime causes of aggression.

Palestine

From Hormuz, Polo traveled overland to his home, the republic of Venice. On his journey east twenty-four years previously, his original starting point, Acre, had been the sole remaining Middle Eastern triumph of the Crusades, and the last Christian bastion in Palestine. Acre was lost to Islamic warriors in 1291, the year before Polo began his return trip from China.

It was Greek and Roman peasants who first called the eastern Mediterranean region Palestina. Three monotheistic religions—Judaism, Christianity, and Islam—are reverently bound to this

territory. In the gradations of sacred space, the Holy Land is the holiest of lands for Jews, just as it is for the Arabs and Christians. From time immemorial it was the Promised Land to the Jewish people. After centuries of persecution, Jews in Russia created the Lovers of Zion movement in the early 1880s, in reference to the mountain on which Jerusalem was built, supposedly the dwelling place of the Jewish God. At the same moment, in the areas bordering the Mediterranean, a pan-Arabism was burgeoning as a political force in revolt against the Ottoman Empire. The Arabs dreamed of creating a unified community in the Holy Land where the Jews dreamed of re-creating their ancient homeland.

Jews began escaping repression in Europe by moving to Palestine in the late nineteenth century. They joined the tiny Jewish community that had inhabited the area for a thousand years. To win Jewish support for the Allies during World War I, the British secretary, Arthur Balfour, wrote to Jewish leader Lord Rothschild to assure him that the British government supported the ideal of providing a homeland for the Jews. The Balfour Declaration laid the foundation for international support to found the modern state of Israel.

After the war, with the disintegration of the Ottoman Empire, Britain gained control of Palestine—the last outpost of its empire in the Middle East—where Arabs were 90 percent of the population. A Hebrew map of Palestine from 1936 (Plate 78) depicts the British-sanctioned Zionist settlements in a peaceful, harmonious green—the symbolic color of life and action and freedom. They resemble healthy, thriving vegetation in a desert landscape. It is Map as Act of Hope. It is a visual metaphor for the values of the mapmaker. (Coincidentally, green is for Muslims the color of Paradise—Quran 55:62–64—and the color of wealth—Quran 18:31.) The Jewish settlements on the map exude a calm that belies the human anguish on the scene. In 1936, the time of this map, the anti-Semitic policies of the Nazis swelled the Zionist settlements, and the Arabs began a three-year revolt against British rule *and* Jewish immigration to Palestine. Thousands of Arabs were killed or jailed when the British responded with full military force, though in 1939 they set a rigidly upheld quota on European Jewish immigration to placate the Arab states, no longer able to annihilate them in this, the imperial sunset.

Palestine remained relatively quiet during World War II. The Arabs were pacified by the British concessions in 1939. Focused on avoiding complete annihilation at the hands of the Nazis in Europe, the Jews supported the Allies and resigned themselves to postponing their dreams of a homeland in Israel. In 1947 the United Nations adopted a plan to divide Palestine into two states, Jewish and Arab, with Jerusalem administered by the United Nations. The UN plan was accepted by the Jews and rejected by the Arabs. In 1948 Britain gave up its mandate and the Jewish Palestinian state, renamed Israel, declared its independence and became a client state of the United States. Six Arab armies attacked Jewish settlements in every part of Palestine. A cease-fire the following year won Israel extended borders and displaced thousands of Arab Palestinians. The wars continued.

A 1987 map by Russell Lenz (see Plate 79) dramatically depicts head-on what Balfour described as the "small notch" of Israel, which he hoped Arabs would not begrudge the Jewish people. It is Map as Haven to Home. It has the urgency of an eyewitness account of an ongoing struggle. Slightly smaller than New Jersey, Israel bears the full historical weight of the fifty-seven Islamic nations on its slender back. Most important, Lenz's map reinvents visually Marco Polo's dream of re-creating in words the vastness of Asian space.

Before Polo's book, the accepted European idea of Asia was the product of biased theological teachings, unreliable classical memories, and fantasy. When twelfth-century Western scholars gained access to Arabic scientific learning, they took little interest in the studies of geography, including Ptolemy, whose *Almagest* (On the Shape of the Heavens) they translated into Latin but not his *Geographia*. Thus Polo's original readers, with no maps at hand, would have experienced a sense of wonder at his travels that is almost impossible for modern readers to comprehend. Fortunately Lenz's map blankets the earth with a metaphysical enchantment. It produces in the viewer a comparable wonder at the earth's shape and vastness. Lenz, like Polo, offers a different take on things and forces reorientation. Also a secular work, Polo's book in its French and Italian versions was titled The Description of the World. Lenz's description of the world is as unique in cartographic history as is Marco Polo's travel memoir.

The Asian landmass dwarfed the Mediterranean world; and as the birthplace of Christianity, the Holy Land loomed immense in its spiritual geography as well. The influential Polo's religion was drenched in Augustine's belief, *Desiderium sinus cordis*—It is yearning that makes the heart deep. (The Christian theologian and philosopher Augustine played a most potent part in the orientation of Western thought.) Both legendary men were explorers. Each sought the truth of existence, a truth made ever present by a love that "groans" for it. It was Augustine who wrote in his *Confessions*, "…groaning with inexpressible groaning in my distant wandering, and remembering Jerusalem with my heart stretching upwards in longing for it; Jerusalem, my Fatherland, Jerusalem who is my mother."

PLATE 78. *Land of Israel.* Zionist pioneer settlements are described optimistically on this 1936 Hebrew map.

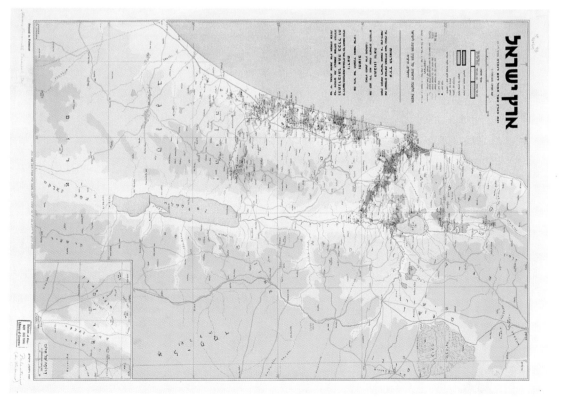

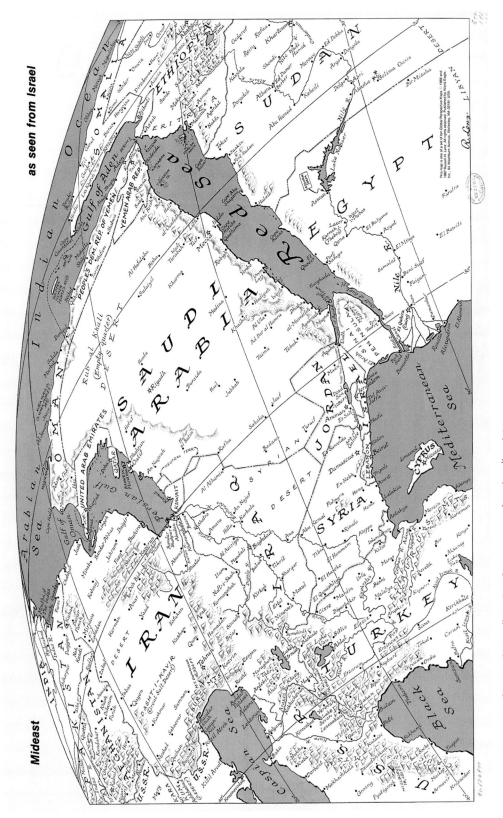

Mideast

as seen from Israel

PLATE 79. *Mideast as Seen from Israel.* Russell Lenz's 1987 map encapsulates Israel's point of view.

AFRICA

Africa, the matrix of the human species, is the second-largest continent after Asia. Spanning 5,000 miles from north to south and 5,000 miles at its widest point, it is bigger in land area than the United States, China, India, and Australia combined. A series of plateaus comprise most of Africa, and they often descend sharply to the sea quite close to the coast, which produces a landmass with a generally narrow coastal plain. This steep decline to sea level creates barriers of falls and rapids in the lower courses of rivers that impede their use as transportation routes into the interior. And Africa's fairly regular coastline affords few natural harbors, while the shallowness of coastal waters makes it difficult for large ships to reach its shores.

The origin of the continent's name is uncertain. The Greeks were Africa's first European colonists. They conquered Cyrene circa 631 BCE and had a strong influence on Egyptian culture. The Greeks called Africa "Libya" (derived from ancient Egypt's "land of the Lebu"—Berber peoples), though their word for "sunny" was *aprica*, not unlike the Phoenecian word *aprike*, "free from cold." When the Romans conquered Carthage in 146 BCE, they replaced "Libya" with "Africa," perhaps because a tribe of Berber people living to the south of Carthage were called the Afarik. The word Africa came to mean the entire continent at the end of the first century BCE, when Rome ruled the entire Mediterranean world.

Africa has extraordinarily varied terrain divisible into six general climatic regions. Yet based on the dense jungles and rain forests of the Congo basin and parts of the western coast—a small proportion of the landmass—Africa was dubbed the dark continent, though there are other meanings ascribed to that famous phrase, including the fact that it remained unmapped for such a long time. In fact, snowcapped mountains, vast river basins, huge lakes, savannas, upland plateaus, valleys, hills, grassland plains, and the greatest desert on earth enchant its topography. These are all places where darkness is vanquished by the dazzling tropical sun.

Africa has the diversity and richness of a long, complex history, the longest human history of any continent. African hominids date from at least 4 million years ago. Thus it is also untrue that Africa was a primitive place, a blank place, an uninteresting place, a barbarous place, before Europeans brought civilization. African history preconquest reveals the rise and fall of many brilliant indigenous civilizations, as well as major contributions by black Africans to ancient Egypt. Ancient Africa's past is recorded in histories of Greece and Rome and written in stones uncovered by archaeologists; and, in North Africa's Mali, ancient history is recalled by the griots, a class of storyteller-historians.

Some of the largest African cities and kingdoms were located in the Sahel, a desert and savanna region immediately south of the Sahara in central and western Africa, where they served as way stations and terminus points for ancient trade routes across North Africa, trade dominated by salt and gold, two of the continent's most valuable mineral resources. Perhaps the greatest of these empires, the Songhay (fl. 500–1400 CE), had several thousand cultures under its control, finally collapsing when its subject peoples revolted. The inventive genius of sub-Saharan Africans had developed metallurgy possibly before anyone anywhere else in the world, and by 1400 BCE, east Africans were producing steel in carbon furnaces. (In the West steel was "invented" in the eighteenth century.)

Elsewhere in Africa, kingdoms flourished. South of Egypt, the Nubian civilization can be traced back to 6000 BCE; its greatest kingdom, Meroe (500 BCE–700 CE), was destroyed by rival Aksumites of Ethiopia, whose trade routes extended from the Mediterranean to the Indian Ocean. There were the Zimbabwe (twelfth to fifteenth centuries), who traded along their Indian Ocean coast, and the Kanem-Borno (twelfth to nineteenth centuries), who controlled the area around Lake Chad. Like their counterparts in Europe and Asia, African kingdoms rose, flourished, and declined for many different reasons. When the Muslims conquered Egypt and brought Islam, a religion of the book (Quran), to Africa in 646, they spread literacy, which is why many African languages use Arabic script. But Islam also brought fragmentation. Institutions and kingdoms collapsed as Muslims declared holy war (*jihad*) against pagan social groups.

Maps have always been a part of the material culture of nonliterate and literate peoples. Aside from the Egyptians, however, there are very few indigenous African mapmakers whose work has survived. The Sudanese writer Jamal Mahjoub touches upon this seeming lack of durable cartography in precolonial Africa in his story "The Cartographer's Angel," in which a modern map of a village is drawn to the complete dissatisfaction of the community at large, who ask, "Where are the angels, and the ghosts, where are the dead spirits, where do good luck and misfortune reside?" Clearly the map in the story does not represent the villagers' world.

It remains a mystery what course African history would have taken, and what the modern maps of Africa would look like, if the Europeans had not interrupted the natural political evolution of a continent where there is no single "African," but about a thousand different cultural/linguistic groups, each one distinct and unique. For the colonist, however, the world was divided into two human species, and what divided the world was race. As Frantz Fanon, the theorist of racism and colonialism, insists, "The colonist makes history. His life is an epic, an odyssey. He is invested with the very beginning: 'We made this land.' He is the guarantor for its existence: 'If we leave, all will be lost, and this land will return to the Dark Ages.'" In short: "Until I see it, it doesn't exist. It is a dark spot on Earth." Colonialism darkened Africa's history into tragedy. This is a story told most brilliantly in maps.

The Sub-Saharan African World

Sub-Saharan Africa was as unknown to Marco Polo and his contemporaries as was Asia. It was a place of myths and legends completely separate in their imaginations from the northern portion of the continent, which had become integrated into the life and history of the Mediterranean world. The entire continent of Africa as we have come to know it became firmly inscribed in the Western world's imagination during the great age of European discovery when, in 1459, on the eve of the Italian Renaissance, a Venetian monk and cartographer named Fra Mauro produced a world map for the young king of Portugal, Afonso V (see Plate 80). Oriented south in the tradition of Islamic mapmakers, the map places Africa top right—up—side down to Western viewers—and depicts the huge landmass almost entirely surrounded by water. This innovative map convinced Portugal's monarch not to send his explorers sailing west across the theoretically empty Atlantic to find the shortest seaway to the temptingly rich Indies, but to have them continue sailing south from Portugal, beyond the two thousand miles to Senegal and Cape Verde, places identified on Fra Mauro's map. In spite of daunting tales of men bursting into flames at the equator, the first recorded sighting in the sky of the Southern Cross already had been safely noted there on previous voyages for the king.

At a time when Ptolemy's *Geographia* was newly reborn in Italy through Europe's Byzantine conquests, and revered by most as a geographical touchstone, Fra Mauro's large, majestic map displayed Italy's mastery of the latest geographical, statistical, and historical knowledge by giving an eastern border to China and by erasing Ptolemy's curving extension of Africa, which had enclosed the Indian Ocean and made it an inland sea. Ptolemy's other allusions, however, are present in the shapes of other regions of the known world, such as India and the oversized Ceylon (Sri Lanka) Fra Mauro portrays the encircling ocean as a narrow, circular band, the way the Greeks imagined it. Visually, by not including any notion of the Atlantic's expanse, he excludes any possibility of sailing west to reach Asia. In fact he eliminates the Atlantic from view. He offers instead a simple, direct sea road to the East around Africa, which, in fact, is as misleading for the modern viewer as it was for the map's contemporary user.

Fra Mauro and his contemporaries knew there was nothing simple or direct about the southern route. The tyranny of Africa's coastal winds and currents and equatorial doldrums made it necessary for Portuguese navigators to sail far out into the uncharted Atlantic in an arcing swing known as the *volta*, toward Brazil, in order to catch and ride the southern trade winds back to the African mainland. Once the winds' unchanging latitudes were recorded on sea charts, few of which have survived, Portuguese sailors mastered the art of finding the winds again by sighting the sun or the polestar with a mariner's astrolabe and noting their route on a map's rhumb lines. Those lines facilitated European seafaring exploration outside the Mediterranean world. By including rhumb lines, Fra Mauro reveals the particularly complex tacking technique involved in riding those lines to fixed points; but *where* the crucial useful winds were captured in the unseen Atlantic he may not have known. They were state secrets, classified for all but the few chosen Portuguese explorers. What look like lines of decoration on the map told tales of great daring to the initiated.

Marco Polo's influence is found in place names. Arab and Persian sources detailed the roads and gave Fra Mauro localities along

PLATE 80. *Fra Mauro's Map of the World.* Portugal's plan for a sea route to India was sparked by this 1459 map of the known world.

the east coast of Africa, facing the Indian Ocean, including Safala and the immense island of Diab (Madagascar). The break at the southern end of the continent may reflect a confusion about the actuality of Madagascar in spite of the mapmaker's multiple sources noting its existence. Its history and civilization were dominated by the Indian Ocean world, separating it from the mainland spiritually and geographically; and the dense forest covering the eastern coasts of both Africa and Madagascar may have added to the spatial confusion. Various church emissaries to Venice from Ethiopia "with their own hands had drawn for me," wrote

Fra Mauro, which explains the great detail he provides for that empire.

His map includes written information, including various legends of navigation in the southern sea. One of the many legends on the map near the southern extremity of Africa says that in 1420 an "Indian" junk was driven by a storm from the Indian Ocean out into the Atlantic, "the Sea of Darkness." Fra Mauro writes, "I affirm that some ships have sailed and returned by this route." Though there is no mention of fiery deaths, or of sea monsters, the map retains a medieval cosmography. It includes legendary places,

PLATE 81: *Female Figure in Manda Style.* The migration paths of African mythical ancestral heroes are recorded in many ways.

such as Prester John's Christian kingdom, mingling with accurate geographic detail. Yet the map also reflects the new intellectual climate of a religious-scholastic world beginning to tilt in favor of scientific rigor and knowledge based on eyewitness accounts.

In 1482, twenty-three years after Fra Mauro's map appeared, Portugal's Diogo Cão became the first European to reach the mouth of the wide and powerful Zaire (Congo) River below the equator. The people then living in the region of the mighty river included the Angolans of the central kingdom of the Congo, who befriended Cão. Also residing there were the Tabwa, a people belonging to the Bantu language group. Drawing upon a religious system based on honoring their ancestors, the Tabwa created maps very different from those with which Europeans were familiar.

The Bantu are a people with a history of migration. Their original home, circa 2000 BCE, was in the area of modern Nigeria, on Africa's west coast above the equator; but in a series of migrations, Bantu speakers spread to the savanna lands of Angola and east to what is today Lake Victoria, then south throughout central and southern Africa. The migration paths of these ancestral Bantu heroes have acquired mythical dimensions. They were inscribed on the human body as part of initiation ceremonies in the Congo. Plate 81, showing a wooden sculpture of an ancestral figure, reflects this Tabwa practice. Each mark on the initiate's body, and each mark on this sculpture, has both spatial and spiritual significance. It is Map as Body Polity.

The elongated figure eight and the line cutting through it, the *mulalambo*—a mark signifying geographical boundaries, such as the familiar bank of Lake Tanganyika—separate east from west, left from right. Left and right, in turn, had particular significance for the Tabwa. As in many other cultures, left had negative associations for them, representing deception and corruption. The right, by contrast, represented strength and integrity. More than a demarcation of opposing forces, however, the *mulalambo* may also represent the route taken by the Celestial Hunter of the Tabwas' origin myth, following the Milky Way southward to where hunters could find game. It may also denote the terrestrial north-to-south route the Tabwa people themselves took during various migrations. This deep consciousness of geography extends to the villages of the Islamic Tabwa, which are laid out north to south with all main entrances on the east, facing Mecca, facilitating for Muslims their five daily prayers offered in that direction.

When they settled along Lake Tanganyika, the Tabwa encountered the Luba, another Bantu people, whose religion was also based on veneration of ancestors, and on paying tribute to spirits. The Luba, who exercised a strong influence on the Tabwa settlers, formed a great empire ruled by a divinely ordained king. It flourished in the environment of lakes, marshes, and river channels at the source of the Zaire River from the 1450s until the 1870s, when it was challenged by Arab slave traders and European invaders. Originally, in order to survive flooding and drought, the Luba co-

operated on large-scale works such as dikes, drainage canals, and dams, which led to political unity and the establishment of a sacred kingdom.

Luba royal institutions were created to counterbalance the absolute power of the king. Its members were responsible for remembering the history of the kingdom, and their interpretations of history could influence the actions of the rulers. Wall maps (see Plate 82) drawn by elders were used in the last two stages of initiation into the royal society. The maps locate the dwelling places of the guardian spirits of their kings, as well as the migration paths of their Bantu ancestors. They also detail the locations of the guardian spirits, chiefdoms, and the all-important waterways essential to the survival of Luba kingship and Luba history. The symbols for those waterways are the only ones easily interpreted by noninitiates.

The maps are mnemonic devices used to teach initiates the precepts and principles of their community as handed down from the founders of the royal culture. These abstract drawings encode

PLATE 81: *Female Figure in Manda Style.* The migration paths of African mythical ancestral heroes are recorded in many ways.

PLATE 82. *Lukala Wall Map.* Luba kingship and history are specified by this African wall map.

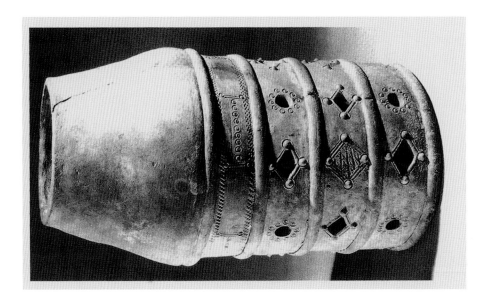

an official history of the Luba state. They capture the shared consciousness of place, and demonstrate the Lubas' sophisticated grasp of vast areas of forests and rivers, an understanding made manifest by their large-scale communal works. They also display a profound commitment to guarding their identity as a people, by intertwining it with their history. It is Map as Social Construction. It inculcates in each individual a respect for the ancestral earth and for others, since each is a part of the whole. Luba wall maps are abstract expressions of territorial pride, laced with a humbling purity celebrating a long legacy.

The Congo people's cosmology was as defined as their geography. On a ribbed ceramic cemetery stele (Plate 83), the Congo cosmos is ideographically represented as a cross of diamonds with circles attached at each end to signify the cardinal points (north at the top) and the position of the sun in its four phases — dawn, noon, sunset, and midnight. The horizontal ribs represent the water, with heaven above and earth extending below. The regular movement of the heavenly bodies in time and space is a metaphor for the flow of human life. It was believed that after death some humans were reborn in the Underworld and became the ruling

PLATE 83. *Congo Cosmogram.* The Congo cosmos is ideographically represented in order to create a poetic metaphor.

spirits in the landscape, those whose territories must be learned during initiation ceremonies.

The place of the Congo in the European and Arab cosmos clashed dramatically with the views of the African cultural groups who lived in the region. Exploitation of African resources, both material and human, became the primary basis of European relations with sub-Saharan Africa from the fifteenth century onward. Angola, where Diogo Cão had first landed, for example, proved a disappointment with regard to gold, though it did provide many slaves for Portugal's colony in Brazil. Portuguese commerce in people was conducted with the assistance of African traders, who brought slaves from the interior to the European traders waiting on the coast. A 1743 German map of the African coast in Latin and French by the great printing house Homann Heirs (Plate 84) depicts the area just north of the equator, and shows the interior as territory still unknown to Europeans 250 years after Diogo Cão.

On it, Africa's large rivers remain a jumble of confusion, with the Senegal River becoming the utterly misconstrued Niger, located here in the Ethiopian territory, historically considered part of northern "White Africa," a place with Caucasian ethnic strains within a mixed population, very different from true "Black Africa." In spite of the waterway mixup, a dense clutch of cities and kingdoms appears in the realm of the Mandingos along these river routes. This urban development reflects the importance of the overland trading activity to the river sites but also suggests the rivers' lack of importance to long-distance trading significant in the evolution of the major Niger civilizations, such as the Mali empire. Mali, familiar to the Mediterranean world across the Sahara, appears on the map as a known world apart, surrounded by desert. For more than two millennia, imperfect geographic information regarding the rivers had been carried to the Mediterranean world

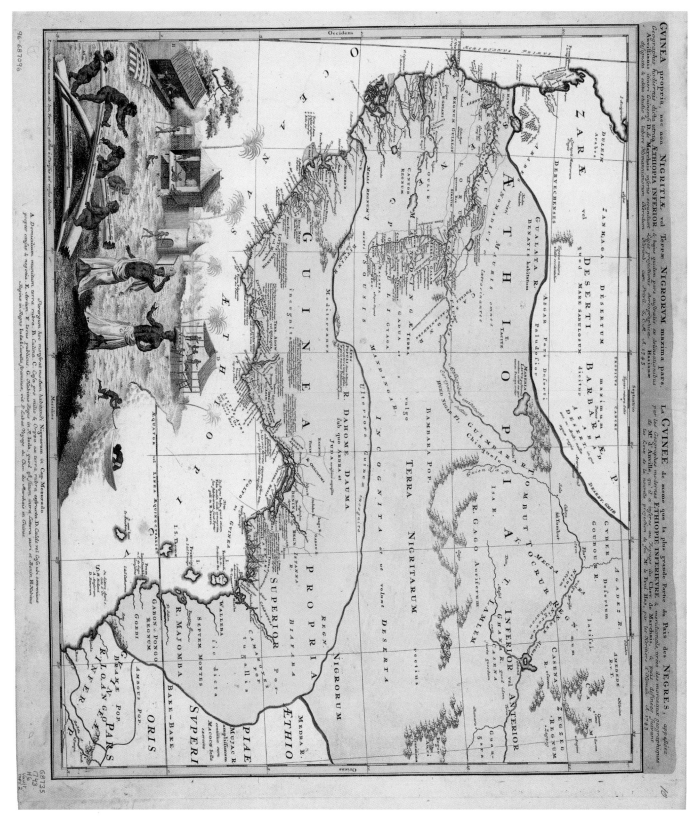

PLATE 84. *West Africa from Gabon in the South to Niger, Mali, and Mauritania in the North. The beginnings of European colonialism are found in this 1743 map of Africa.*

along ancient dromedary trade routes established in the quest for Senegal's gold. The Portuguese sea route considerably weakened the value of the overland route, and the navigable rivers, as the charted "roads" to the ships at anchor, replaced its use in such trading ventures.

Meanwhile the coast is dotted with European names, and the mouths of conspicuously truncated rivers display European saints' names. Most dramatically, in spite of there being no natural ports on the African coast, a tiny cluster of supposed ports on the lucrative Gold Coast in the "Ethiopian Ocean" are marked with symbols of ownership: *H* for Holland, *A* for Britain, and *D* for Denmark. It is Map as Herald of Colonialism. Sovereignty over the African coastline was initially the white traders' primary goal; once ashore, and before they could reach the salubrious uplands, many of them succumbed to the myriad fatal diseases of the tropics. The map recognizes African control over the interior by dividing it into kingdoms (*regnum*) with no sign of European influence, though many local authorities were already being undermined by the slave trade wars. Human enterprise proved more fateful to Africans than the forces of nature.

Landscape as a subject for painting had emerged in the West in the seventeenth century. The map's large cartouche places this second way of picturing the world beside the more reliable, measured representation, the map. Unlike maps, however, landscape art can shift elements in creative ways, and the cartouche takes advantage of this fact. It depicts an unspoiled, indigenous community on Cape Mesurado, practically on the west coast of the African bulge, with, inexplicably, an idealized king and queen of Juda transported from their homeland above the Gulf of Guinea. Putti, a standard European cartographic decoration, appear colored black—symbolic of the peoples south of the Sahara—and work with a boat nearby on one of the most valuable exports from the continent, ivory. The small boat also contains valuable transportable "merchandise" in the form of a native person, one as easily moved by the traders as the king and queen of Juda by the artist. The main catchment area for slaves was the West African bulge depicted on the map.

Arab traders, too, were masters of the slave trade. Links were established to connect Persia and Arabia and East Africa during the first Islamic expansion in the seventh century, and market towns, such as Sofala, prospered as hybrid civilizations—half Arab, half African—from trade in gold, ivory, and slaves. It is no coincidence that in 1803 Africa was the subject of one of the first published Muslim maps in the Western cartographic tradition that used longitude and latitude (Plate 85). The royal printing house of the Ottoman Empire in Istanbul translated the portions of an English atlas by William Faden with a focus on the areas surrounding the empire itself. The maps were done as part of the "New Order," an attempt by the Turkish emperor to westernize the sciences in order to deal with European imperialism at a time when the Sudan was an Islamic stronghold and the Ottomans controlled Egypt. It is Map as Common Language.

Arabs dominated trade in the central Congo Basin. They were a familiar, knowledgeable presence to European explorers through-

out Africa. Yet the Turkish map pointedly ignored the various African kingdom boundaries, the territorial identifications, and the blank spaces in the heart of Africa as they appeared on the English model map. The entire interior is labeled by the Arab mapmaker "Kingdom of Unbelievers," framing everything in terms of his Islamic religion for the business of slavery. The Quran prescribed a humanitarian approach to slaves: free men could not be enslaved. But as the empire of Islam expanded, the laws were interpreted more narrowly. Thus people *outside* the Islamic empire, unbelievers, were considered acceptable candidates for slavery. The Arabs had traveled widely as traders, using a universal system of barter in lieu of valueless money, and this map shows that no terra incognita existed for its audience.

The Arab slave trade in Africa was entrenched for more than six hundred years before the Europeans arrived. The great trade networks across the Sahara were as much about transporting slaves as other goods. At the time this map was made, however, the expansion of Russia had ended the Ottoman Empire's slave trade in Caucasians, which made Africa even more precious to them.

The English names Gulf of Guinea and Gold Coast are to the Arabs Gulf of Gold Mines and Elephant Tooth, and the British-identified Slave Coast lying next to the Gold Coast does not appear at all in Arabic, because the Arabs had their own slave outlets within the northern Islamic empire. West Africans captured by Arabs were sold in Morocco and Tunisia; east coast captives were sent up the coast to Egypt, or shipped from eastern markets to the Persian Gulf. Trading did not extend over vast distances. Goods acquired were turned over to caravans for marketing as quickly as possible, which is why scale on the Arab map is given in caravan hours: 2.5 British miles equals one hour. Likewise, the Arab mapmaker clearly marked the Islamic empire's boundaries to the north, because although castration of male slaves raised their market value as eunuchs, mutilation of slaves was forbidden by Islamic law. The job had to be done before the Arab caravans carrying slaves crossed into the Islamic empire. Instead of shifting zero degrees longitude to Istanbul (it was common practice for each country to make its own capital city zero degrees longitude), the Turks left the British demarcation of London on the map to avoid confusion over localities.

The pope being the arbiter among the Christian monarchs, a papal bull in 1455 had chartered Portuguese imperialism by granting Portugal a monopoly on navigation and trade south of the Canary Islands to the Indies. The coming of the Protestant Reformation, however, diminished papal power, and this, combined with their own overextension, soon erased the Portuguese from maps of Africa. But it was only a matter of time before other Europeans found a way into the heart of the continent, always with the assistance of African guides, without whom they would have been perilously lost in the mazes of forest and undergrowth, or eaten alive by predatory beasts.

Many eighteenth- and nineteenth-century writers report map-making assistance from African natives of various cultural and linguistic groups. In 1824 the British explorer Hugh Clapperton (1788–1827) became the first European to visit the court of Mohammed Bello, sultan of the Sokoto and the most powerful man in all of western Sudan. Clapperton was seeking the course of the mighty Quarra (Niger) River, the crescent-shaped river that dominates western Africa. Extending over 2,500 miles, it rises 150 miles inland from the Atlantic, then runs eastward, away from the sea into the Sahara before sharply turning southeast to the Gulf of Guinea. Its course had baffled Western geographers for two millennia. Incorrectly, they had connected it to the Senegal (farther north) and to the Nile (farther east).

Extremely welcoming at first, Bello then forbade Clapperton to travel to the river, although he "drew on the sand the course of the river Quarra, which he also informed me entered the sea at Fundah." On their parting, the sultan presented Clapperton with "a map of the country." It is Map as Obfuscation. An adaptation of the sultan's gift appeared in the 1826 *Narrative of Travels and Discoveries in Northern and Central Africa*, a book written by Clapperton and published the year before his death in Africa from fever.

In the Eastern cartographic tradition, Sokoto, being the center of the sultan's world, is placed at the center of his map (see Plate 86). However, that is not the only geographical adjustment the sultan made on the portable map. Most important, the map does not reveal, as the sand drawing had done, the Quarra's relationship with the Atlantic. This fundamental change shed light on Clapperton's having been forbidden to visit the river, and he wrote in his journal: "I could not help suspecting the intrigues of the Arabs to be the cause, as they know well, if the native Africans were once acquainted with English commerce by the way of the sea, their own lucrative inland trade would from that moment cease."

The sultan also falsely described in Arabic and English the course of the Quarra, "which reaches Egypt, and which is called the Nile." He knew, possibly from Clapperton himself, that European myths had the Niger flowing up, via Lake Chad, to become the Nile, and rather than reveal the Niger's unexpectedly direct descent into the Gulf of Guinea, he wanted to confuse things further. As it

PLATE 85. *Turkish Africa.* This is the first published map by Muslims using European cartographic methods.

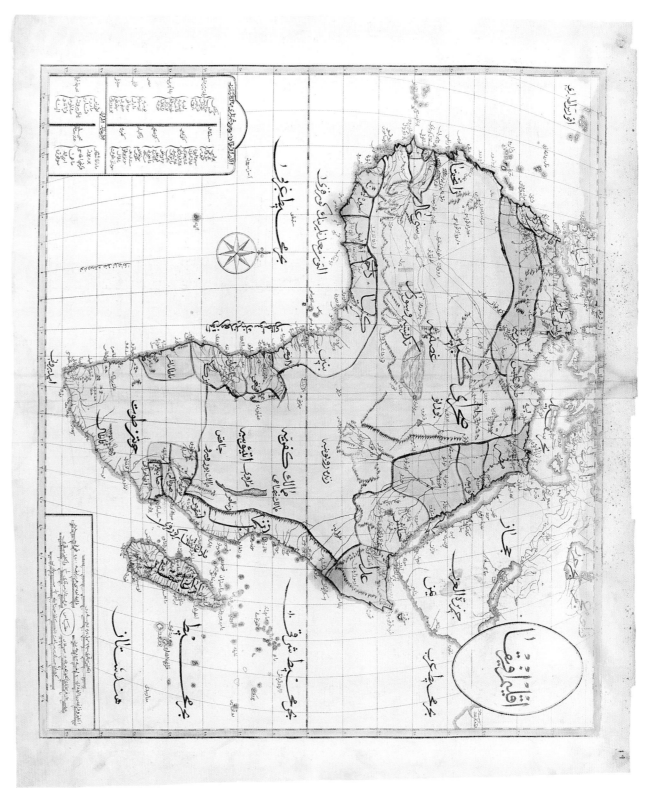

happened, just before visiting the sultan, Clapperton had been on an unsuccessful expedition to Lake Chad to check out the Nile theory, and in his book he credited the sultan's change of story to the fact that "strangers would come and take their country from them, if they knew the course of the Quarra."

Perhaps the most famous explorer-adventurer-writer was Henry M. Stanley (1841–1904), who after fighting on both sides of the American Civil War, went to Europe as a foreign correspondent for the *New York Herald* and in 1869 received the assignment to find the Scottish missionary David Livingstone, lost on the hunt for the source of the Nile. (Stanley found him in 1871 in Tanganyika, greeting him with the immortal words, "Dr. Livingstone, I presume?") Returning to Africa from 1874 to 1877, Stanley followed the Congo River from its source to the sea, which gave him an intimate knowledge of the region. This knowledge served him well when he embarked in 1879 on his notorious third expedition to the African heartland at the invitation of Belgium's King Leopold II, who was convinced his subjects would not support the acquisition of colonial territory, but who was determined to endow his own royal lineage with an independent fortune of such magnitude that it would control his country's economic and political history in spite of parliament. Stanley's job was to help Leopold organize a private colony under the guise of the International Association for the Exploration and Civilization of Africa. Owned by Leopold, it was to be international in name only.

A map of equatorial Africa from 1884 has annotations added by hand in blood-red ink (Plate 87). These few innocuous lines sketch the very rough boundaries of Leopold's Association, and bring home to the viewer how simple it is to communicate life-changing events via the graphic form of the map. The absence of all signs of human habitation on the map adds a sense of innocence to the lines. It is as if Africa in 1884 were an uninhabited piece of real estate. Yet during his third expedition Stanley had negotiated treaties with 450 chiefs in the Congo basin permitting Leopold to build "stations" or "free ports" along the banks of the powerful river, the most dominant natural feature on the map. In fact the treaties transferred to the king the rights to everything but villages and gardens. Twenty million people were defrauded, forced into labor, degraded, mutilated, tortured, or murdered, as Leopold, with no previous colonial experience, acquired a field of action sixty times his kingdom's size. The absence on the map of any indigenous territorial markers allows the eye to scan the width of the continent unimpeded and to see the scope of Leopold's ambitions. Those few red lines on this map were a sign that the world sanctioned his ambitions. It is Map as Unprecedented Scam.

PLATE 86. *Sultan Bello's Map of the Niger River's Course.* The intent of this African map was to baffle, not enlighten, a British explorer.

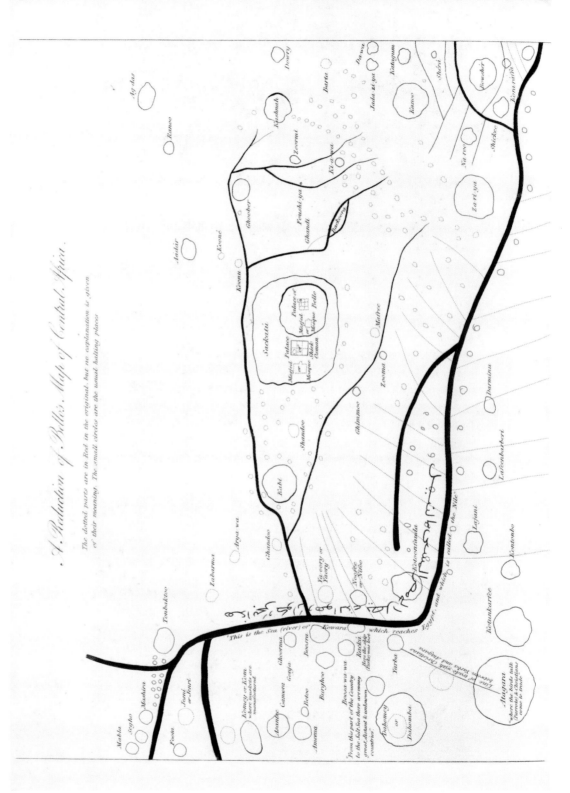

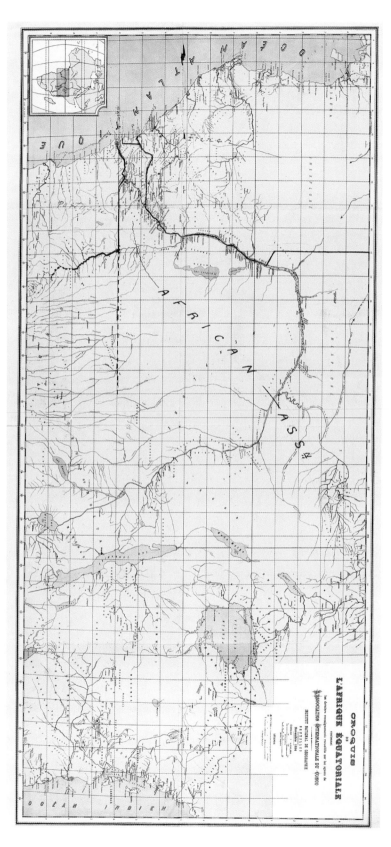

The map records King Leopold's success immediately following the Berlin West African Conference in 1884–85. Convened the same year the map was drawn, the conference intended to prevent wars between European powers over what came to be called "the scramble for Africa." At the time of the conference, 80 percent of Africa was controlled by about one thousand indigenous cultural groups not represented on the map. Fourteen European countries, as well as Turkey and the United States, recognized Leopold's sovereignty over his loosely configured Association when the interior of Africa was divvied among the major players, all still confined to the coast.

The red annotations for equatorial Africa's sectioning were made by the U.S. minister to Berlin. They were part of his official dispatch making the United States the first nation outside Europe to accept the terms of the Berlin Conference. (In fact the map took the Belgian parliament by surprise. They had not been consulted about their king's new sovereignty; and they granted him a second crown only after his assurances that his second kingdom would pay for itself.) The tiny opening on the Atlantic claimed by Leopold at the mouth of the Congo River is a perfect metaphor for the amount of access the world was going to receive when the Association was renamed the Congo Free State. Around this time, 1888, Nietzsche was writing about the human being's natural aversion to truth. He could have used Leopold's successful scam as an example of nature operating in terms of survival and strength rather than authenticity and openness.

The Congo state, the Belgian premier promised, was "an international colony to protect, effectually the aboriginal inhabitants of Africa." With a total trade monopoly soon in place, however, Leopold posited that he was not trading, he was "harvesting" his own produce, and in 1903 a Congo administrator declared that the native "is not entitled to anything." The colonizers' abuse of the Con-

golese people led to an international outcry, forcing the Belgian government in 1908 to officially annex the king's property and assume responsibility for its administration as the Belgian Congo.

The red-line mapping by the Association and its two European neighbors provides an outline sketch of hypothetical boundaries along longitudes and latitudes. It was done with an offhand geometric flourish as the basin of a river is not easy to define. The mass of squiggly lines at the bottom of the map acts as a shorthand for the intense river activity in the region, as well as a justification for Leopold's effective occupation to accomplish a survey while dealing with Arab wars and Bantu uprisings. An undated map of the Belgian Congo (Plate 88) reveals how much Leopold relied upon the absence of African surveys to expand the vague frontiers he had been granted in Berlin. The same map shows how Leopold expanded his territory to the Nile when he defeated the Babuja tribe north of the Congo in 1890, ignoring British claims to the region.

The "Belgian Congo" blazons forth on the brightly colored map as an overblown Belgium in the heart of Africa. It proclaims Leopold's stated goal to "open the darkness of Africa to a ray of light." It shows the vast territory cut to the pattern of tiny Belgium, which is presented in an inset as the model for the plan. It is Map as Colonist's Dream. It literally makes Belgium civilization's prototype—a ray of light—and it demonstrates how Leopold's visual acuity created nationalist enthusiasm for his royal estate, the way a photo of a tiny, helpless child in a parent's likeness would inspire the impulse to protect it. The replication also inspired fervently Catholic Belgium to fund an "African crusade" to stop Muslim expansion among the "pagans." This administrative map presents Belgian Congo provinces in big red letters and districts with mostly transliterated native names in solid black. The larger

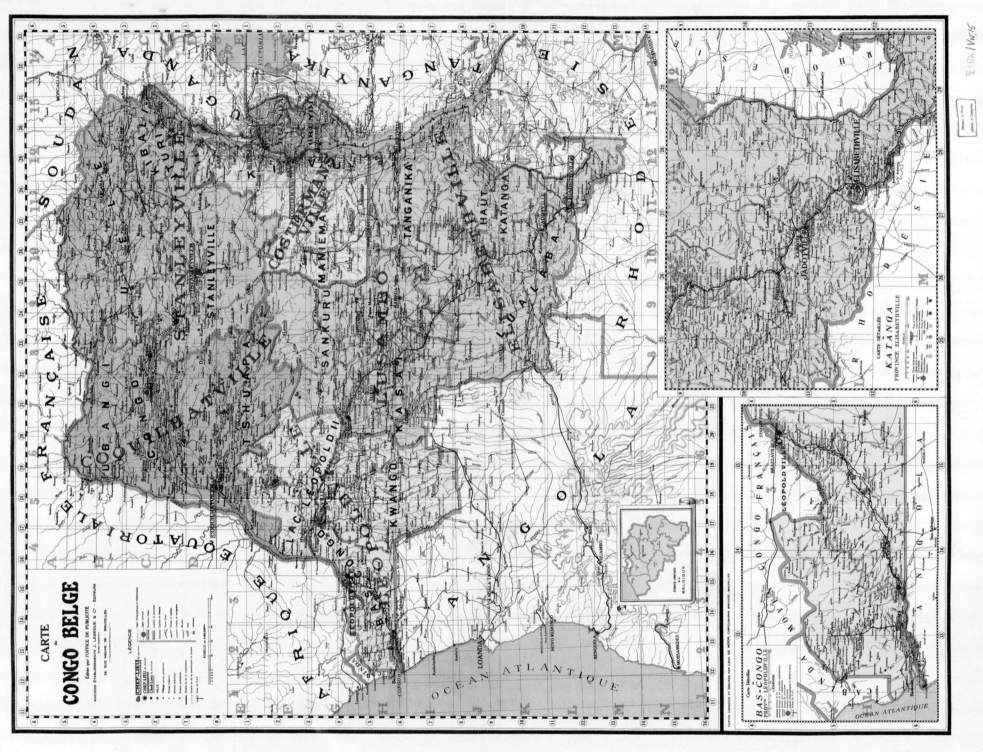

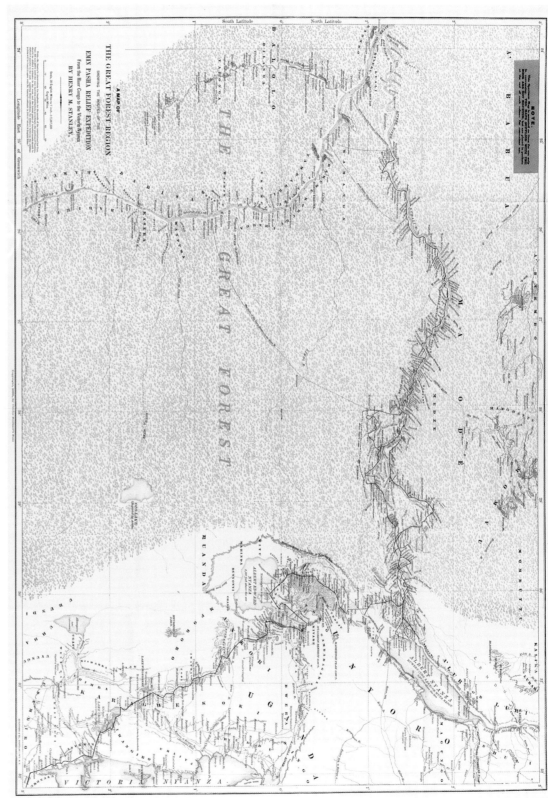

A MAP OF
THE GREAT FOREST REGION
SHOWING THE ROUTE OF THE
EMIN PASHA RELIEF EXPEDITION
From the River Congo to the Victoria Nyanza
BY HENRY M. STANLEY.

insets represent the most populous areas. A celebration of Belgium's consciousness regarding Africa at the end of the nineteenth century, the map reveals a world without causality, sequence, or depth, a world embroiled in the feverish acceptance of surface, along with a consciousness suffering from delusions of grandeur.

Agitation by the native people forced Belgium to grant independence in 1960. Christened the Democratic Republic of the Congo, the country became Zaire in 1971 and reverted to the former name in 1997.

Throughout the nineteenth century, explorers sought to fill the void of European and American ignorance about Africa. Without exception, each benefited from the geographical knowledge of the indigenous people. Most owed their lives to that knowledge. Thus any explorer's map in effect bears witness to the cartographic expertise of the local inhabitants of Africa.

Stanley's fourth and final expedition (1887–89) took him through central Africa on an expedition to rescue German physician and explorer Eduard Schnitzer. Known as Mehmed Emin Pasha in his capacity as governor of the southernmost province of Egyptian Sudan (Equatoria), Schnitzer had retreated to the shores of Lake Albert (located between what is now the Democratic Republic of the Congo and Uganda) during the uprising inspired by the Sudanese mahdi (holy man) Muhammad Ahmad. Stanley journeyed over 1,400 miles from the mouth of the Congo River by steamboat and canoe, and on foot through the Ituri forest in the northeast Congo basin. His overland march was documented on a map showing the western half of equatorial Africa (Plate 89) and was sold with his subsequent successful book *In Darkest Africa.*

Instead of following the known Zanzibari traders' route across the forest, Stanley mapped his own geographical path and described it discursively in his book. It sometimes ran parallel to the established way and sometimes diverged. Although the trade route remained the Africans' choice, modern tourists still refer to "Stanley's Way." It is Map as Plot for Travel Book. Stanley inscribed both native and European names on his very detailed map. He used dotted lines for rivers "reported by Arabs" and scrupulously noted

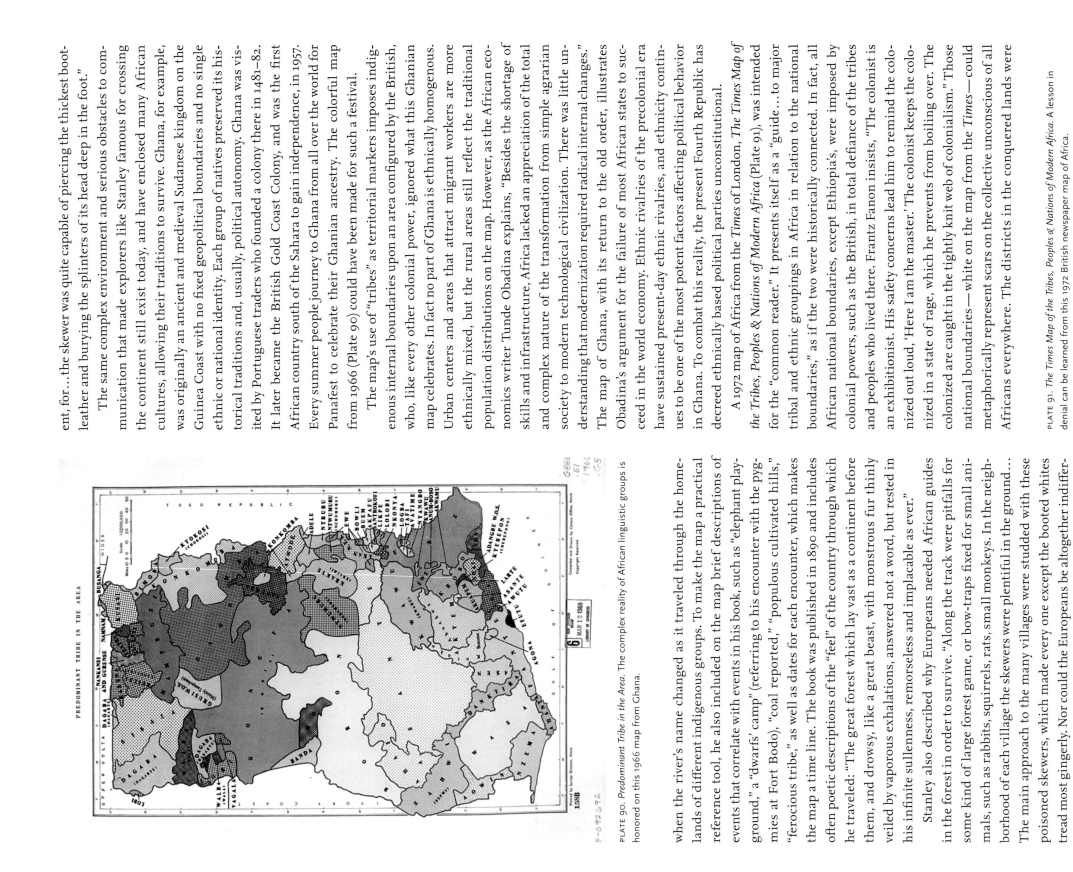

PLATE 90. *Predominant Tribe in the Area.* The complex reality of African linguistic groups is honored on this 1966 map from Ghana.

PREDOMINANT TRIBE IN THE AREA

ent, for... the skewer was quite capable of piercing the thickest boot-leather and burying the splinters of its head deep in the foot."

The same complex environment and serious obstacles to communication that made explorers like Stanley famous for crossing the continent still exist today, and have enclosed many African cultures, allowing their traditions to survive. Ghana, for example, was originally an ancient and medieval Sudanese kingdom on the Guinea Coast with no fixed geopolitical boundaries and no single ethnic or national identity. Each group of natives preserved its historical traditions and, usually, political autonomy. Ghana was visited by Portuguese traders who founded a colony there in 1481–82. It later became the British Gold Coast Colony, and was the first African country south of the Sahara to gain independence, in 1957. Every summer people journey to Ghana from all over the world for Panafest to celebrate their Ghanian ancestry. The colorful map from 1966 (Plate 90) could have been made for such a festival.

The map's use of "tribes" as territorial markers imposes indigenous internal boundaries upon an area configured by the British, who, like every other colonial power, ignored what this Ghanian map celebrates. In fact no part of Ghana is ethnically homogenous. Urban centers and areas that attract migrant workers are more ethnically mixed, but the rural areas still reflect the traditional population distributions on the map. However, as the African economics writer Tunde Obadina explains, "Besides the shortage of skills and infrastructure, Africa lacked an appreciation of the total and complex nature of the transformation from simple agrarian society to modern technological civilization. There was little understanding that modernization required radical internal changes." The map of Ghana, with its return to the old order, illustrates Obadina's argument for the failure of most African states to succeed in the world economy. Ethnic rivalries of the precolonial era have sustained present-day ethnic rivalries, and ethnicity continues to be one of the most potent factors affecting political behavior in Ghana. To combat this reality, the present Fourth Republic has decreed ethnically based political parties unconstitutional.

A 1972 map of Africa from the *Times* of London, *The Times Map of the Tribes, Peoples & Nations of Modern Africa* (Plate 91), was intended for the "common reader." It presents itself as a "guide…to major tribal and ethnic groupings in Africa in relation to the national boundaries," as if the two were historically connected. In fact, all African national boundaries, except Ethiopia's, were imposed by colonial powers, such as the British, in total defiance of the tribes and peoples who lived there. Frantz Fanon insists, "The colonist is an exhibitionist. His safety concerns lead him to remind the colonized out loud, 'Here I am the master.' The colonist keeps the colonized in a state of rage, which he prevents from boiling over. The colonized are caught in the tightly knit web of colonialism." Those national boundaries—white on the map from the *Times*—could metaphorically represent scars on the collective unconscious of all Africans everywhere. The districts in the conquered lands were

when the river's name changed as it traveled through the homelands of different indigenous groups. To make the map a practical reference tool, he also included on the map brief descriptions of events that correlate with events in his book, such as "elephant playground," a "dwarfs' camp" (referring to his encounter with the pygmies at Fort Bodo), "coal reported," "populous cultivated hills," "ferocious tribe," as well as dates for each encounter, which makes the map a time line. The book was published in 1890 and includes often poetic descriptions of the "feel" of the country through which he traveled: "The great forest which lay vast as a continent before them, and drowsy, like a great beast, with monstrous fur thinly veiled by vaporous exhalations, answered not a word, but rested in his infinite sullenness, remorseless and implacable as ever."

Stanley also described why Europeans needed African guides in the forest in order to survive. "Along the track were pitfalls for some kind of large forest game, or bow-traps fixed for small animals, such as rabbits, squirrels, rats, small monkeys. In the neighborhood of each village the skewers were plentiful in the ground… The main approach to the many villages were studded with these poisoned skewers, which made every one except the booted whites tread most gingerly. Nor could the Europeans be altogether indiffer-

PLATE 91. *The Times Map of the Tribes, Peoples & Nations of Modern Africa.* A lesson in denial can be learned from this 1972 British newspaper map of Africa.

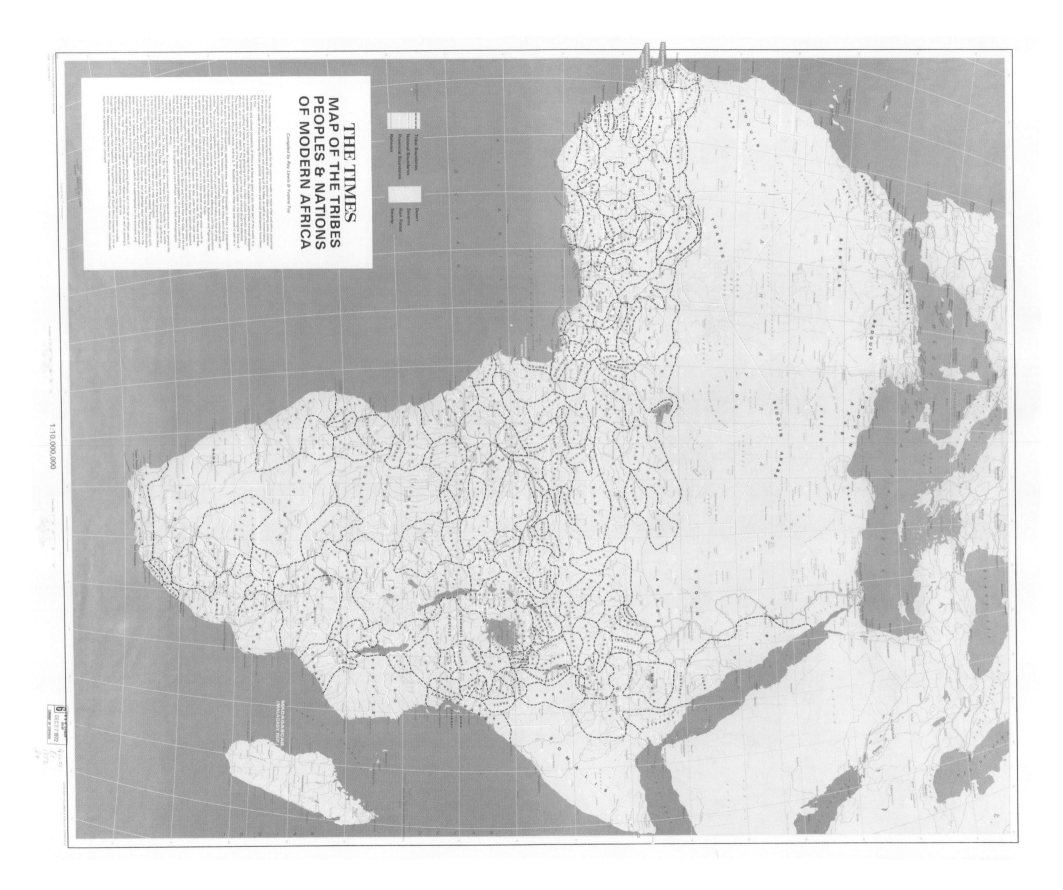

PLATE 92. *Royal Tapestry.* This map is encoded with metaphorical meanings for the people of Cameroon.

palace literally inscribed the spirit of the people on the landscape. Whenever fire or other disasters destroyed the palace compound, the Bamum replicated it on the same sacred ground. The oral tradition was dominant until Sultan Njoya invented an alphabet so that

often named after the vanquished. On European maps such as the one from the *Times,* the names resemble cemetery markers, though the peoples named were far from dead.

Without any explanation, the map's text declares that "emphasis on tribal differences is very unpopular among Africans, but… 'tribe' has clearly emerged as a profound influence on events, as well as posing a challenge to African statecraft, which was not anticipated during colonial rule." Perhaps the British and the other colonizers did not "anticipate" political difficulties from the "tribes" because as colonial invaders they held prevalent social theories that their own cosmopolitan industrial civilization would gradually break down the older, localized African identities featured on the map. To most educated Africans, the word *tribe* fosters a sense of sameness, of a primitive timelessness. The word *tribe* harbors a prejudice that was used first to justify slavery, then colonialism.

The British, like every other colonial power, understood perfectly the social reality of "tribal differences" in Africa, which they manipulated to secure their territory. They relied upon the cooperation of African communal leaders from the colonial web of "units" on the *Times* map to implement their colonial system of indirect rule. If a particular ethnic group in a British territory did not have a dynastic king but was organized according to a system of self-government, the British chose a ruler among the collaborators in the community, offering him wealth and power in return for cooperation, often at the expense of the welfare of the community.

The tribe often posed a serious challenge to colonialism's statecraft too. It took 450,000 British troops to end the 1879 war resulting from Great Britain's invasion of the Zulu homeland in South Africa. The *Times* map's text acknowledges that "tribal divisions inside countries…produce internal stresses or find political expression." Those internal stresses can only have been exacerbated by the artificial boundaries and mergers of native peoples created by conquering colonialists, who behaved as if the inhabitants of Africa were one extended black family and not diverse groups with as many as ten thousand different polities. Though tribal differences have been used by unscrupulous African leaders to perpetuate neocolonialism and to destroy burgeoning nationalism, the differences were far from "very unpopular." Six years before the *Times* map appeared, Zambia's first president after independence in 1964 respected and honored these differences by using ethnic balancing in his appointments to cabinet and other key government positions.

An early twentieth-century royal tapestry map (Plate 92) epitomizes the self-image of the Bamum community. It depicts the palace belonging to Sultan Bedou Njoya, the sixteenth of his dynasty. Njoya ruled the Grassfields kingdom of Bamum from 1889 to 1933 in what had become the northwestern part of the German colony of Cameroon after the 1884–85 Berlin Conference. His palace, as with all palaces of chiefs, was the locus of political power in the kingdom, the center of culture and identity for the local population. It was a complex of bamboo raffia buildings connected by many hallways and courtyards.

In 1897 Njoya created a palace museum, one of the first, to hold the substances of the chiefdom in trust for future generations. His

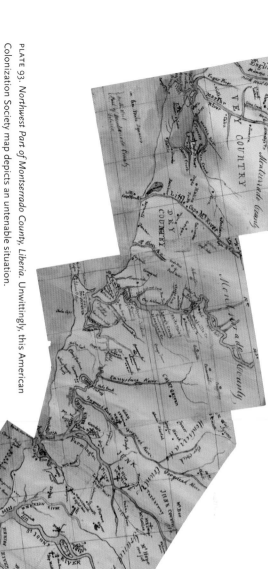

PLATE 93. *Northwest Part of Montserrado County, Liberia.* Unwittingly, this American Colonization Society map depicts an untenable situation.

"man's speech could be inaudibly recorded." In 1912 he wrote the history and customs of the Bamum to assure their survival. He told his subjects, "I will give you a book that talks without making a sound."

When the old palace burned down in 1913, the new one that Njoya built ingeniously incorporated bricks similar to those used to build the home of a German colonial official as a testament to ethnic affiliation and a way to naturalize colonial power. At the same time, a royal tapestry was created depicting an idealized ground plan of the old palace. The Bamum were renowned for their textiles and this tapestry blueprint is a map that talks without making a sound. Although the new brick palace used line and form as a means of compromise and survival—"All kings who resisted the white men were defeated," Njoya said—the palace map was a rallying cry for the Bamum to hold tight to their unique identities.

All colonialists played one group off another. The Germans regarded Muslim Africans, with their glorious past, as belonging to a "higher" civilization than non-Muslims. The French collaborated with southern negroid peoples in Chad when Muslim northerners spurned their attempts to educate and assimilate them; after Chad's independence from France in 1960, a southerner was elected the country's first president and France provided loans and grants and substantial military support for decades. The most devastating fallout from this colonial technique of divide and conquer was in Rwanda in 1994, when 800,000 of the Belgian-favored Tutsi community, along with moderate Hutus, who favored power-sharing, were victims of genocide. They were massacred thirty-two years after independence by extremist Hutu government administrators and military leaders with age-old grudges entrenched in memory.

People have always encoded metaphorical meanings into maps. The royal tapestry expresses the fundamental importance of the power of the chiefs and the attachment of a people to their place. It is Map as Repository of Tradition. A similar symbolic message is found on the map's border, which resembles a spider's web. According to Bamum legend, the spider symbolizes wisdom. Spiders

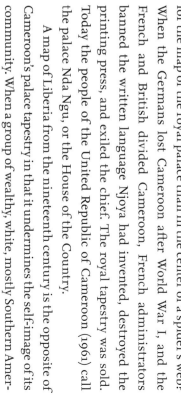

carry messages between humans and the Creator. What wiser place for the map of the royal palace than in the center of a spider's web?

When the Germans lost Cameroon after World War I, and the French and British divided Cameroon, French administrators banned the written language Njoya had invented, destroyed the printing press, and exiled the chief. The royal tapestry was sold. Today the people of the United Republic of Cameroon (1961) call the palace Nda Ngu, or the House of the Country.

A map of Liberia from the nineteenth century is the opposite of Cameroon's palace tapestry in that it undermines the self-image of its community. When a group of wealthy, white, mostly Southern American men created the American Colonization Society (ACS) in 1816, they aimed to preserve the institution of slavery by preventing slave revolts, thought to be provoked by free blacks—"the incubus of the Negro population." The men worked to send native-born, Christian black people "home" to a colony in Africa named Monrovia (after U.S. president James Monroe), under the paternalistic supervision of white men, as the British had imposed freed Christian blacks from Britain and Canada on a congeries of native peoples already in thrall to Islam in Sierra Leone.

The immigrants were to bring "the sun of righteousness" to "the dark continent," meaning they were to promulgate Christianity. The first two groups of settlers were rebuffed when the Africans learned they intended to end the lucrative slave trade. Cape Montserrado was finally "purchased" in 1821 at gunpoint from the king of the region. An undated nineteenth-century manuscript map of the northwest part of Montserrado County—ten square miles—was drawn on separate sheets (Plate 93). Its irregularity of form

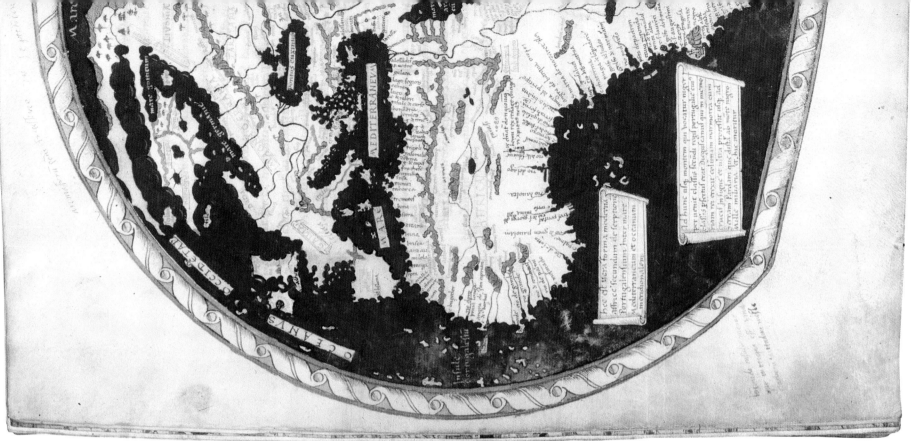

captures the unorthodox way the white leader imposed his deeply religious black transplants on the coast of West Africa after palavers (meetings) had failed to deal with the natives.

A short war ensued. The settlers won, a fact they viewed as a victory over a "barbarism" in need of westernization. But the colony, named Christopolis, needed fortification, and the nineteenth-century undated map makes plain the cost of its violent beginning. Even though negotiated treaties had extended the settlement, Liberia was a contested, jagged, an isolated coastal strip 30 to 40 miles wide. Africa's interior, full of perceived and actual enemies, was inaccessible to the settlers, which is why there is no sense of it on the map. American-based Protestant churches inculcated their social norms and forged the settlement into a religious colony with a seventeenth-century New England Puritanism at its core, and Americo-Liberians used their culture to provide a basis of social stratification. The map reflects those ubiquitous churches, just as the names of the communities—New York, Maryland, Virginia, New Georgia—reflect a disconnect with the world around them, where Chief Barbona and Chief Palm Tree live in Vey and Dey and Bassa Counties, named for the original African communities found there.

Monrovia transformed itself into the Commonwealth of Liberia in 1839, then declared itself a republic in 1847. The map is part of the American Colonization Society's collection and was made to sell Liberia as a destination. It is Map as Failed Advertisement. In 1855 William Nesbit, a disenchanted black, wrote of Liberians, "They constitute a sort of cod-fish aristocracy…I have visited all these settlements, and do unhesitatingly say, that I am not able to imagine any more abject state of misery." By 1855, of the 27,000 immigrants, fewer than 5,000 survived the rigors of the African environment; and by 1900 only 15,000 people with American antecedents could be found there. Less than 5 percent of the population, they remained the incompetent governing elite until a civil war between rival warlords (1989–95) overthrew them, leaving total social and economic devastation in its wake.

In 2003, a fourteen-year civil war ended in Liberia, and the United States sent armed support for the West African peace force already in place. Again Liberia was a country out of joint, just as it appears on the nineteenth-century map.

The Portuguese first visited the Liberian coast in 1461 and, on sighting vast grain fields, named it the Grain Coast. By 1487, under Bartolomeu Dias, they had successfully continued their journey south of the Congo River. The 1489 world map by Martellus that resulted from Dias's rounding of what he accurately named the Cape of Storms—but which Portugal's King João II instantly renamed the Cape of Good Hope—converted European geographical hypothesis about Africa into knowledge, albeit displayed on this map with a radical readjustment (Plate 94). It is Map as Truth Compromised. Martellus amended and expanded upon Ptolemy's worldview under the instruction of Bartolomeu Columbus, Christopher's brother—a mapmaker living in Lisbon—who had been summoned by the king of Portugal for the royal interview with Dias after the explorer's return from his sixteen-month voyage.

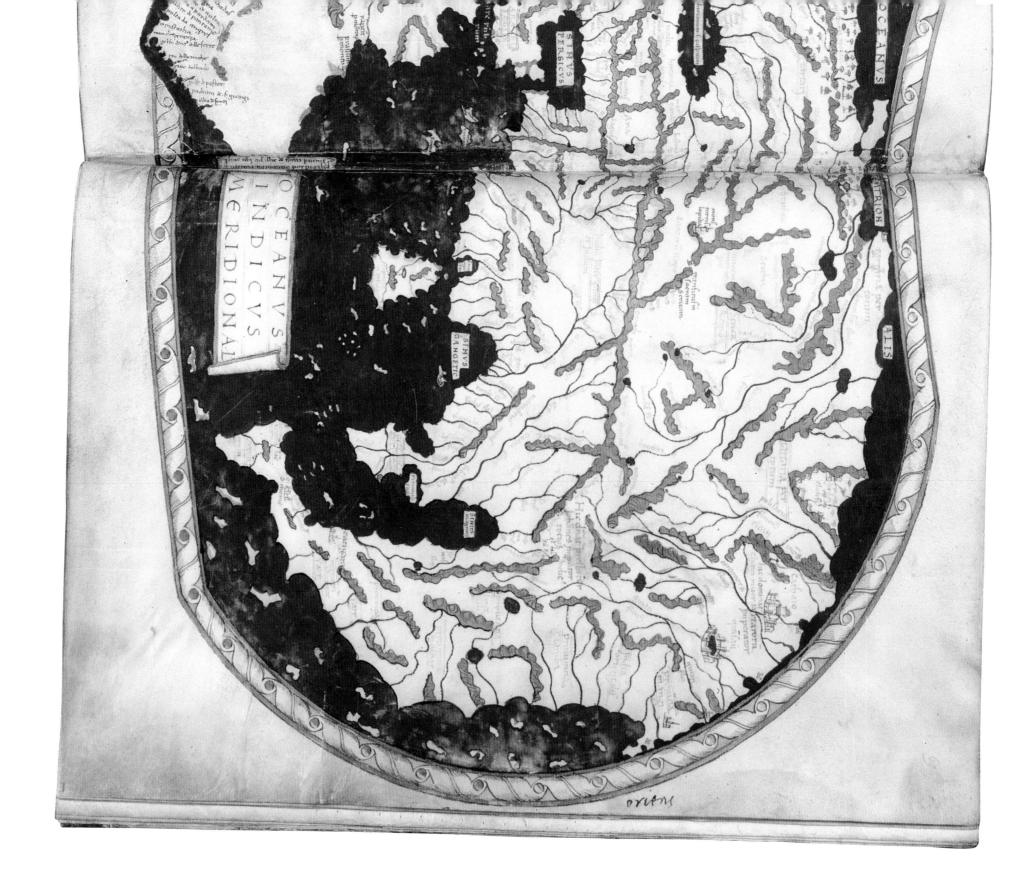

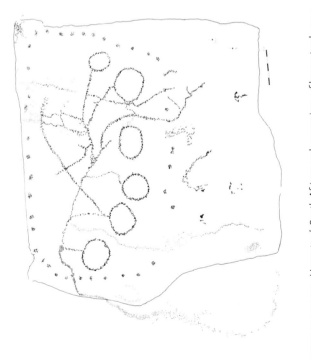

Dias had followed the coast south six hundred leagues beyond where it was already navigated, until the winds forced him southwest, out into midocean. Experimenting on a bold scale with winds for thirteen days in the unknown, seemingly infinite sea, he reached south 39 degrees latitude, where he found a zone of favorable winds that carried him back to the meridian where the coast of Africa had been sighted last. Africa had vanished. Turning northward, he made landfall with a strong, warm current flowing from the northeast. His pilot shot the sun using a terrestrial astrolabe: south 35 degrees latitude (actually 35°51'). Dias had rounded Africa but only reached the point where the cold Benguela current of its Atlantic west coast merged with the warm Agulhas current of the Indian Ocean. Refusing to go any farther, his exhausted crew insisted he return home.

League by league, Dias related his Cape journey to the king using a navigational map, and the king instructed Bartolomeu Columbus to record the sighting, "which place he found by astrolabe to be at a distance of 45° below the equatorial line." And Martellus drew his map accordingly, in the style of Ptolemy, complete with the strings of mountains. It was reasonable to João II to disseminate false information on his map as a means of deterring Spanish competition. Knowing how the Columbus brothers were vastly underestimating the size of the globe, João II would later encourage Christopher Columbus to sail west for India, to continue distracting the Spanish crown from going south around Africa in 1492.

Using the venerable Ptolemy as his template, Martellus may have hated to tell the lie. The way he dramatically broke the frame of his map with the protruding tip of Africa undeniably impresses the viewer with Portugal's great achievement. Yet it can be seen as the cartographer's need to tell the truth. "We are stretching the facts here! Properly drawn, Africa belongs within the border!"

Besides latitudes, Dias reported herdsmen and their cattle at the "world's end." A few sailors had disembarked upon the unknown shore and tried to make contact, but to no avail. Dias killed one native with a crossbow during a stone-throwing incident before departing for home. About these natives he learned nothing,

though maps engraved by them in stone do tell some of their story. Had he progressed inland, he would have come upon Bantu-speaking people, who for millennia lived in settlements built on elevated locations where there were few trees. A circular stone wall, identified from ruins, served as the cattle pen, which was central to each family homestead for these agriculturalists.

In southern Africa, rock art has been dated to at least 25,000 years ago, and one Kwazulu-Natal map fashioned on a rock (Plate 95) shows the most complex form of community homesteads in the Zulu kingdom of precolonial south Africa. Six cattle pens ringed by huts are linked by a network of paths. The actual uphill orientation of this homestead is replicated by the mapmaker-artist, who engraved the cattle pens opening up the side of the rock with the paths descending through the circle of huts, as if going to a stream at the bottom of a valley. It is Map as Three-Dimensional Model. This type of precolonial homestead became extinct in the nineteenth century. It exists only in ruins and on rock engravings. The maps are a form of written history. They are classic records of spatial knowledge expressed in domestic patterns, and they show the timeless human impulse to document place. The rocks may also have been used by the engraver to create an ideal homestead site, the way an architect might sketch examples to be studied. Or they could have been part of a religious ritual, some form of communication with a spirit-god.

In 1498 Vasco da Gama bravely completed what Dias began in 1488 by sailing via the Atlantic into the Indian Ocean around the southern tip of Africa and on to India. The decade's delay was due to the confusion spread among the Portuguese by Columbus's achievement. If he had really reached the Indies first, where were the spices? Where were the stories of the great cities of Cathay? But why, if these were not the Indies, had Spain signed a treaty with Portugal surrendering the African route to India? One of the first Western printed maps (Plate 96), and the first of Africa (1508), celebrates da Gama's achievement. It is a woodcut; and in spite of its geographic distortions of Africa's width due to Ptolemaic influences, it became the prototype of modern images of the continent. Produced in Milan,

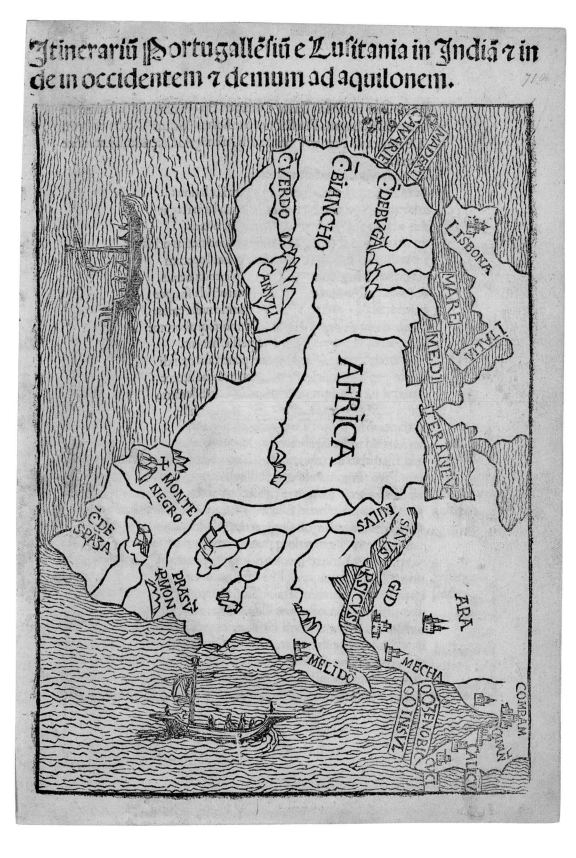

Itinerariũ Portugallẽsiũ e Lusitania in Indiã z in de in occidentem z demum ad aquilonem.

Italy, it occupies the title page of a collection of essays by Fracanzano da Montalboddo on great voyages. There are few inscriptions on the map, and the only European town is Lisbon, marking the composition as Portuguese. It is Map as Transformation of Maritime Space.

Da Gama's triumphant voyage, symbolized by oversized ships on the map, revolutionized the history of the Atlantic Ocean. He successfully linked a barely explored sea with the world's oldest tradition of long-range trade, while connecting Africa, Asia, and South America. Superseding the Indian Ocean, the Atlantic soon became the world's busiest freeway. Da Gama had dared to sail far into its unknown waters in search of winds that would carry him beyond the Cape of Good Hope. It was a dizzying act of bravado, one of unprecedented duration for a European ship. Its audacity and daring are inadvertently commemorated by the cartographer's use of ships as decoration on the Montalboddo map. Two sailing ships, one upside down and one sideways, produce a joyful feeling, almost giddy at first, followed by a frisson of fear for all the sailors lost attempting to navigate what Dias, who died in a tempest there in 1500, had christened honestly the Cape of Storms.

When the map is turned upside down to right the ship, however, the vessel (along with the Portuguese possession of Africa) is viewed from royal Lisbon, and a theatricality comes into play. The ship of the hero da Gama effortlessly, serenely approaches King João II's rechristened placid Cape of Good Hope. On the opposite side, at the Cape of Agulhas in the Indian Ocean, there is no sign of Madagascar. It is as if Montalboddo's mapmaker decided Fra Mauro's island off the southern coast of Africa was mythical.

Portugal's Prince Henry the Navigator (1394–1460) was the first European to attach the lateen (triangular) sail of Islamic vessels to his three-masted, small ships called caravels. The lateen sail allowed ships to sail directly into the strong trade winds and hold a course accurately, regardless of ungovernable currents, just like the ships on the map. With their contrasting directions, the waves on the map convey the Atlantic and Indian Oceans as discrete universes, while the continent's tip nearly meeting the map's frame forever keeps them contending entities in the cartographer's lexicon. The ships make the subject of the map as much about humanity's power over sea spaces as about Africa pinned down at last by the Portuguese—and ripe for invasion.

Whenever the Portuguese rounded the Cape, they preferred to refresh themselves after their immense journey in the sheltered harbors of what is today Mozambique. The encounter of Portugal and Africa is at the heart of Portugal's national epic poem by Luis

PLATE 96. *Montalboddo's Africa.* This 1508 woodcut is one of the first printed maps of Africa.

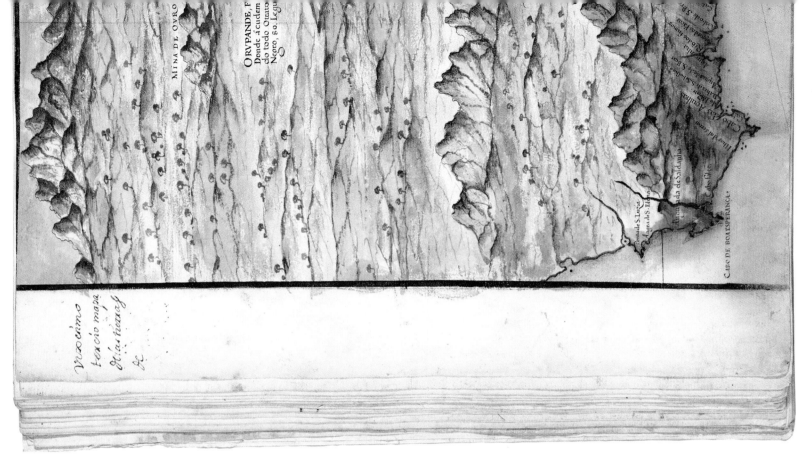

de Camões (1524–80), *The Lusiads.* In it the Cape is personified by Adamastor, a Titan metamorphosed into the "boundless stature" of Africa by the angry gods. Da Gama, the hero of the epic, is confronted by Adamastor, who exists at the crossroads of human desire and nature, where ancient maps noted: "Here be monsters!" He exists, in Camões's words, "to lead these kingdoms and folk into what deaths, what horrors must they swallow now." A 1630 manuscript atlas, known as "Secret Maps of the Americas and the Indies from Portuguese Archives," gives a comprehensive portrait of a doomed empire. The hand-painted atlas was prepared by João Teixeira (fl. 1602–48), cosmographer to the king. One map (Plate 97) depicts the south of Africa with mountains color-coded to represent various mineral areas—gold, silver, copper. It is Adamastor's crossroads of human desire and nature.

The vastness of Africa is metamorphosed into a symbol of empire's riches. It is Map as Epic Vision. Like *The Lusiads,* it reflects the deepest ambitions of an entire nation and epoch. Teixeira, seemingly inspired by Camões, used the Cape and its environs to honor the memory of Portugal's brief period of greatness while foretelling a disastrous future. There is a dreamlike emptiness in the world of the map, akin to the poet's "empty nothing we call fame." The rich mineral deposits beckon unimpeded. Yet, the Rozwi empire of Mwene Mutapa in the middle Zambezi Valley withstood Portuguese attacks from 1571 to 1575, when it triumphantly set up a gold trading relationship with them.

Eventually it was the gold in Teixeira's mountains that kept Portugal's empire afloat. With the Indian Ocean transformed on the map into a placid Portuguese lake, the compass rose gives out directions, the only sign of activity. But just as there is no sign of human habitation on the map, the only sign of political realities is in the absence of place names. Portugal had been displaced from this coastal realm by the Dutch when Spain annexed Portugal in 1580, but in Teixeira's map the memory of Africa's treasures lingered on.

The Dutch became the principal beneficiaries when Portugal's empire crumbled. They set up a colony on the Cape, which drew settlers from various European countries. The British eventually took the Cape by force in 1806. Sir John Barrow, private secretary to the British military governor of the Cape, described in his book, *An Account of Travels into the Interior of Southern Africa in the Years 1797 and 1798,* how the "weak and peaceable" indigenous Hottentots had "a predominant passion for spirituous liquors." Able to buy a whole district with a cask of brandy, the first Dutch settlers easily spread northward. Barrow's book makes plain the tension between many native groups and the Boers ("farmers" in Dutch), who were white South Africans of Dutch, German, French Huguenot, and Belgian extraction. The progenitors of modern Afrikaners, they believed themselves ordained by their Calvinist God to be rulers of a segregated Cape. In 1828, when slavery was abolished in all British possessions, the Boers, one-quarter of the Cape's white population, moved north to escape British jurisdiction. They founded their own republics, which the British took by force (1880–81 and 1899–1902) to form the Union of South Africa in 1910.

The Afrikaner majority began passing laws denying blacks their civil rights; but in order to achieve complete segregation, black people had to be "consolidated," the chosen word of the South African government. This entailed mass removals of about 3 million people, sorted into ten tribal groups regardless of their ethnic realities, and resettled as citizens of ten "homelands," or "bantustan," which they could not exit without passes. The Homeland Resettlement Policy of 1968 was designed to create labor pools for the white economy while stripping the black workers of political,

social, and economic rights in the designated white area of the country—87 percent of South Africa's land.

Five years later, a map from the Republic of South Africa depicted the ten tribal-group homelands (see Plate 98). These brightly colored areas on the map resemble lakes—natural topographic features. The overall visual effect is one of normalcy, as if there were nothing unnatural about the plan. Each homeland is not a single unit because too many people might make crowd control difficult. Rather, each is split into several manageable units. The reality of

the 87 percent statistic hits home when viewed in the language of cartography. It is Map as Blueprint for Hardship. Joyce Harris, past president of Black Sash—a nonpartisan, nonprofit, antiapartheid South African organization—wrote: "People were moved from places where there was employment to places where there was none, [from places] where they could do some subsistence farming to places where this was impossible. Huts were burned down to force people out...the places where people were so unceremoniously dumped were without shops, clinics, schools, or even running water."

The map shows the black reservations largely clustered in South Africa's northeast area in a semicircle, presumably to act as a buffer zone between white South Africa and its black African neighbors. The plan projected an "independence" for these homelands stipulating the loss of South African citizenship. When Bophuthatswana (1977), Venda (1979), and Ciskei (1981) became independent, more than 8 million people were turned into foreigners needing permits to enter an urban area in South Africa.

Growing violent uprisings by the black population and international sanctions finally ended apartheid in 1994, when free elections gave black South Africans formal possession of their government and their homeland.

The colonialists' dream that their "civilizing" influence would erase tribal differences, and that Africa's diverse ethnic communities would evolve into European-style bureaucratic states, seems to

have been fulfilled on a CIA map from 2003 (Plate 99). It is Map as Denouement. In fact African independence did result in a continent composed of separate nations in the European tradition. This map represents the cartographic apotheosis of the human impulse to substitute what is familiar for what is alien. By placing Africans in Europe's traditional cartographic structure, the map, like all modern maps of Africa, visually concludes the hectic nineteenth-century "scramble for Africa." Modern maps depict the ideal of sameness for nation building and long-term security in the modern world economy. The colors on the CIA map, for example, unite Africa, Europe, and the Middle East in the viewer's inner eye, making them all equal players in world history. Africa is disciplined, normalized, a part of a whole, if generic, world. Cartography is a way of imposing order onto cultures. The implied equality of nations on maps becomes pure mockery in the face of the enormous economic differences that exist between Africa and most Western civilizations.

Like the word *tribe*, maps generalize the occupants of each area. A map's traditional format assures the viewer visually that each state

PLATE 98. *South Africa Black Homelands Consolidation Proposals.* The South African government's plan to achieve total segregation was articulated by this 1973 map.

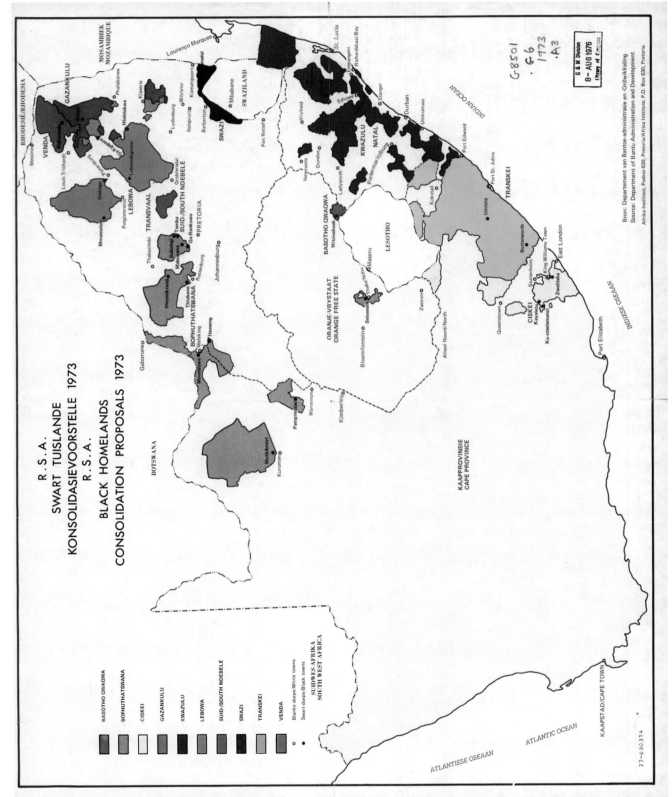

is a source of identity for its citizens, who engage with a national community of their own making. With a map of Africa or the Middle East, it is as if colonialism never existed. In the case of Africa, where indigenous, organic boundaries were violated for selfish gain—as opposed to settlement of a world war—this map becomes *the* symbolic representation of the empty containers of nationalism the more than one thousand ethnic groups inhabiting the land were left to fill. What the map of Africa might have been without the intrusion of colonialism is the fascinating question raised by this map, which offers no self-image of the African peoples.

Historical geographer J. B. Harley contends: "Where maps are ordered by government (or are derived from such maps) it can be seen how they extend and reinforce the legal statutes, territorial imperatives, and values stemming from the exercise of political power." If maps are seen as integral in the struggles to alter power relations, the CIA map tells many stories. The simplicity of the map, for example, removes all sense of place. (This is exacerbated by the presence of several major rivers offering routes for exploration.) Protesters opposed to the abuse of third world labor by international corporations, the modern form of colonialism, could compare the emptiness of the map to dehumanization, and a way of whitewashing human rights issues. All states in the world of the map seem created equal. It is Map as One Side of the Story.

A mapless state would be economically, politically, and militarily unmanageable. World maps also imply that every state pictured has imposed the rules of social order. This is not the case with many of the tumultuous, undeveloped, devastated areas of the world, but especially with modern African states, where military conflicts have aided and abetted the absence of economic diversification, lack of physical and human capital, poor trade facilitation, and generally weak national infrastructures, such as inadequate transportation networks resulting in 90 percent of the continent's villages and towns living in isolation. As the journalist Peter Winkler explains, "In an environment in which the swift vacating of settlements was a priority for centuries, either to escape from slave hunters or because climatic conditions often made a quick move necessary, history was not written in buildings or in road construction." Though the Western world's knowledge of Africa has grown immensely in the twentieth century, the world's simplistic image of Africa is recalled by maps like the CIA map. In all basic reference maps, Africa is reduced to its bare outlines, like newspaper headlines of wars, poverty, famines, AIDS, genocide, refugee camps—which is why geography is not cultural history.

The Ethiopians are the one African people unfettered by European domination. In the fifteenth century, when the seafaring Roman Catholic Portuguese rounded the Cape, they succeeded in building a relationship with the Ethiopians, Africa's only Christian community at the time. Theirs was a great, impregnable highland civilization. Geography again influenced history. The Portuguese helped the Ethiopians repulse Muslim invaders in 1541, but the Europeans' zealous condemnation of the Eastern form of Christianity practiced in Ethiopia since the fourth century led to their expulsion in turn in 1640. Their bigotry sowed a deep hostility to

Europe's Western Christians that continued to the end of the nineteenth century when Ethiopians made brilliant compromises in order to maintain their independence following their landmark triumph at the famous Battle of Adwa in 1896.

A map-style oil painting, probably done by a monk near Addis Ababa circa 1970, celebrates Ethiopia's liberty, which is the true victory of the Battle of Adwa (see Plate 100). The scene of the battle has been reimagined ritualistically in a traditional manner. The conflict's roots lay in the Conference of Berlin (1884–85), when Italy was presented with Ethiopia. Italy's main force, 17,000 troops, infantry and artillery, and their supplies, occupied the highlands of Ethiopia's northern coastal province of Eritrea and then crossed into its heartlands.

After coming to power in 1889, Emperor Menelik II had united Ethiopia's various leaders and kings to create a coalition army of 100,000 rifle-bearing soldiers, a feat marked by placing gunfighters center stage on the map. Rather than attack piecemeal, Emperor Menelik applied the Ethiopian military strategy of long marches to confront the enemy by moving his army for almost 150 days to meet the Italians. The map shows the Ethiopians, dressed in differing traditional uniforms and decorations, defeating the Italian army of General Oreste Baratieri at Adwa on March 9, 1896, and capturing Brigadier General Matteo Ailertone (bottom row, center left). The throned emperor, with the actively involved empress at his feet, was chief strategist. The flying horseman at top is a testament to Ethiopia's long history of military genius.

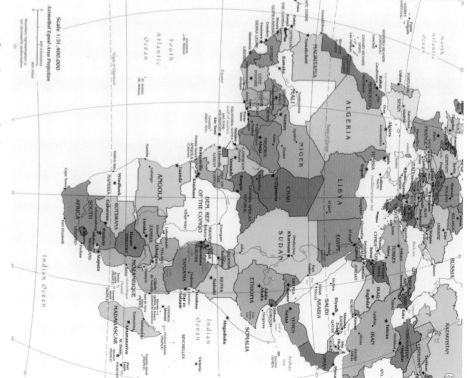

PLATE 99. *Africa.* The tyranny of tradition in the twenty-first century is behind this 2003 CIA map.

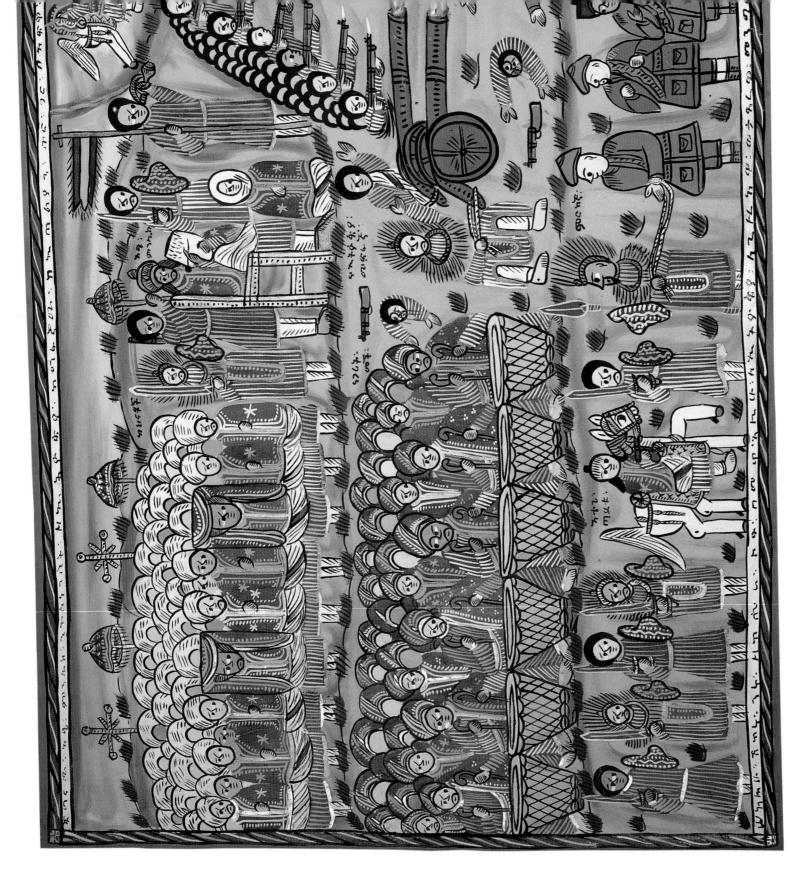

PLATE 100. *Battle of Adwa.* This pictorial map memorializes a key event in African history.

As the painting-map attests, the main battle was initially a "meeting engagement," a clash of troops advancing toward each other. In the Ethiopian strategic culture, however, actions were not performed in the manner of Italy's linear battle formations. Rather, they were dominated by individual initiatives, mobility, and energy fueled by the map's drums; *and* — unlike with the Italians — there was no dependency on firepower. Though the painting-map shows a parallel formation that organized after the Italians' surprise attack — the tented sleepers on the right may symbolize the unreadiness of the Ethiopians — there was a rapid closing of the two sides. (Or the tented sleepers under the red cross may be an acknowledgment of the

work done by the Russian Red Cross, invited by Emperor Menelik to treat the more than three thousand wounded Ethiopian soldiers after the battle. The Russian medical corps established a hospital in Addis Ababa.) The traditional swordsmen in the center are symbolic of the time-proven Ethiopian military strategies that confounded the Italians' plans. The Ethiopians' flexible formations, expressed by clusters of soldiers on the left, made for easy regrouping and for strikes along the regimented Italians' outer flanks, actions expressed on the map by Italian body parts on the battle's fringes.

For the first time, a non-Caucasian nation defeated Europeans with lasting results in Africa. The stunning victory brought hope

CARTOGRAPHIA

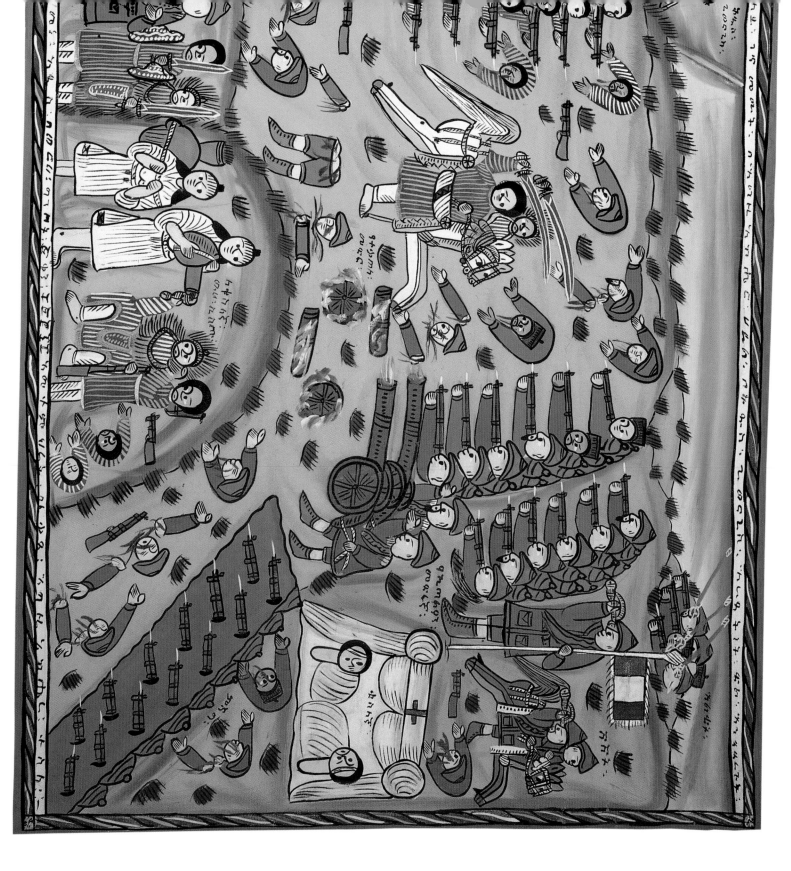

to Africans everywhere of future emancipation from colonial rule. It symbolized the power of African political resources to create multiethnic cooperation among independent communities with interactive histories of more than two thousand years.

The Italians may have been forced out of Ethiopia's heartland, but after the Battle of Adwa, Italy landlocked Ethiopia by taking Eritrea, its maritime frontier, as a colony in 1889. An Ethiopian map from 1923 (see Plate 101) shows the results of the Ethiopians' disregarding the seventeenth-century rift with Western Christians when survival was at stake. To secure its boundaries, and to stall aggressive Italy, Ethiopia began to compromise with the invad-

ing Europeans. A political chess game was begun by their helping Christian France gain a piece of neighboring Somalia in 1898, and continued by their assisting Britain—a former invader—to restore order in Britain's piece of Somalia. By 1908, to Ethiopia's relief, the three colonial powers had signed a treaty to maintain the political status quo. The European powers accepted Ethiopia's borders flanked by themselves on the north (Italian Eritrea), northeast (French Somaliland), east (British Somaliland), south (British Kenya), southeast (Italian Somaliland), and west (Anglo-Egyptian Sudan). The map prepared in 1923 by the Ethiopian court geographer, Kh. P. Papazian, celebrates Ethiopia's survival. If the nation

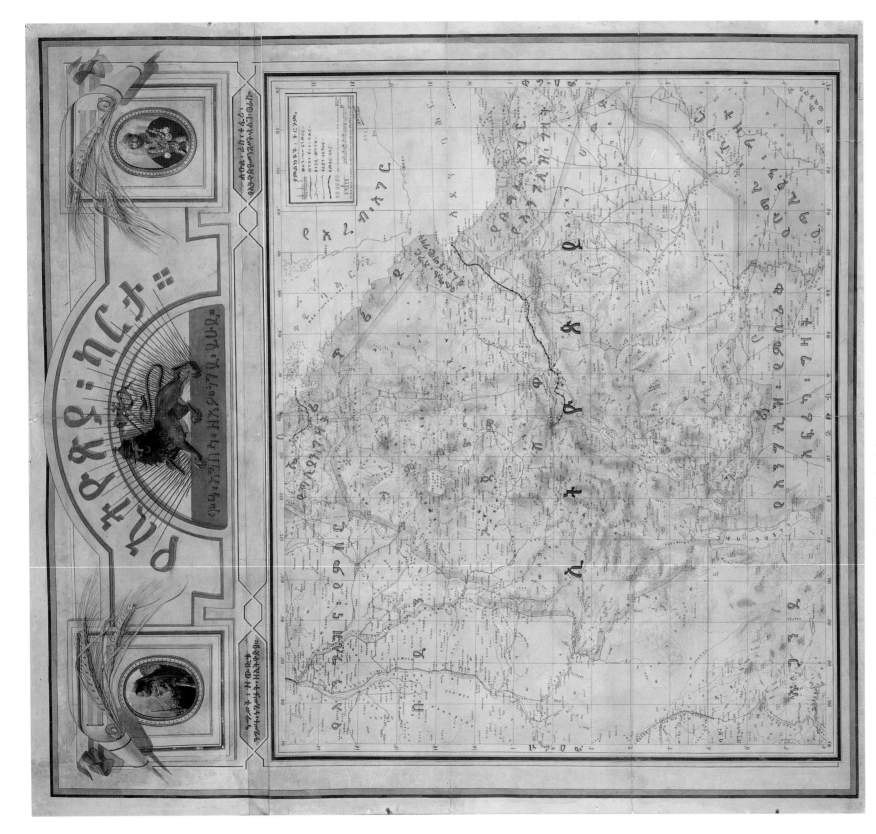

PLATE 101. *Map of Kingdom of Ethiopia.* Ethiopia's hard-won survival is celebrated with this 1923 African manuscript map.

collaborated with the colonial powers for self-protection, its car-tographer later collaborated for self-projection. It was a life-and-death game of political chess. It is Map as Checkmate.

The legend and all the place names are in Amharic, the official language of Ethiopia. Physical features include Lake Tana, in the north, the source of the Blue Nile's journey to the Mediterranean,

which was Britain's chief interest, and the French-built railroad running from Addis Ababa to Djibouti in French Somaliland, which was France's chief interest for the territory it traversed. But the map fills only three-quarters of the large sheet. The remaining upper quarter is ornately illustrated with potent images attesting to Ethiopia's long history of independence. In the left-hand

CARTOGRAPHIA

{120}

PLATE 102. *Earth's City Lights*. There are many different lessons to be learned from this NASA satellite image.

corner is a portrait of the queen, and in the right is the Prince Regent Ras Tafari, soon (1930) Emperor Haile Selassie. Between the two leaders is the crowned Lion of Ethiopia bearing the Christian cross on its right shoulder. Imperial Ethiopia claimed direct descent from King David of Israel, hence the crowned lion of Judah. (One of the emperor's titles was the Conquering Lion of the Tribe of Judah.) The lion was the only image on the first flag of Ethiopia hoisted in 1897, the year after the Battle of Adwa.

Without acknowledgment, the map is based on a 1918 British War Office map of "Abyssinia." The cartographer reversed the colonial process and reclaimed Ethiopian heritage by translating the English names back into Amharic. At the heart of the map is the ancient, undefeated royal realm. It is a source of pride and life, like the wheat that forms a sheltering sky over the royal heads. When Haile Selassie was overthrown in 1974, the lion's crown on the flag was removed and the cross finial was changed to a spear point.

The Portuguese charted their way around Africa by means of the stars. Centuries later, an image of Africa made from amid those stars confirms current sorrows. Over time, the notion of the "dark continent" came to mean many things, mostly negative, as Africa endured colonization and struggled with political chaos, famine, and disease during and after decolonization. Plate 102, a composite NASA satellite image from 2000, adds another meaning to the famous description of Africa.

Capturing the entire earth at night with its networks of blazing electrical power grids, NASA also gives a new meaning to the notion of power. If every map reflects the social order of a particular period and place, NASA's revelatory map makes Africa's current struggles with darkness (in all its forms) visible. As the historical geographer J. P. Harley insisted, "To those who have strength in the world shall be added strength in the map." And, seemingly, those who are weak, low on "energy," will be erased in the map.

In the twenty-first century, Africa's darkness on the map most obviously signifies the absence of "progress," which, by extension, means a disconnect from the electronic communication revolution quickly becoming the heartbeat of the global economy. This particular isolation from the onrush of the future deepens the darkness and likens it to the bottom of a well.

Today, according to the nonprofit Freedom House, only about one-fifth of sub-Saharan Africa would qualify as "free." And "democracy" is no guarantee of sound governance. Most movingly, the darkness denotes the absence of a moral imperative on the part of the world economic community. Overtaken by the darkness, the great continent of Africa seems to have slipped into the dreaded realm of the terminally ill. It looks on the verge of being extinguished, being blown out. It is Map as Silence Equals Death. When asked what the twenty-first century's most pressing moral question will be, social historian Samantha Power replied: "Where were you when Africa disappeared?"

EUROPE

Continents are described by most people as large, discrete landmasses. If mapping is nothing more than describing reality, the question naturally arises: "Why is Europe called a continent?" Europe, like India (which is larger than Europe), is a huge peninsula attached to Asia. And Asia, in turn, is actually attached to Africa!

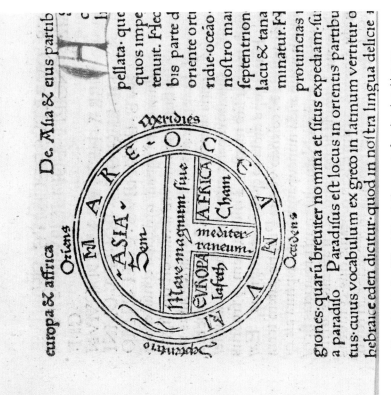

Undeniably, "Europe" is a distinct entity in the spatial unfolding of world history. The postmodern cartographers might say that "Europe" is a culturally constructed geographical classification. Like Latin America, sub-Saharan Africa, South Asia, and Central Asia, Europe can be classified legitimately as a "world region," a place where several countries have historical and cultural bonds. Yet Europe stubbornly remains a continent.

The Romans had inherited the ancient Greeks' notion of a three-part world. From their base in Rome, they saw Europe as the western part of their empire and Asia as all that stretched east. When the Western Roman Empire fell, the Mediterranean world and northern Europe were divided among non-Roman tribes who were either Catholic or Arian Christians, with the exception of the shamefully maligned Attila the Hun, who ruled the rich, vast region north of the Danube and refused to be "Romanized" or send soldiers to Rome as the Barbarian tribes had done for centuries. Attila's "defeat" and vilification—totally fabricated by a self-serving Pope Leo I circa 452 after Emperor Valentinian, lacking an army, had instructed the Pope to surrender Rome to the sophisticated pagan warrior king—helped create the mythic authority of the Pope, who took the pagan title *pontifex maximus* and became master of the imperium in the same way the warrior shogun came to dominate the emperor in Japan. The Catholic Church and its laws became the basis for a new form of Western civilization. Then the Germanic Franks ("free people") settled in Belgic Gaul and after converting to Catholicism, conquered and converted all of Gaul circa 507 using Christ as their battle god. (Centuries later they resumed their religious crusade to take Jerusalem.) The warrior Catholic Christ was already the inspiration for the destruction of all that was not faith-based in the Roman Empire. With the loss of early Celtic Irish, Arian Christianity, the Greek language, and the Roman libraries, entire systems of thought vanished—including Ptolemy's system of coordinate mapping—as well as the independence of mind associated with the Greek civilization.

Public life in Europe became inseparably intertwined with religion, which again dominated the mind of Western man as it had done before the ascension of Athens. By the end of the fourth century, only 10 percent of the Roman population was still pagan. Having achieved great secular power, the Roman Catholic Church made scholarship and cartography handmaidens of religious tradition and of the Bible, which was interpreted literally. Throughout Europe, people lived in scattered communities. In time, cultural zones became unique. They defined themselves with the help of imaginative cartography. Eventually, in the early fifteenth century, when the work of Ptolemy reappeared in the West, Europe was formulated and defined by the art and science of cartography, soon a common and unifying language. Though each nation used the same basic scientific formula for making maps, each found ways to translate its national ethos into the geographical image. Meanwhile, the Age of Discovery created among these Europeans a Eurocentric vision of the world. It became an absolute necessity for Europe to be perceived as a mighty continent. There mapmaking was implicitly about the geography of power.

Europe Conceived

In the new Christendom, dating from late antiquity through the early Middle Ages—a time of change, ferment, and creativity too intense to be called Dark Ages—the few surviving classical works became tools for interpreting scripture. Christian scholars utilized the ancient Greek three-part scheme of the known world, but translated it into a prayer with the aid of Genesis, translated into the Vulgate by Saint Jerome (died c. 420): "Noah gave each of his three sons, Shem, Ham, and Japheth, one of the three parts of the world for their inheritance, and these were Asia, Africa, and Europe, respectively." Theological construct became historical "fact" cleansed of Greek paganism in what is known as the T&O (*orbis terrarum*—Latin for "globe of world" or "wheel of the world") map.

These earliest European world maps were simple, theological views of space, oriented east where the Garden of Eden was believed to be. Thus Asia appears on the top half of the circle, with Europe on the bottom left quarter and Africa on the right. Asia is separated from Africa by the Nile and from Europe by the Don. The Mediterranean separates Europe from Africa. The world's ocean (*mare oceanum*) flows around the edge of the flat earth, an emblem of the binding Catholic dogma.

The first printed map in Europe (1472) was a T&O map that appeared in the encyclopedia of Isidor, bishop of Seville (Plate 103). Compiled between 622 and 633 during a time of meager learning, the manuscript's essential knowledge was sequestered in monasteries and convents. The map illustrated geography lessons. It is Map as Catholic Symbol. Its purity exemplifies men who scorned the flesh and the world, men who denied direct observation and experience in favor of pure abstraction. "Divine revelation, not reason, is the source of all truth," wrote the Christian theologian

Tertullian of Carthage (150–225). This contempt for the world had a tremendous influence on Western mores and attitudes.

The map honors the theologian Augustine of Hippo, the begetter of Christian puritanism. He was the first to marry the Greek philosophical tradition with the Judeo-Christian religious and scriptural traditions. The marriage spawned the T&O map, which is the summation of its age. The Greek's three-part known world was transformed into the form of a tau cross, a mystical Christian icon. Conveniently, the form placed Jerusalem at the intersection of the horizontal and vertical axis, satisfying the Bible, which has Jerusalem at the center of the lands (Ezekiel 5:5). It was Augustine who also gave the Roman Church's theologians grounds for fighting the "Just War" in Christ's name, a teaching that eventually evolved into the Crusades to reclaim from Eastern infidels the center of the lands on the T&O, the Holy Land.

By 800, the pope had elevated a Frank king, Charlemagne (724–814), to the position of Holy Roman emperor. All the Western tribal kings saw themselves as Caesar's successors. An imaginary ancient Rome became their inspiration. Charlemagne fostered a broad literate culture in his new civilization, his Carolingian empire, yet another attempt to construct a Europe dominated by one people. While the Vikings attacked from the north, he unified what are today France, Germany, northern Italy, and parts of the Slavic lands. In his library were three silver tables with, according to his biographer Einhardt (770–840), the "entire circuit of the earth" divided into three continents on one and detailed plans of Rome and Constantinople on the others. Charlemagne's realm was totally within the unyielding grip of Christianity, for the Church remained the supreme relic of the Roman Empire west of Constantinople.

As they were integrated into the Church, where books were fundamental for the promulgation of dogma, the kings were forced into literacy. Like Charlemagne, they founded monastic schools. Their monastic model formed the European mind. An early seventeenth-century French map (Plate 104) shows the lasting effects of their lessons. And, paradoxically, the seeds of what became known as humanism, the hallmark of modern Western civilizations—the revival of classical letters, the birth of individualistic and critical

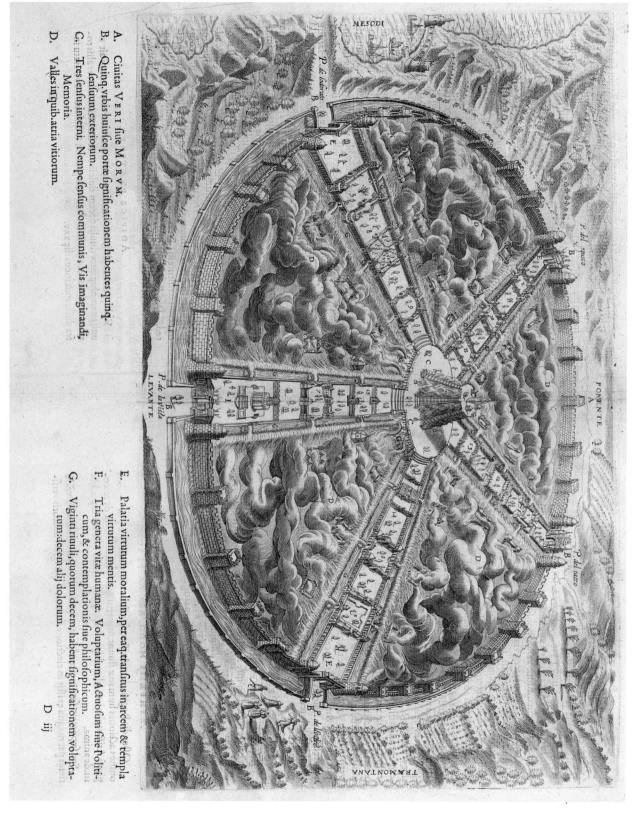

PLATE 104. *The City of the Soul.* The medieval Christian notion of the soul was adhered to in this 1609 French map.

A.   Ciuitas VERI siue MORVM.

B.   Quinq; vbis huiusce portæ significationem habentes quinq;

C.   Tres sensus interni. Nempe sensus communis, Vis imaginandi, Memoria.

D.   Valles in quib. aria vitiorum.

E.   Palatia virtutum moralium, per eaq; transitus in arcem & templa virtutum mentis.

F.   Tria genera viræ humanæ. Voluptariam, Activam siue Politicum, & contemplationis siue philosophicum.

G.   Viginti riuuli, quorum decem, habent significationem voluptarum: decem alij dolorum.

D iij

spirit, and the emphasis on secular concerns—were planted. At first, the monks, in thrall to Augustine, saw sinful humanity fused into a sinister mass by a vengeful God. Suffering was at the center of the early medieval Christian message to the world. Traditional rational norms of justice—equity—were unknown to its God or to its kings. Then, in the early twelfth century, with the Church's inception of purgatory as a place in the Christian afterlife where the punishment was made to fit the individual crime, human beings became differentiated sinners with unique personalities. This liberation from communal slavery to the Church and kings generated revolutionary ideas.

The French map of the soul's city touches the core of what became the European sensibility. Using the Book of Revelations, Augustine had relied upon the common belief in otherworldly places, such as Heaven and Hell, when he invented the Eternal City of God, a place made visible in the Church. The City of God was a particular destination, the specified goal of a Christian life. For him, the temporal City of Man on earth was a unified kingdom, a counterpart to the celestial one. Thus, things visible allowed mankind to see and know with intellectual, inward sight, things invisible. Over a millennium later, this idea still flourished.

The engraving from 1609 conceives of the soul as a fortified space. A city of truth or morals, it protects and encloses the virtues. The city of the soul is entered by five gateways, each identified with a physical sense. Because of its promotion of sexual activity—sex was isolated by Augustine as an element of evil, even in marriage—touch is the only sense in the Christian realm given a neg-

ative evaluation. Augustine's legacy of repudiating pleasure became a fundamental reality in the evolution of all modern Christian traditions. The seventeenth-century map chronicles its passage through time. It is Map as Internalized Christian Guilt.

Unlike imperial Rome, the medieval Western world, with its distinct awareness of both temporal and otherworldly places, functioned almost entirely without a cartographic science. The French illuminator of a 1494 manuscript copy of Boccaccio's 1348 biographical tales, *On the Falls of Famous Men (Des nobles malleureux)*, shows a peasant giving directions to a knight on the road (Plate 105). Without maps, such "performance mapping"—this pointing and gesturing—was a common occurrence in the Middle Ages, partnered with verbal itineraries or list maps. Giving verbal directions is possibly the oldest method of passing geographical information and one that is still practiced today. It is Map as Performance Art. Using biographies of primarily Mediterranean world classical figures, Boccaccio, a diligent student of the Greeks and a strong proponent of humanism, provided abundant examples of errors of judgment kings and princes should avoid. Most important, according to the critic Louis Brewer Hall, "the characters are punished here on earth, and this change in setting from Hell to Earth is one of the milestones of literary history." The rulers of the City of Man must use any means to find "the right path," even if it involves taking instructions from their lowly subjects. The illustrator of Boccaccio's moral guide took the message literally when he supplied for the prologue what was a generic image at the time.

It was the theologian and philosopher Peter Abelard (1074–1142), in Paris, who spurred this philosophical humanist revolution. After the fall to Christendom in 1085 of Spain's Toledo, where the Islamic culture had preserved the philosophy and science of the Greeks, the work of the ancients found its way north, most notably to the major European kingdom, France, and its great university in the royal city of Paris, the premier city in medieval Europe and the first modern city to achieve the stature of Rome. For many Europeans, Paris *was* France, and the ultimate City of Man.

Plans of Paris were part of the French cartographic stream from the sixteenth century onward. One of history's most elaborately beautiful city plans was made of Paris in 1739 by Louis Bretez, a member of the Academy of Painting and Sculpture. Proposed by Michel Étienne Turgot, comptroller general of France, it covers twenty large sheets, each showing and identifying its portion of every Parisian street, house, park, and monument. All are as entrancing as the one showing the Île de la Cité, the heart of old Paris (Plate 106). The entire map serves as the visual memory of the architectural reality of a long-gone medieval Paris during the ancien régime.

Besides being a major work of art, Bretez's map had a very specific job to do. Its primary function was to reestablish Paris as the universal model of a capital city. It is Map as Public Relations Tool. The map was to convince the world that Paris was the place to be, the place to locate the home office of your international business,

PLATE 105. *A Knight on Horseback.* The most common form of mapping is illustrated in this 1494 book illustration.

the place *très chic.* Other cities, such as Vienna and London (twice the size of Paris), had stolen some of its limelight, and the Bretez plan was to force them all further back in the queue for urban supremacy. Contemporary newspapers, such as the *Journal de Trevoux,* trumpeted the map, surmising what could have been learned of ancient Rome's passions, interests, and daily life had a similar map of the capital of the ancient world been available for study. One hundred years later, Bretez's map had become just such an invaluable primary historical document, giving access to a lost world.

There were also other ambitions capering around Bretez's creation. Throughout the Western world, the sixteenth-century dream of applying the rationalist approach to urban design became the goal of many rulers. French monarchs had dictated house alignments, building heights, and facades to little or no effect in Paris. Like all medieval cities, Paris grew helter-skelter, as the map makes plain. It grew to meet the demands of its inhabitants. At the time of Bretez's map, the crown was attempting unsuccessfully to halt the growth of Paris and its disease-infested, rabbit-warren slums so evident on the map. To succeed, urban planning needed the cooperation of many disciplines: architecture, engineering, surveying, landscape architecture, and mapping. It was fostered by economists, social workers, public health specialists, and municipal administrators with the attention span of a cartographer like Bretez.

This dream of a modern Paris was finally achieved between 1852 and 1870. Louis Napoleon, or Napoleon III, granted his deputy, Baron Haussmann (1809–91), almost dictatorial powers. Georges-Eugène Haussmann demolished as much as 60 percent of Bretez's medieval city, regardless of its historical value. He then dissected the neatly reordered city with many grand boulevards, replacing those that had simply encircled the old maze. He built a mammoth system of sewers to deal with the ongoing problem of water pollution for the city's 1 million inhabitants. On the Île de la Cité, he razed everything but Notre Dame, the Sainte-Chapelle, the Conciergerie, and the Palais de Justice, leaving 15,000 people homeless. The new center of Paris was located in the northwest, the area where rich Parisians had been migrating for centuries. Whereas Bretez's map advertised the city as a great human achievement, building the new Paris was to advertise the power and efficiency of its emperor, whose concern about the high rate of unemployment was influenced, no doubt, by stories of a disruptive social event that royalty did not want repeated. One of the triggers of the French Revolution had been similarly high rates of unemployment in France. Descendants of the mobs that had rampaged through those streets immortalized on Bretez's map were put to work by Haussmann. The streets may have been removed from the earth's surface, but what happened on them is encoded in this map as vividly as in the novels of Victor Hugo and Charles Dickens.

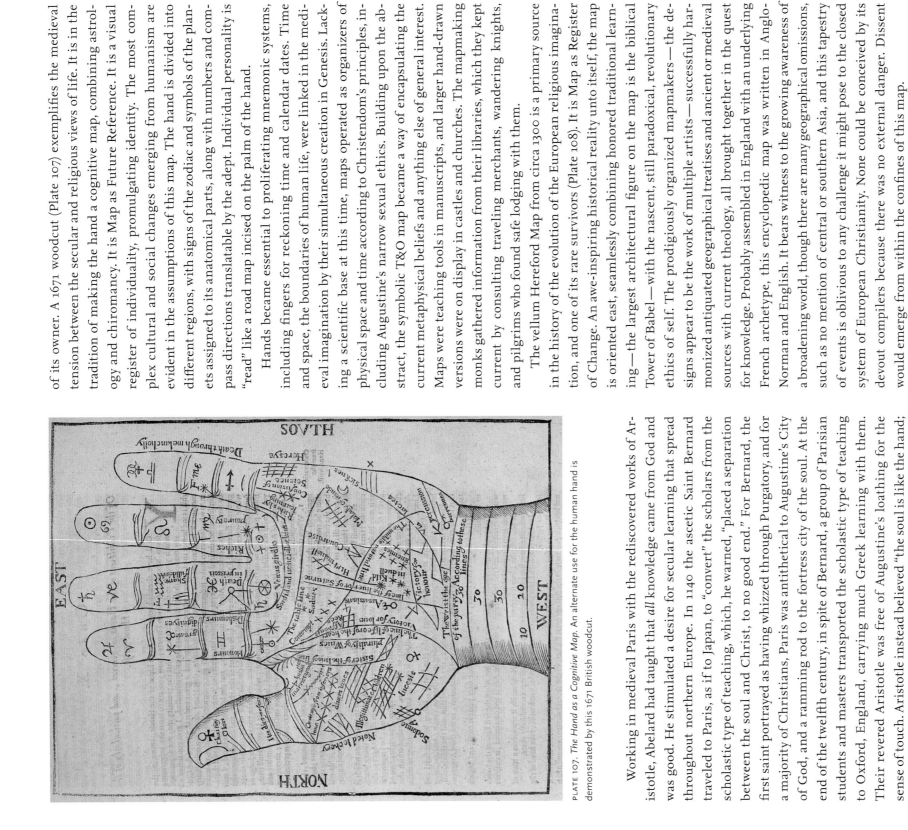

of its owner. A 1671 woodcut (Plate 107) exemplifies the medieval tension between the secular and religious views of life. It is in the tradition of making the hand a cognitive map, combining astrology and chiromancy. It is Map as Future Reference. It is a visual register of individuality, promulgating identity. The most complex cultural and social changes emerging from humanism are evident in the assumptions of this map. The hand is divided into different regions, with signs of the zodiac and symbols of the planets assigned to its anatomical parts, along with numbers and compass directions translatable by the adept. Individual personality is "read" like a road map incised on the palm of the hand.

Hands became essential to proliferating mnemonic systems, including fingers for reckoning time and calendar dates. Time and space, the boundaries of human life, were linked in the medieval imagination by their simultaneous creation in Genesis. Lacking a scientific base at this time, maps operated as organizers of physical space and time according to Christendom's principles, including Augustine's narrow sexual ethics. Building upon the abstract, the symbolic T&O map became a way of encapsulating the current metaphysical beliefs and anything else of general interest. Maps were teaching tools in manuscripts, and larger hand-drawn versions were on display in castles and churches. The mapmaking monks gathered information from their libraries, which they kept current by consulting traveling merchants, wandering knights, and pilgrims who found safe lodging with them.

The vellum Hereford Map from circa 1300 is a primary source in the history of the evolution of the European religious imagination, and one of its rare survivors (Plate 108). It is Map as Register of Change. An awe-inspiring historical reality unto itself, the map is oriented east, seamlessly combining honored traditional learning—the largest architectural figure on the map is the biblical Tower of Babel—with the nascent, still paradoxical, revolutionary ethics of self. The prodigiously organized mapmakers—the designs appear to be the work of multiple artists—successfully harmonized antiquated geographical treatises and ancient or medieval sources with current theology, all brought together in the quest for knowledge. Probably assembled in England with an underlying French archetype, this encyclopedic map was written in Anglo-Norman and English. It bears witness to the growing awareness of a broadening world, though there are many geographical omissions, such as no mention of central or southern Asia, and this tapestry of events is oblivious to any challenge it might pose to the closed system of European Christianity. None could be conceived by its devout compilers because there was no external danger. Dissent would emerge from within the confines of this map.

Large wall maps, such as this one now displayed in Hereford Cathedral, which is 5 feet 2 inches tall by 4 feet 4 inches wide, blended geography and literature, ethnography, history, zoology, cosmology, and theology in a cartographic image easily explained to illiterate people standing in front of it. It contains nearly eleven

PLATE 108. *Hereford Mappa Mundi.* The goal of this c. 1300 large wall map of the world was not to represent reality.

PLATE 107. *The Hand as a Cognitive Map.* An alternate use for the human hand is demonstrated by this 1671 British woodcut.

Working in medieval Paris with the rediscovered works of Aristotle, Abelard had taught that *all* knowledge came from God and was good. He stimulated a desire for secular learning that spread throughout northern Europe. In 1140 the ascetic Saint Bernard traveled to Paris, as if to Japan, to "convert" the scholars from the scholastic type of teaching, which, he warned, "placed a separation between the soul and Christ, to no good end." For Bernard, the first saint portrayed as having whizzed through Purgatory, and for a majority of Christians, Paris was antithetical to Augustine's City of God, and a ramming rod to the fortress city of the soul. At the end of the twelfth century, in spite of Bernard, a group of Parisian students and masters transported the scholastic type of teaching to Oxford, England, carrying much Greek learning with them. Their revered Aristotle was free of Augustine's loathing for the sense of touch. Aristotle instead believed "the soul is like the hand; for the hand is the instrument of instruments." In the medieval world, the topography of the hand became a memory device, or an "artificial memory," by providing a multitude of "places" in which to harbor memorized letters, words, numbers, images, and their associated concepts. Then humanism produced another use for the hand's topography—chiromancy, or palmistry.

Like a landscape, every hand had distinctive characteristics that, according to some, revealed the interior life and unique fate

now the face of man, since Christ became man through her human body. It is based on: "Blessed is the womb that bare thee, and the paps which thou hast sucked" (Luke 11:27). As a faithful reflection of Western man taking his place as an agent of creation, this map is a quintessential cultural landscape.

European man's new role as an agent of creation, his humanity to be prized, was most radiantly honored in the ground plan for the medieval Gothic cathedral. By 1224—the central Middle Ages—the Greek science of logic was perceived as the basis for all the progress the mind could make, the mind that comprehended the order of creation, the mind for which mathematics and cartography were primary tools.

The royal abbey cathedral at St.-Denis (Plate 109), north of Paris, was the first complete piece of European architecture to have a ground plan born of the science of logic and mapped with reclaimed Greek geometrical and arithmetical instruments gleaned from the Muslim world. Those plans completed the ascension of the urban art form called Gothic, a way of structuring buildings in Europe, not a style (except in Italy). It is Map as Luminous Prototype. At St.-Denis, the city of the soul was entered through the sanctified portal of sight. The requisite spiritual condition of being made "pure and ready to ascend to the stars"—*puro e disposto a salire a le stelle* (Dante's final line in *Purgatorio*)—was achieved by a few strokes of the cartographer's pen.

Abbot Suger (1081–1155) rejected the inherited architectural forms in order to express his ideas in stone. Celebrating the sense of sight, his ground plan embodied the teachings of Saint Denis,

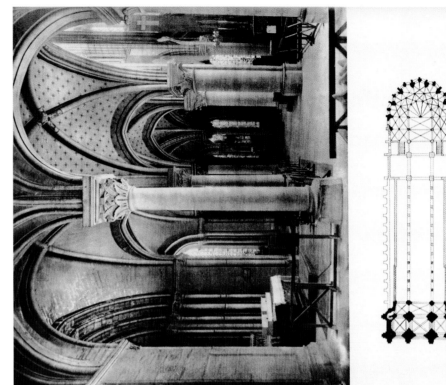

PLATE 108A. Detail from the *Hereford Mappa Mundi* showing the Virgin Mary baring her breasts.

hundred inscriptions, mostly in Latin, from classical and medieval texts, along with nearly as many symbolic decorations and painted scriptural and historical scenes. The morality and science it teaches held sway for centuries; some of its fables—such as the Anthropophagi—were still being told to Desdemona by Othello in 1604. The Hereford Map offered an ordered beginning to studies for those "who shall hear, or read, or see it," as a legend on the map makes plain.

Medieval *mappae mundi* like Hereford's were not about representing geographical reality. They were more concerned with being true to their beliefs. At the top, Christ thrones beyond the circle of earth. By the Middle Ages, Augustine's and Paul's distinction between the flesh and spirit had become absolute. Just below Christ, on Earth in the east, are Adam and Eve in a circular Garden of Eden, a lost world believed to exist within the known world. In Genesis, their sin was of the spirit: an appetite for knowledge. But by the time of the Hereford Map, their sin was linked to sexuality—hence they cover their genitals—and sexual abstinence was taken as evidence of the highest spiritual prowess. "For if ye live after the flesh, ye shall die," wrote Paul (Romans 8:13). Remembrance of Adam and Eve's punishment, Death, put the fear of God in everyone looking at the map. Yet if salvation was to be achieved by renouncing the sins of the world, the world of the Hereford Map was an enticing place full of City of Man marvels and tantalizing adventures depicted in warm colors encouraging assimilation of its double messages. There are little miniatures of notable cities; walled and unwalled towns are differentiated. Jerusalem is still at its exact center, but it is one city among many now, an adjustment to Europe's having lost the Crusades. The sight of the Virgin Mary, the personification of purity, kneeling bare-breasted beneath Christ at the top (Plate 108A), instructed the viewer that the face of God was

PLATE 109. *St.-Denis Floor Plan.* The ground plan of the first French Gothic cathedral evolved from the science of logic.

the patron saint of France, who asserted, "God is light." Since light was the least material substance on earth, and closer to the world of true spirit, the goal of Suger's ground plan was to produce an ecstacy of stained-glass light; the history of its use in church windows around the world begins with him and his ground plan.

Begun in 1140, the new chapels were supported by stone buttresses; their spherical outer walls were pierced by tall windows that reduced the wall surface to the dimension of window frames. The walls appeared transparent. Over the central doors were immense spherical windows, geometric stained-glass confections shaped like roses and drenched in primary colors to provoke the primary emotions (Plate 110). Suger's ground plan used geometry to create a luminous path to enlightenment. The plan made perfection visible.

Suger believed the City of God could be imagined only in a beautiful City of Man. Esoteric gnosis holds that in what was Belgian Gaul in the twelfth and thirteenth centuries, a group of cathedrals (all named for Notre Dame, the Virgin Mary) trace on earth the form of the constellation Virgo, the Virgin: Chartres represents the star Gamma, Bayeux is Epsilon, and Amiens is Zeta in that constellation. Terrestrial and celestial geography were mystically merged in this way in the spiritual realm of cartography.

PLATE 110. *West Rose Window of Strasbourg Cathedral.* The Gothic rose window is a geometric representation of a spiritual proposition.

French Gothic cathedrals were clearly the most gigantic artistic undertakings and the largest fiscal investments of the medieval period. They were built hands-on by the entire community, whose members joined forces to pull the great stones out of the earth with ropes. It had taken centuries for the French Capetian kings, descendants of Hugh Capet (d. 947), to consolidate their power and build a royal bureaucracy that, by the close of the thirteenth century, made France the largest, wealthiest, and best-governed monarchical state in Europe. Trade flourished. A 1484 wall chart on vellum by Arnaldo Domenech, a Catalan cartographer, was created for converting from one system of weights to another between pairs of towns (see Plate 111). Its geographic significance lies in its graphic presentation of the economics linking Europe and the Mediterranean world. It records one of the major social changes in European history. It is Map as Nascent Old-World Capitalism. The only one of its kind, Domenech's wall chart explains the rise of the urban mercantile middle class that made cities hubs of activity, as in Roman times. Begun in the eleventh century, the expanding trading systems gathered momentum in the fourteenth, and as commercial wealth began to compete with traditional wealth of rural landholdings, the ensuing rise of cities marked the end of the feudal social order of the Middle Ages and the creation of the Western world's bourgeoisie, a major building block for the invention of Europe as a continent.

Social fluidity occurred as money became more valuable than land in underpinning military might. Money was a key factor in Europeans' building 150 churches and cathedrals as embodiments of civic pride on the continent between 1150 and 1250. These changes in the game of life are documented in maps. Domenech's chart gives the lie to the myths of medieval Europe slowly emerging from a deep sleep (the Dark Ages) only after the dawn of the Italian Renaissance (1420–1600). The chart fairly hums with life and activity. Europe sits in dialogue with Africa and Asia fully awake. And the loosening grip of the Catholic Church is further documented as merchants are shown ignoring the Pope's threats of excommunication for doing business with Islamic infidels.

The humanism that defined national characteristics took a unique turn in Italy. The Italian Renaissance seems to be a thing apart, to have a life of its own, driven by the arts or *studios humanitates*—what is called today the humanities—rather than by the sciences, though it was the Italians who revived an interest in classic geography by first printing in Bologna (1477) Ptolemy's *Geographia*. It had reached them via the Islamic world. With the works of Ptolemy other influences from the East came to Italy, just as in Islamic Spain. There are striking similarities between the Italian schools of learning and the Islamic literary tradition (*adab*), such as the subjects of study, the manner of teaching, and even formal institutions. In both societies, art was not an isolated discipline. It engaged the full life of the people; and as in China, too, education and culture often took the lead in political affairs. With its superb access to the latest geographic information and the delicacy of its craftsmanship, Italy became the first center of Europe's early mapmaking industry. A beautifully wood-engraved Venetian map of the world

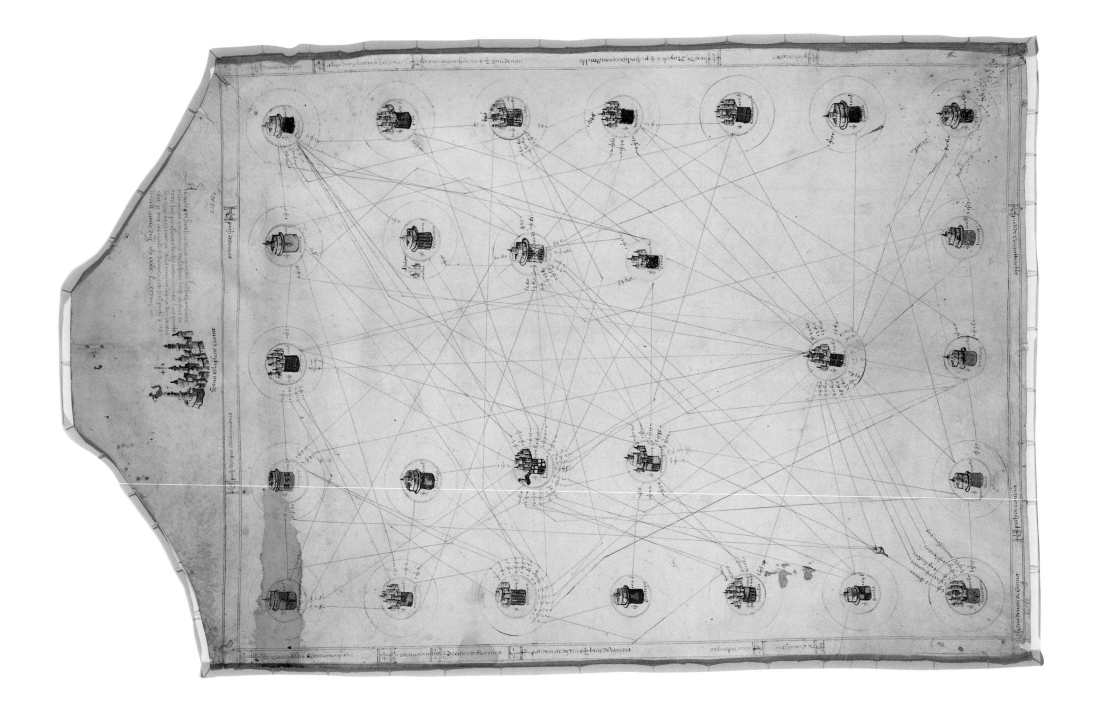

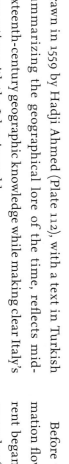

Before the sixteenth century, scientific and geographic information flowed principally from the East to Europe. Then the current began to reverse itself. The Hadji Ahmed map is a perfect example of this profound change in the balance of knowledge and power between Europe and the Ottoman Empire. It is Map as Power Shift. It is also the first European map in any Turkic language, and the first secular, geographic, and scientific text prepared for

drawn in 1559 by Hadji Ahmed (Plate 112), with a text in Turkish summarizing the geographical lore of the time, reflects mid-sixteenth-century geographic knowledge while making clear Italy's connection with the Islamic world.

PLATE 112. *A Complete and Perfect Map Describing the Whole World.* The Islamic world's influence upon Italy was affirmed by this 1559 world map.

PLATE 111. *A Fifteenth-Century Guide to Weights and Measures for European and Mediterranean Cities.* These 1484 trading links chronicle the end of the feudal Middle Ages.

PLATE 113. *Du Pinet's Europe.* There is deep symbolic resonance at a time of massive change in this 1564 French map.

printing in any of the languages of Islam. Hadji Ahmed, a citizen of Tunis, was captured and brought to Europe as a slave. Hoping to gain his freedom, he created the map from European images for Turkish noblemen and scholars. He worked with the University of Padua, from which the course of public instruction throughout the Venetian dominion in Italy was controlled, and with the medieval princely geographer Abulfeda. The projection used by Ahmed is "cordiform," the world drawn within the outlines of a heart, credited to Johann Werner, a German mathematician. Nonetheless, the map's publisher, Marc' Antonio Giustinian, was arrested, tried, and though found innocent of trafficking with the infidel, was forbidden to publish his Arabic world map because it contained current information that could be of use to the enemy.

At the time, Venice was severely weakened by wars fought on the mainland. The success of the Portuguese in opening a sea route to India had erased Venetian trade monopolies, while the onrushing Turkish presence created another serious threat to the last great

Christian sea power of the Mediterranean world. Banned, the map was forgotten until 1795, when the wood blocks were discovered in the Venetian Secret Archives.

In Italy where it was the humanities, especially the study of law, that led to dreams of a unified national destiny, the Gothic cathedrals, with their use of geometry and light and pointed arches to achieve the transcendental, held little appeal. Italians preferred traditional frescoes—pictorial art on plaster surfaces in Romanesque structures. As different nationalities coalesced into distinct European nations, the philosophy of humanism made "the world" a thing separate from nature, a thing humanity dominated and no longer held sacred, a thing to be divided and mapped. Yet as descendants of Rome with direct links to Christian antiquity, the Italians still retained ties with a sacred hierarchy. Thus Florence's Galileo (1564–1642) died under house arrest, condemned of heresy for teaching Copernicus's theories of Earth revolving around the sun. Paradoxically, personal merit replaced divine judgment first in Italy. Anyone, regardless of lineage, could become an Italian king.

Thanks to burgeoning trade, out of kingdoms grew European territorial states—the markers of the modern age. A map of Europe in a rare 1564 atlas, the first city atlas, was written and compiled by Antoine du Pinet (c. 1510–c. 1584) (Plate 113). He has turned Europe upside down by orienting it in the Islamic manner. (The direction of the type confirms that the map was not bound into the book incorrectly.) In 1564, the year John Calvin died, du Pinet was a Protestant in Lyons, France. Calvin had tried to bring religious tolerance to Catholic France. Though he failed, he and, in Germany, Martin Luther (1483–1546), managed to turn the European world on its head with their reordering of medieval life through the tenets of their reformed churches. Unlike the Catholic hierarchy, the evangelical Protestant one of du Pinet's time resembled that of the Muslims, who saw no contradiction between the legacy of Greece and their faith, and who condemned icons as a form of idolatry. At a time of massive social and religious change, the southern orientation by du Pinet has a deep symbolic resonance. It takes the focus off the Mediterranean world, where Catholicism reigned supreme. For him, the action had moved north, as would the evolution of Western cartography.

A terminal blow to the bondage of Catholic dogma behind the T&O map was the fact that Calvin believed humanity was responsible to no earthly ruler (and especially not to the pope!), only to God. This astounding reversal of the status quo can also be felt in the topsy-turvy orientation of du Pinet's map. It can be seen to depict a state of mind. The new urban commercial class now had the power to reject authority in accordance with its members' individual consciences. Several of the German provinces in the center of the upside-down map were Lutheran states whose bishops reported to the princes. For a time, Catholic France supported those heretic Protestant princes because they were at odds with Charles V, the Holy Roman emperor, who was also king of Catholic Spain, France's mortal enemy. The map is a monument to a pivotal moment in the making of modern Europe. It could be a visual pun dramatizing this turning point, this advocacy of humanism at a time when constraints were overthrown and the tables turned on once all-powerful Rome.

It was no accident that du Pinet's map coincided with the fervent production in manuscript and printed editions of the rediscovered *Geographia* of Ptolemy, the wellspring of cartographic reasoning in Europe. The outline of du Pinet's Europe and its mountains are straight out of Ptolemy. It is Map as Autobiography.

As an early form of Western cartographic writing, it constructs a second subject to the "I," or the emerging human individual: Europe. Maps on the order of du Pinet's work easily equate profiling a country with discovering the contours of a self. Thus, the individual cultural identities being expressed in medieval literatures across the continent are repeated in the language of cartography. Living in geography allows for delineating national *and* personal space. In both cases, natural boundaries are honored. Maps like du Pinet's began to make observations on the poetics of character.

The guile of the cartographer extended from fictions about geography—about shapes and patterns—to the larger matter of feigning place, and the compounding of this exercise in narrative. His map visualized theological divisiveness. On it Europe was no longer a single entity. Maps and cartographic history became both the product and the summary of individual and collective histories.

Though lacking the precision of portolan charts, less accurate maps, such as du Pinet's Europe, dramatically influenced history. While Italy dominated the European map trade, books of stylized island maps known as *isolario* were introduced for travelers in the early fifteenth century, long before specialized atlases appeared on other subjects. Probably developed from exacting *portolani*, or seaman's guides to ports, the island guides initially focused on the Mediterranean world. But by Benedetto Bordone's time, his printed atlas, *Libro* (1528), covered most of the known world. Though his map of Ireland (Plate 114) has official-looking navigation symbols at compass points, the shape of the country plays upon the disjunction between the known and the imagined lore. There are symbolic castles and cathedrals along the coasts, as well as major rivers, information that would have appealed to cosmopolitan book buyers and tourists.

The *isolario* tapped into the magical character of islands fostered by the Christian idea that they had emerged after the biblical flood, each isolated and unique, with singular creatures and ways of life. (When explorers discovered similarities in flora, fauna, and animal life on them, theologians were confounded.) But at a time when imaging as a mental act was prized, and when scholars and sailors had prodigious memories—a carryover from before the printing press—maps were present to the mind's eye and had an unquestioned veracity.

In 1588, during the Anglo-Spanish War (1585–1604), Catholic Spain's Armada, comprising 130 ships, launched an attack in the English Channel against Protestant England. Only forty pilots were on board the Spanish ships. A series of twelve hand-colored plates, engraved in 1590, are a primary source for the history of this famous military campaign, and the best contemporary evidence of the Armada's sailing order. Number Five (see Plate 115) re-creates the final battle off Gravelines (Flanders) and Portland Bill (England);

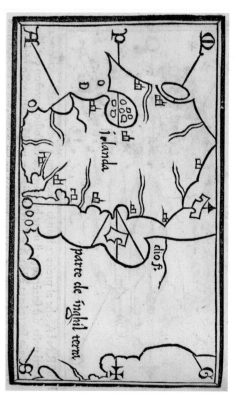

PLATE 114. *Bordone's Ireland.* The stylization of islands was in a cartographic tradition with lethal consequences.

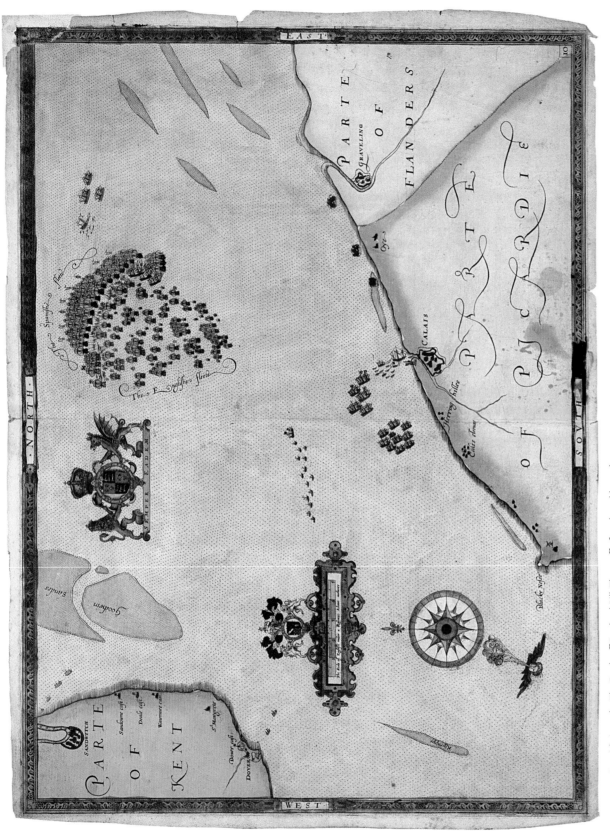

PLATE 115. *Spanish Armada: The Battle off Portland Bill.* The stuff of myth and legends abounds in this accurate 1590 British military map.

it shows the English attack on the *San Lorenzo*, flagship of the Spanish galleons division, and their sinking of four other ships. It is Map as Rhetorical Text. It is the closest thing we have to a sixteenth-century snapshot.

The fifth plate tells of unqualified triumph, a victory that has become the stuff of legend. In truth, even taking into account England's witches, who have claimed that the rise in the winds was of their doing, nature's unpredictability joined forces with visualizations of Ireland based on popular but inaccurate maps (such as Plate 114) within the seafarers' minds to defeat Spain. Being in northern waters, Spanish senior officers advised their defeated, homebound fleet to sail high up toward Norway and far out into the Atlantic in order to avoid floundering on the coasts of Scotland and Ireland. None who followed the specific latitudes and longitudes given by the pilots was wrecked on Ireland's coast. However, constant headwinds, frequent gales, wild storms, and ships wounded by gunfire brought into play those memorized certainties that Ireland's western coast was a fairly straight line. Thirty or more Armada ships crashed on the bulging coast of County Mayo,

which gave rise to another Armada myth: the one about the black-haired Celts' origins.

Legend has it that the Spanish were vanquished entirely from that day forward and Britannia ruled the waves with undisputed glory. Actually, the Spanish regrouped their naval forces and defeated the English the next year, a fact rarely added to the saga of the Spanish Armada heroically depicted in the 1590 engravings. And it was the Dutch who followed the Spanish as rulers of the sea in the late seventeenth century, not the triumphant English. Their day would not come until the mid-eighteenth century. By then, maps of Ireland bore no resemblance to Bordone's borrowed fancy.

The Low Countries

From about 1570 to the 1650s, the center of the map trade shifted northward, from the Mediterranean world of Rome and Venice to the Dutch Low Countries. Mapmaking thrived in the city of Antwerp in Belgium, the second-largest but most active port city in Europe, then moved to Amsterdam. Its locus shifted because Europe's power axis shifted, and maps express shifts in power. The Flemish

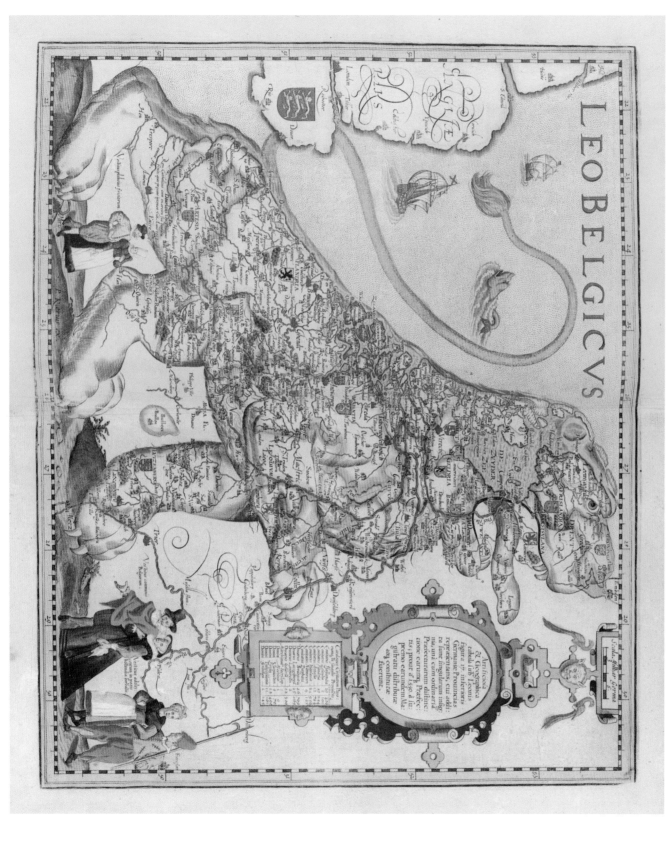

LEO BELGICVS

and the Dutch took the crown for map production, though the entire area assigned to the mostly Dutch-speaking Low Countries consisted of seventeen provinces situated between France and Germany. Variously called Germania Inferior, Les Pays Bas, Nederland, or Lowlands, these areas were active players in the Northern Renaissance. Maps of Belgium (the whole of the Netherlands, including Holland) in the form of a lion— *Leo Belgicus, inferioris germaniae*— were published beginning in 1583. One by Pieter van den Keere (1571–c. 1646) was printed in Amsterdam in 1622 (Plate 116). It delightfully sums up the region's self-image. It is Map as Emblem of Power.

All social, political, and economic life at this time was concentrated in cities. The rise of the mercantile middle class, its cities and city-states, which had begun in the eleventh century and gained momentum from the fourteenth, marked the end of the social

order of the Middle Ages. Though most of the cities remained walled in the ancient tradition, by the sixteenth century, as in Roman times, the city had become the symbol of organized social and cultural life, and the focal point of trade. With the flow of travelers to cities throughout Europe greater than ever—merchants, students, tourists, pilgrims, and every kind of wayfarer—an atlas of cities was a bookseller's dream.

Though technically not a product of the Low Countries, having been printed and created in Cologne, Germany, *Civitates Orbis Terrarum* (1576?–1620?; six volumes), the first uniform collection of plans of cities of the world, belongs to the cartographic school of the Netherlands, and was an obvious result of the printing-press revolution. The *Civitates* was conceived in Antwerp as a companion volume to Ortelius's *Theatrum Orbis Terrarum* (Antwerp, 1570), the first systematic world atlas based on contemporary knowledge since Ptolemy. The city atlas not only echoed the title of the world atlas but also supplied similar supplementary text, and reflected its style of engraving, along with its urban-theatrical sensibilities,

PLATE 116. *The Low Countries Depicted in the Shape of a Lion.* This 1622 map of the Netherlands roars for itself.

PLATE 117. *The City of Cologne.* After the rise of the "common man" came the first systematic atlas of cities, *Civitates Orbis Terrarum.*

such as picturesque compositions framing the city plans. The Civitates was edited and written by Georg Braun, with drawings from many sources engraved in Cologne by Frans Hogenberg, who was also working with Ortelius in Antwerp on his atlas, and Simon van den Neuvel. Braun favored depicting cities from an oblique angle, believing they "should be drawn in such a manner that the viewer can look into all the roads and streets and see all the buildings and open spaces." It was clearly a practical enterprise approached with creative gusto.

As a printed visual record of medieval Europe, the book's lovely images appealed to all people, and this book of maps became one of the bestselling works of its time. It is Map as the Rise of the "Common Man." Though over a period of forty years more editions were printed in scholarly Latin than in German and French—Plate 117 is from the French edition, *Théâtre des cités du monde*—the names of places, churches, and gates were given in the vernacular on the maps. Braun wrote his intentions to Ortelius. "The unlettered...will see his own native town skillfully depicted, with places named in a form familiar to him." In his preface to Book III (1581), Braun also described the newly emerging print culture of the "lettered": "What could be more pleasant than, in one's own home far from all danger, to gaze in these books at the splendor of cities and fortresses and by looking at the pictures and reading the texts accompanying them, to acquire knowledge which could scarcely be had but by long and difficult journeys." "These town plans were the only form of topographical representation in which spatial relationships were correctly expressed. They spurred a visual revolution."

Building on the experience of the great Flemish mercantile and cultural centers, such as Ghent, Bruges, Antwerp, Brussels, and Leuven, the Dutch created a commercial empire run by the prosperous middle classes concentrated in the cities pictured in *Civitates Orbis Terrarum.* Primarily of Germanic stock, the Dutch were major participants in the process of transforming the world into a capitalist system, one born in conflict, not in peace. Their global seaborne "gunpowder" empire made them the greatest power in seventeenth-century Europe. By publishing atlases, they popularized the map-making art and pioneered new techniques, which facilitated the growth of their Dutch East India Company, founded in 1602. With its cartographic offices in Amsterdam, the Company soon held a monopoly on trade with the Orient.

The Dutch saga began in 1581, several years after the publication of the first volume of *Civitates,* when the seven northern Protestant Dutch provinces declared independence from the rule of Spain, and became the Republic of United Netherlands, forcefully enunciating the principle of self-determination. The Roman Catholic town council of Amsterdam was against breaking with Catholic Spain; it was replaced by a Protestant council. The anti-Catholic excesses of the Protestant Reformation, which was initiated when Martin Luther challenged papal authority and its commercialism of his faith in 1517, were modified throughout the Dutch Republic. Religious tolerance was encouraged to ensure that traders of Catholic countries were not antagonized, and to eliminate any further debilitating Christian

PLATE 118. *Christian Celestial.* This 1660 Dutch celestial map was a courageous act of the
Counter-Reformation.

religious wars, which were decimating Europe. Yet in 1660 the Dutch forbade exercise of the Roman Catholic religion. The same year, Andreae Cellarius (1596–1665) published his *Harmonia Macrocosmica* (Harmony of the Universe) in Amsterdam. This glorious celestial atlas with thirty color plates is the only one of its genre published during the golden age of Dutch cartography. In it, the artist courageously thumbs his nose at the prevailing political policy.

Ostensibly spatial depictions of the heavenly systems of famous astronomers, the book includes Ptolemy and Copernicus, among others. Also included, however, is a depiction of the night sky with constellations fashioned in biblical forms boldly displaying a Roman Catholic ethos both above (New Testament) and below (Old Testament) the ecliptic (Plate 118). It was published the very year such iconic Catholic representations were expressly forbidden in the United Netherlands. It is Map as Counter-Reformation Activity. The baroque style of the apostles in their colorful flowing robes perched on the ecliptic; the sentimental approach to the New Testament symbols, such as Peter's boat; and the depiction of Eve sprawled on the bottom in a provocative pose exuding female wantonness as she clutches the apple—all these made an emotional appeal to the senses of the kind begun by French Gothic cathedrals and reviled by the Reformation's proscribed austerity. The overall conception of the plate was taken from the work of Julius Schiller, who published his *Coelum Stellatum Christianum* in 1627 without the rebellious subterfuge.

On Spanish and Portuguese celestial maps, the Southern Cross was purposely misplaced to befuddle sailors. Cellarius symbolically assures the viewer of his not having corrupted his data to keep it secret by making Noah's ark, depicted to the left of Eve, a Dutch ship. It stands as a testament to his integrity even if it was the custom of the day to use indigenous craft. The Ptolemaic night sky recorded 48 constellations. The sixteenth-century Western tradition deviated from ancients by adding more, and by the eighteenth century, celestial maps displayed 108 constellations in what was then their current location. The nineteenth century rejected additions, though by that time there were 300,000 named stars—too many to translate into images. In 1928 the number of constellations was officially reduced to 88 by the stellar authorities in the Western world and "constellation boundaries" were introduced. Today, with the link to classical iconography broken in the popular imagination, only in the names of the brightest stars do we have the remains of the Ptolemaic constellations.

Still believing the uncharted New World to be no more than a narrow strip of land close to the Far East, and prevented by English privateers from going west to the Indies, the Dutch unsuccessfully sought a northeastern route through the Arctic to Asia. The Spanish edition of Joan Blaeu's *Atlas mayor* (1662) was produced, like all the various language editions, in twelve oversized volumes for the wealthy and the intellectual bourgeoisie to display in their growing libraries. While its hand-colored maps—printed on heavy paper in an unrivaled large format with luxury bindings—rest among the highest expressions of Dutch cartographic art, they also remind the viewer that humanism is not a matter simply of attitude and

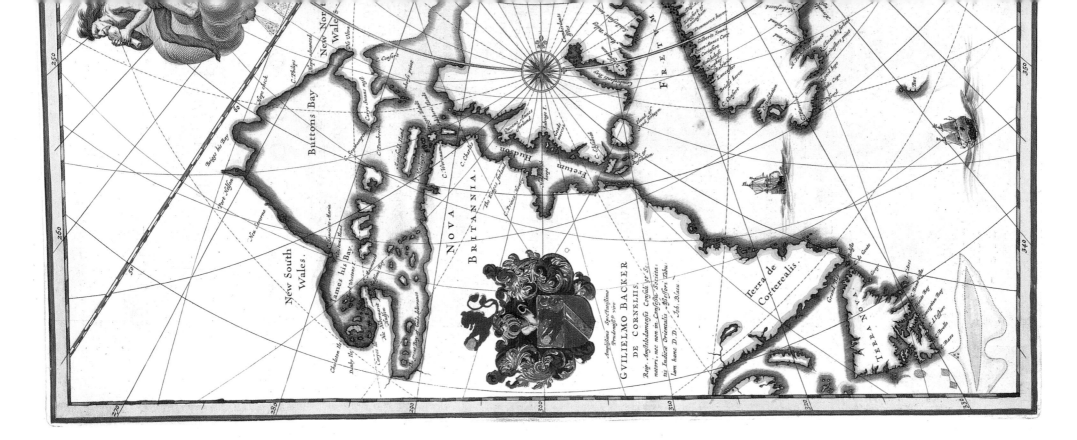

substance, but of communication too. In the spirit of the Netherlands' cartographic camaraderie, only 194 of the atlas's 600 maps were new. In this anthology, Blaeu's original map of the regions below the Arctic pole (Plate 119) is about the long-held Dutch desire to find another, quicker route to Asia, to shorten the length and expense of a trip around the Cape of Good Hope. It is Map as Last Resort. It reveals how the power of imagination conditions the objectives of exploration, the behavior of explorers, and the gathering of geographical information for more interpretations, modifications, and cartographic inventions. It was decades in the making.

The vast, time-consuming expanse of the Atlantic was documented. The profits gained from the New World were minimal compared with the treasures of the Orient. The Dutch search for the legendary Northwest Passage began in 1609, when the Dutch East India Company hired the experienced British explorer Henry Hudson to find a quick way to the "islands of spicery." (As he sailed up the Hudson River beside Manhattan under the flag of the Company, establishing New Netherland [1609–64], Hudson thought he had found it.) His previous explorations in 1607, around Iceland and into Canadian waters, supplied much of the information used on Blaeu's elaborate Arctic map fifty-five years later.

Having failed to find the Northwest Passage via the Arctic, the Dutch then sailed south. Taking on one of their Iberian enemies, overextended Portugal, they successfully attacked Portuguese colonial possessions in Africa and Asia, thereby gaining the economic resources to plunder and wage war for more than sixty years. The Dutch-Spanish war (1595–1609) had been the first inter-European struggle for power to take on a worldwide dimension, another supporting factor in Dutch map production. In 1609, while Hudson was busy staking claims in the New World, the ten southern Catholic Dutch provinces were liberated from Spain, and the Golden Age of the Dutch Republic reached unprecedented economic, political, and cultural heights. The Netherlands boasted the biggest navy in Europe and the largest merchant fleet trading internationally—all requiring maps for practical use, for study, and for display. Its geographical position made it a commercial crossroads and a meeting point for men of ideas and letters, as Venice once had been. Dutch artists as renowned as Rembrandt (1606–69) and Vermeer (1632–75) worked to take a clear-eyed look at the real nature of the physical world. They possibly inspired Braun and Blaeu and Jacobus Cruquius, who introduced decimal scale to maps and developed the polder map—a map that describes any piece of land reclaimed from water for farming—one of the very earliest types of large-scale topographic maps of a limited area. The speed and energy with which the culture of the young republic developed a character of its own, while successfully opposing the military might of Spain, is unparalleled in European history.

For more than two thousand years, the Dutch and their ancestors, the Frisians, added to their shoreline. A quarter of the Netherlands is below sea level on land wrested from the North Sea,

PLATE 119. A *Map of the Arctic Circle*. This 1662 map makes no secret of the Dutch desire to find their own way to the Indies in a time of swirling change.

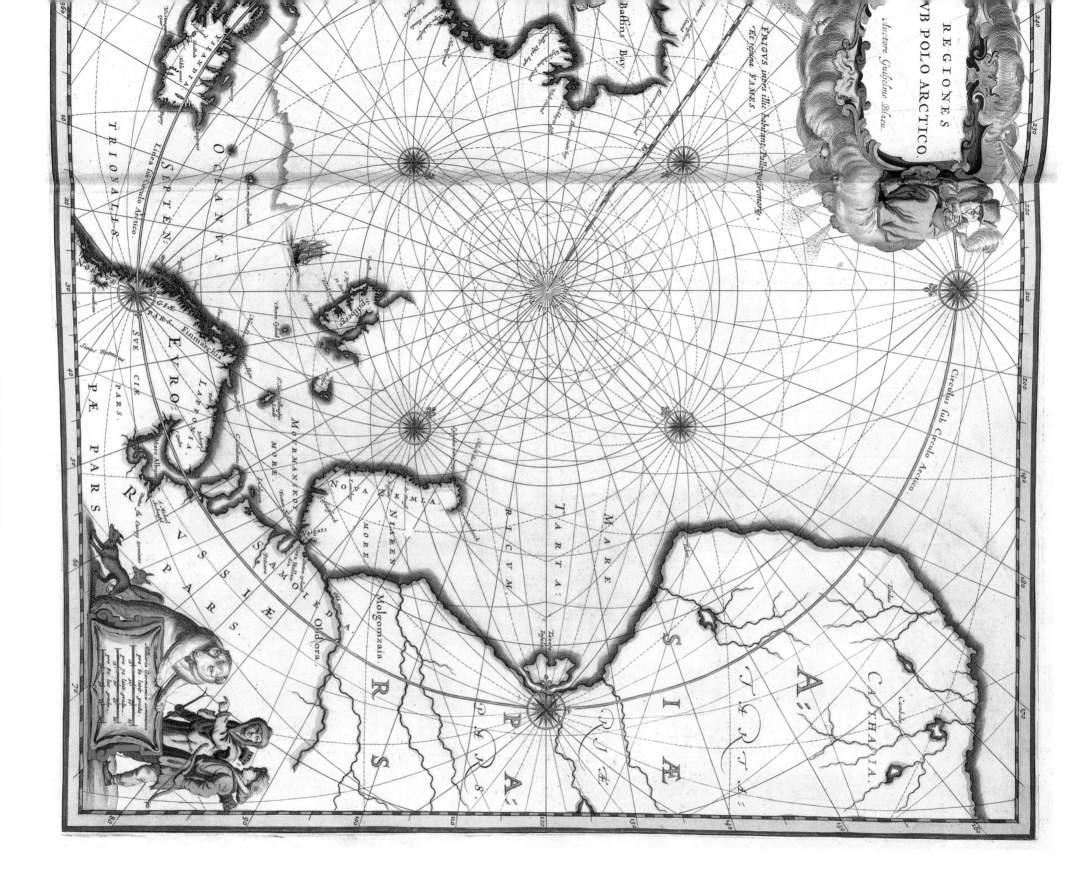

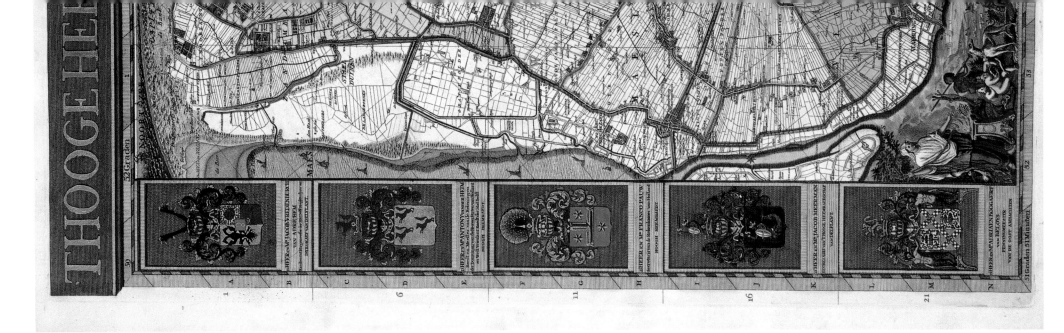

PLATE 120A. Detail from *Index to Atlas of Polder Maps* showing warring ships.

the Rhine, or the River Meuse by 10,000 miles of dikes, dams, weirs, flood barriers, and artificial dunes, all aided by pumps, holding ponds, and windmills. Another quarter is low enough to be regularly flooded in the natural course of events. A Dutch saying insists: "God created the world except Holland; it was taken by its inhabitants from the sea." Building the world's most sophisticated water-management system was a collaborative effort that also produced a societal cohesion in spite of provincial separatism and religious conflict. This collaborative spirit gave birth to the spirit of tolerance for which the Dutch Republic is justly famous to this day, and possibly to the atlas of Ortelius—a bound collection of uniform map sheets made by different cartographers. Representing the high point of Dutch polder cartography is the work of Nicolas Kruikius, a surveyor, who, with a team of engravers, produced an atlas and a map in 1712 of the polder district, or authority, of Delfland based on triangulation surveys (Plate 120). It is Map as Process of Self-Actualization.

These twenty-five sectional map plates and a title plate of the entire Delftland polder district are beautifully colored and illuminated with touches of gold leaf. The title plate is embellished with coats of arms on the right and left margins, ships at ongoing war probably with England off the north shore, and agricultural scenes in the lower margin. The prosperity broadcast by the map gives the battle depicted in the North Sea (Plate 120A) the value of annoying mosquitoes. At the same time, the magnificent national defense system is made as obvious as the canals by the tracing of various lines of fortifications on the map. Military engineering is embedded in the civil engineering, which is the country. Also neatly visualized are public and private property and the major industries: fishing, agriculture, and forestry. The map is a monument to the competence of the district managers and of their governing boards, who, with the polder maps, demonstrated the Dutch genius for urban and regional spatial planning. In their suggestion of space, pattern, and depth working in concert, the maps are as sublime as a painting by Vermeer.

PLATE 120. *Index to Atlas of Polder Maps*. This 1712 map eloquently expresses the engineering ingenuity of the Dutch.

Today, after centuries of managing nature, the Dutch are confronting the ravages of global warming. Because of the carbonization of the atmosphere and the melting of the polar ice cap, Holland is endangered by rising tides and rivers. One plan is for the republic to buy out some polder farmers, lower the dikes, and let the rivers flood the level fields when necessary. Another plan is to create a new outlet channel for the Rhine, altering the map of Europe. A worst-case scenario described by the physicist Marty Hoffert predicts: "The earth is going to become an ecological disaster, and… somebody will visit in a few hundred million years and find there were some intelligent beings who lived here for a while, but they just couldn't handle the transition from being hunter-gatherers to high technology."

Military enterprises dominated the period of the Baroque when the Dutch came into full flower. It was an age of opulence inspired by the court of Louis XIV of France (1638–1715) and was driven by the new wealth of the middle class. The visual arts blended the naturalist and the classicist styles, producing grandeur, vitality, and emotional exuberance in a manner intensely theatrical, or, to be more precise, operatic. (Opera was the child of the seventeenth century.) Baroque battle plans, such as the one by Romanus de Hooge, *Plan of the Siege of Namur* (1695; Plate 121), evoke a state of giddiness by overwhelming the senses in a painterly way familiar from the work of the Van Eyck brothers and Rembrandt—masters of topographical "realism." Engraved by Pieter Persoy of Amsterdam, Hooge's plan is a bird's-eye view of the city and chateau of Namur. It is Map as Epitome of the Baroque. The ten-month siege commanded by the king of England defeated Louis XIV's army and made it clear that Louis, France's Sun King, was not destined to become dictator of Europe. The English also successfully battled for the Dutch territories, winning Bombay (1661), New Amsterdam (1664), and Gibraltar (1704).

With only four years' respite, the seventeenth century saw continuous warfare. Thus early modern Europe has been described as a "military revolution" owing to the great changes in the way that war was waged. Initiated by the French, huge, professionally trained armies in the late fifteenth century needed maps to perform tactical maneuvers with their new firearms led by officers trained in burgeoning military academies. The heaviest financial burden borne by the states consisted of fortresses, naval arsenals, and other military structures, which needed specially trained officers to design and construct them. This group of officers took over the title "engineers." A plan showing the fortifications for a French city of Saint-Louis on the River Saar in the German Lorraine (see Plate 122) was made by Gaspar Baillieu, engraved in Paris in 1708, and printed in The Hague. It is Map as Nation's Strength. It witnesses the more classical elements in the Baroque style applied in the pattern of thick low walls and bastions—"bastioned traces"—built to replace the medieval city's high curtain-walls, easily demolished by cannon fire. These supplementary bastions of Sar-Louis forced the attacker to fire at a remove from the city center. It was the Italians, in response to French attacks, who first developed the complex, extraordinarily expensive system of bastioned traces, which required the purchase of immense tracts of land surrounding the cities to ensure a field of fire. To accurately calculate the angles of fire, these fortifications could not be built without mapmakers.

Centuries later, a different form of complex and expensive fortifications appeared in the same part of Europe. After the first battle of the Marne (September 5–10, 1914), the German army was forced to retreat, having failed to take Paris and compel France into an early surrender. In order to keep gained territory and to protect themselves from the advancing French and the new machines of warfare — the machine gun, poison gas — the Germans dug trenches, elaborate, multitiered, sprawling, and interconnected — baroque webs of trenches. The French followed suit. Soon the trenches spread from the North Sea and the English Channel to Switzerland — an estimated 600 miles of trenches dug into the countryside. A 1915 British Ordnance Survey map makes clear the scale of these trenches (Plate 123). Like inverted mud castles of defense, they were so detailed and huge an undertaking as to be similar in scope to any seventeenth-century fortification.

For more than three years, these twentieth-century enemies were stuck in trenches and reduced to the level of rodents until freed by another new war machine — the tank. They faced each other across a treacherous, muddy strip of no-man's-land, a wasteland of craters, blackened tree stumps, barbed wire, and the occasional shell of a building. Usually around 250 yards wide, the separation between the adversaries varied from 7 yards at Zonnebeke to 500 yards at Cambrai. Some of the costliest battles in the history of human warfare were fought in this amazingly narrow, bloody, shell-churned swath of Belgium and France as each side strove unsuccessfully, using outdated army traditions and head-on infantry charges across infernos of firepower, to break out of the geographic stalemate along what became known as the Western Front. (The 1930 film *All Quiet on the Western Front* captures perfectly the horror of trench warfare.) Over one-third of the Allied casualties were sustained in the trenches. It is Map as War Butchery.

PLATE 122. *Fortification for Sar-Louis.* This 1708 plan for an elaborate defense system witnesses the more classical Baroque style.

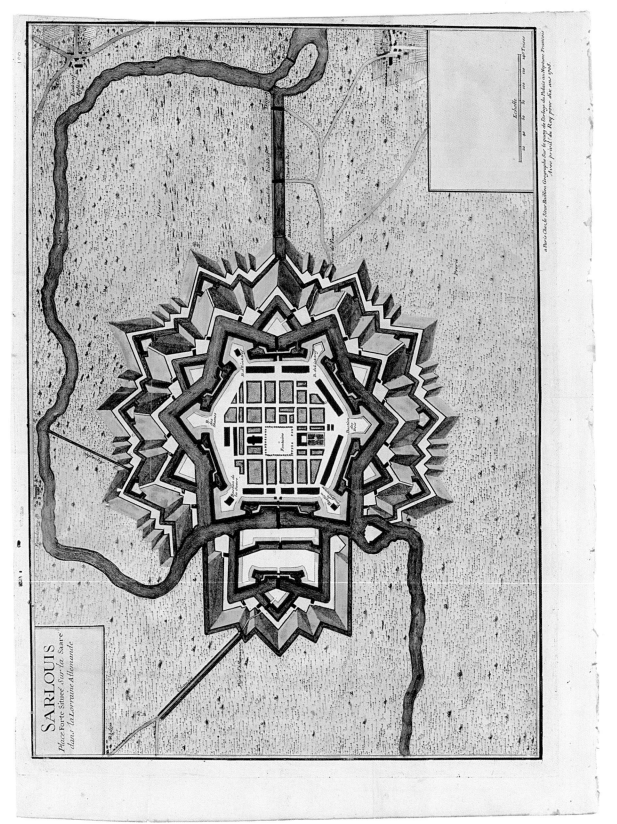

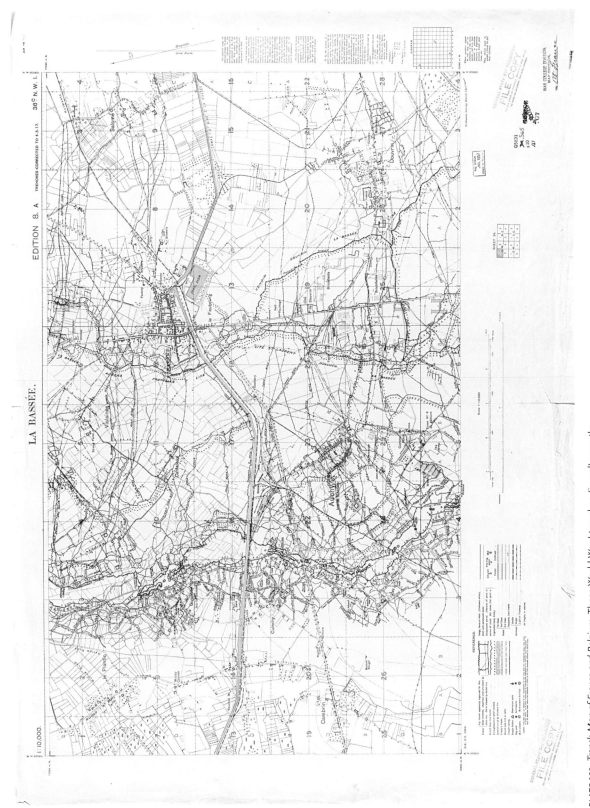

PLATE 123. *Trench Map of France and Belgium*. These World War I trenches (in red) were the deadly result of the new machines of warfare.

In the trench area near the River Somme, approximately 1,120,000 soldiers died in five months of horrific fighting.

In these trench realms, where each network extended three or four miles, there were front lines, support lines, and reserve lines, underground rooms, communications trenches, forward positions for machine gunners and sharpshooters, as well as tunnels deep beneath the trenches for placing explosives under the lines of the enemy. The high cost in human lives of trench warfare ended their use. Trenches are truly a metaphor for the Theater of War. When the curtain fell on World War I in 1918, with approximately 10 million dead, the trench stage set was struck—most of the trenches were reclaimed for farming, villages, or woods—and the scale of the epic visual trench melodrama can be experienced now only in maps that have an added poignancy. There was no single public memorial where the names of the dead soldiers were inscribed one by one to honor their stunning sacrifice, the way the courageous American soldiers who died in Vietnam were eventually honored in our nation's grieving memory for their equally deadly missions. The trench maps are a memorial to the dead, who silently insist through them, "Remember Me!"

France

The center of the European map trade began to shift from the Low Countries to France in the 1650s. French geographers with their precision measurement placed cartography on a firm scientific footing during the eighteenth century, and many of their maps reflect original surveys or firsthand accounts obtained from French engineers, explorers, and missionaries. In fact, it was the French who made military maps of primary importance during their late fifteenth-century campaign against the Italians under Charles VIII (ruled 1483–98).

It was a French king, Henry IV (ruled 1589–1610), who first used the visual language of mapping to delineate his kingdom, a much more trustworthy means of communication than performance mapping or giving verbal descriptions. Capable of making a field sketch of a proposed fort, he was acknowledged to be a man who thought everything out in images. When he reunified France legally by various treaties following decades of civil war, he then used a map of the entire country to document his successful efforts. As he so brilliantly intuited, it became a visual metaphor for his omniscient presence. Meta-mapping was born. Drawn by Joanne Joliveto, the

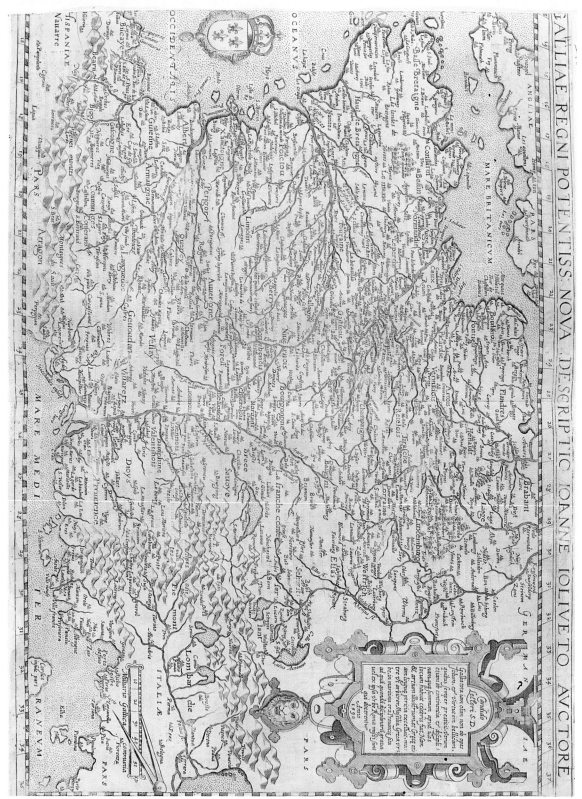

PLATE 124. *General Map of France.* This 1594 map helped create a nation.

"new description" of France (Plate 124) appeared in the first atlas of the country. Edited by Maurice Bouguereau, *Le théâtre françoys* was published in 1594, and ostentatiously dedicated to the king via an engraved portrait and nine quatrains written to honor him and to dramatize his triumph. It was the prototype of all future French atlases. The map became Henry's throne from which he could invent "France" in space and history. The disorder and political rivalries of the individual wartorn provinces, along with some of their contentious allegiances to Spain, are nowhere to be seen. The provinces appear gathered in an organized and seemingly objective, stable manner. Their marriage is sanctified by Henry's divine right as the sixty-third successive king, a fact documented by a list beginning in 417 with Haramond. It is Map as Space Becoming Place.

Henry IV was the first French king to implement a systematic program of cartographic inquiry. He used maps to settle territorial disputes between provinces and surrounding nations. Administrative linear boundaries replaced dynastic frontier regions. Thus his surveyors were used to combat threats from within as well as from outside his kingdom. Cartography became synonymous with royal authority. It endowed the king with godlike powers in the national space *he* constructed. Henry relied heavily upon the rhe-

torical power of maps as instruments of persuasion and as forms of narration. Encouraged by the political needs of Henry IV, Joliveto tells a story about the physical and conceptual nature of his world predicated on the belief that France is an extension of the king's body. The interlocking proximity of the French provinces on his map implies a network of fluid relations overseen by a prudent legislator, a single, thinking royal planner who has carefully woven them together in the theater of his own sovereign vision.

The mathematics, particularly geometry, used by Henry's surveyors, and by his son Louis XIII's cartographers, led the great French philosopher René Descartes (1596–1650), a devout, conservative Roman Catholic, to create a theory of the universe adhering to medieval theology and the Bible, which contradicted Galileo's "heretical" belief in the earth's revolving around the sun. However, living as he did during the Scientific Revolution, which was precipitated by the rise of rationalist science in modern Europe, Descartes was also fully committed to higher mathematics, with its necessitating clear and distinct ideas, and logical deduction. This age-old conflict in belief systems pushed him to scientific extremes.

Unlike Galileo, who applied mathematics to physical reality and became the founder of mathematical physics—the heliocentric sys-

114 Principiorum Philosophiæ

PLATE 125. *Descartes's Mechanical Universe.* The ideas behind this 1644 map of the universe came to dominate modern Western thought.

tem embodied a physical truth—Descartes refused to distinguish between physics and mathematics. He reduced all natural phenomena to a branch of mechanics, all science to a form of applied mathematics. "I do not accept or desire," he wrote, "any other principle in physics than in geometry or abstract mathematics, because all the phenomena of nature may be explained by their means." Discarding the qualitative aspects of nature, he concluded its order was solely mathematical, and the physical world an entirely mechanical one divorced from all spirituality, transformed—as Henry's France had been by the mathematics of mapping—into an object. This rationalist view of the world, this purely quantitative understanding of the order of nature displayed in Descartes's map of the universe, came to dominate modern Western philosophy and science, completely obliterating the religious and qualitative one. The mathematics of nature became the philosophy of nature. Earth and Heaven lost all metaphysical and cosmological sense when the West wholeheartedly adopted this new "mechanical philosophy."

While Henry, the creator of modern France, strove to bring all France under one system of government using cartography, Descartes, the father of modern Western philosophy, strove to reduce all natural phenomena to one system composed of motion. The map of the universe he created for his book *Principia Philosophiae* (1644; Plate 125) shows it as a continuously running machine, which God set in motion. It is Map as the New Order of Nature. Since his religious beliefs rejected Galileo's theory of planetary motion and Newton's theory of gravity, as well as the idea of a vacuum in space, Descartes argued that the universe was composed of a "subtle matter" he named "plenum," which swirled in vortices, like whirlpools, and actually moved the planets by contact. In his map, these vortices carry the planets on their rounds. His idea, like Henry's map of a unified France, assumes all tensions between competing factions are resolved. Both maps changed the world in which they appeared.

In discourse with Descartes and his idea of nature as a machine, allegorical maps became a seventeenth-century vogue in France. The most famous, *La carte de Tendre* (Map of Tenderness) by Madeleine de Scudéry, appeared in her ten-volume heroic novel, *Clélie, Histoire romaine,* in 1654 (see Plate 126). Drawn without scale, though the legend claims it adheres to the Leagues of Friendship (*Lieues d'amitié*), and with a purposeful return to a time before scientific methods came to dominate cartography, the map offers a utopian world where women are in charge. It is Map as Sensibility of the Heart. By charting a field of possibility, not of certainty, it created an image of emotional subjectivity diametrically opposed to both Descartes's certainty of mind and Henry's nationalist claims for cartographic objectivity. In Scudéry's novel, the heroine Clélie disobeys her father and creates her own gauntlet for her admirers to run—both male and female—in order for them to achieve her highest accolade: Tender Friendship. Thus, the field of geography was transformed on her map into a realm of allegory, with the towns representing courtship strategies: The villages of Pleasing Verses and A Gallant Letter are important stops for the initiate in the land of Tender.

If Clélie was not captivated, her pursuer might get lost in the *Lac d'indifference,* while others moved directly from *Nouvelle amitié* up the *Inclination Fleuve* to *Tendre*—Tender Friendship. The map illustrates the novel's central theme: the ultimate goal of the human heart and its most profound gratification is asexual psychological intimacy, a variant of courtly love, medieval France's *gai sabar* (gay science, or happy wisdom), which was a form of paganism that redefined traditional Christian ideals of love, marriage, manhood, virtue, and femininity. *Tendre* was reached only when relationships were viewed as a courtship adventure; they were a matter of Clélie and Scudéry's personal selection, not mechanistic, preordained social orders. The map can be read as a fantasy world of a powerful feminist devoted to theoretical discourse, who ruled over her weekly salon like a queen, with adherents situated like loyal subjects within her topography of love and desire. *La carte de Tendre* was a meeting of science and the poetry scorned by Descartes. It was a literary excursion into the language of cartography that refused to disengage the representation of space from the visual language of art.

Under Louis XIV's seventy-two-year reign (1643–1715), France became a world power and a cultural leader in Europe. Louis used

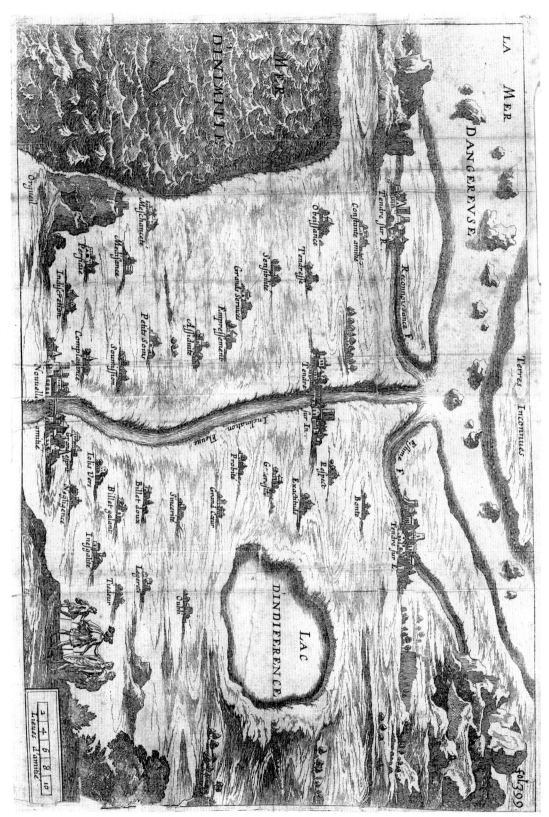

the bourgeoisie to build his centralized bureaucracy. Curtailing local authorities, he created specialized ministries, filled by professionals responsible directly to him. His comptroller general of finances, Jean-Baptiste Colbert (1619–83), was one of the great exponents of mercantilism, an economic system dependent upon foreign trade for gold that superseded the medieval feudal organization of Western Europe. Colbert's goal was to make France economically self-sufficient. To this end, he constructed shipyards, arsenals, and harbors while developing a navy and placing hydrographic surveying on a scientific basis. And as a great patron of the arts and science, he contributed significantly to the splendor of Louis XIV's reign.

In the 1650s, Colbert commissioned a group of mathematicians and astronomers of the Academy of Sciences, which he founded along with the Paris Observatory, to map the coasts of the European continent from Norway to Gibraltar. Supported by Colbert's passions for art and science, the French Admiralty published in Paris *Le Neptune françois* in 1693. A pirated edition with exquisite plates created by Romanus de Hooge was printed in Amsterdam the same year. It was the most opulent and the most expensive sea atlas the Dutch published that century. It was never intended for use on board ship, but was created for commercial offices and libraries.

It is Map as Mercantilism. The French towns shown in the elaborate cartouches on the page from the atlas showing the environs of L'Isle d'Oleron (Plate 127) were living symbols of successful trade.

Although the Dutch dominated the market for charts and sea atlases throughout the seventeenth century, French hydrographers transformed the science of charting the waters—oceans, rivers, lakes—at a time when Dutch maritime power was declining. (By 1682 hydrography was being taught in French public schools, and three naval-guard schools had been created in France.) The shortcomings of the Dutch charts were emphasized by the scientific precision of the French hydrographers, and France soon became the center of geographical science extravagantly funded by royal edict.

The maps were generally drawn on the mathematical projection created by Gerard Mercator in 1569; it transformed the curved surface of the entire earth into a flat surface, and replaced the projections constructed by Ptolemy to deal with only a small portion of the globe, his known world. Mercator's goal had been to produce a new map sailors could use, a map with straight lines that were

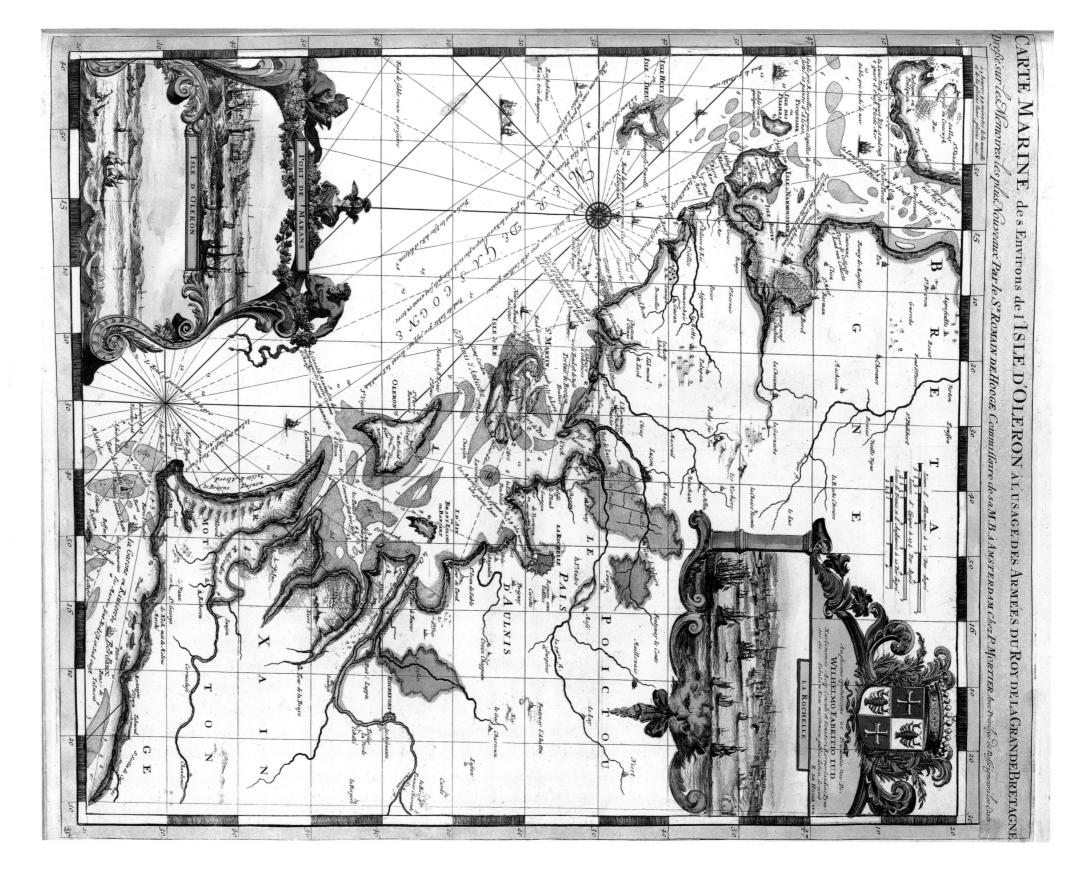

like rhumb lines on the curving sea. His projection, he wrote, "spreads the surface of the globe out flat so that places are in the correct position relative to each other, both as regards direction and distance, and with the current latitudes and longitudes." Though the projection caused gross distortions of landmasses, born of its time, it depicted the world as a stage for trade by successfully producing a map with lines of constant bearing in the tradition of portolan charts. It was the perfect choice for a nautical atlas.

Along with nautical maps, Colbert wanted *useful* maps of France in order to build roads and canals and bridges. The need to fully grasp the actuality of his territorial domain inspired Louis XIV to invite Giovanni Cassini, astronomer and surveyor of fortifications, to move to Paris from Bologna in 1669. Cassini had expanded upon Galileo's tables of the eclipses of Jupiter's four major moons as a means of fixing longitudes on Earth. His work reconfigured France's coastline, and all the maps of Europe were deemed obsolete. The

CARTE DE FRANCE LEVÉE PAR ORDRE DU ROY PREMIERE FEUILLE

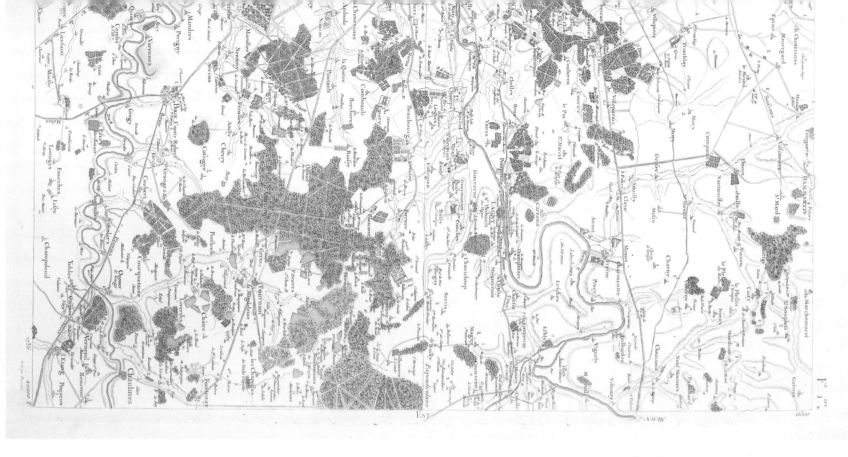

invitation also produced the first multisheet (182), topographic map series of an entire country using uniform standards and symbols but very different realistic symbolism to render the terrain: forests are actual clusters of trees, mountains are descriptively rendered, and all is seen from a single viewpoint above the earth as if through Apollo's eyes and by extension through the eyes of Louis XIV, the Sun King. The Italian Cassini seems to have brought with him, and introduced to cartography, Leonardo da Vinci's teachings on drawing from life. Four succeeding generations of the Cassini family worked over one hundred years to complete, in 1789, *Cartegéométrique de la France*, or more commonly, *Carte de Cassini*.

The assembled map forms approximately a 36-foot square, and was based on a network of some 40,000 meticulously surveyed triangles. They established the basic principles of national mapping still in use today. The Cassinis' accuracy of geographical knowledge and the efficiency of their surveying techniques constructed what is essentially a spatial paradigm fit to accommodate a national vision. Their work was also of immediate political relevance for the fate of the monarchy. Unlike Joliveto's general map of France in Bouguereau's atlas of French provinces, which promulgated the ancient dynastic identification between the land and the body of the monarch, the Cassini atlas, with its recognizable topography and land use (cultural landscape) contributed to a conception of nationhood by articulating the terrain owned by French citizens. What people saw was what they knew. It is no accident that the Cassini project was published during the French Revolution. No longer the sole property of the king, the rivers of France became the economic circulatory system of these new citizens of France. The coastline itself, the lines for rivers, and the lines depicting both the natural features and the buildings of France are equated with the lines for administrative borders. It is a fusion of geography and history. It conceives of space not only in terms of political power but also in terms of its social and cultural uniqueness, since the space is configured as France.

Unlike the profoundly negative symbolic function of a map at the start of *King Lear*, where the cartographic image of a unified kingdom is a visual prelude to a process of political disintegration, Louis XIV's Cassini map of France became, for the revolutionary government, a symbol of the nation's new, cohesive order of existence. It is Map as Mirror of French Society. The Cassini map helped redefine the relationship between the self and the space of the world. The People of France, not the king of France, became the ideal substance of Cassini's map.

One goal of the French Revolution was to make study both patriotic and pleasurable. To this end, the eighty-three departments created to replace the old geographical system of provinces were made to function as a board game in 1795 (see Plate 129). Derived from one of the most ancient of all known children's games, Game of the Goose, the numbered departments were arranged in a spiral leading to a winner's circle. In the center, revolutionary rhetoric permeates the instructions on how to play the game. The winner's circle, for example, contains various symbols of the Revolution and the phrase *Liberté, égalité*. (Ironically, the innermost department in the spiral is the island of Corsica, home of Napoleon.) The individual maps of the departments are quite detailed and are assembled in the form of France in the circle on the map's lower right corner outside the parameters of the game, mimicking, in theory, what was occurring in the children's heads within the parameters of the game. Though annexed by France in 1791, Avignon (on the

PLATE 128. *Department of Paris*. The French Revolution found new meanings in this map, from the Cassini family's topographic survey of France.

the wealthy. The region was also known as the Woodland because, when viewed from above, the dense growth of trees created a blanket of green, as on the map. In the south, supported by the disgruntled Roman Church and encouraged by England, a provisionary government was formed, intending to march against Paris and drive the revolution onto the rocks—wishful thinking encour-

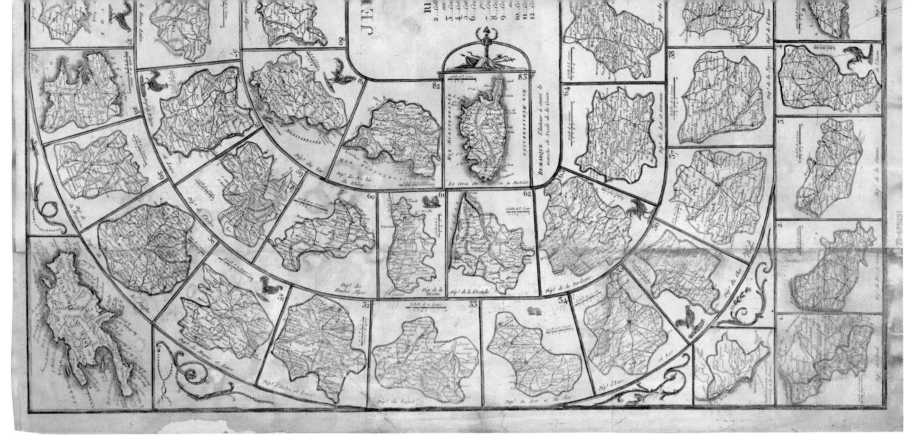

far left) is also not included in the game, because the annexation of the former papal state was not sanctioned by Rome until 1797. The city of Paris (Ville-de-Paris), center of the uprising and evermore the symbolic heart of France, has its own square on the game board because it is one of the country's departments.

The expulsion of the Jesuits from France between 1762 and 1764 for preparing students only for ecclesiastical careers had a great impact on French education. The religious order had managed 106 colleges—about one-quarter to one-third of the "secondary" schools in the kingdom. The reformers wanted standardized geography textbooks and reasoning to replace memorization in order for the students to grasp the elementary principles that lifted geography into the category of sciences. Knowing the importance of winning the support of the young if France's new incarnation were to last, the leaders of the Revolution adopted and systematized these plans. Maps were to be useful tools in making the French people citizens of the world, while supporting the political actions of the Revolution.

The first official French school atlas after the Revolution was an atlas of the new departments. The resulting game board offered children the same information in a form they could enjoy. As with all play, the game became a joint enterprise, just as the Revolution had made France a communal enterprise for everyone. It is Map as Game Plan. Old and abusive France had been replaced by a new, regenerated, remodeled France of which her children were to be aware and proud. Everything was different, even the contours of France's face.

Appearing in England at around the same time as the cartographic game was a propaganda cartoon map of France (see Plate 130) that literally transformed the new republic into an unmoored ship of state on the rocks. It is Map as Wishful Thinking. Published in London in 1796, the map was made in support of the monarchy and memorializes in a central box below the image the beheaded Louis XVI, Marie Antoinette, and the rest of the dead aristocrats. Its text condemns the influence of the "assassins" of the Revolution in all the "provinces," except those in the south and west. They are distinguished as land on the map to the upper left of the ship, and as rocks to the south. The metaphoric loosed anchor is below the broken mast on which a fleur-de-lis flag is shown floating, and a rowboat, inhabited by counterrevolutionaries (identified on the map), approaches to save it—"The Vendeans, remaining steadfast in the royal cause...are supposed embarked to recover the lost standard of their ancient constitution."

The map is a paean of praise for the Vendée revolt (1793–96), which began in the region surrounding the Loire River. This rural Roman Catholic area was loyal to the fallen king and opposed the new republic's taxes, conscription, abolition of ancient regional and local privileges, and selling of confiscated Church lands to

PLATE 129. *A Geographical Board Game of the Republic of France.* The aims of the French Revolution are glorified by this map.

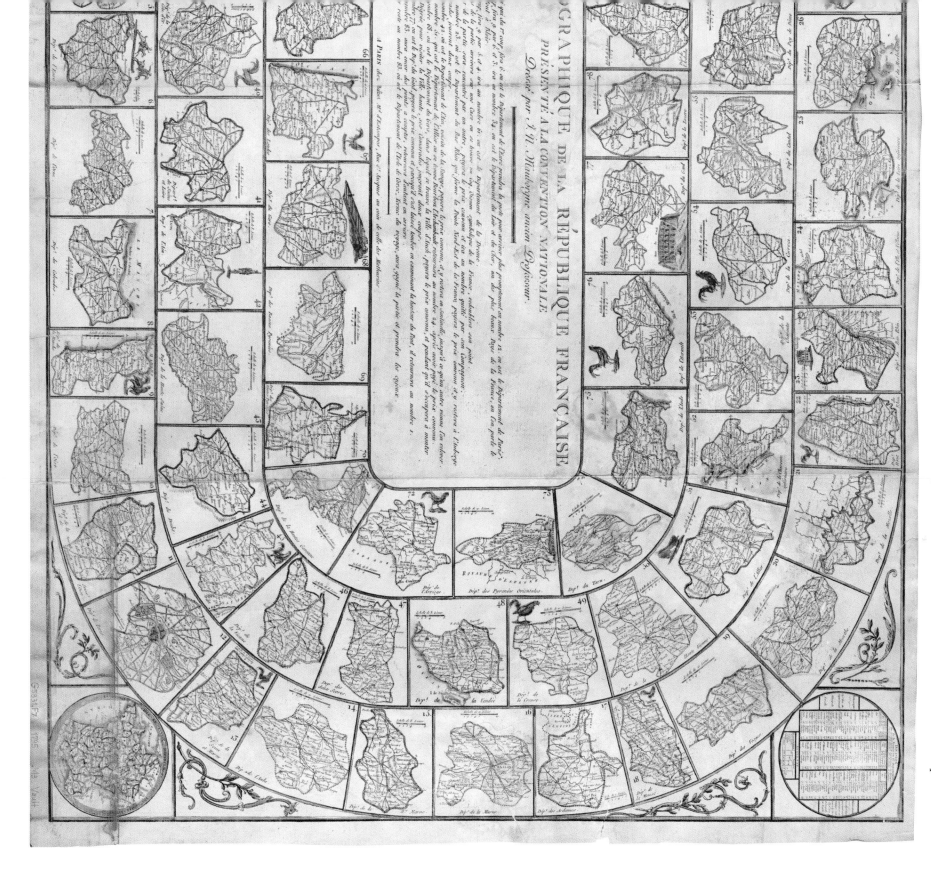

aged by the English map. Two hundred thousand died fighting in the unsuccessful insurrection, the denouement of the French Revolution.

Ironically, whether the English monarchists intended it or not, the French king's privileged inner space of a kingdom has been replaced on the map by the universal symbol of wide-open vistas

and liberty—a ship. This map inadvertently reflects the changed terms of the game of life in France at the end of the eighteenth century. Even the rocks on which the ship "founders" had a different symbolic meaning for the French revolutionaries, because it was with rocks that they broke the stained-glass windows of St-Denis to protest the links between church and state. Liberty was the ideal

England and Ireland

In the eighteenth and nineteenth centuries, when they ruled the world, the English came to dominate the map trade. However, it was in the late sixteenth century that their commitment to the visual language of mapping came to the fore. It gained preeminence in the property market. Originally estate boundaries were casually set by perambulations, another form of performance mapping. Until the 1540s, disputes were settled by the verbal testimonies of twelve "good and lawful" parish men. Then, inspired by French surveying advances, a new form of Western mapping appeared in England: the meticulously detailed estate map. Like the Japanese, who often mapped only the territory under discussion, leaving the surrounding areas blank, the English estate map concerned itself solely with the property at hand. As demonstrated by John Franklin's 1767 hand-colored plan of Robert Earl Granville's mansion house, land, and gardens (Plate 131), it focused on one privately controlled property, one form of rural enterprise. It is Map as Social Evolution. If the subject's occupied land was not of a piece, the disparate portions were connected by simple boundary outlines of the intervening properties. Franklin's estate atlas of twelve manuscript maps, mostly by Franklin himself, provides a graphic inventory of the earl's entire estate, divided into tenanted properties in the vicinity of Hawns Parish, Bedford County (Bedfordshire).

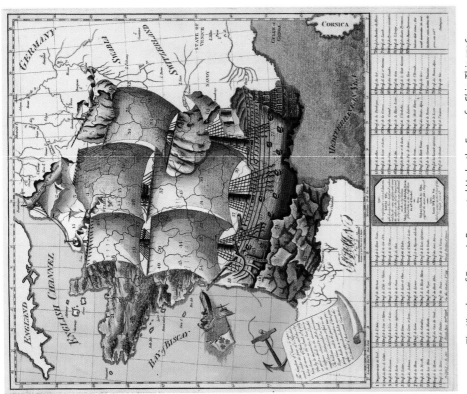

PLATE 130. *The Kingdom of France Is Represented Under the Form of a Ship.* This 1796 English map transforms the new Republic of France into an unmoored ship.

toward which Europe had slowly progressed. The abstract, theoretical notion of liberty, evolving through the late Middle Ages, the Italian and Northern Renaissance, and the Reformation, became a political reality when the French Revolution, in theory, freed the peasant holdings from their feudal dues. The 1789 Declaration of the Rights of Man and of the Citizen remains a landmark in the history of freedom and a cornerstone in the development of European civilization. Liberalism, its attendant philosophical doctrine, strove for freedom of thought, maintaining that religious unity was not necessary for social or national unity.

Along with maps of the departments in schools, the values of France, and certainly its secular imperatives, were inculcated in the students from the earliest age. They were, and still are, taught that "France" was an idea of citizenship, an identity forged in the neutral space of its public schools, a place apart, which Jules Ferry, the nineteenth-century educator, called the *école sanctuaire*. Children were to be guaranteed freedom of thought and of expression in schools, at liberty to explore the world with wide-open vistas before them, but forbidden to display religious symbols.

To a revolutionist, the idea of France as a ship of state is another form of serious play. By its very nature, being a work of art, the map makes the spectator a player in *its* game of shipboard life, as it boldly evokes Descartes, who said, "One must always serve the interests of the whole of which one is a part." Cut free of its anchor to the past, France seems to be flying into the future on the map, secure in any coming storm.

For centuries, to avoid state bankruptcy, the rulers of England sold off the royal forests to aristocratic entrepreneurs, who indiscriminately cut them down to build houses and, most urgently, ships with which England could conquer the world and maintain national security. Trees were known as the "wooden walls" of the kingdom. (Rumor had it that the wreckage of the Spanish Armada's flagship *San Lorenzo* contained a note from King Philip ordering the destruction of England's great Forest of Dean.) With a large ship requiring two thousand mature oaks, the enclosure laws came to mean clearance permission. Presciently, the Dutch had bought entire Norwegian forests. Their successor in the power game with England at the end of the seventeenth century was France, where the royal forests were protected from deforestation by laws initiated by Abbot Suger of St.-Denis when he was regent of France in 1147. Suger became aware of the need for reforestation when he had trouble finding tall, old-growth trees to support the columns during the construction of his Gothic cathedral. English environmentalists took a leaf from the French history books. In 1758, nine years before Franklin's drawings were made, prizes were given by the Royal Society for the Encouragement of the Arts to the landowners who planted the most acorns to renew England's supply of the national oak, which became a symbol of both wealth and patriotism.

Keeping track of landed gentry's property was not new in England. Written records were maintained as far back as the middle of the eleventh century. However, estates of the landed gentry grew rapidly after Henry VIII (ruled 1509–47) broke from Rome in order to divorce his first and fourth wives and execute his second and fifth. (The Pope's refusal to grant Henry an annulment was a political miscalculation, since he had done so for others.) Henry distributed confiscated Roman Catholic Church lands to his obedient, wealthy subjects, and consolidated open fields through enclosure laws. Local land surveyors drew large-scale plans, and hand-colored and elegantly decorated them. Picture maps were sometimes done in watercolor of the landholdings, but the estate map quickly evolved into a more scientific exercise, such as the 1767 one by Franklin, whose drawings provided an inventory of the rural landscape, especially its valuable and controversial trees (see sidebar).

When an English "estate" was an entire country, such as Ireland, the map took a more general approach. Historically, the Gauls or French Celts (Keltoi) are the true ancestors of modern Europe. According to the popular historians Jones and Ereira, Celtic settlements on the Atlantic coast represented a network of interlinked societies, possibly indigenous, that spanned the continent and paralleled the Greeks along the Mediterranean as far back as the fourth century BCE. By Shakespeare's time, however, the propagandizing Roman and Catholic historians had transformed the great Celts, whose Celtic-Christian monks had helped save Western civilization, into barbarous

Irish animals. Ireland was synonymous with political unrest and rebellion, which could spread to England if not contained by strong intervention.

Between 1775 and 1790, Lt. Col. Charles Vallancey made a military survey of Ireland in case the British needed to defend it *after it* had been invaded by France or Spain. On his map showing Bagenbon Bay between Waterford and Wexford is a note observing that "Strongbow"—Richard de Clare, Earl of Pembroke—landed there in 1171, having backed the losing side in England's civil war. "If an enemy invades this island," Vallancey wrote, "it will certainly be with a sufficient force to keep possession of it for some time." Thus the detailed overview of the landscape—the roads, the cultivated fields, the bogs, the mountain passes. Landlords, tenants, and tiny villages are rarely identified, signifying the absence of a notable culture in the mapmaker's mind. The scale is given in both English and Irish measurements.

Another map (see Plate 132) shows the survey from the River Barro to Clonegall through the pass of the Black Mountains, and part of the road from Ross to Dublin through Tullo. For the most part, on Vallancey's survey maps all the local names in Ireland became a jumble of the Irish with approximate English sounds, or were replaced with

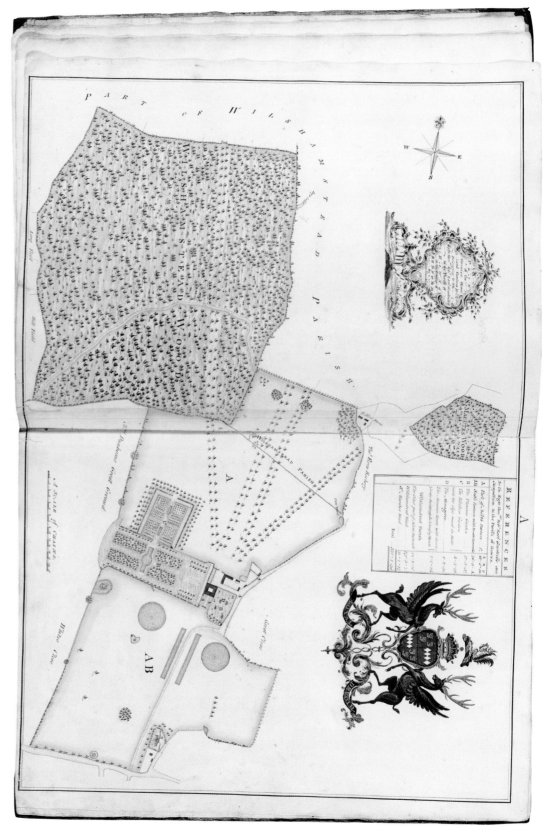

English names—the Irish Sea is "St. George's Channel," for instance. It is an eradication of history, a final act of reprisal against the obstreperous Irish, and the changed names on the landscape created a further barrier between the Irish and the English. Erasure of local identity is a spiritual and mental invasion. It is Map as Intellectual Appropriation of Space. It advances the social vision of the conquerors by writing the defeated people out of history, because names contain the record of a complex relationship with place. Vallancey's focus on the landscape, and not on the proprietary boundaries imposed on the regional topography, reveals a military, not political or economic, basis for the work he undertook as a cartographer. His map embodies a specific form of power and authority. It is working to create a different reality in Ireland, one that never

took root in the history-laden Celtic soul, though a stratum of ethnic consciousness did disappear from there forever, thanks to the imperialist British and maps like this one.

By the time of Vallancey's map, Ireland had been assigned a fixed place within an international British constellation. In need of safekeeping, it was a royal plantation for English and Scottish colonizers in the geographic neighborhood of the British Isles. Of all the changes wrought by the English on the Irish landscape, the destruction of its trees was probably the most devastating. Irish oaks provided the roofs of great buildings and the masts of British ships. Once covered by trees, Ireland had only one percent of its forests left at the time of its independence in 1922. This map is about Ireland's forced integration into the British economy, and except for an Irish-sounding name, Ireland is addressed visually as one of many British colonies under military occupation.

A scientifically accurate map of Ireland was made by Queen Victoria's Ordnance Survey team from 1833 to 1846. Every historic site, every church, every school, every gravel pit, every spring, every road, every parish pump, house, and business, and everything else of note was recorded on the six-inch maps (six inches to the mile). The place names on the OSI (Ordnance Survey Ireland) map were based on the work of John O'Donovan, an Irish scholar employed to verify them. Names were standardized, which was assumed less a cultural oppression than Anglicizing or changing them. So, for example, Bun Abhann, signifying "river mouth," which was where the parish was situated, became Bunowen. And Bogan Buidhe' (yellow soft ground) became Bogganboy. Except in the Gaeltacht areas, where Irish was spoken, these English-friendly names became second nature to the local people, who still recognized an Irish geography in the landscape.

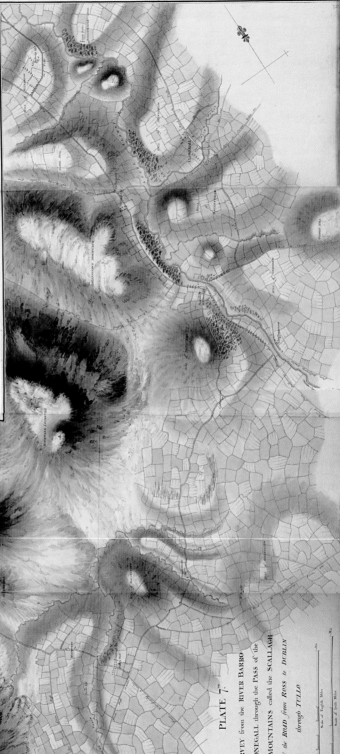

PLATE 132. *The Military Survey of Ireland.* The intellectual appropriation of space is the story behind this 1776 British map of Ireland.

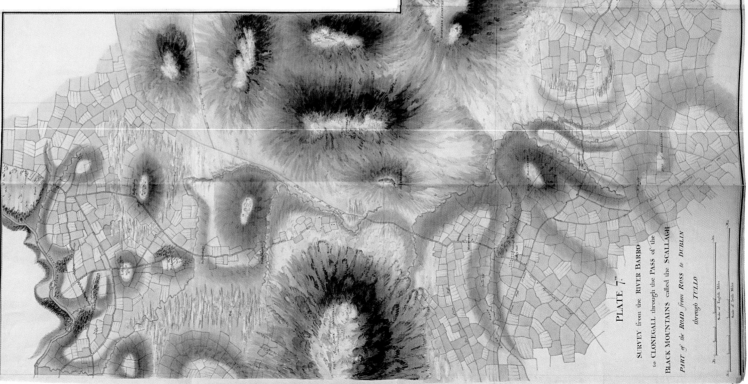

PLATE 7.

SURVEY from the RIVER BARRO
to CLOSEGALL through the PASS of the
BLACK MOUNTAINS called the SCALLAGH

PART of the ROAD from ROSS to DUBLIN
through TULLO

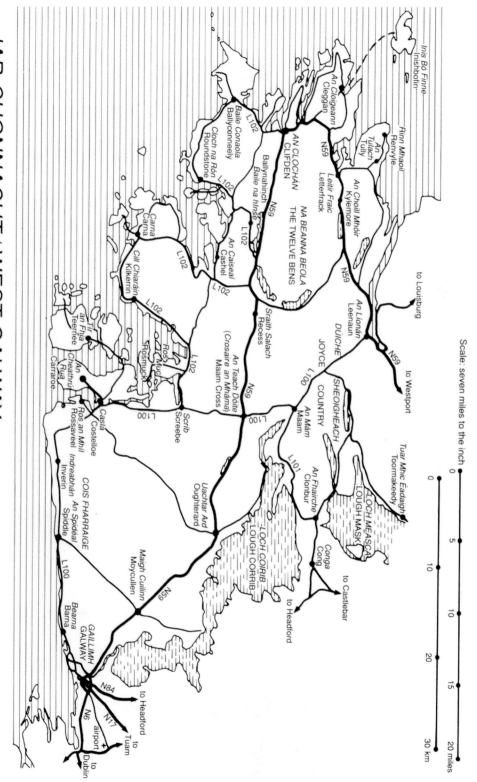

PLATE 133: *A Basic Bilingual Route Map. Cultural heritage is made manifest by this 1990 map of Ireland.*

When recently mapping Connemara, a Gaeltacht region in the county of Galway and the province of Connacht, Tim Robinson, an award-winning British writer and cartographer, relied upon the names as he heard them spoken, even if they were grammatically suspect. Wherever an English or Anglicized name was most used, he placed it on his 1990 map (Plate 133), though he often substituted the Irish name: "My justification of this bias," he wrote, "is implicit in the map as a whole." It is Map as Cultural Restoration. It restores the commercial nature of his mapping in a culture that valued scientific knowledge as a means to gain power over nature. For him, knowledge from geology offered the physical means to subdue nature. Like the Reformation and the French Revolution, the Industrial Revolution left no one unaffected. Along with Descartes and his mechanistic universe, it is a key to the origins of modern Western society.

Ireland's spatial and political integrity. It demonstrates how power is exerted on cartography, as well as *with* it. The basic topography of his map is that of the British Ordnance Survey of 1898, brought up to date by Robinson's 1982–89 fieldwork on foot and bicycle. His translation of geography and the man-made world into a graphic image uses the power of language to capture the spirit of the place and to transform cartography into a personal, expressive art steeped in self-esteem.

From the beginning of the nineteenth century in Great Britain, geological maps were used regularly, especially in conjunction with mining operations. The developing Industrial Revolution in England was fueled by coal, mined since the thirteenth century. As a child of this revolution, the so-called father of the science of geology, William Smith (1769–1839), married geology to its economic value. His cartographic work was one of the engines transforming the society in which he lived. Smith was a man of his particular time and place, and his pragmatic goal was to apply his observations and ideas to the everyday needs of the canal builders, quarry and mine owners, landowners, and agriculturalists, who were optimistic and progressive like himself. He was perfectly clear about the commercial nature of his mapping in a culture that valued scientific knowledge as a means to gain power over nature. For him, knowledge from geology offered the physical means to subdue nature. Like the Reformation and the French Revolution, the Industrial Revolution left no one unaffected. Along with Descartes and his mechanistic universe, it is a key to the origins of modern Western society.

Coal miners were aware of regular successions of workable coal seams, but Smith recognized, through direct observation as a canal-site surveyor, both the chronological succession of fossils in the rock strata and the fact that sedimentary rocks could be identified by the fossils they contained. Traveling for his work, he discovered these rocks always arranged in the same order all over England. He drew up a table of successive strata in their descending order, an early version of the geological column, from chalk to coal, beyond which not much was known. He then devised from the fossils present the age of geological formations, and, while laying the foundations for a new science, almost dislodged the popular Christian belief that the world had been created at 9 a.m. on Monday, October 23, 4004 BCE, in six days as described in Genesis.

In 1799 Smith drew and colored his first geological map of the area around Bath, England, and in 1801, he produced a small geological map of England and Wales. It colorfully illustrated the outcrops of seven geological formations, and revealed what lurked beneath the cultural landscape. Then, in 1815, he produced the first geological atlas of a country, England, titled *A Delineation of the Strata of England and Wales*, applying the same coloring technique. Among the fifteen maps in the atlas, the one of southwestern England (Plate 134) typifies the vivid hand-applied watercolors used to indicate various geological strata—dark green is chalk; deep gray is coal. It is Map as Means to Subdue Nature. His work was instrumental in the establishment of the Geological Survey, which undertook in 1835 the geological mapping of Britain at the scale of one inch to a mile. Thanks to having the first European central bank and a developed credit market, a labor surplus from the unemployment due to enclosure laws, few constraints on domestic economy, no environmental consciousness, and enough coal to run all the machines, England became the first industrial nation on earth. Smith's map displayed the supporting skeleton beneath the new body politic.

Germany and the Balkan Peninsula

The year William Smith was born in England, 1769, Alexander von Humboldt was born in Berlin. An assiduous traveler and mapmaker of Western Europe, South America, and North America, Humboldt became a friend and geographic adviser to Thomas Jefferson, possibly inspiring the Lewis and Clark expedition. It was Humboldt, one of the founders of modern geography, who developed and publicized the concept of empirical research in nature, to him too vast and powerful ever to be subdued. All of Western

PLATE 134. *Geological Map of Southwestern England.* One of the cornerstones of modern society rests in this 1815 geological map.

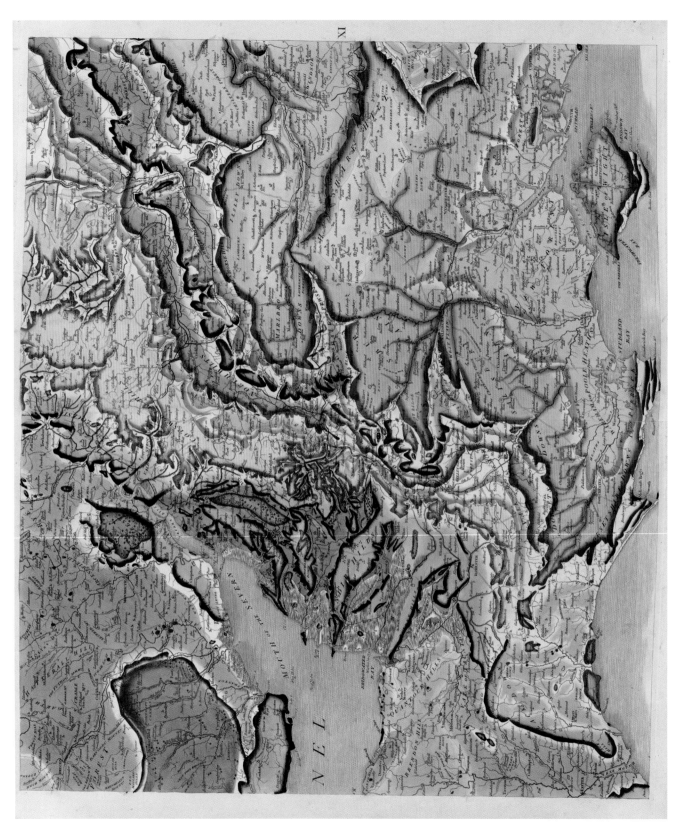

natural science was influenced by his genius. He lived and worked in the nineteenth century when "Germany" was a confederation of thirty-nine sovereign powers, and Europe was experiencing the unification of people with common cultures into national states as a way to quench revolutions and restore a semblance of order after decades of war.

With his enduring diligence and devotion to duty, his conscientiousness in the smallest details, and his passion for knowledge, Alexander von Humboldt epitomized the idealized German character—one of the great ethnic complexes of Europe and a basic stock in the composition of the peoples of northern Europe. These "Germanic" attributes were expressed in the language of cartography for centuries in various places, including the Low Countries, and were admired throughout central Europe and Russia. (In Prague, Kafka wrote in German.) Following France, Germany became the primary center of influence, and much of the nineteenth century's scholarly research in geography, cartography, and art history emerged from there. The language of mapping, however, had already been codified elsewhere. For the most part, the Germans

PLATE 135: *Plant Geography.* The "Germanic" sensibility is embedded in this 1845 map.

poured their genius into perfecting existing forms, many born in the Germanic imagination as it flourished in many peoples.

Though Humboldt did develop graphic techniques for portraying his data, it was his colleague Heinrich Berghaus (1797–1884) who perfected a new cartographic image to provide a quickly grasped overview of complex and varied data. The famous Larousse encyclopedia in 1867 declared Berghaus, not the world-renowned Humboldt, the "most illustrious representative" of the science of geography, probably as a result of his great *Physikalischer Atlas* (published in installments, 1838–48). Based on Humboldt's idea, it was the first atlas designed to describe the earth's physical characteristics. The atlas also relied upon Humboldt's vision, data (his botanical collection alone contained about sixty thousand plants), and his cartographic techniques. For example, to illustrate in Plate 135 the distribution of various types of vegetation growing on the vertical plane at different altitudes on mountains, Humboldt provided the sketch of the Andes (top left), and Berghaus produced the other four using data from the Danish natural scientist Joskim Schouw (1789–1852). Schouw also contributed the data for the

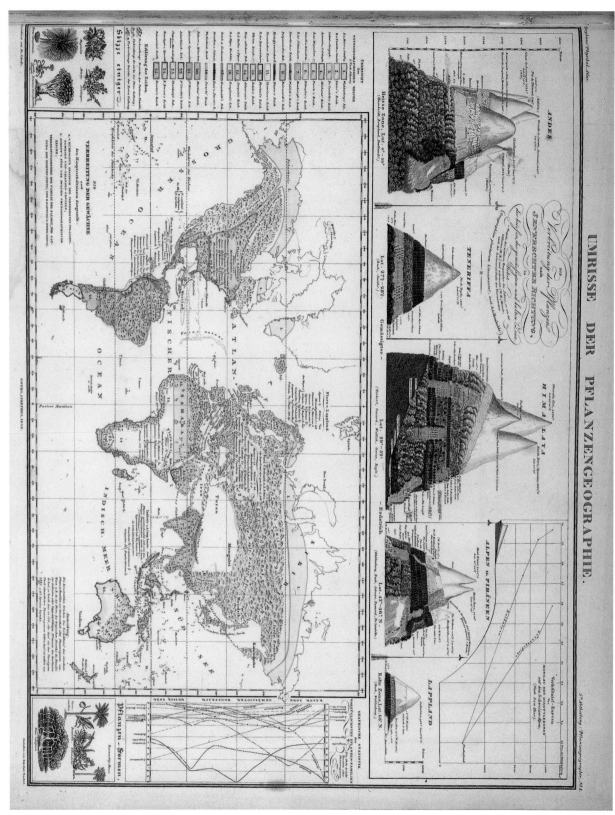

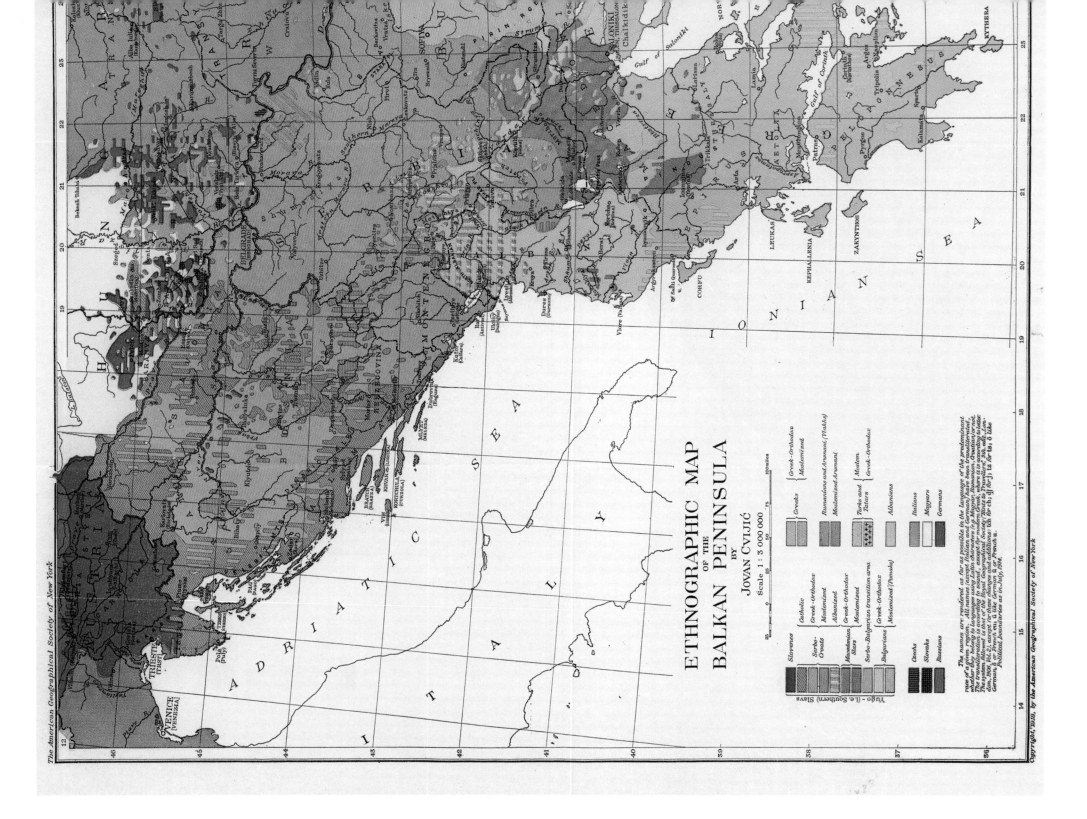

ETHNOGRAPHIC MAP
OF THE
BALKAN PENINSULA
BY
JOVAN CVIJIĆ

Scale 1 : 3 000 000

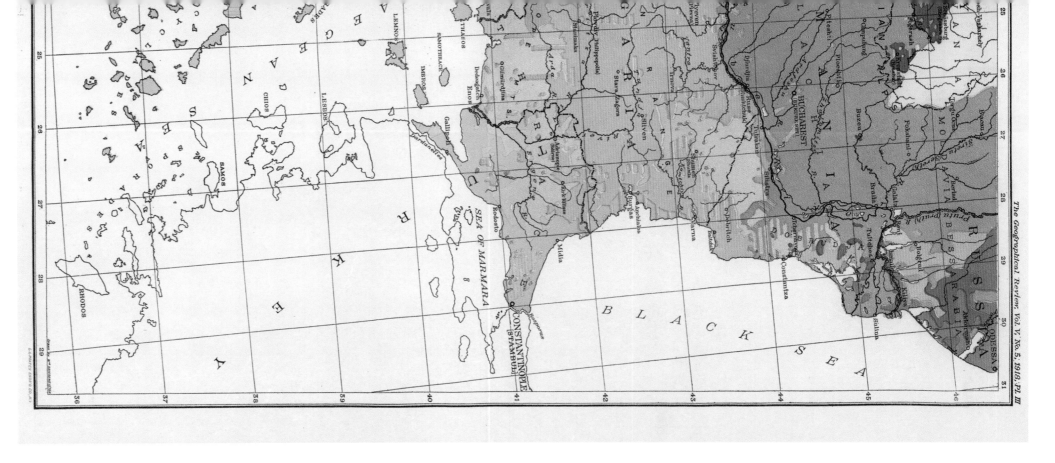

The Geographical Review, Vol. V, No. 5, 1918, Pl. III

variations in plant life on a horizontal plane—the entire earth. The colors and numbers identify the plant groups listed to the left of the world map; nine plant forms are illustrated in the lower corners. Percentages are given of the plants as well.

Basically the map is an illustrated mini-textbook. It tried to *picture* the world. With the emotional force of landscape painting, it aimed to mirror nature. It is Map as Treasury. It placed nature at the center of human experience, and made nature the place from which humanity emerged, not something lodged in the eye, disposable, like coal dust. The physical atlas opened new vistas to the curious and the traveler eager to see with his or her own eyes what only Germany's most insatiable scholar and dark alter-ego, Faust, had been able to see when carried around the earth in the arms of Mephistopheles. And the physical atlas had a much lower price tag than Faust's journey.

In 1918, at the end of World War I, Jovan Cvijić, a Serbian nationalist, published an ethnographic map in the tradition of Humboldt (Plate 136). But Cvijić had a political agenda with horrifying consequences. It is Map as Inspiration for Ethnic Cleansing. By using alternating blood-red dots and dashes, he redrew the boundaries of the six republics that formed Yugoslavia, merging them into two: Greater Serbia and Montenegro. His rationale was to include geographically all areas in which there were any Serbs, even only a handful. Since they were practically ubiquitous, he rejected the legitimate boundaries of historical Yugoslavia, and most regions were mapped as Greater Serbia. Then, by differentiating between Catholic Serbs, Greek Orthodox Serbs, "Muslimized" Serbs, and "Albanianized" Serbs, he set up divisive distinctions among the Serbs themselves.

The eastern European concept of an ethnic group having its own "True National State" differed from the western European nation-state idea, where the entire citizenry had a common loyalty to a monarch, or where a democracy granted citizenship to the inhabitants of a territory. The ethnic approach to unity was born in the various German states and lands. There people decided that ethnic nationalities with a mappable distribution could form a country. Though many people had regional identities stronger than their ethnic ones, this made no difference if the dominant ethnic group expelled them.

Cvijić's map inspired much slaughter during the violent restructuring of the territory once known as Yugoslavia. In Kosovo, for example, Albanians composed 90 percent of the population and Serbs only 6 percent; yet in the late 1980s, Yugoslavia's tribal leader, the Serbian nationalist Slobodan Milošević, initiated ethnic cleansing of the Albanians and the geographical elimination of Kosovo. The ensuing ethnic cleansing and war in Yugoslavia originated in Serbia. In contradiction to Milošević's arguments, it was not caused by age-old hatreds, nor was it a civil war, nor a war to save Europe from Muslim fundamentalism. Before he was overthrown by a

PLATE 136. *Ethnographic Map of the Balkan Peninsula.* This 1918 map made by a Serbian nationalist destabilized Yugoslavia and inspired a war.

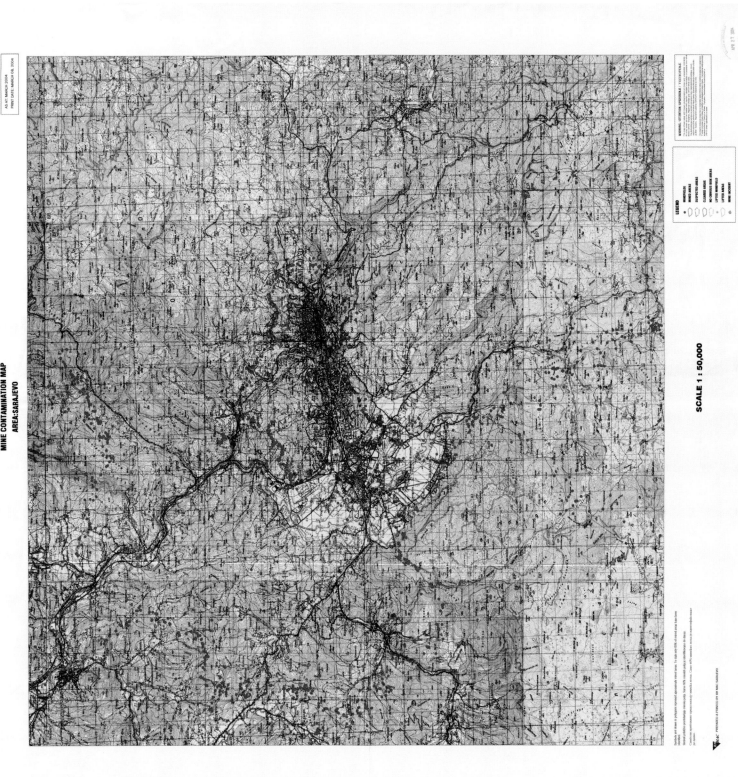

MINE CONTAMINATION MAP
AREA:SARAJEVO

SCALE 1 : 50,000

PLATE 137. *Mine Contamination Map, Area: Sarajevo.* The legacy of terrorism and ethnic cleansing are graphically depicted in this 2004 map.

popular revolution in 2000, Milošević's "vision" was responsible for the deaths of hundreds of thousands of people deemed by his nationalist followers as aliens in their own lands.

All of the republic of Bosnia was seen by Cvijić and his followers as part of Greater Serbia. In May 1992, the capital city of Bosnia, Sarajevo, with a population of 500,000, was blockaded and partly occupied by Milošević's Yugoslav national army. His allied Bosnian Serbian terrorists bombed and shelled the uncaptured areas of the city from the surrounding mountains with the in-

tent to create widespread destruction of institutions of learning and memory—hospitals, schools, synagogues, mosques, churches, libraries, and museums. As the social critic Susan Sontag explained, "It is precisely because Sarajevo represents the secular, anti-tribal ideal that it has been targeted for destruction." Sarajevo was home to most major archives, libraries, institutes, and museums in the republic of Bosnia. Every day, some 4,000 shells hit the city, many aimed specifically at people waiting on lines for bread and water. The Oriental Institute with its priceless Ottoman manuscripts, and the National and University Library with its 2 million books, were both completely destroyed, as planned by Milošević.

The siege lasted until February 1996, making it the longest continuous siege in modern history. When the Serbian aggressors left, 10,615 Bosnians were dead, 50,000 had been wounded, and enough land mines had been planted to be the subject of a map. It was the Germans who first realized the importance of keeping track of land mines. After World War II, the victorious Allies acknowledged the sagacity of the defeated Germans by adopting their values regarding mapping the presence of land mines, something that seems born of common sense.

The *Mine Contamination Map, Area: Sarajevo* (Plate 137) was prepared with a numbered military grid to make reproducing sections easier. Printed in the mined city by a local organization in 2004, the map is in Croatian, Serbian, and English, with a warning that reads: "This map shows area with known contamination of mines and unexploded ordnance. All other areas are to be treated with caution." It is Map as Antidote to Terrorism. Lacking a central government, the Bosnian postwar political structure had opposing nationalist forces in charge of the various governmental bodies in Bosnia's ten cantons. This has produced other ways to destroy particular institutions of learning and memory, mostly by not funding them if they are not dedicated to the nationalist agendas promulgated by the governmental bodies in charge of them. Unexploded mines on the map, shown as red dots, are emblematic of the festering wounds of ethnic hatred cataloged by Jovan Cvijić and waiting to flare into new violence, very like the yellow flames used to symbolize a "mine incident" on the map.

Russia

Just as in most European countries, from the fifteenth century onward maps in Russia were, for the most part, the product of the monarchy (tzar), expanding and centralizing power in the massive Russian state, which spans eleven time zones and is unevenly populated by dozens of ethnic groups. Maps existed to create a single Russian reality. As always, the creation of the maps involved the local people, and the Romanov dynasty, established in 1613, broadened the administrative apparatus necessary to centralize the vastness of space and to focus the energies of its subjects.

Organizing property rights for the aristocrats, estate maps performed the same economic role as in England, but they served another social function in Russia as well. Used as local-dispute maps among small landowners, they often brought people into court, where far-flung and notoriously independent-minded people were "tamed" by the single administrative judicial process dictated by the state. However, the local land-dispute cases often engendered complex twists and turns, lies and falsifications, that would have delighted the gambler in Dostoyevsky. Though they could drag on unresolved, the cases did offer local communities a way to express their immediate concerns while at the same time withholding their local knowledge to undermine the functioning of an all-powerful central government. Thus, as well as centralizing power, maps in

Russia expressed an anarchy of spirit and an impulse to be silent and secret, to harbor hidden agendas, that came to dominate the programs and the public cartography of the ruling Soviets in the twentieth century.

Atlas Mira, the national atlas of the Soviet Union, was published in two volumes by Moscow's Scientific Research Institute in 1937–39. Issued just before World War II, the atlas was withdrawn from circulation by Soviet authorities because it contained many physical and economic maps of a detail previously unavailable to foreigners. Two additional volumes planned by the Soviets apparently were never published. The specialized economic map from volume two (see Plate 138) shows the region surrounding Moscow, and is typically revelatory of the thematic maps in this atlas. It focuses on the famous five-year plans devised to strengthen the Russian economy. Many of the symbols on the map were innovative and have since been adopted by mapping establishments of other countries. It is Map as Transformation and Terror.

The five-year plans were created in 1928, a year after Stalin gained full, autocratic power. Their goal was to transform Russia from a semifeudal agricultural country into a modern, self-sufficient, industrial state by means of a "revolution from above," which meant using extreme, militaristic tactics to increase production on all fronts. Instead of a classless society, the dream of the 1917 communist revolution—"From each according to his ability, to each according to his needs"—a totalitarian one came into existence, with Stalin's Communist Party controlling every aspect of Russian life. The economy was centralized. Small-scale industry and businesses were nationalized, including farms, which were merged into large collectives, reintroducing a form of serfdom. The wealthiest peasants, known as kulaks, resisted; but lacking the court system to apply the old local land-dispute techniques, they initiated the destruction of livestock property, contributed to a general famine resulting in the deaths of 5 million to 7 million people, and were either slaughtered or exiled to Siberia.

When the first five-year plan failed to meet its unrealistic production targets, Stalin ended it after four years by declaring it a success. (A joke among dissidents of Soviet Russia seems appropriate to the map: "We are pretty certain about the future; it is the past that is always changing.") The second five-year plan (1933–37) had more realistic goals and was more successful, whereas the third, begun in 1938, was redesigned to emphasize armaments owing to the threat of international war, though the all-powerful Stalin had convinced himself his genius would prevent Hitler from invading Russia. Thus the atlas, with its detailed maps, was published in 1937 by a proud and triumphant Stalin who, from 1934 to 1938, was instigating purges of his Russian "enemies," amounting to an estimated 7 million murders. To Stalin's literally paralyzing shock, Hitler invaded Russia in 1941.

As the map clearly shows—obviously too clearly—the Union of Soviet Socialist Republics, created in 1922 of eleven republics, was transformed into the third-largest industrial state in the world, after the United States and Germany. Life for the average Russian, however, was not equal to the opulent display on the economic

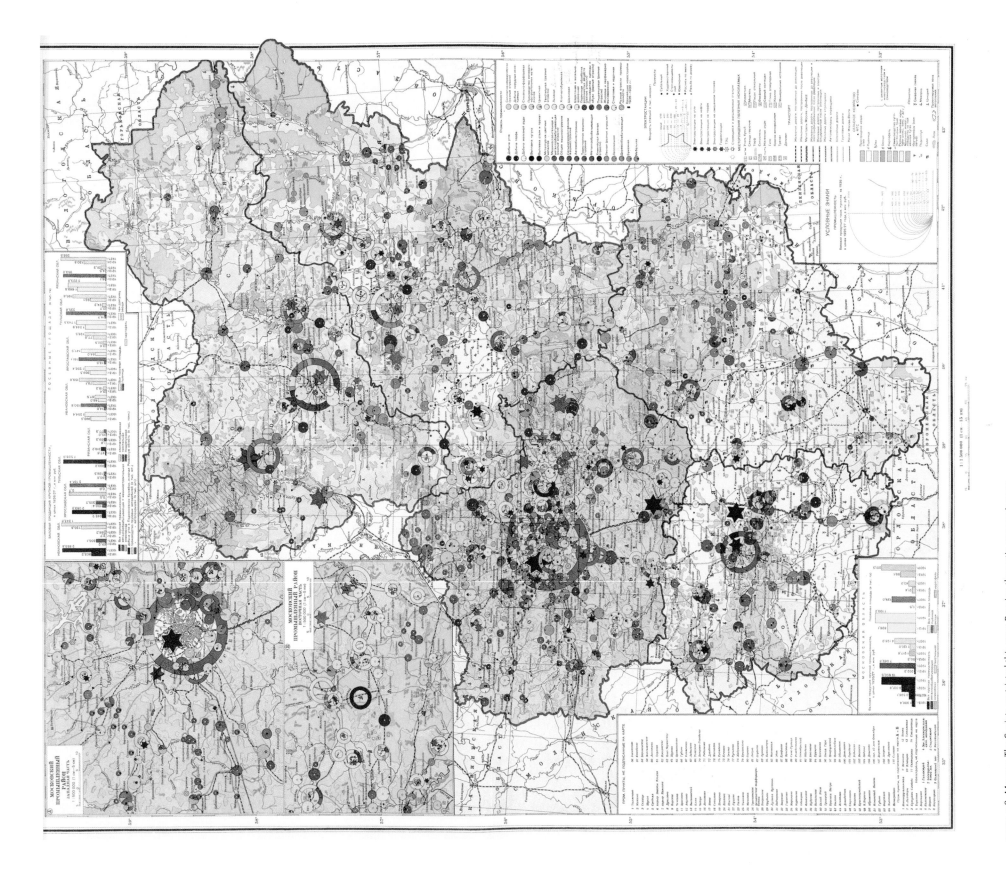

PLATE 138. *Moscow.* The Soviets restricted this 1939 Russian thematic economic map.

map in the *Atlas Mira*. Commodities were in short supply and agriculture, exploited to finance the industrialization drive, showed poor returns well beyond the date of the map. The face of transformation present on the map offers a false sense of abundance, somewhat akin to the maps produced by the Soviets in the Cold War period, in which place names were changed and buildings omitted to deepen the shadow of secrecy.

Europe Reconceived

Although the most important, the Treaty of Versailles was only one of the treaties that concluded World War I. Signed on June 28, 1919, it was drawn up between Germany and the Allied powers—including Britain, France, Italy, Japan, and the United States. It was eventually ratified by every country involved except the United States and Russia, which did not participate in formulating or signing the treaty. The terms of the treaty were sweeping, affecting the geographic, economic, and political order worldwide. As Plates 139 and 140 show, the treaty provisions redrew the maps of Europe and Asia Minor. The map dated 1924 clearly articulates the new shape of power politics. Gone entirely are two major players in world history: the Austro-Hungarian and the Turkish Ottoman empires. Enter a whole new cast of characters to the world stage, including Yugoslavia and the modern Middle East. As history proves, moving lines around on a map does not solve problems. It is Map as Curtain Raiser.

The vengeful Allies at Versailles rejected German attempts to negotiate, forcing the country to accept every stipulation exactly as presented to them, along with the "war guilt" clause, which placed all responsibility for the war on German aggression. These harsh terms have often been blamed for fueling antagonisms that erupted into World War II. But basically, the underlying tensions that had preceded World War I were still very much alive. Reconfiguring the 1914 map did not end conflict between communist, democratic, and later fascist ideologies, colonial and nationalist forces, or ethnic and religious groups. In fact, the treaties and the continued political infighting proved that peace had been a secondary concern, way behind the victors' gaining control over world trade and resources, labor and agriculture. France and England divvied up North Africa and the Middle East—a descriptive term devised by the British ("middle" was in relation to England and China, which was the Far East). Defense and security were higher priorities than respect for all nations. General Tasker Bliss, chief of the American military delegation to Versailles, concluded there, "What a wretched mess it all is. If the rest of the world will let us alone, I think we had better stay on our side of the water and keep alive the spark of civilization to relight the torch after it is extinguished over here."

In 1952, soon after the horrors of World War II, six European countries—Belgium, France, the Federal Republic of Germany, Italy, Luxembourg, and the Netherlands—came together to create the European Coal and Steel Community (ECSC). In direct contrast to the Treaty of Versailles, they pooled their coal and steel resources in a common market controlled by an independent supranational authority. Thus began the institutional framework for the construction of a united Europe, a new political entity, and a place, theoretically, with a common future. The idea was born out of the desire to prevent another war by economically intertwining community members. There has been no war between states in Western Europe now for more than sixty years.

In 1958 all economic sectors of the member nations were merged in a common market called the European Economic Community

PLATES 139 AND 140. *Europe and Asia Minor in 1914*, and *Europe and Asia Minor in 1924*. Europe and Asia Minor before and after World War I.

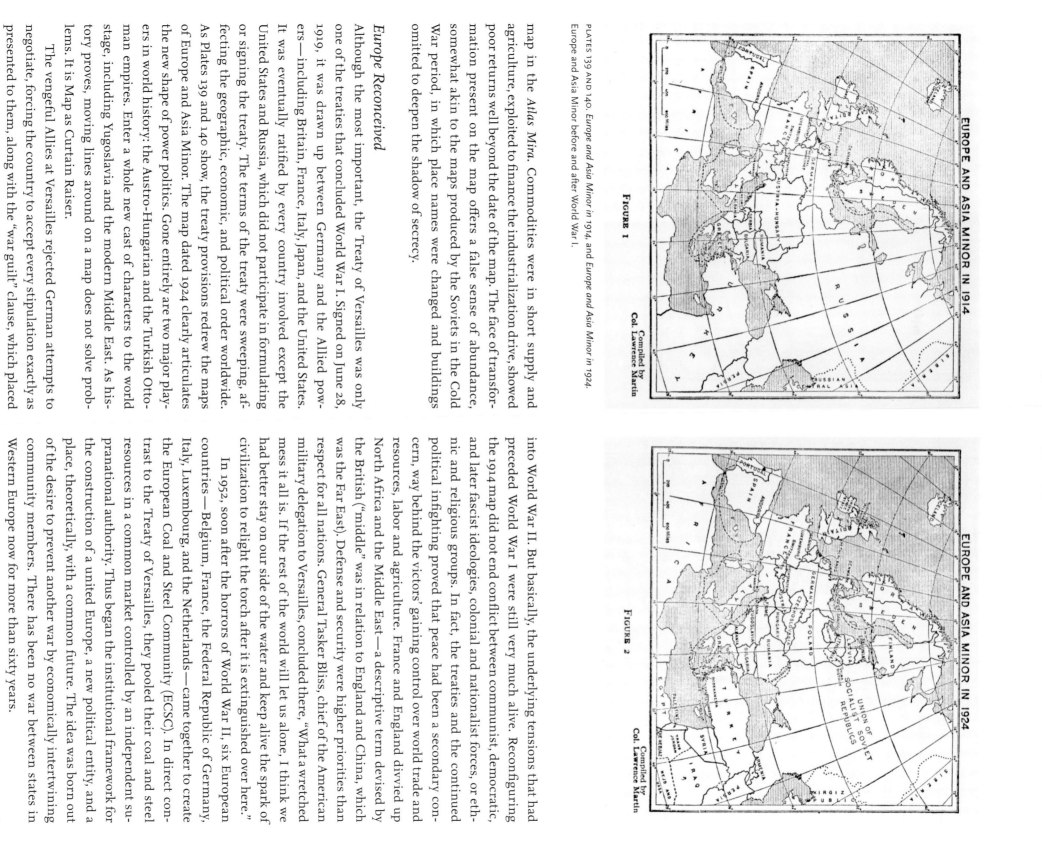

EUROPE AND ASIA MINOR IN 1914

Compiled by Col. Lawrence Martin

FIGURE 1

EUROPE AND ASIA MINOR IN 1924

Compiled by Col. Lawrence Martin

FIGURE 2

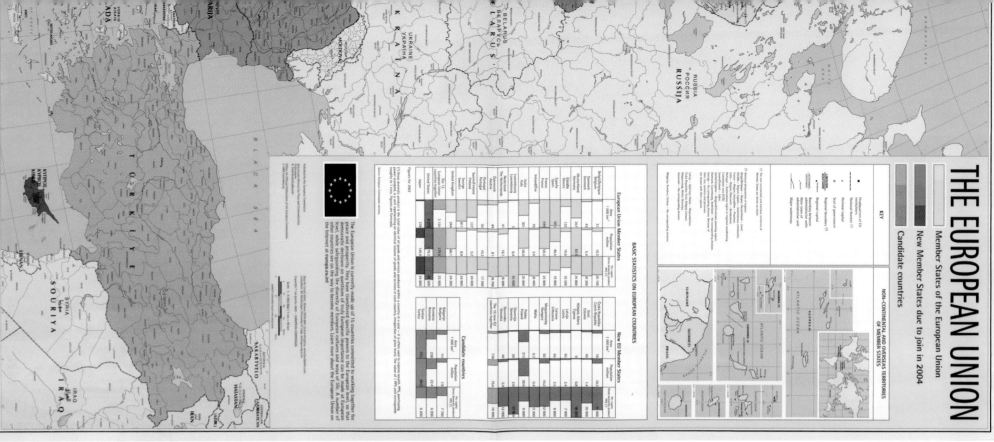

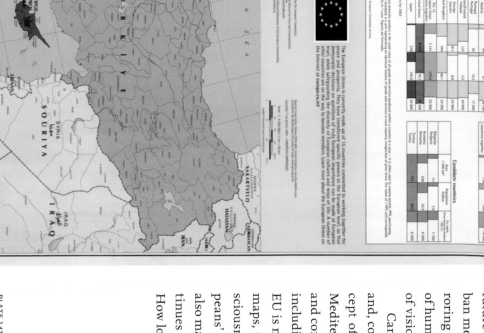

(EEC), which became the European Community (EC) in 1965. Eight years later, the United Kingdom, Ireland, and Denmark joined the EC, and a European Parliament was elected in 1979. Greece expanded the Mediterranean world's presence in 1981, followed five years later by Spain and Portugal. In 1993, the Treaty on European Union (Maastricht Treaty) was ratified by all its members. Austria, Finland, and Sweden were welcomed by the EU as members in 1995, bringing the family of nations to fifteen. (A common currency called the euro was accepted by twelve of the EU members in 1999; only Great Britain, Sweden, and Greece abstained from joining the monetary union.)

EU25, with more than 450 million people, came into existence in 2004 when Cyprus, the Czech Republic, Estonia, Hungary, Latvia, Lithuania, Malta, Poland, Slovakia, and Slovenia joined, eradicating the centuries-old cartographic concept of an Eastern and a Western Europe to create an image on a 2004 EU map (Plate 141) similar to that of medieval Catholic Christendom. It is Map as Historical Anthropology. Charlemagne would recognize this geography, centered as it is around Brussels and Strasbourg, the heart of his realm. But as was not the case in the Carolingian empire, national antagonisms and national identities survive in the EU. Yet national histories, just like single national maps, will not produce a cohesive realm without a new perspective shared by its member states. Formed as an economic unit, the EU of the 2004 map recalls the 1484 wall chart on vellum for successfully converting different systems of weights and measures in different civilizations. The answer to the future of Europe may lie in the melding of its continent-wide urban mercantile middle class to form one, great City of Man, mirroring what happened in the Middle Ages when cities became hubs of human activity and "Europe" was invented by maps in the hands of visionary geniuses from various cooperating civilizations.

Candidate countries now include Bulgaria, Croatia, Romania, and, controversially, Turkey, a fact that entirely reinvents the concept of "Europe," though the Ottoman Turks ruled one of the Mediterranean world's great seaborne empires. History saw a long and constant flow of technology and ideas into Europe from Asia, including Ptolemy's *Geographia*. The acceptance of Turkey into the EU is noted on the 2004 map, just as it is on the 1914 and the 1924 maps, when Turkey was very much a part of the European consciousness. These maps combined provide a visualization of Europeans' long-overdue acknowledgment of the Eastern influence. It also makes visible a geographical place called Eurasia. Europe continues to be reimagined and reconceived. A new question arises: How long will Europe remain a continent?

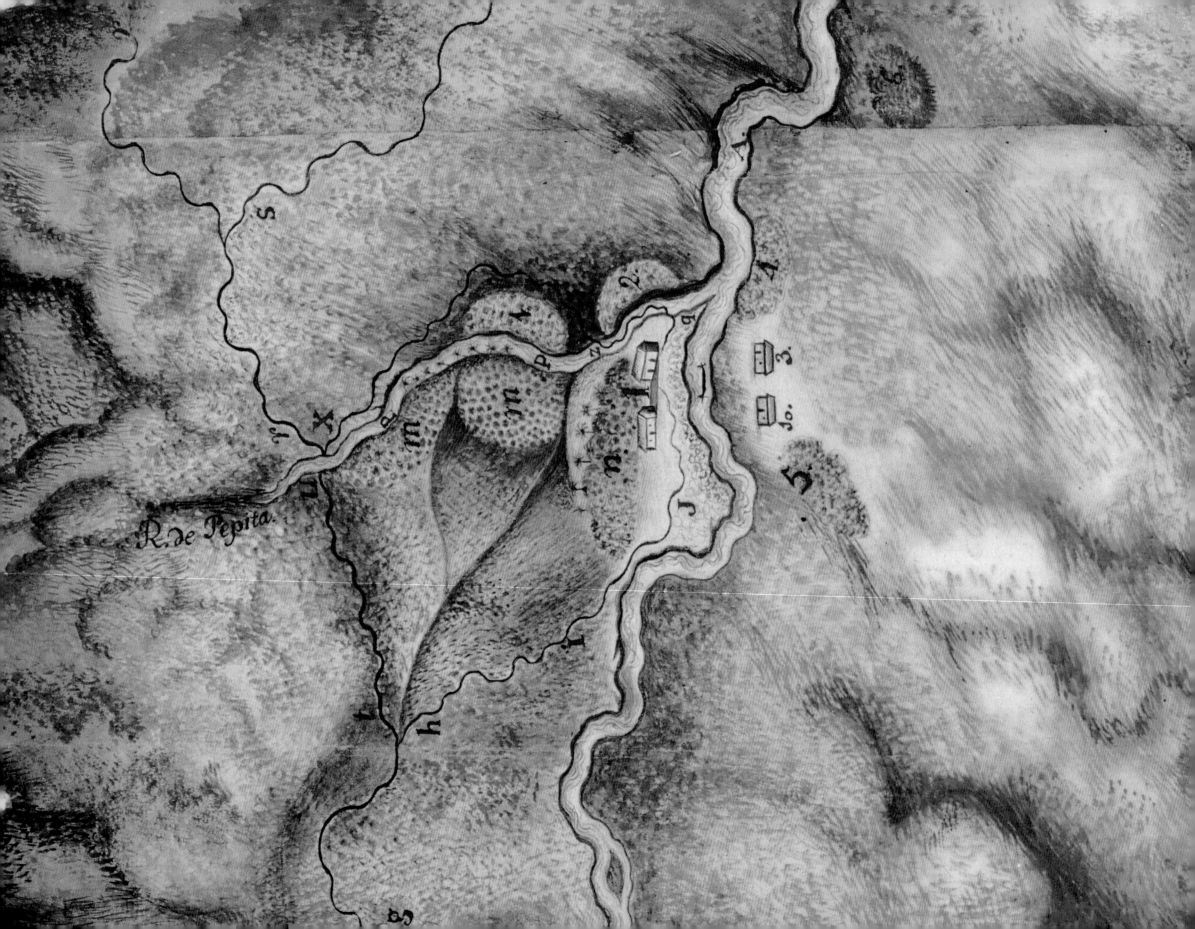

R. de Pepita.

THE FOURTH PART: THE AMERICAS

PLATE 142. *Ruysch Map of the Known World.* Comprehending the 1492 news from Columbus is the goal of this 1507 European map.

OVERLEAF: Detail from pages 190–91.

J ust as Marco Polo was not the first European to travel to China, so Christopher Columbus was not the first to reach the landmass known as America. Like Polo's, however, Columbus's journey was the first to have a lasting impact on human life. It unwittingly precipitated the first encounter of two separate and flourishing parts of the world. Neither had been aware of the existence of the other. It was an intercultural encounter, with dire consequences for millions of indigenous people, who were viewed as pliable, atheistic aliens by Columbus, who wrote in his diary, "They should be good and intelligent servants." His ambitious followers had similar ideas. European weapons of war and diseases annihilated whole, brilliant cultures on the continent of America. As with the geography of Asia and Africa, the setting of this drama slowly came to be visualized by the West via the character of maps.

The very shape America took in the human imagination, the discrete northern and southern portions, was a balancing act, a cartographic construction by mapmakers, who, according to the geographer Carl O. Sauer, "delineated the two New World continents at their narrowest connection, the isthmus of Panama." In fact, climate, land formations, language, culture, all led eventually to the creation of a middle region called Central America as a way of redressing the geographical and cultural imbalance caused by visually and politically driven cartographers placing mind over matter on the drawing board. Since America's boundaries are not scored on the land—though they are the results of colonialist exploration on the ground known as "traverse surveys"—it is more efficacious while mapping civilizations to dismiss the commonly accepted three-part division of America and to consider the cultural evolution of present-day Anglo (North) and Latin (South) America (Canada and the United States being Anglo in theory, and from Mexico southward being Latin, in practice). By taking this "spatial" approach to the history of empire in America, both the victors *and* the victims of New World maps are represented.

Portugal and Spain were in the vanguard of Europe's overseas expansion in the search for a route to the Indies and its spices, a priceless commodity that drove the Western world's economy and influenced global politics, as oil does today. Thus the Iberians were the curators of the rapidly changing conception of the world. At the apogee of their powers, their joint empires were known as the Luso-Hispanic world. It included significant portions of America.

America was born for western Europe with Columbus and Vespucci. Having set off from Spain in 1492, traveling westward at about one hundred miles a day with a paucity of exact information, Colum- bus was hoping to reach Japan in thirty days, then Cathay (China), then India. Sailing through the Bahamas to Cuba, he thought he was in the Indian Ocean off the coast of Asia. He stuck to this story to his death in 1506, even after Vespucci and European geographers with a knowledge of his faulty estimates of the size of the Atlantic contradicted him. It was Amerigo Vespucci who turned the European cartographer's world upside down. In his 1505 published letter, "Mundus Novus" (New World), he claimed to have sailed 2,000 miles down the eastern coast of Columbus's "Asia" in 1501, along today's Brazil into the Southern Hemisphere, nearly to Cape Horn. The place he had explored was not Asia, with its fabulous cities, but an entirely different place, large and diverse, one that was most definitely a "continent." It was a New World of which his ancestors had no knowledge.

Before Vespucci's astounding revelation, newly circumnavigated Africa, Europe, and Asia comprised the accepted European three-part worldview presented by Ptolemy. Even after Vespucci, however, a new fan-shaped map with a conical projection, engraved on copper, appeared in a 1507 reprint of Ptolemy's *Geographia*. The new map (Plate 142 and title page) was by Johann Ruysch, a native mapmaker of Antwerp. Living in Germany, he labored to fit the news of the discoveries on the other side of the Atlantic into the geographic framework of Ptolemy. It is Map as Delusional Moment. Ruysch, like most educated people of his generation, could not jettison Ptolemy's revered theory of the world. Ignoring Vespucci's seemingly far-fetched and self-aggrandizing claims, he could not imagine a fourth part of the world in the Western Hemisphere. An entire New World? His map is the most beautiful visual record we have of the general confusion engendered by the initial voyage of Columbus to "Asia." It is a moving human document, a priceless primary source for researching a state of mind in sixteenth-century Europe. Offering direct access to the past, Ruysch's creation makes each viewer a time traveler.

Enough was enough for Ruysch. He had already updated Ptolemy with considerable help from Marco Polo, Fra Mauro, Martellus, da Gama, and many other Luso-Hispanic explorers. Then, literally not knowing what to do with Columbus's landing site, he neatly inserted a large island as King Ferdinand's property underneath Asia, just below the Tropic of Cancer. "This map," he wrote beside Columbus's much-touted discovery, "is left incomplete for the present, since we do not know in which direction it trends." There is still a wide ocean passage to "the land of the spices." In spite of its being on maps Columbus was known to have studied, Japan is missing entirely, though Ruysch does admit he is unsure of its location

PLATE 143. *Waldseemüller Map of the World.* The sources behind the assumptions of this 1507 map still remain a mystery.

PLATE 143A. Detail from the *Waldseemüller Map of the World* showing how it named America.

and guesses that "Spagnola" (Haiti) might be it. Reached by John Cabot in 1497, Greenland and Newfoundland ("Terra Nova") appear as peninsulas of Asia just below the Arctic Circle.

There were other states of mind on display at the time. The same year Ruysch expressed his, the most revolutionary visual statement of the period was made by Martin Waldseemüller, a German scholar, humanist, cleric, and master mapmaker living in St.-Dié, France, among scholars recruited by the cathedral's canon to produce another new edition of Ptolemy. Inspired by Vespucci's vision of the world, along with other empirical evidence, Waldseemüller created the first modern map of the world (Plate 143) depicting a separate and full Western Hemisphere, with the never-before-documented Pacific Ocean as a huge body of water between Asia and the new discovery, "an island," he wrote, "inasmuch as it is found to be surrounded on all sides by the ocean." He christened the immense island America, to honor the recognition of the discovery's true geographic significance by Vespucci, who is pictured above the main map at the right, opposite Ptolemy and beside the portion of the globe bearing his name. The newly acknowledged fourth part of the world is shown there as one piece with a different configuration, not divided as it is on the main map, where "America" appears on its southern segment, just above the Tropic of Capricorn (Plate 143A).

"Now these [three] parts of the earth have been extensively explored," Waldseemüller wrote, "but now a fourth part has been discovered by Amerigo Vespucci." However, when this map was published in the new edition of Ptolemy in 1513, Waldseemüller replaced "America" with "Terra Incognita," perhaps suggesting that he had second thoughts in the face of major controversy about honoring Vespucci exclusively for this astoundingly prescient image of the New World. It was too late. The name stuck. A reported one thousand copies of the 1507 map were printed, which was a sizable print run in those days. The single surviving copy shown here exists because it was kept in a portfolio by a German globe maker, who probably had acquired it for his own cartographic work.

The map has been called America's birth certificate. It is Map as Decisive Moment. Printed from wood-block plates on twelve separate sheets, each 18 by 24 inches, and measuring 4 by 8 feet across when assembled, the map, considering the vastness of its subject, is appropriately the largest and the grandest map ever printed to that date. Its full title is "A Drawing of the Whole Earth following the Tradition of Ptolemy and the Travels of Amerigo Vespucci and Others."

Just how did the mapmaker know not only the existence of, but also the breadth of the Pacific Ocean, which—according to standard history texts—was not discovered by Europeans until Balboa crossed the Isthmus of Panama in 1513? The renown the map acquired by its naming the new continent after Vespucci has overshadowed the great questions raised by the "and Others" in its title. Who were Waldseemüller's informants? Who gave him the approximate correct shape of South America's western coast in the inset, and word that the far coast of the continent was mountainous? In the literature of maps, there are few more haunting questions about the spread of knowledge in Europe nearly five hundred years ago.

It has been conjectured that long before Columbus, the Portuguese, who sailed way out into the Atlantic in order to catch the trade winds and ride them back around the tip of Africa, may have been blown around Cape Horn into the Pacific or driven there on a tsunami and, once there, explored up the western coast. The secretiveness of their mapping culture could have been breached and word of their travels, even copies of their drawings, smuggled to St.-Dié.

Or, like Vespucci, Waldseemüller could have deduced from other available evidence. A sixth-century adventure of Hoei-Shin is reported in Chinese histories; he supposedly sailed 4,000 miles east of Japan to a continent he named Fusang, in honor of trees he found there bearing fruit like red pears, possibly the maguay tree of Latin America. Added to his exploits are those of multilingual Chinese mariners who, beginning in 1405, made epic voyages in vast treasure fleets involving 27,800 men to explore the oceans and to build, diplomatically, an international commercial empire with the "barbarians." Since the Chinese believed they ruled all under heaven, they had no interest in establishing a colonial or military empire. They also sought knowledge for China's multivolume encyclopedias and vast libraries of printed books covering every subject known to man, libraries constructed centuries before Europe existed. The massive oceangoing teak ships (junks) were nearly 500 feet long, dwarfing the 150-foot ships used by Portuguese, Spanish, and Venetian explorers. Chinese drawings and notes on explorations of the western coast of America could have been given to Venetian merchants or Portuguese sailors in India, for example, where Chinese fleets often appeared on their way to Africa.

Similar to Ruysch's work, Waldseemüller's map is a captured moment of time. It is Western mankind's progress in envisioning the earth. Nothing shares better the sense of life's mystery on earth that fired the imagination of the explorers and their monarchs. It is a primary source in the history of the imagination—a unique dimension of history—and a historical reality unto itself. The fantasies of the late Middle Ages wane and a finite world is born, with a mapmaker assembling the pieces. As the French medievalist Jacques Le Goff concludes, "To study the imagination of a society is to go to the heart of its consciousness and historical evolution." Waldseemüller epitomizes the ambition and the daring of the Age of Discovery. He tells a story with his poetic image as close to a cliffhanger as visually possible, and the encounter it announces is, in some respects, one of the saddest stories ever told.

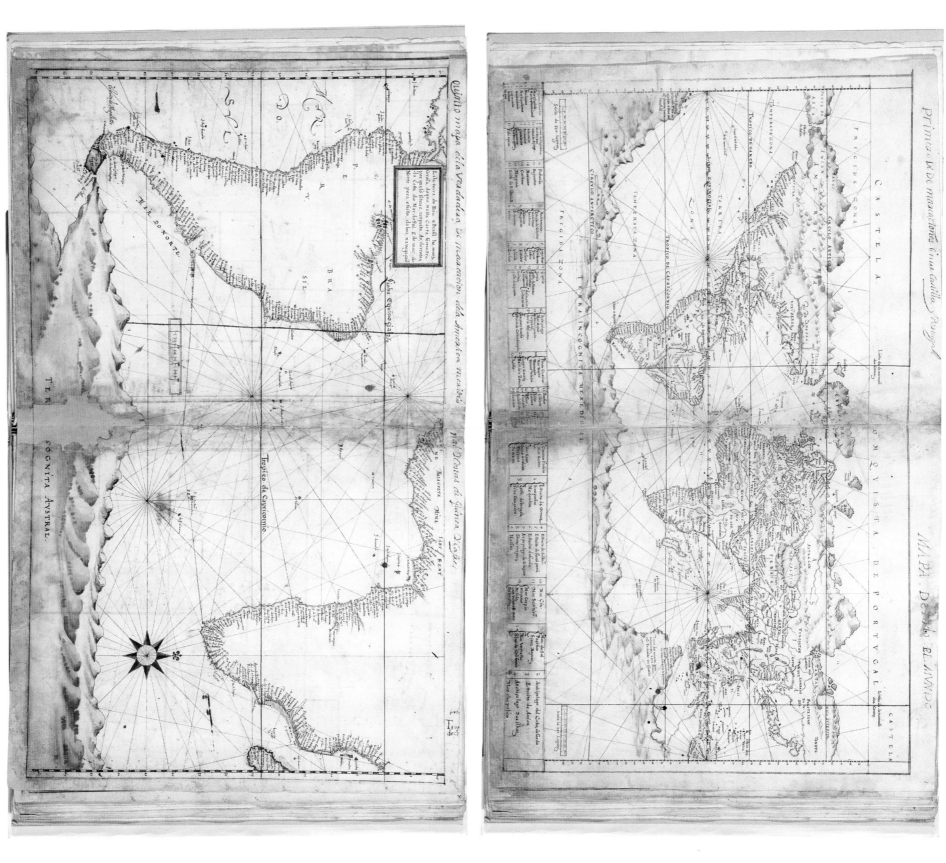

PLATES 144 AND 145. *World* and *South Atlantic*. Greed and duplicity are on display in the marking on these 1630 maps.

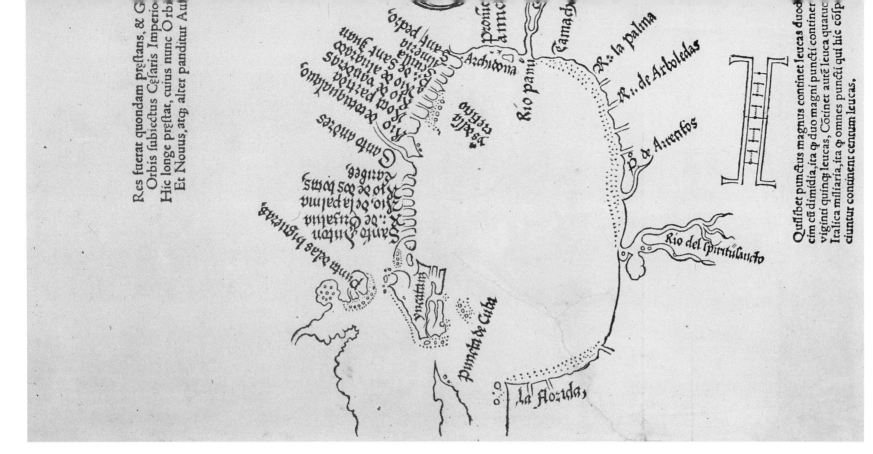

PLATE 146. *Map of Mexico City and the Gulf of Mexico.* Tenochtitlán, the monumental capital of the doomed Aztec empire, is the focus of this map.

The interaction between Spain and Portugal in America also had its dark side. From the fifteenth to the seventeenth century, the two monarchies vied for possessions around the globe. In 1493 Pope Alexander VI (the notorious Rodrigo Borgia), being the most influential person in the Western world at the time, and also a protégé of the Spanish monarchy, issued a papal bull at Columbus's request using maps to create an imaginary longitudinal line of demarcation. It legally divided the world between Spain and Portugal 100 leagues west of the Cape Verde Islands. (One Spanish league was approximately four miles.) His line effectively gave America to Spain, which did not sit well with Portugal, though the Portuguese did secure their hard-earned African route to India by similar papal intervention. The two countries held several diplomatic congresses to dispute the placement of the line, which was shifted in 1494 to 370 leagues west of Cape Verde, giving Portugal a piece of Latin America.

A sea atlas compiled in 1630 by João Teixeira Albernaz I, cosmographer to the king of Portugal, and the most notable Portuguese cartographer of his day, contained sea charts, plans, and views of cities and harbors of colonial and commercial interest to the Portuguese, and, most interestingly, two maps with the line of demarcation in two different places, casting doubt on the accuracy of both (see Plates 144 and 145). To the great advantage of the Spanish, the second map's crudely drawn line was moved farther east, "expelling" Portugal from the New World. It is Map as Reckless Moment. The skullduggery makes an abstract conflict tangibly human.

Considered confidential or secret, the atlas had been locked away in the Library of the City and Royal Archives in Lisbon. In 1681 it was removed by bribery (paid for by the viceroy of New Spain) and presented to the king of Spain. It was the Spanish who moved the red line on the book's second map, and offered it as evidence that Portugal knew it had no legal claim to the New World. The stakes were high. The line was about which side of the line lay the great estuaries of the Amazon and the Plate, the paths to the hinterland, the local people, and the resources. There is wide disparity in the continent's shape and accordingly in the line's position among contemporary New World maps still in existence. With the evidence gleaned from the two Teixiera maps, this sometimes intentional disparity reflects conflicting agendas, none of them very hidden. The changing line illustrates how stationary maps became a moving force in history, and how easily maps can be made to lie.

LATIN AMERICA

A few hundred miles from where Columbus landed in San Salvador, across the expanse of Mexico, the Aztec empire was at the height of its power. North of the Aztecs were the peaceful Indians of the pueblo, living as they had lived undisturbed for at least a thousand years. And much farther north and east of them was the League of the Iroquois, the Five Nations. Unbeknown to Columbus, and to many who followed him, America was inhabited by a complex mosaic of human societies.

In 1519 the conquistador Hernando Cortés began Spain's conquests of Mexico and Peru. For twenty years, before invading the great central areas of Western Hemispheric civilization, Spain had focused on the islands of the Caribbean, with Cuba as its base. There, knowledge of Indian rivalries and how to take advantage of them was acquired. Without any large-scale military organization, several hundred Spanish immigrants from all walks of life believing in divine preordination slaughtered millions of indigenous people in less than twenty years, taking control of central Mexico (1519–21) and Peru (1532–34, 1536–37) by dint of Indian allies, steel weapons, the horse, and by seizing the local leaders. One of the most famous examples of this last technique involved the seizing

of the wealthy Aztec emperor Montezuma, with a domain of over 200,000 square miles, which he controlled by terror tactics. Disgruntled Indian guides led Cortés and his band of fortune-seeking adventurers across desert plateaus and up into a valley ringed by jagged mountain ranges 7,500 feet above sea level into Montezuma's extravagant metropolis of Tenochtitlán, where the Aztecs were

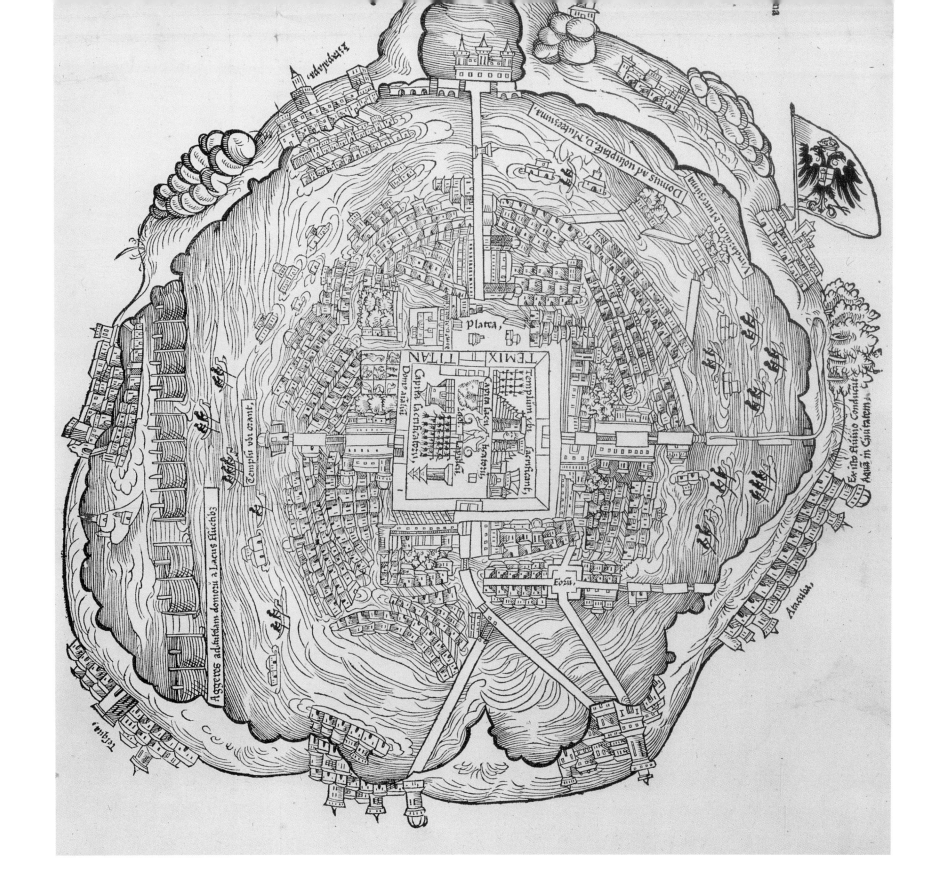

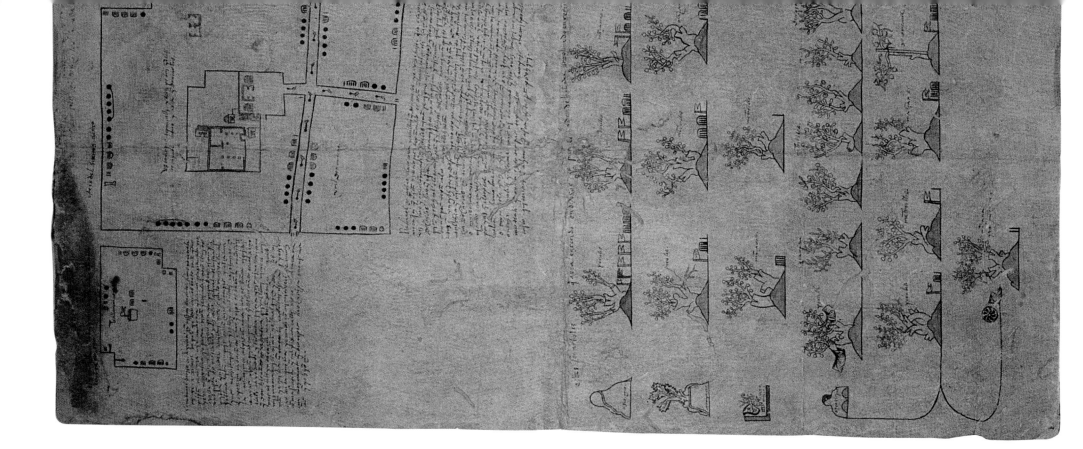

the dominant community of a small confederacy. Rising from a dike-tamed lake, the brightly painted, dazzling island city, with clustered neighboring cities around the lake joined by causeways, was home to about 80,000 people. Cortés wrote that its Great Temple was of such "great size and magnificence" that no human tongue could describe it. "There are as many as forty towers, all of which are so high that in the case of the largest there are fifty steps leading up the main part of it, and the most important of these towers is higher than that of the cathedral of Seville."

A map of the Gulf of Mexico and the monumental stone city of Tenochtitlán (now Mexico City) was printed on a single sheet and published in 1524 with a letter from Cortés to Charles V, the emperor and king of Spain (see Plate 146). There is much in both of these maps to suggest that the drawings supplied to the Nuremberg engraver who prepared the printer's woodblock were based on lost Aztec originals and were faithful to the Aztec idea of Tenochtitlán. It is Map as Vision of Lost Greatness. In 1522 Cortés had sent his lieutenant, Juan de Ribera, to the Spanish royal court with numerous Aztec maps, one of them described as a "native painting representing the town of Tenochtitlán with its temples, bridges, and lakes." Another report told of "castles or royal dwelling places, crowned with turrets and watchtowers." In fact, Tenochtitlán's built environment was not radically different from that found in many contemporary European urban settings. However, its square ceremonial precinct, set within a circular city, set within a circular lake, is a native, not a European, conception of a city. As the cartographic historian G. Malcolm Lewis explains of Amerindian cartography, "Indigenous maps were based on different assumptions than European maps and created for different functions. They were born of experience and oral tradition, not an inscribed archival history in the Western sense."

In Aztec myth and poetry, their capital city was portrayed as a majestic place—the center of the universe in both horizontal and vertical space. Rich in Aztec symbols, the map affirms this belief by suggesting a vertical photograph taken from above the city with a fish-eye lens. Not only does the exaggerated scale of the Great Temple enclosure reveal the imprint of Aztec mythic and cosmic models, but it also makes the temple dominate the plane of the map to stress its importance; it appears to be raised vertically above the rest of the crowded city and above the circling lake shores beyond. In fact, there was not one circular lake, but two lakes joined by a canal. The inclusion of a decapitated victim in the temple with flowing banners on its arms (blood?) honors the practice of sacrifice central to the Aztec religion.

The schematized map focuses on the island capital. Its geometric perfection reflects the highly cultivated Aztec understanding of how the center of empire was patterned after their perceived order of the larger cosmos. (The cleft between the temples was aligned with the rising sun of the equinox, which is on the map.) Like the ancient people of the Mediterranean world, the Aztecs believed

PLATE 147. *The Oztoticpac Lands Map.* This c. 1540 land litigation map is crammed with valuable economic and cultural data.

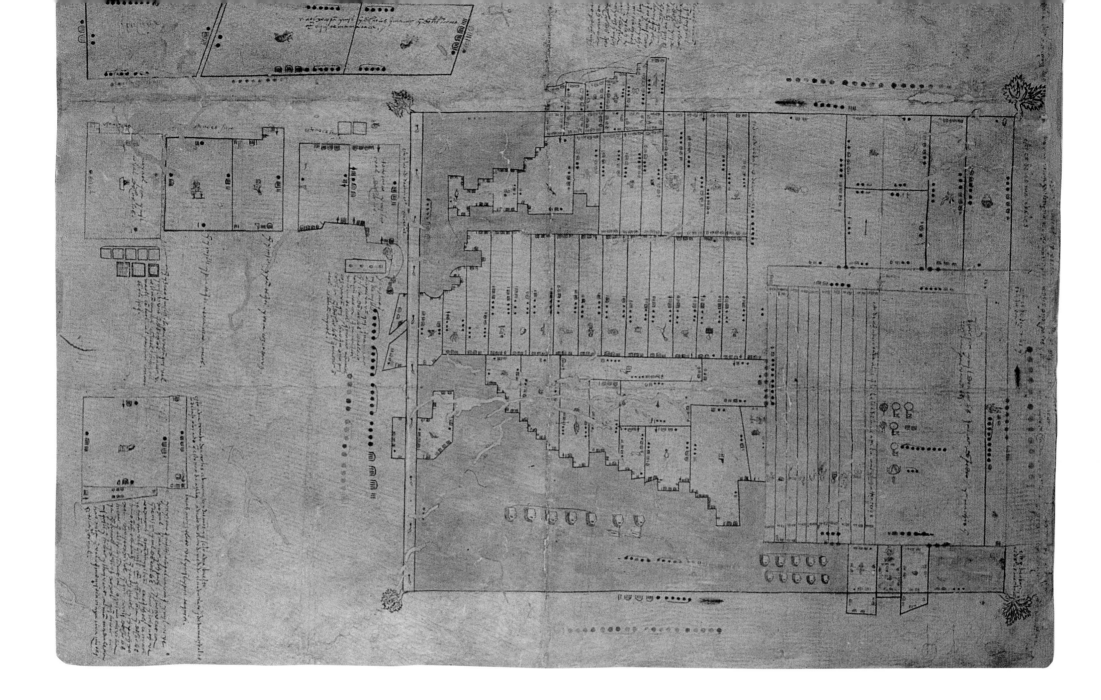

the earth was surrounded by a great expanse of water. Their city was the navel of the cosmos. By the time the map appeared in Europe, Tenochtitlán had been razed to the ground by Cortés and tens of thousands of Indian allies eager to throw off an onerous Aztec yoke. With the treasure-rich Aztecs vanquished, other Spaniards with similar ambitions cast their eyes toward the lands forming a great arc north of the Gulf of Mexico.

Most Indian documents, including books, maps, and paintings, were systematically destroyed by Cortés, his fellow conquerors, and zealous Catholic priests. Regrettably, such destruction was common among conquerors. (The Aztecs destroyed the historical records of those they conquered because, as they wrote, "these paintings contain many lies, for many in the pictures have been hailed as gods.") Plate 147 shows a land litigation map in red and black ink, created in about 1539 or 1540 by one or more skilled Indians. The map concerns the ownership of properties claimed by various royal descendants, including Don Carlos Ometochtli Chimecatecotl, grandson of the king of Texcoco, a city in Mexico's Central Valley and a well-documented Aztec place of importance.

Following the Spanish conquest in Mexico, painted manuscripts in various native artistic traditions continued to be produced. In civil and economic matters, Indian peoples and Spanish alike found that maps, tribute registers, and cadastral and census documents derived from native tradition met a common need. Don Carlos was executed by the Spanish Inquisition for possessing, among other things, an ancient Aztec book of paintings and an Indian calendar that set forth the "Count of fiestas of the Demon." The offending antiques were destroyed. However, the execution of one of the powerful lords of Texcoco, for whatever reasons, proved to be a critical event. It damaged the prestige of the Inquisitor Bishop Juan Zumárraga, who was officially reprimanded for his zealous action.

The Texcocan lords drew revenues of various kinds from their own private estates, as well as from tribute-paying communities, some of which are shown on the map with their returns. Oztoticpac, an estate within Texcoco, was one of the properties owned by the family, and most of the drawings on the *Oztoticpac Lands Map*, which is less than a yard square, are plans of fields with indigenous measurements and place glyphs. There are also Spanish and Nahuatl (Aztec) glosses. Near the upper left is the plan of several houses within a precinct. On the upper right is a map showing about 75 plots of land. The profiled heads, a distinctly Amerindian cartographic symbol, indicate via attached numbers the Indian families who owned or rented the plots.

Important to the suit concerning the estate of the late Don Carlos was the orchard inventory pictured in the lower left of the map. A grove of trees—identified as pears, quince, apples, pomegranates, peaches, and grapevines—is depicted. A number of grafting techniques can be identified in the tree and vine symbols. Since no other Indian maps show the blending of native fruit trees with European varieties, the clear depiction of these horticultural practices places the *Oztoticpac Lands Map* among the most important Indian pictorial documents. It is Map as Grafting the Old World onto the New. Besides being the earliest known recorded lawsuit in New Spain's horticultural literature, it provides valuable economic and cultural data about Spain's civil courts in Mexico's immediate postcontact period.

Encompassing America was a contentious affair among sixteenth-century European powers. The authoritative source of American geographical knowledge was the work of explorers and navigators, as interpreted and plotted by the official cartographers of the crowns of Spain and Portugal. Spanish pilots accompanying an exploring expedition were obliged to keep a log and to make charts of sightings. Upon returning home, every scrap of information had to be given to the Casa de Contratación (Board of Trade), housed in the royal palace of Seville to emphasize its all-encompassing power. It was the central authority for Spanish travel to America and custodian of charts and sailing directions to the Western Hemisphere; it was responsible for the *padrón real* (royal chart)—the master copy for charts distributed to all ships leaving Spain. Its first *piloto mayor* (chief pilot), administrator of its navigational school, was Amerigo Vespucci.

Diego Gutiérrez (1485–1554) was a chart and instrument maker, and a pilot who worked in the Casa de Contratación from 1534 to his death. His posthumous map of 1562 (Plate 148) is a catalog of the American data acquired by Spain. After only four decades of European exploration and settlement, Latin America looks remarkably complete. The map is filled with images and names that had been popularized in Europe over several years: parrots, monkeys, mermaids, Brazilian cannibals, Patagonian giants, and an erupting volcano in central Mexico complement settlements, rivers, mountains, and capes. Although containing fanciful imagery, Gutiérrez's map correctly recognized the existence of the Amazon River system, other rivers, and a myriad of coastal features on the eastern coast of America, while the Holy Roman Emperor Charles V (Charles I of Spain) is represented as the reincarnated Caesar in his chariot whizzing across the Atlantic toward Florida to lay claim to America—all of it!

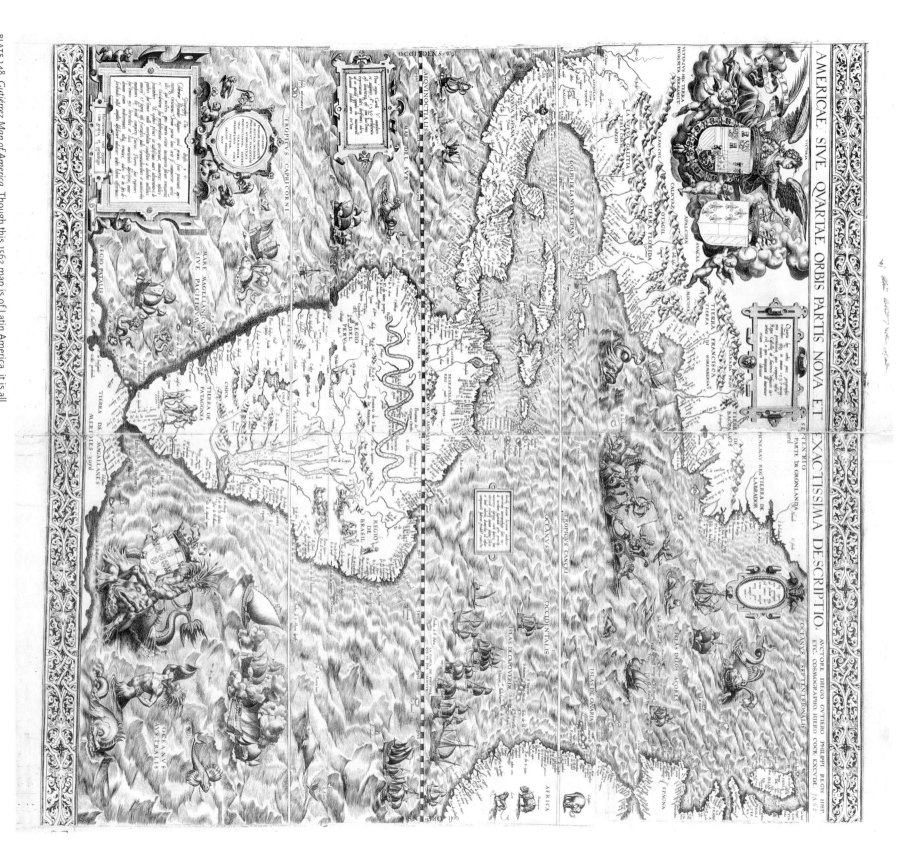

PLATE 148. *Gutiérrez Map of America.* Though this 1562 map is of Latin America, it is all about Spain.

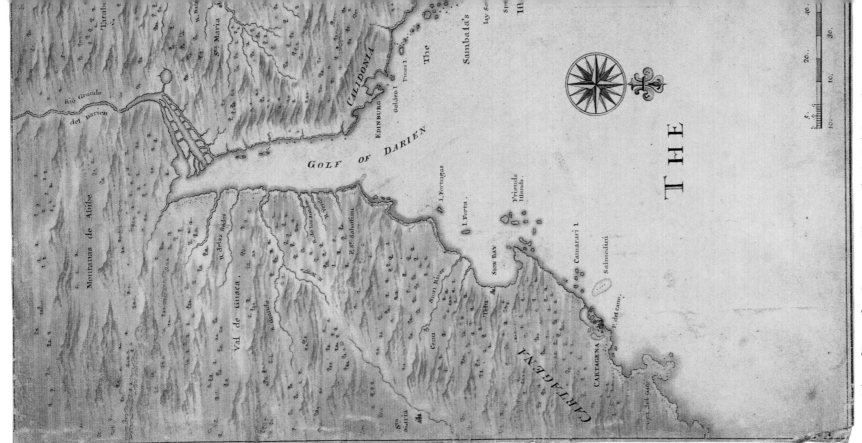

THE

PLATE 149. *Isthmus of Panama from Cartagena to Nicaragua Showing Both Coasts.* The Scottish settlement on this c. 1700 British map was abandoned before the map, which is oriented south, was made.

This great map is a celebration of the "other" hemisphere…all of it. The tiny piece of Portugal's Africa to the far right, with exotic lions, rhinos, and elephants, heightens the sense of "otherness" achieved by Gutiérrez. This fragment of the rival's holdings seems a taunting slap in the face of the "loser" nation, though it had taken intrepid Portugal twelve expensive expeditions, made within twelve years, to sail safely around that tiny piece of Africa to Cape Bojador in 1434, and their success led to great financial gain for the Portuguese. Yet by promulgating the belief that the people inhabiting the New World were "other," like the Africans with their dark skin and their unique animals, conquest and destruction, exploitation and extermination, were easier to rationalize. "Otherness," that age-old psychological power play, still successfully operates today. It dimmed the vision of the colonists, who became blind to the wisdom of human traditions different from their own.

In reality, Portugal had the wealth of the Indies to finance expensive explorations, and had been secretive about its successes to the point of threatening loudmouths with execution in 1504. Spain staked public claims wherever its ships landed, though secrecy was a primary concern. On the Gutiérrez map, King Charles I, Holy Roman Emperor, triumphantly rushes to his American colonies, although in truth his wars with France, with Reformation Protestants, and with Ottoman Turks were leading to Spain's financial ruin. He lacked the funds to give much support to his American dream, which is one of the reasons immigrants and explorers fought the Aztecs and the Incas (1532–33) on their own. In fact, under his son, Philip II, Spain went legally bankrupt. Money from America and the overtaxed Spanish peasants — the nobility was exempt from taxes — barely kept Spain afloat. The lack of investment in industrialization sent the traders elsewhere. Then the colonies in America and the Indies evolved and were able to provide for themselves. Spain's wealth was illusory, and the map played a key role in maintaining the facade.

As the largest one-sheet printed map of the Western Hemisphere up to that time, the Gutiérrez image dictated the boundaries of Spanish empire to the encroaching French in Florida and the Portuguese in Argentina by deploying the interlopers' coats of arms as calling cards near their claims. This is an artistic manifesto of Spain's ownership of the entire Western Hemisphere. It is Map as Lion's Share. Immense Spanish galleons seem to guard the precious treasure on both sides. This is also the cartographic debut of the name "California," soon to be as famous as "America." The word appears in the present-day Gulf of California, just above the Tropic of Cancer (Plate 148A).

A sensitively rendered English manuscript map in colored pen and ink from circa 1700 depicts the Isthmus of Panama, the Caribbean coast from Cartagena to Nicaragua, and the Pacific coast from Colombia to Costa Rica (Plate 149). In 1698 two Scottish colonies, Caledonia and Edinburg, were established on the Caribbean coast of Panama, the center of the isthmus having been locked by the Spanish into colonial rule. Along with the coastline, which the understaffed Spanish could not close, the map (which is oriented south), includes coastal features, navigational hazards, streams, other bodies of water, pictorial representation of vegetation and relief, and various Spanish towns and settlements, which are treated as neighbors to the two Scottish colonies. The map gives the impression that the Scottish settlers were there to stay. It is Map as Wishful Thinking. In fact the English-speaking colonies were abandoned in 1699 and reconfigured immediately as New Calidonia and New Edinburg, only to be abandoned again in 1700, the assumed date of this map.

The fact that many Indians spoke Spanish should have been a key to Indian survival tactics for the naive Scottish. Instead of frightened slaves, the Scottish and French met confident Indian men eager to pool resources, full of good faith and integrity, who had learned quickly how to manage the activities of the invaders. Yet when the welcoming Indians warned the Scottish of upcoming Spanish aggressions, they were ignored and dismissed as unreliable liars looking for gifts, or as two-faced connivers playing one

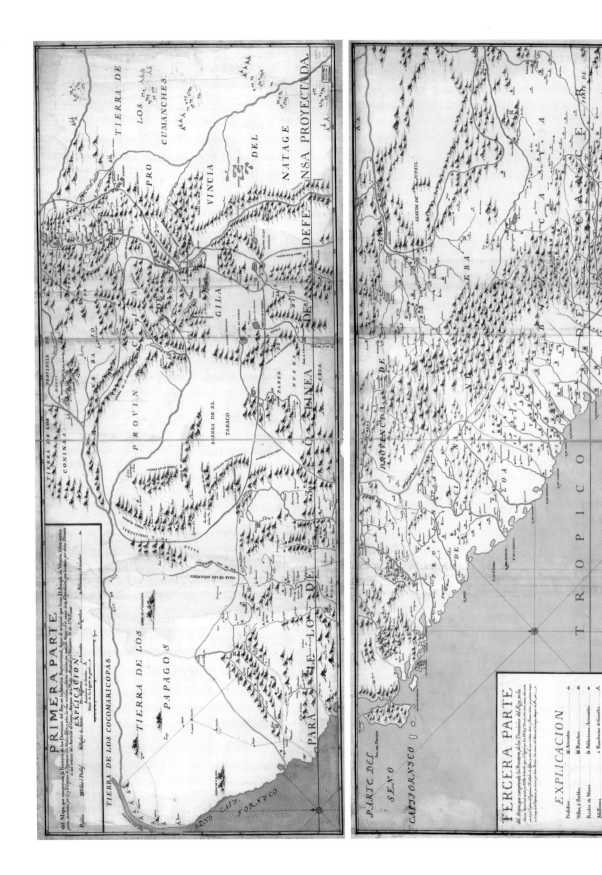

side against the other. More important, the Spanish were wrongly perceived to be incompetent pushovers for tolerating French pirates on the coast and for having allowed the Scottish to set up camp in the first place. Overextended the Spanish may have been, incompetent soldiers they were not.

The "otherness" of the Indians in Latin America blinded *all* the Europeans to the difference between wise political maneuvering as a method of survival, and duplicity. It was a complex situation, an intricate balancing act for the natives, similar to the delicate handiwork on the English map made after the English-speaking colonies were vacated. Some settlers had sailed home disillusioned about acquiring easy fortunes, having dangerously divided their vulnerable Scottish Company with factional fighting and mutiny; some died of tropical diseases or were killed by the Spanish; some deserted the desperately hard living conditions after England's King William III forbade his subjects to do business with them.

Stories of the brutality of the legendary Spanish conquistadores set up simplistic and false impressions about the relationship between the surviving indigenous people and their conquerors. It was generally assumed in Europe that the subjugated Indians wanted nothing to do with the Spanish and kept their distance. It was also assumed, incorrectly, that the Indians formed a single tribal community, a monolithic group of interrelated people like the Spanish, the Germans, the Italians, or the French, with a social system in the European manner, complete with a hierarchical administration in charge. The internecine feuds among Indian groups were seen as disruptive family squabbles, rather than as attempts by the Indians to defend their personalities from being obliterated by the colonists. As in Africa, these feuds continued long after the colonists had replaced genocide with corrupting native leaders, many of their own making, murdering only obstreperous types who could not be bought with gifts, and subduing the remaining people by converting them to a Christianity dominated by controlling priests.

PLATE 150 (ABOVE AND OPPOSITE). *Map of New Spain's Frontier.* The actual northern extent of Spanish settlement in America by 1768 is revealed here.

Alta California, on the far northern frontier of New Spain where Gutiérrez placed the Spanish crest on his map, was officially established in 1769 by Father Junípero Serra and Gaspar de Portolá. All of Hispanic California belonged to the king of Spain, and was administered for him by the viceroy of New Spain in Mexico City, founded on the site of the destroyed Aztec capital, Tenochtitlán, with its lakes drained. Provincial civil and military authorities oversaw local land grants to individuals until the end of the Spanish regime in California, in 1822. A detailed map of the internal provinces of New Spain—northern Mexico and southwest United States—was prepared as a result of the 1766–67 expedition at the viceroy's request to inspect Spain's frontier military posts (presidios), such as Monterey and San Diego (Plate 150). It is Map as Imperial Stocktaking. The engineer Nicolas de la Fora recorded the distances, directions, and astronomically determined points of the route survey in his journal of the trip, which extended to the present Arizona-Sonora boundary (in the northwest), to El Paso, Santa Fe, and Taos (in the north), and, in Texas, to San Saba, San Antonio, and Los Adaes (in the northeast).

José Urrútia drew a number of local maps and played a major role in the preparation of what is essentially a realistic appraisal of New Spain as it existed in a territory too vast for even Spain's Caesar to control in its entirety. The gigantic map measures 4½ by 10½ feet in four sheets. It included administrative boundaries, pictorial representation of relief, selected European and Native American towns and settlements, mines, missions, presidios, haciendas, Native American nations, rivers, streams, lakes, mountains, coastlines, and coastal features. This personal examination of most of the frontier provinces by a pair of trained cartographers was locked away for political reasons and never made available to commercial mapmakers. One of the recommendations of the official tour of inspection was for a reorganization of the northern presidios in order to meet the Native American menace more effectively. The map's elaborate details made planning projected military battles easier. It leaves no doubt that Spain, in spite of increasing difficulties, was in America for the long haul, but with a growing awareness of the necessity to consolidate its power and focus on what could be locked into place.

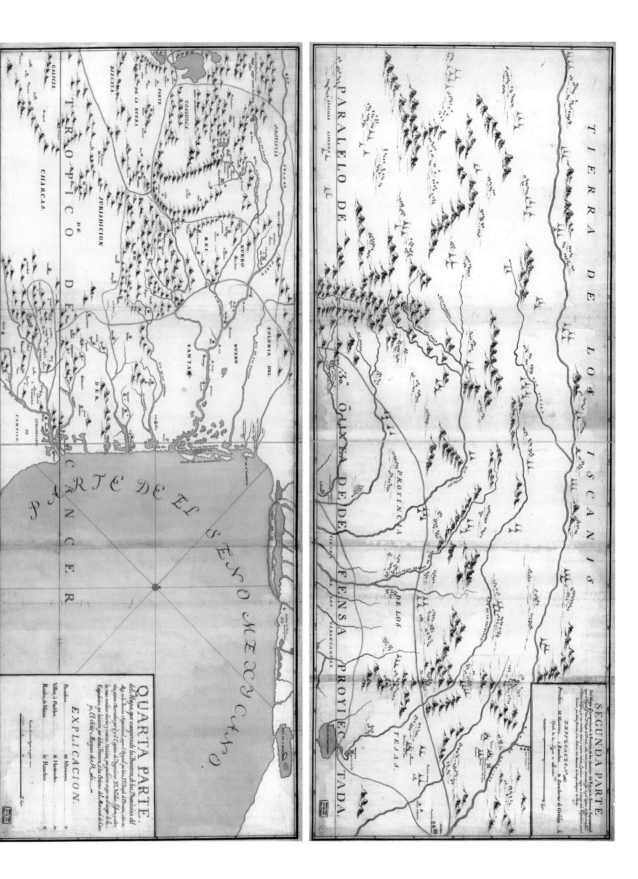

The Indian menace reported by la Fora and Urrútia was probably one of the reasons the Spanish did not try to possess all of the American continent. In theory, they could have gone north of Taos to the Arctic Circle with their claims. In practice, they were struggling to keep what they had in check. By judiciously giving substantial tracts of land to military veterans, and later as rewards in the contentious political environment of Mexican California, governors of New Spain and later the Mexican Republic engaged these American settlers in their struggles to retain Alta California. They actually succeeded for several generations, aided mightily by la Fora and Urrútia's great cartographic achievement, which showed them *where* they actually were on earth.

The 1777 Treaty of San Ildefonso between the Iberian crowns stipulated the need to more accurately define the boundaries of their possessions in the giant southern mass of the American continent. To ensure veracity of the survey, a joint commission of experts was named to mark the line. Four teams (*partidas*) were formed, each with a different sector of the 5,000-mile border. However, the entire northwestern region, with the hellishly inhospitable Amazon basin, a 4,000-mile area, was assigned to the fourth *partida*, governed by the Spanish engineer and mapmaker Francisco Requena and by the hostile Portuguese commissioner, Lieutenant Colonel Chermont. Spain, being at war with England, could send no supplies for the six officers and thirty highland Indian "soldiers" beyond a used set of survey instruments and an old map, neither of which arrived. The wealthy Portuguese had a huge team, including a military escort of five commanders and 45 soldiers, 220 Indian boatmen for fifteen riverboats, and four expert surveyors. They had already explored and made maps of the region, maps they refused to show Requena, who wrote, "If limits are not placed on the Portuguese in South America, they will arrive very soon to dominate there, alone."

Facing every imaginable hardship, and losing most of both teams to tropical diseases, the few remaining Portuguese continued to survey while Chermont antagonistically disputed the ownership of every geographical position with Requena, who continued to draw maps—with and without Chermont—and to travel the Amazon on his own, until his return to Madrid in 1794. Two years later, he presented his map of his survey commission and other maps to the king of Spain. The accompanying letter stated his goals directly: "To permit your Majesty to appreciate the injustice and ambitious pretensions of the Portuguese commissioners." It is

Red capital letters on his composite map (Plate 151) denote specific survey explorations along the Spanish-Portuguese border in the Amazon River Basin. With a keyed legend, there are extensive networks of rivers and streams, Native American settlements, European towns and cities, missions, abandoned settlements, ecclesiastical jurisdictions, administrative centers by categories, sites of longitude and latitude readings, pictorial representation of relief, coastline, and coastal features. An Amazon landscape is the subject of an elaborate cartouche, probably the work of Requena, who was also a noted watercolorist. The art of painting the land as

a means of capturing it is married to the science of mapping space as a means of owning it. Also, the incredulity induced by the complex river system on the map is heightened by the large human presence in the cartouche, despite the fact of a sizable reptile, perhaps a not-so-subtle reminder of Requena's torments on the site. The ease with which the map takes us from the fantasy to the form of the Amazon highlights the genius of cartography, the eye of history. The complete 5,000-mile line that was recognized by the Iberian powers remained a common boundary for more than a century. In 1876, after Venezuela and Brazil both won independence, Requena's maps were involved in settling their border disputes. Maps are the gestures that establish borders. They inaugurate the vast future work of the history of limits.

In the 1760s, with the Spanish empire in America disintegrating, while both France and England were flexing their muscles fighting the Seven Years' War in Anglo-America among the northern European colonists, first attempts were being made by Spanish settlers in Latin America to organize and map areas of economic interest. Beautiful watercolor maps were made by agricultural laborers or miners to help the authorities, particularly in litigation. One very detailed map (see Plate 152), oriented south, artfully shows the vicinity of the present-day Pacific coast city of Buenaventura, Colombia, when it was known as the estuary of the winding Rio Dagua, where the island of Sombrerillo was key to this part of the Viceroyalty of New Grenada. (It was used to change cargoes from large ships to small boats able to take freight up the river.) Besides the waterways, impeccable detail is given to roads, called King's Highways, and their routes to plantations and across streams.

According to the legend on the map's lower half, the region had a few farms growing bananas, avocados, cocoa, guava, and other agricultural crops, as well as pasturelands. The area was enclosed by tall mountains on all sides, and the river's course is shown from an exquisitely drawn ship (far right) at the estuary to where its chief tributary, the Rio de Vitaco, branches to the north. The map appears to be part of a legal document, and allusions to failed crops and other disasters might have involved bankruptcy proceedings, with properties reverting to the king. Its freedom of orientation, extraordinary colors, design, and precise details recall older portolan charts. Because of the Spanish requirement for secrecy, only general maps of Colombia existed until around 1810, when the legendary German scientist Humboldt took an interest in the Magdalena River, which allows egress 1,060 miles into the interior from the Caribbean coast without having to change boats. (Few maps of the complex waterways of the Pacific coast were ever made.)

This detailed map makes clear that for legal cases, geopolitics were put aside: Spain allowed defendants to be specific geographically on a canvas larger than an estate map in order to tell their side of the story. They were given the right to question authority's truth and were encouraged to trust in the power of truth. It is Map as the Art of Governing. The map tells of a colonial administration in America that eventually cared deeply about the troubles caused for Spanish settlers and colonized natives by land and climate. Interestingly, no church or mission is shown on the map, but there is

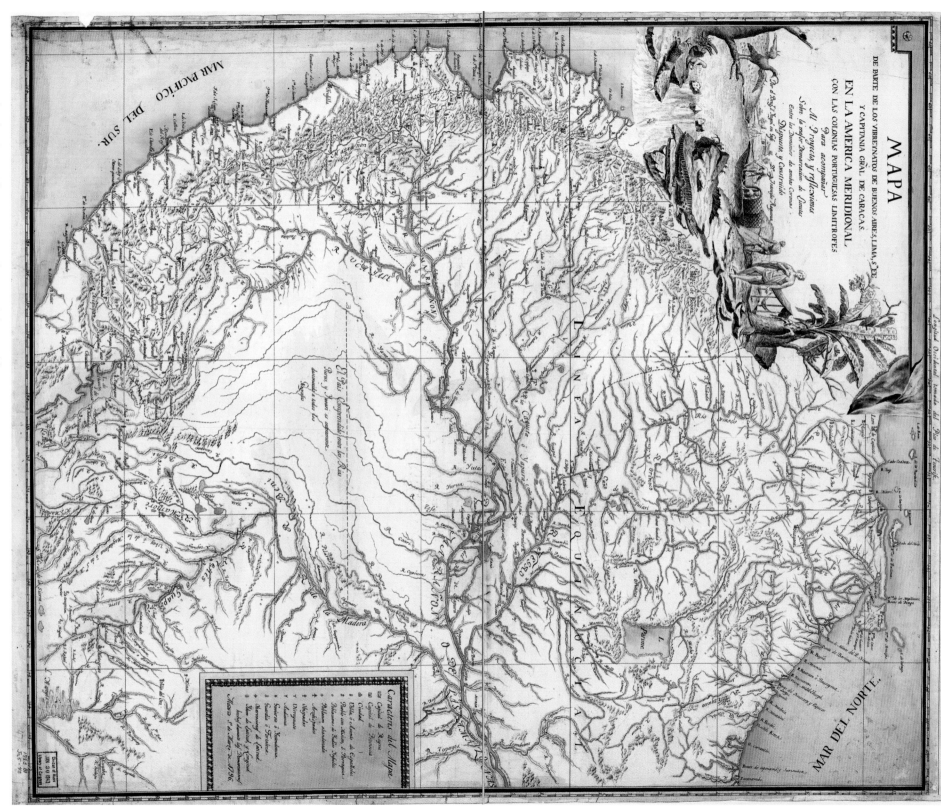

MAPA
DE PARTE DE LOS VIRREYNATOS DE BUENOS AIRES, LIMA, S.ᵗᵉ FE
Y CAPITANIA GRÀL. DE CARACAS,
EN LA AMERICA MERIDIONAL,
CON LAS COLONIAS PORTUGUESAS LIMITROFES

Caracteres del Mapa.

MAR PACIFICO DEL SUR.

MAR DEL NORTE.

PLATE 151. *Map Based on the Joint Spanish-Portuguese Boundary Commission's Work in New Spain.* This 1796 Spanish map was the result of a collaboration from hell.

PLATE 152 (OVERLEAF). *Map of Dagua River Region, Colombia.* A unique glimpse into life in the farthest reaches of New Spain is offered by this 1764 map.

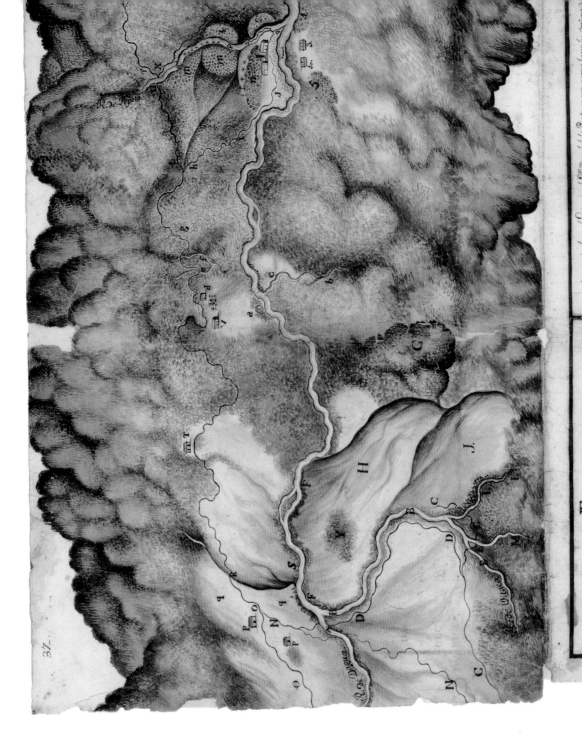

37.

Explicacion.

AAA. Rio de Dagua.

BBB. Rio de Vitaco, cuyas aguas internan en el de Dagua.

CCC. Camino Real antiguo de el Rio de Vitaco, q̃ passando por Sabaletas, cuja por el Potrero de los Chancos, hasta el Rio de Dagua.

DD. Desecho q̃ buxa costeando el Rio de Vitaco, y passa dicho Rio de Dagua.

E. Passo antiguo del Rio de Vitaco: En este passo se concluieron por el Dr. Bernardo Alphonso de Sa. las medidas que se practica, y se expresan en el titulo de Merceð librado á fabor de Franco. de Roa, de los Chancos.

FF. Rio de Dagua, q̃ en el intermedio de estas letras toma el Nombre de los Chancos.

G. Montaña de la derezera de Calima, cuyas faldas se eleban sobre el Potrero de los Chancos.

H. Potrero de los Chancos.

Y. Aguada que está sobre una Meseta q̃ haze dho Potrero de los Chancos.

J. Potrero de Sabaletas.

LL. Quebrada de Sabaletas.

M. Rio Grande, q̃ haze su entrada en el de Vitaco, sobre cuyas Juntas se halla demarcado el passo del Camino Rl antiguo, como se demuestra en su correspondiente lugar.

NN. Camino Real y nuebo de los Simarronas, q̃ toma union en la hazienda de Dagua, con el que cxa de esta Ziuðað, y passan en uno, haz...

O.O. Camino Real antiguo que sale de esta Ziudad, y passando por dha Vitaco, q̃ conducen á las Provincias del Raposo, y el Chocó.

P.P. Casas y Hazienda de Dr. Antonio y Dr. Roman Garcia llamada de Dagua.

q.q. Potrero de Dagua.

R. Vajada del Camino Rl. antiguo del Potrero de Dagua, y es el mismo que unido con el que Simarronas forma su marcha en la conformidad que ha exordio.

S.S. Quebrada Seca, cuya derrota, atrabesando por el camino Real que se dha Vajada de Dagua. Sigue arrojando sus aguas, guiando las tiene, á frente de los Chancos. Esta es donde Dagron los Vatigos términos las medidas que por este lado presentó Dn. Bern. de Sa, y sobre de intervo á la Feliz de Dagua q̃ posée Dn. Antonio Garcia, que fue uno testigos para este acto.

T. Sitio de los Oxos.

V. Sitio del Cerrojo.

a. Casa q̃ se nombra Rancho, y pertenece al que se halla agregado en el Naranjo, á qual dirro...

b. Centinela á un corto CañaDazal q̃ frente este en la Vega del Rio de Dagua según se halla.

b.c. Quebrada cuyo nombre no se puðo aberiguar, q̃ occidente á dho Rio de Dagua por intre...as de las Eleuadas Montañas q̃ en este Vega se demuestran.

d. Casa de la Brūña, que Sirve de Estanquillo al arrendador de aguardiente hasta Ziuð...

e.f. Quebradas de Gimenez, cuyas aguas en breue instante se pierden de vista, por ðo agu... tacienda, hasta q̃ hacen su entrada en el nominado Rio de Dagua.

g. El Cerrito. Sigue el mismo curso entrada, como las antecedentes Quebradas.

h.i.j. Camino, ó Desecha moderno, que apartandose ðel antiguo de mas, q̃ hasta oy existe... pendiente, espesa Montaña de Yegñtos, y Inmiðiato: sobre la Playa del Esperito R... gua, llega á descansar á las Juntas con las gentes y cola de que le pueðen trafa...

2001-662577

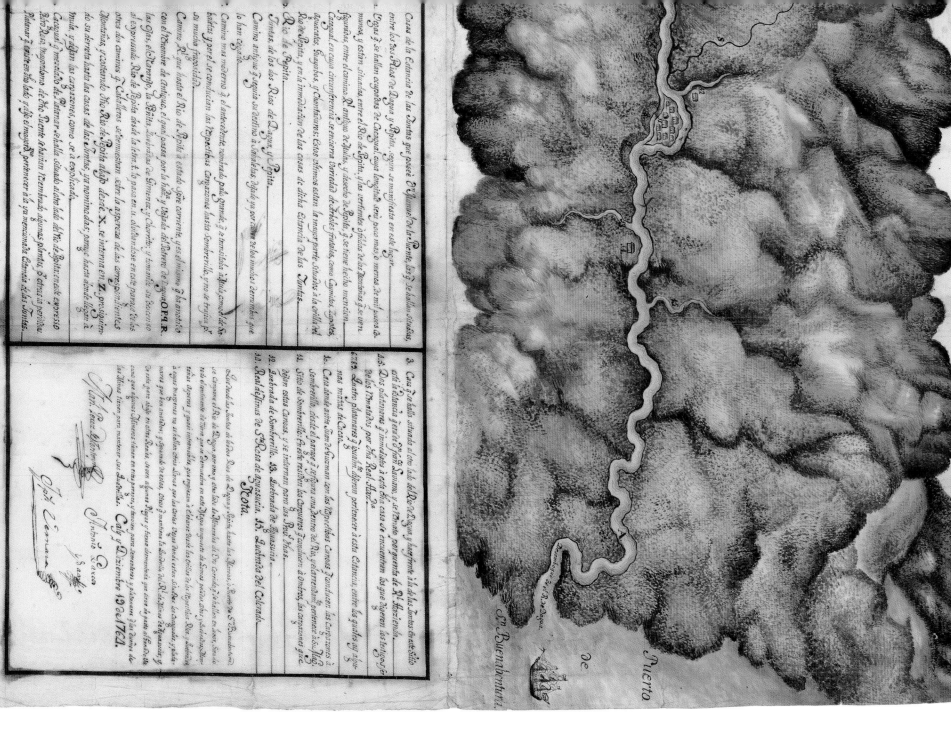

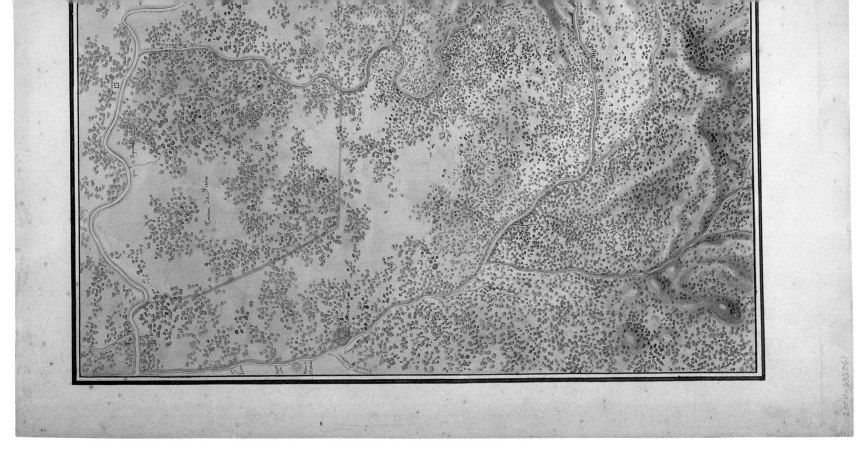

a tavern. Attempts by Spanish apologists to deny the savagery of the conquistadores and the early colonists are often based on the judicial fairness displayed in maps like this one. They accept maps as social proclamations, tools to facilitate the geographical expansion of social systems, but they deny that the truth espoused in each map is specific to its time and place. Maps exist in historical context. Originally, Spain in the New World held the view of Christopher Marlowe's Tamburlaine: "Give me a map, then let me see how much / Is left for me to conquer all the world."

In 1819 a political union of the present-day neighboring nations of Panama, Colombia, Venezuela, and Ecuador was achieved. This federation was known as Gran Colombia. It was led by Simón Bolívar, whose life was devoted to establishing a nation and government in the midst of the continuing struggle for independence from Spain. Despite attempts to consolidate the central government in Bogotá, the period between 1819 and 1830 witnessed considerable internal dissensions that climaxed with the secession of Venezuela and Ecuador from Gran Colombia in 1830. It was during these difficult times that Gran Colombia arranged for a loan of 2 million pounds sterling from Great Britain. In partial repayment of the loan, British creditors were granted lands in various provinces of Gran Colombia, which they, in turn, attempted to sell to immigrants. This led to a commissioned map, a dazzling, colored, pen-and-ink map of a portion of Mariquita Province (now Tolina Department) west of the Magdalena River in Colombia (Plate 153). It includes roads, streams, towns and settlements, delineation of government and private lands, and carefully rendered pictorial representation of vegetation, cultivated fields, and relief. It exists to extol the immense advantages of Colombia for colonists and merchants. It is Map as Real Estate Promotion. Oriented with east at the top, this seductive map includes a well-executed, impressive shield of Gran Colombia to add to the grandeur of the enterprise, while an elegant cartouche adds a classy touch. Roulin, the mapmaker, worked for a British-sponsored agricultural association involved with various colonization schemes in Gran Colombia. He was, in effect, a local artist helping to sell a piece of the "real" world he knew firsthand. His map is a representation of place with a practical bent. It has a dream-like quality appropriate to its aim of selling dreams of success in exotic places. Maps satisfy Freud's description of dreams as "picture writing."

Nation-states evolved from the work and passions of immigrants to the southern landmass of America, and with independence from European colonialism came governmental agencies inventing other uses for maps. The world's great tropical forests, which once seemed so forbidding and impenetrable to explorers and cartographers such as Requena, became prime targets for economic exploitation and development. One way to make them available to colonists was to declare traditional European-style maps the only way to claim land rights. Since the ancient and efficient cartographic languages of indigenous tribes were not compatible with European forms of mapping, the tribes and their rain forest habitats became endangered species. In Brazil, for instance, the Indians, who had lived in harmony with their diverse forest environment for

thousands of years and had numbered an estimated 5 million to 10 million in hundreds of tribes throughout the country, were reduced to fewer than 300,000 to 1 million by the twenty-first century; and every year an area of forest the size of Louisiana is cleared.

In the course of their work in the rain forest, some conservationists and scientists built close personal relationships with indigenous peoples. Perceiving a need for a new kind of conservationist organization, one that could be a partnership with local peoples in Brazil, Colombia, Costa Rica, Mexico, and Suriname, the founders of the Amazon Conservation Team (ACT) met in 1995 to curb ecological and cultural degradation in tropical and subtropical America. By combining tribal knowledge of the land with

Western science, highly accurate, invaluable maps were produced by the indigenous peoples with the assistance of ACT in partnership with the Center for the Support of Native Lands and the Central Bureau for Aerial Mapping. One of the maps emerging from ACT's Land Use Mapping Project shows the homeland activities of the Trio peoples in southwestern Suriname (see Plate 154). There

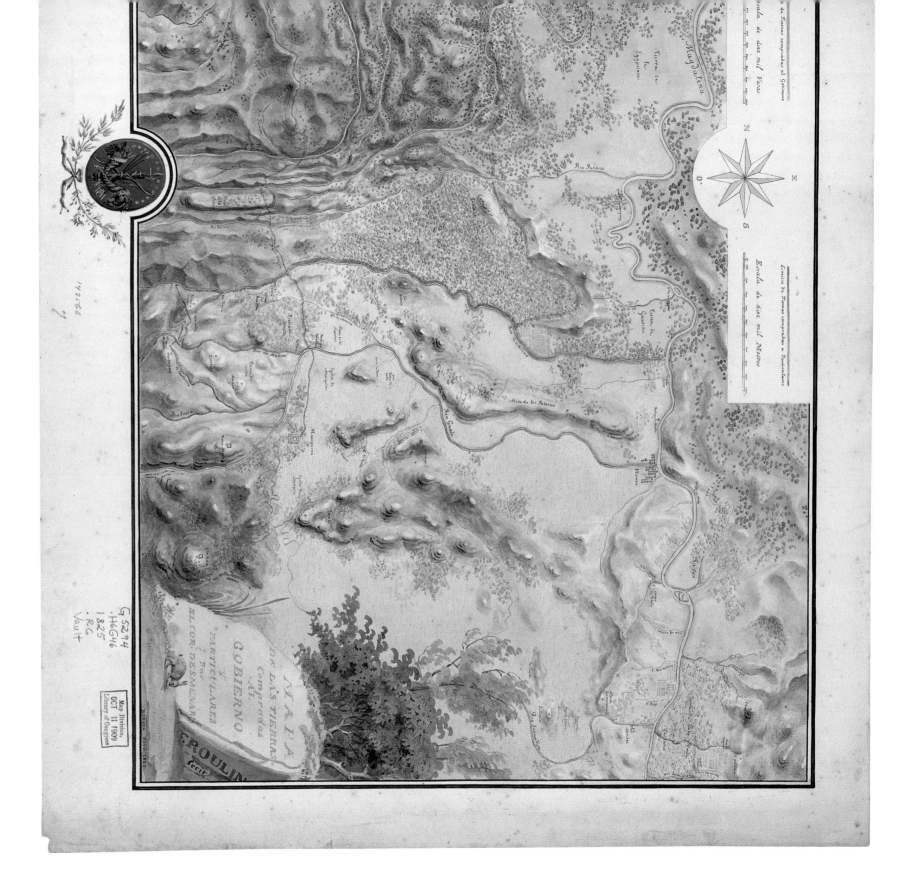

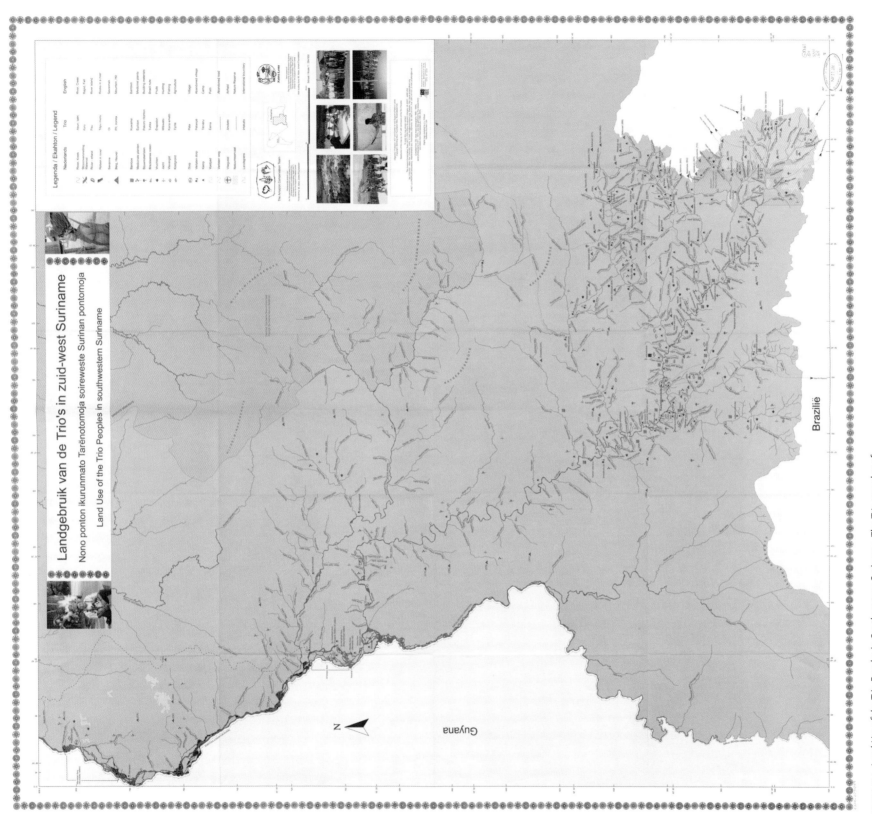

PLATE 154. *Land Use of the Trio Peoples in Southwestern Suriname.* The Trio peoples of Suriname were assisted in making this map to save their ancestral home.

are currently about 2,000 Trio living in Suriname and Brazil. It is Map as Act of Survival. It contains a legend in three languages, including Trio. The Indian symbols used on the map of their ancestors' territory are also identified.

These maps made it possible for the indigenous peoples to defend their homes from destructive miners and loggers, and by extension to strengthen tribal leadership, to perpetuate traditions that have sustained the forests and rivers for millennia, and to develop the area in a positive way. The mapping process relied upon their oral traditions and stressed the links between their history and their particular territory. The map provided the transformational energy they needed to break free of the complex web of colonists' subjugating constraints and legal impediments. Their claims could be categorized in court as "ancestral rights," which are now internationally recognized, and their map could be submitted as evidence in land rights negotiations.

The tropical forest ecosystem is extremely fragile. When the trees are destroyed, erosion takes the soil, clogs the rivers, and the area quickly becomes a "red desert" for all time. Believing they will reap greater profits, planners are beginning to employ Indian subsistence techniques as an alternative design to environmental destruction for tropical forest use. The survival of the planet rests upon the attitudes presented in the indigenous map by the Trio people of Suriname.

If the visual imprint of human activity is called the cultural landscape, then the Landsat image taken from space by NASA (Plate 155) reveals contrasting cultural landscapes along the Mexico-California border, or between Latin and Anglo America. The dark patch at the top of the image is the Salton Sea, the agricultural drainage reservoir for all the productive agricultural valleys that adjoin it. These appear on the Landsat image as bright colors representing growing vegetation throughout California's Imperial Valley, a $1.5 billion enterprise resulting from a man-made ecosystem based on imported water. The marked break, where irregularly shaped fields and less prosperous agriculture appear, is the Mexicali Valley below the Mexican border on the Landsat map. It is Map as Contrasting Resource Development.

The Salton Sea, California's largest lake, was created in 1905 when the Colorado River flooded and filled the Salton Sink. The flooding river also created the Alamo and New River channels. The Salton Sea became a transboundary watershed. Its primary water source is drainage from the neighboring 500,000 acres of irrigated California farms. It acts as a repository for that runoff. California's agriculture industry would dry up without the Salton Sea's watershed system, including the Colorado River, which is the only significant source of surface water in the southwestern United States. Thirty dams control the river and its tributaries, and two immense reservoirs store its water for U.S. farms and cities. Aqueducts and canals siphon off its water for seven western states and northern Mexico. Legally, every drop of its water is claimed or currently under litigation. The Morelos dam on the Arizona-Mexico border sends virtually all of the remaining Colorado River water to irrigation canals in the Mexicali Valley below the Salton Sea, and farther on to Mexicali and Tijuana, and finally into the Bay of California.

In 1944 a water treaty between Mexico and the United States specified that 1.5 million acre-feet of the Colorado River was to reach Mexico annually. The Landsat image shows how resource development differs on opposite sides of the border. The failure of the Mexican government to encourage and support the creation of a man-made ecosystem in the Mexicali Valley, an extension of the thriving Imperial Valley, has profound economic repercussions for the Mexican people, such as the absence of jobs and the loss of tax revenue for the nation. It demonstrates poor government supervision of the precious water, which is also evident in the pollution of the New River in Mexicali from human and industrial waste.

The sense of responsibility to the Mexican people that was historically, after a time, the hallmark of New Spain, visually manifested in ancient maps, has been lost in the transition to modern times by its leaders in independence. This truthful map seems to prove the colonialists' warning: "If we leave, you will revert to the condition of barbarism we rescued you from by our efforts. Without us, you are nothing." In fact, the map shows how colonialism reduced people to nothing. Ensnared in Western culture, the colonized people were left with distorted, disfigured, and destroyed memories of once great civilizations of their own making. Truth, as expressed in maps, is what hastens the dislocation of the colonialist regimes after decolonization. Truth is what fosters the emergence of thriving nations. By mapping civilizations, the past can be reclaimed. As Frantz Fanon insists, "Reclaiming the past

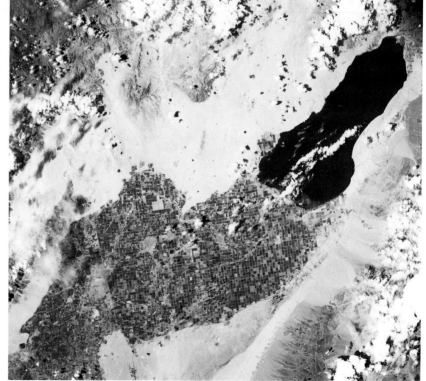

PLATE 155. *Colorado River Basin.* Contrasting cultural landscapes are captured by this NASA image of the Mexico-U.S. border.

PLATE 156. *North East Coast of North America*. New France was partially mapped by its founder, Samuel de Champlain, with the assistance of its indigenous inhabitants.

ANGLO AMERICA

If the European invasion of Latin America was the result of ruthless conquest, Anglo America's invasion was the result of gradual colonization. France, England, and the Netherlands engaged in wars against financially strapped Spain in an effort to undermine vulnerable Iberian preeminence in the distant New World. The first real description of the North Atlantic coast was made by Giovanni da Verrazano, who was sent out by Francis I, king of France, in 1524, when France's claim to a New France was colonies in Canada and Louisiana. They were essentially trading areas for fur, leather, and fish. The people of France were not eager to emigrate, which left the Indian populations of the territories fairly undisturbed at first. As traders, not settlers, the French gained the support of the various tribes with whom they lived peacefully, often marrying into them. By the 1590s, however, the French crown, stimulated by revenue from furs, offered trading monopolies in the St. Lawrence region to entrepreneurs who would settle colonies there.

In the southeast and southwest, French activities were hampered by the Spanish, but in the far north, the French initially moved around unimpeded. Stimulated by the possibility of a trading monopoly, Samuel de Champlain (1567–1635), explorer and founder of New France, made his first voyage to Canada in 1603. Most of the great maps of the European Age of Discovery were drawn by professional cartographers, but his portolan-style chart on vellum—the first thorough delineation of the New England and Canadian coast from Cape Sable to Cape Cod—he drew himself in the winter of 1606–07 (Plate 156). The shorelines were drawn from the rail of his ship, but he also incorporated Indian cartography. In the French manner, he established relatively unambivalent friendly relations with the Indians, and relied on their comprehensive and helpful geographical intelligence.

For this map, Indians accurately drew Massachusetts Bay and the Merrimack River for him with charcoal, and, as he wrote, they "placed six pebbles at equal intervals giving me thereby to understand that each one of these marks represented that number of chiefs and tribes." It is Map as First Relationship Encounter. They also drew maps of places they had visited, and told him all about them. A number of habitations are shown along the shoreline, the larger ones representing French settlements and the smaller ones Native American villages. The Indian presence on Champlain's map is not a symbolic one, though, more important, the absence of any record of their individual territories does open the door for the creation of New France in what appears to be an undivided wilderness.

does not only rehabilitate or justify the promise of a national culture. It triggers a change of fundamental importance in the colonized's psycho-affective equilibrium." Much has been achieved in Latin America since independence was reintroduced as a way of life, but as the NASA map shows, much more wisdom remains to be culled from the perfection of the indigenous Latin American spirit.

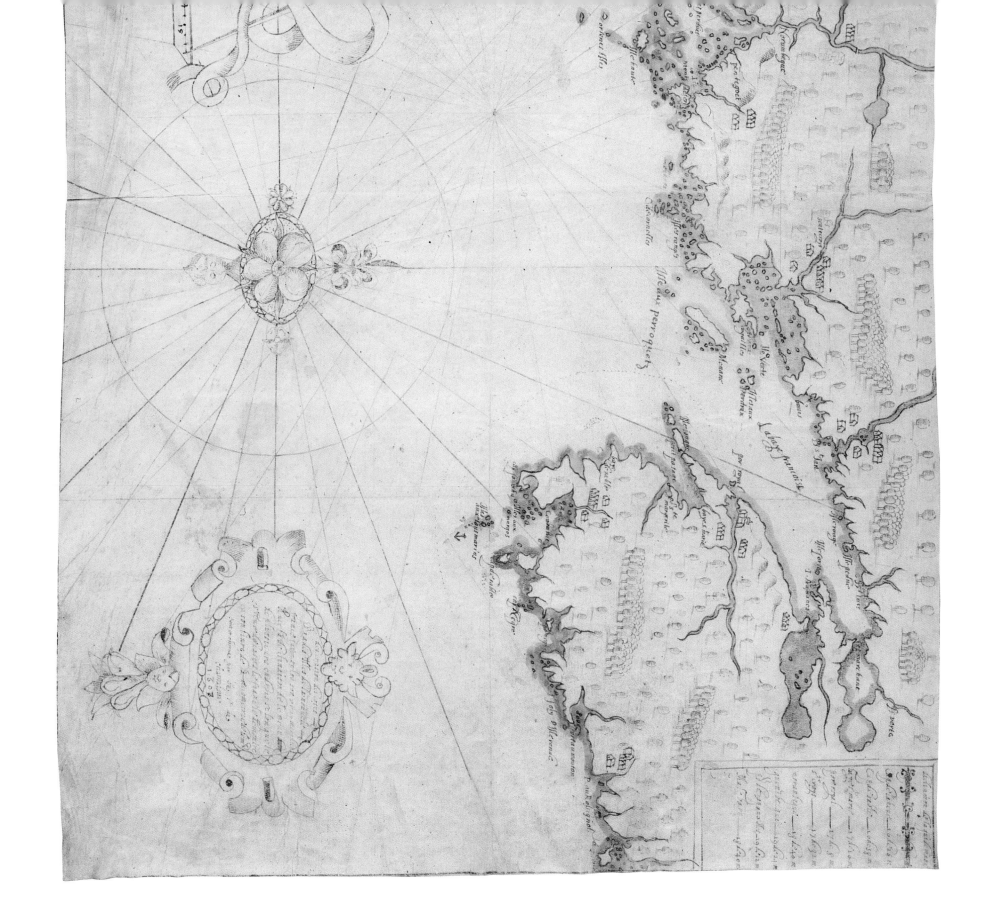

In 1608 Champlain founded the first European settlement at Quebec. The same year, he joined a successful war party of Huron and Algonquins against the Iroquois, who were shut out of the trading empire. For allies, the Iroquois then turned south, encountering the Dutch, who would trade them muskets, and later the English, after they replaced the Dutch. Meanwhile, French missionaries were converting members of many tribes, including members of the Five Nations, dividing them internally, a fact that would also seriously weaken the French during their Seven Years' War with England.

To compete with the Spanish and the Portuguese in America, the Dutch formed the United East India Company (1602). In 1609 the Amsterdam Chamber of Commerce employed Henry Hudson, an Englishman, to search for a Northwest Passage to India. He explored the area charted by Champlain before sailing south to Virginia, then north again into the Hudson River. There he came upon an idyllic, lush ecosystem called Lenapehoking — "where the Lenapes dwell" — the Lenapes being about a dozen discrete Indian groups of approximately 65,000 people who inhabited seasonal campsites in what became New York City with all its boroughs and parts of Long Island, New Jersey, and Connecticut. Astonished by the area's beauty and natural abundance, Hudson sailed up the Hudson looking for a route to the Pacific, but turned back at Albany, where he initiated friendly relations with the Iroquois after claiming the entire unknown region for the Dutch. "The land is the finest for cultivation that I ever in my life set foot upon," he wrote. In 1614, a Dutch fur trading post was established on Castle Island in the North River just below modern Albany, and the next year one was built "about the Island Manhattans," derived from Manna-hata (island of the hills) at the mouth of the Hudson River.

When the Dutch West India Company was created in 1621, its encompassed the Hudson River Valley, from the mouth of the river, actually a fjord, to Albany. The Company sent agents to colonize the lucrative area. In contrast to the other American colonialists, such as the Pilgrims in 1620, with their religiously driven quests, most of the Company people had no intentions of staying. They worked as fur traders rather than as farmers, forcing the Company to maintain its own farms. Since the Dutch were not eager to leave flourishing Holland, thirty families were sent, mostly Walloons from Leyden who had been denied permission to settle in Virginia; they were scattered to establish outposts on the Dutch territory's western and eastern boundaries. Other Walloon families followed, along with Danes, Swedes, Norwegians, English, Moroccans, and religious outcasts from other colonies and countries, such as Quakers, Sephardic Jews, English Calvinists — all drawn to the colony's tolerance for diversity and dissent. Unlike the other colonies, New Netherlands welcomed foreigners, an attitude already established in tiny Holland, dependent upon world trade for survival. Anyone could go to this Company settlement and deal in furs, as long as they did all of their business with the Company, both trading and buying supplies. The Company's profits from liquor sales ran second to furs, with fully one-quarter of its buildings consisting of "grog-shops" devoted to tobacco and beer. The daily "mischief and perversity" fueled by immoderate drinking was another difference between New Netherlands and the other colonies.

Many of the early settlers succumbed to illness or were driven off their farms by Indians wanting their campsites back. In 1626 Company director Peter Minuit "purchased" Manhattan Island from the Lenapes for sixty guilders' worth of trade goods, and christened his settlement New Amsterdam. A majority of the Company's shareholders, however, favoring trade over colonization, considered New Amsterdam a commercial "factory" or trading post. A map drawn about 1639 depicts this hybrid colony centered on Manhattan (Manatus) with a section of its surrounding area (Plate 157). It is the result of the first careful survey of the area. It is Map as World Apart. It gives the names of the diverse and dispersed settlers who worked the twenty-two farms (bouweries). The few structures are identified as "under construction." The Lenape longhouses in what is now Brooklyn make the extent of the integrated Indian presence plain. Also, the house provided for Company slaves is on the Manhattan shore opposite what is now Roosevelt Island. The specter of slavery already haunts the New World, though the Dutch did not adhere to the American South's system of absolute racial subjugation; slaves in New Netherland had the same judicial procedures as whites, could own property, testify in court, bear arms in times of emergency, and be legally wed.

Six years before the Manatus map, a new Company director general, Wouter Van Twiller, tried unsuccessfully to create a border between New Netherlands and New England with a fort in what is now Hartford, Connecticut. When the British ignored his efforts, he abandoned the entire Connecticut River Valley to them. He was replaced in 1647 by Peter Stuyvesant, a man determined to "tame" New Amsterdam's tumultuous inhabitants and to make the town appealing to the orderly Dutch temperament. Good schools, a police force — both missing on the Manatus map — were created, along with a well-regulated economy that dealt with privatized real estate, ultimately creating a bustling cosmopolitan colony that still lured, he wrote unhappily, with its promises of "an imaginary liberty in a new and, as some pretend, a free country." In 1660, Charles II became king of England, and his younger brother, James, Duke of York, grew determined to drive the Dutch out of American colonial trade. On September 8, 1664, the flag of the Dutch West Indies Company was struck peacefully, and both New Amsterdam and New Netherlands became New York. Its financial success and its adherence to religious freedom appealed to the now King James II. It was allowed to remain a world apart in the New World.

The English continued to create a colonial empire in the New World along the Atlantic seaboard, which evolved over time into the original thirteen colonies of the future United States. The conflict between the English and the French in America erupted into the Seven Years' War (1754–66), or what the colonists called the French and Indian War. While destroying France's American empire and the diplomatic system in which Native Americans played a central balancing role, the war enlarged England's territory to

the point of unmanageability, and proved to be a turning point in the history of the New World. Foremost, the insensitive British behavior to their colonial subjects determined the allegiance and the actions of the next (American revolutionary) generation and their resistance to helping pay British expenses incurred during the French and Indian War by raised taxes, such as taxes on stamps and tea.

In 1755 a map published by John Mitchell of Virginia, an amateur cartographer, showed the extent of the British and the French settlements in America (see Plate 158). The political map includes roads and the positions of the principal Indian tribes, who played an enormous role in the war, as well as extensive notes regarding the dates of various settlements. It was undertaken at the request of the British Board of Trade, and it was drawn from actual surveys of the British colonies with their 1.5 million inhabitants. Colored bands represent the claims to western lands made by the individual colonies beyond their official boundaries. The map's text explains the extensions westward across the Mississippi River to the western border of the map as being the result of the original 1609 charters granting the colonies land "from sea to sea." Its prescience regarding "manifest destiny" blurs the fact that to the

British colonists at the time, the map spoke only of their being part of—what naively seemed to them then—the world's most enlightened empire, endangered by the French and their Indian allies. It is Map as American Dream. It was about England's need to control the Ohio Valley, along with the Trans-Appalachian west. Ironically, this was the map Benjamin Franklin used in Paris in 1782–83 negotiating the treaty that terminated the Revolutionary War and granted independence to the United States after the states agreed to consolidate their individual rights to those western lands.

But first came the Seven Years' War, without which the American Revolution would not have happened when or as it did. The struggles between the French and the British over the waterways of the Gulf of St. Lawrence protecting French Quebec and French traders were joined by struggles over the unsettled Ohio River Valley. When the French began to move down from the Great Lakes and up from their forts on the lower Mississippi, the British colonists began to fear for access to their "western lands." A map

PLATE 158 (OVERLEAF). *A Map of the British and French Dominions in North America.* This 1755 map is one of the most important in the history of the United States.

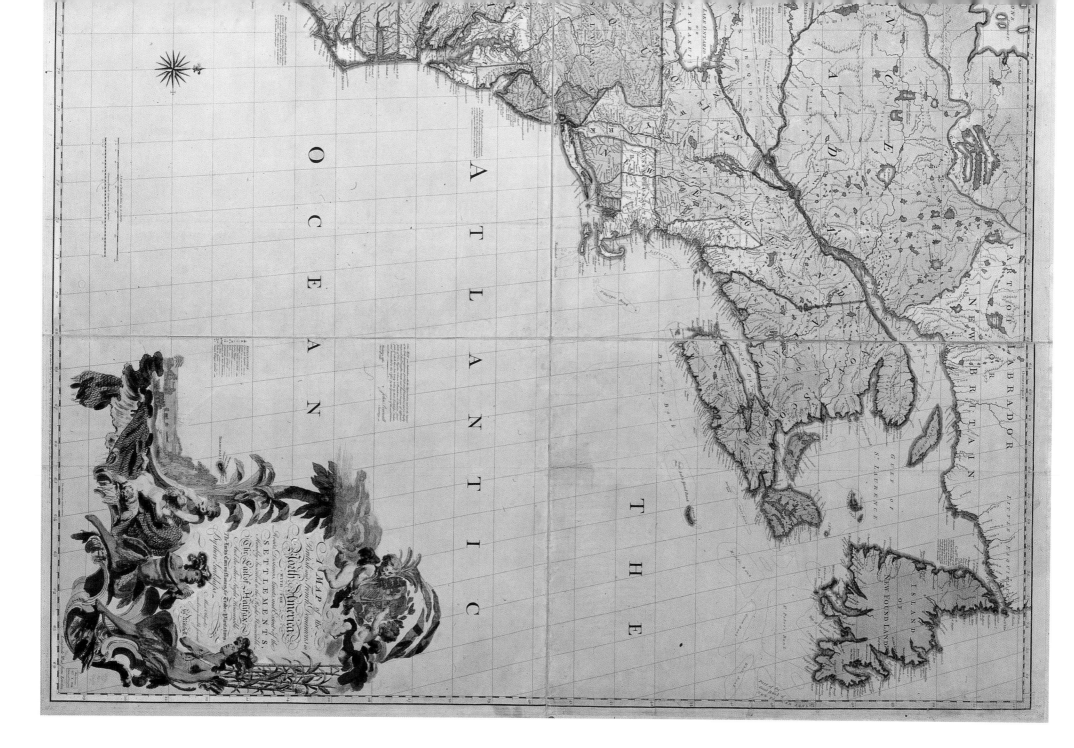

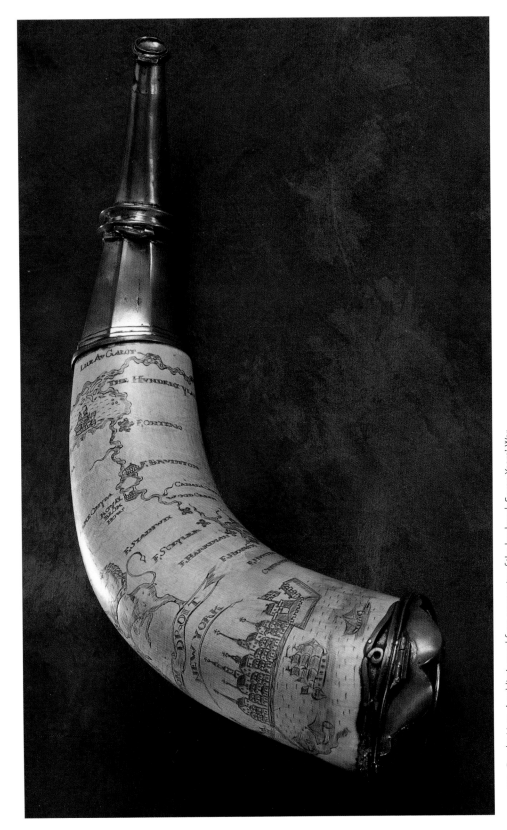

inscribed on a powder horn (Plate 159) between 1757 and 1760 shows the Hudson and Mohawk River Valleys, as well as Lake Champlain and Lake Ontario waterways, which served as the major arteries of travel between New York City (portrayed pictorially at the bottom of the horn) and the St. Lawrence River Valley to the north, and the Great Lakes to the west. Numerous towns and forts along the route are named, and houses, windmills, boats, and other details enliven the design. The horn also bears a British coat of arms, suggesting the owner was an American colonial or a British soldier. Fashioned out of cow or ox horns, gunpowder horns were married to their muskets during the late colonial period. Since maps were scarce, it is possible this map was a guide for its owner or was a record of the area traversed on military campaigns during the Seven Years' War. It is Map as Indispensable Companion.

The image of the ship is critical to the war's story, since it was the British defeat of French fleets in 1759 that denied the French the ability to easily reinforce their garrisons. First Quebec fell, then Montreal, then the Great Lakes, then the Ohio Valley. At the Treaty of Paris, the French ceded Canada and all their lands west of the Mississippi to Britain, whose ally, Spain, gave the British Spanish Florida because the French gave them the Louisiana territory, which included the entire area between the Mississippi and the Rocky Mountains. Great Britain became the world's greatest colonial power, but found itself in need of money to run its phe-

nomenal enterprise in America, the most immediate beneficiaries being the colonists. This led to those taxes, which the colonists riotously rejected. (Benjamin Franklin called the Boston Tea Party an act of piracy.) Then the British attempted to reform the administration of the colonies to gain more direct control over the colonists, who were challenging and resisting any fiddling with the balance of power by refusing to submit to the loss of local autonomy while steadfastly remaining loyal British subjects. When the first spontaneous shots of the Revolution erupted at Lexington and Concord, Massachusetts, on April 19, 1775, they were the inevitable result of Britain's being unwilling to allow its rebellious colonists to dictate the terms of empire. (Samuel Johnson called the Americans "a race of convicts.") Far from being a beginning, the Revolution was actually the culmination of a process of souring relations that had begun during the Seven Years' War.

In June 1775, after a crippling defeat in Boston, the British retreated to Canada. A whole year later, after the Declaration of Independence, hundreds of British ships and 32,000 soldiers under General Sir William Howe arrived in New York, considered a nursery of loyalty to the mother country because the monied New Yorkers knew what they stood to lose if the empire failed to keep its grip on Anglo America. However, the flight of thousands of affluent, aristocratic Tories, the impending invasion of the British army, the presence of George Washington's Revolutionary army, and the prodding of the well-organized and militant Mechanics Union had completed the shift to radical rule. When a royal pardon was offered the colonists, it was rejected, even though General Washington had only 19,000 inadequately armed and poorly trained soldiers, and no navy at all.

The British camped in New Jersey for the winter. A hand-drawn intelligence map by General John Cadwalader was sent to Washington only days before his surprise attack on the British (Plate 160). After crossing the icy Delaware River on Christmas night 1776, in sleet and snow, he defeated the unprepared Hessian troops first at Trenton and, on January 3, 1777, at Princeton, shattering Howe's notion of a quick triumph for his king, who had received word of Howe's smashing successes at White Plains and Fort Washington, successes that had driven General Washington into Delaware in early December. However, Washington had learned his lessons well when fighting with the British in the Seven Years' War; he knew his enemy. The map's strategic intent for the American infantry is reflected in Cadwalader's notation at lower right: "This road leads to the back part of Prince Town, which may be entered anywhere on this side — the Country cleared, chiefly, for about 2 miles…few Fences." It is Map as Wake-up Call. The effect of Washington's triumphs on the colonists' spirits was immense. As the historian Henry Steele Commager wrote, "The Old World imagined the Enlightenment and the New World realized it. The Old World invented it, formulated it, and agitated it; America absorbed it, reflected it, and institutionalized it."

The French, meanwhile, were settled offshore in the Caribbean, waiting for an opportunity to return to the mainland of America with a resurrected New France. In the Louisiana territory, where the majority spoke French, the customs of the Creoles were honored by the Spanish, who governed from their base in Havana, which established the colony's strong Gulf-Caribbean orientation. In 1795 the United States concluded negotiations with Spain for river rights on the Mississippi and docking privileges in New Orleans, in large part because the aggressive United States — according to Louisiana's Governor Miró — "had no other means of shipping their produce than the navigation of the Mississippi." Bankrupt Spain could ill afford another war so far from home. The realities of a possible Louisiana invasion by England or the United States forced Spain to "retrocecede" the vast province of 529,402,880 acres back to France in 1801. Two years later, the French leader Napoleon, in need of money to fight his war with England and realize his imperial ambitions in Europe, concurred with Spain's conclusion: the vastness of Louisiana was impossible to defend. He sold it to the United States for $15 million. The Louisiana Purchase amounted to one-third of the future United States; but at the time, it doubled the size of the young American republic. President Thomas Jefferson saw a different importance. "This removes from us the greatest source of danger to our peace," he wrote.

With the purchase came the method of land allocation used by the French in the province. Colonization required some method of patterning land parcels, and in America the invaders and colonists ignored any indigenous forms of ordering the land. They created a tabula rasa upon which they could impose any design they fancied. It was natural for seafarers to lay claim to land along the river, and a system evolved by the French used the highway-river as a boundary with long lots marked off in uniform blocks, usually rectangular, ten times as long as they were wide. Easy on surveyors, this gave everyone access to the river, and an equal share in the alluvial soils in the river valleys. When the river land was allocated, roads were built parallel to the river, and the long-lot process continued inland.

A map of the Lower Mississippi from 1858 by Marie Adrien Persac (see Plate 161) shows the survival of the French long-lot survey system. It is Map as French Cultural Landscape. It features the names and owners of plantations and primary crops, including sugar, cotton, and indigo, which are designated in different colors. Vignettes framing the map include a cotton plantation, a sugar plantation, a view of New Orleans looking upriver from near Elysian Fields Avenue, and port activity at Baton Rouge. The map serves as a prime source for comparative data on crop production along the river and the dimensions of antebellum plantation

PLATE 160. *Plan of Princeton, Dec. 31, 1776.* Britain's wartime illusions were shattered thanks to this 1776 British colonist's spy map.

THE FOURTH PART: THE AMERICAS

{203}

system was problematic because rivers do not stay the same shape over the years, and as lots were divided among children and grandchildren, each person's slice became impossibly narrow. But more important, Jefferson's choice perfectly expressed his philosophy at the time, and the philosophy of the Federalists, who favored a strong central government capable of providing the political and economic structure required by a unified, prospering, extensive republic. For Jefferson, the rectangular system served the emerging belief in the states that land was a commodity to be bought and sold; it was not only part of the family inheritance. He also wanted the parcels to be manageable for individual family farmers in what he conceived to be essentially an agrarian society where everyone was equal, like their small squares of land. An 1861 map created and published by M. H. Thompson of Knox County, Illinois, shows Jefferson's plan in action (Plate 162). It is Map as Jefferson's Vision. His plan is still operative in a majority of the United States. The insets, containing enlarged plans of villages, views of important buildings, and portraits of notable (rich) residents, were introduced soon after the first printed U.S. county maps in 1808.

The format of county maps was rapidly standardized to include political boundaries, roads, railroads, villages, mills, factories, churches, schools, houses, and names of residents, as well as geographic features, such as rivers, streams, and mountains. Before beginning a county map, business-savvy publishers like Thompson would seek the support of county officials, lawyers, bankers, real estate dealers, and other prominent men of the community. Generally their endorsement appeared in the local newspapers, along with an appeal for financial assistance from every citizen. Canvassers were then sent to every farmstead to solicit subscriptions for the proposed map. Business and home owners were charged from $36 to $60 to have their properties depicted in the views. Actual work did not begin until the canvassers had obtained enough signatures to assure the financial success of the enterprise. Selling for around $5 apiece, about 1,000 copies of each map were printed. The lithographic stones were then cleaned and reused for a new map of another county. Previously not available in cartographic form, this wealth of information on the use of geographical space eventually made these maps large and unwieldy, giving rise to the county atlases in 1864.

The U.S. Constitution details many principles for the political organization of geographical space. The framers of the Constitution wanted the former colonies to retain some self-governance, and their initial debates in Philadelphia were centered on the issue of who got how much power. Since there were big states wanting votes according to population, and small states clamoring for equal representation regardless of population, a compromise had to be struck about territorial representation to the federal government: Two chambers were formed in the legislative branch. The Senate was structured with two members from each state, no matter its population. The House of Representatives was struc-

PLATE 162. *Map of Knox County, Illinois.* Thomas Jefferson's favoring the Rectangular Land Survey System was about political geography.

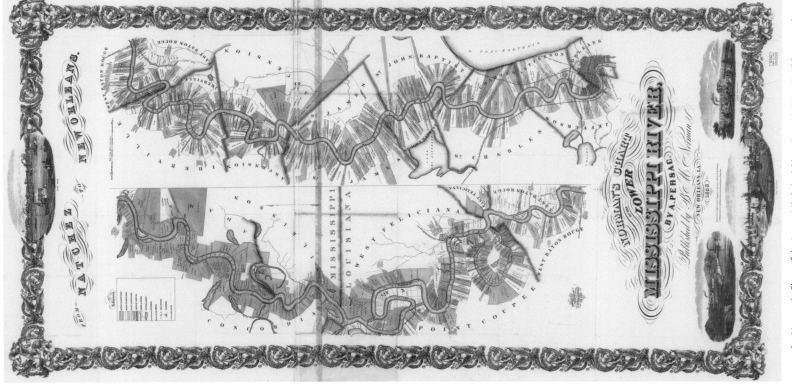

PLATE 161. *Norman's Chart of the Lower Mississippi River.* France's New World geographic legacy is immortalized by this map of the Lower Mississippi River.

properties. For the French, with their shortage of immigrants, the long lots spread the population thinly over an area in an orderly manner while the narrowness of the plots kept the houses fairly close together, giving a sense of community.

After the 1783 Treaty of Paris, Thomas Jefferson was assigned to draft a policy for the new nation on the management system for lands in the public domain. He rejected the French long-lot system in favor of a geometric grid based on latitude and longitude lines known as the Rectangular Land Survey System. The French

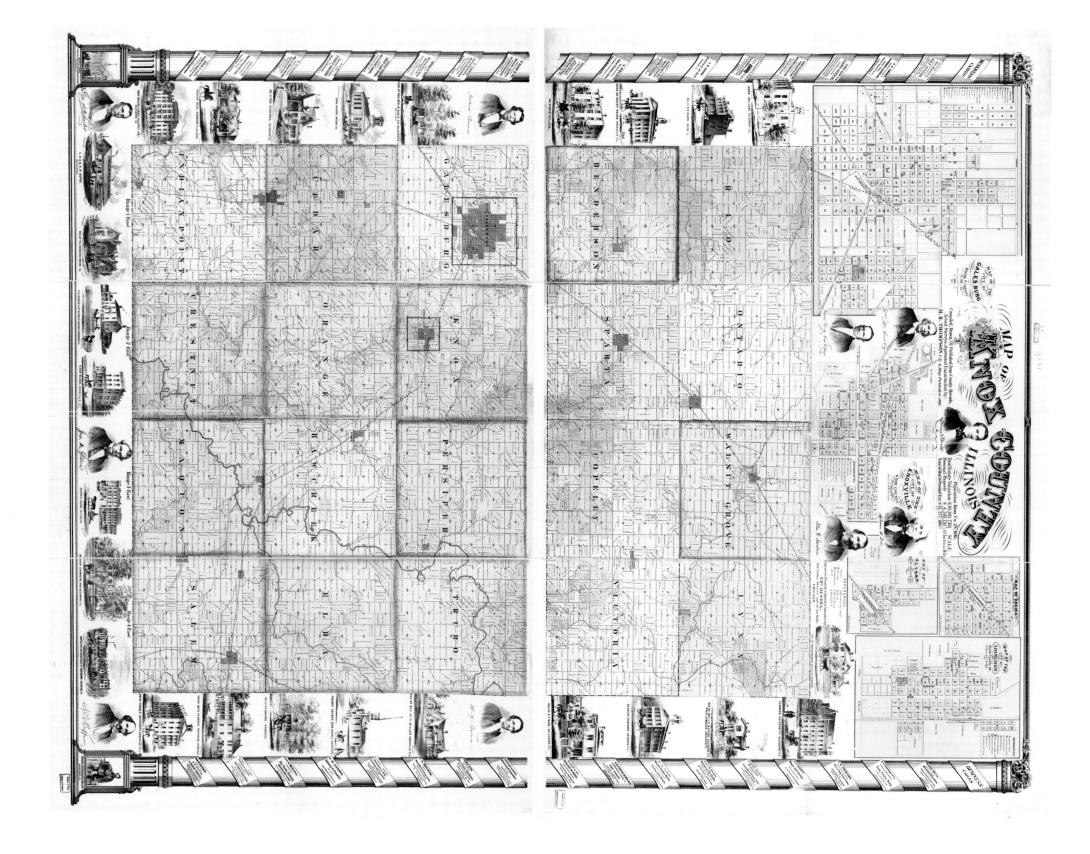

Gerry's party controlled the state legislature and was thereby entitled to redraw congressional district boundaries in the remapping that followed the 1810 census. In order to dilute the Federalist presence in the Boston area, Gerry's cartographers manipulated one district's shape to include dense areas dominated by his own party members. It was like selecting the brightest stars in the night sky and then drawing the resulting constellation. The new district, long and thin, embraced the northern, western, and southwestern fringes of Essex County. Tisdale's geopolitical, often pejorative term when used by the disillusioned electorate came to describe any arbitrary redistricting for political purposes—a common practice in American electoral politics ever since. Political scientists see it as a manipulation that is part of the political process. But, the geographer Mark Monmonier concludes, "because the way political cartographers relocate district boundaries affects who runs as well as who wins, a remap can strongly influence, if not determine, what a government does or doesn't do, what activities it bans or encourages, and which citizens absorb the costs or reap the benefits." The resulting barely readable maps perpetuate the myth that all districts enjoy equal clout, but they also divert the attention from the need for election reform and public referenda. They reveal the complex relationships among geography, demography, and power in the United States of America.

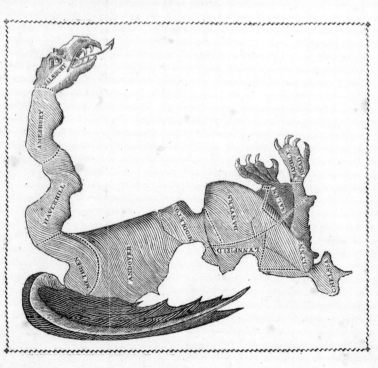

THE GERRY-MANDER.

A new species of Monster, which appeared in *Essex South District* in Jan. 1812.

" O generation of Vipers! who hath warned you of the wrath to come?"

PLATE 163. *The Gerry-mander.* The cunning business of redrawing congressional districts is mocked by this 1812 history-making engraving.

tured with a membership based on state population as counted by census every ten years, and the seats adjusted accordingly. Legislators wasted no time figuring out ways to make the system work for them.

Not only are seats reallocated in the House with shifts in populations, but also billions of dollars in federal and state aid based on population estimates are reapportioned when election districts for Congress and state legislatures are remapped after each ten-year census. In 1812 the engraver Elkanah Tisdale of Salem, Massachusetts, created a legendary image for a political broadside that he named *The Gerry-Mander. A new species of Monster, which appeared in Essex South District in Jan. 1812* (Plate 163). His work immortalized his opinion of the cunning business of redrawing congressional districts by adding fangs, wings, and claws to a map of the new voting districts in Essex County, Massachusetts, where boundary lines were redrawn solely to assure the Jeffersonian Democratic-Republican Party's dominance over the Federalists in the state senate. It is Map as Political Positioning. It answers the question of how far politicians will go to consolidate and expand their hold on power, while reminding the viewer why election districts matter. The Gerry-mander is a hybrid of "salamander" and the last name of the governor, Elbridge Gerry, who forced the partisan bill through the Massachusetts legislature.

An even more complex relationship between maps and reality is revealed by the fallout from Major Stephen H. Long's 1823 *Map of the Country Drained by the Mississippi* (see Plate 164). Long, an explorer and mapmaker, was hired in 1819 by the federal government to find out what lay between the Mississippi River and the Rocky Mountains in the unknown realm acquired by the Louisiana Purchase and not explored by Lewis and Clark. He traveled west through what is now Nebraska and Iowa, then south through Oklahoma and Arkansas. In the journals and reports accompanying his map, he wrote, "I do not hesitate in saying that the entire area is almost wholly unfit for cultivation. And of course it's uninhabitable by a people depending upon agriculture for their existence." Buffalo, wild game, and goats might live there, but not people. Using large type, he labeled this region on his map "Great Desert." In time this area would be renamed the Great Plains, and, with the assistance of approximately 170,000 wells and windmills drawing water from the massive High Plains Aquifer, would become the largest area of irrigation-sustained cropland in the world, growing much of the nation's produce and grain. However, at the time of Long's visit, the semiarid region was suffering from one of its twenty-year cyclical droughts. (The most famous drought, aided by poor farming methods, caused the Dust Bowl evacuation of the region in the 1930s.) Just as a stopped clock is correct twice a day, so Major Long was correct in labeling the region a desert.

As a result of Long's map, this "uninhabitable" region remained sparsely settled until it gained new importance in the eyes of those whites eager to remove the Indians east of the Mississippi. The Great American Desert, as it was also known, was renamed on maps

Indian Territory. After more than a decade of warring and treaty maneuvering in the east, famed Indian fighter Andrew Jackson successfully initiated the Indian Removal Act of 1830, a year after becoming president. (He was aided by a Supreme Court decree that Indians could occupy but not hold title to U.S. lands because the "right of discovery" was superior to the "right of occupancy.") The removal was touted as a voluntary action to the Indians, who had already lost over three-quarters of Alabama and Florida, as well as parts of Georgia, Tennessee, Mississippi, Kentucky, and North Carolina.

President Jackson urged the Indians, "Young chiefs! Forget the prejudices you feel for the soil of your birth, and go to a land where you can preserve your people as a nation." The Indians who chose to remain as citizens of their southern states surrendered to the "white men's laws," yet were hounded off their untitled lands, and those who resisted were forcibly removed by Jackson during the Second Seminole War (1835–42). Eighteen thirty-eight brought the nightmare for the Cherokees known as the Trail of Tears, when 16,000 of them were forced by 7,000 U.S. troops to march to Long's West, at the cost of 4,000 Indian lives. As historian Robert Remini concludes, "From start to finish, the operation of the removal policy was a horror. Deliberate fraud, corruption, mismanagement, and theft marked almost every stop of the process. The Indians were abused and mistreated. Indifference and exploitation characterized white behavior toward these unfortunate people."

By 1837, forty-six thousand Native Americans had been removed from their land east of the Mississippi, and their 25 million acres were opened to white settlement and to slavery. Ignoring the treaties that legalized the Indian Territory, whites then moved into the territory in order to farm, to mine for gold, and to build railroads across the plains, and pressured the politicians in Washington to have Indian rights to it abolished. In 1861 the federal government ordered the Indians to surrender this land; and in 1864, the Cheyenne and Arapaho Indians were driven out of what had become the Colorado Territory into the Oklahoma Territory after many of their women and children were massacred at Sand Creek by the Colorado Volunteers, who were eager to be kept safe at home fighting Indians rather than fighting in the Civil War. From 1868 to 1874, Indians were mercilessly attacked by the U.S. Army of the West, increased in size by thousands of officers and soldiers who preferred the "action" of the plains to retirement after the Civil War. As Dee Brown explains, "Lack of a definite [Indian] policy in Washington resulted in a great deal of confusion, and a corresponding ascendancy of authority given the army in the West." Also, the Indians' primary food source, the buffalo, was reduced by white traders and sportsmen from an estimated 13 million to two hundred by 1885. From about 1850, Indian reservations were mandated by the Department of War, through its Bureau for Indian Affairs, as a solution to the problem facing white settlers, who were constantly being attacked as encroachers by irate Indians. An 1892 map made for T. J. Morgan, commissioner of Indian Affairs, shows all of these segregated enclaves (see Plate 165). It is Map as Cultural Devastation. It graphically places the Indians in geographic containers.

"Indian Territory" vanished from maps in 1907, when Oklahoma entered the Union. Ironically, thanks to the Indian Gaming Regulatory Act of 1988, the Cheyenne and Arapaho Indians in 2005 offered Colorado a gift of $1 billion in exchange for five hundred acres near Denver on which they hope to build a leisure center, complete with a huge gambling casino. As Clara Bushyhead, a spokesperson for the tribe, explained, "It is the dream of our elders to complete our life cycle, to come back to Colorado from which we were driven. Oklahoma was never our home." (Interestingly, all land ties east of the Mississippi seem to have vanished from the collective unconscious of the "Westernized" elders.) There are now 411 tribes operating casinos with a gross 2004 revenue of $18.5 billion, employing 553,000 people. Some tribes without a reservation, but with gambling rights, are being accused by their critics of "reservation shopping" when they work the system and try to acquire land near cities for lucrative casinos. In the near future, an Indian reservation may appear just outside Denver on a map of Colorado.

In spite of Jefferson's agrarian vision for the United States, the commercialization of the northeastern states known as New England produced increasing numbers of urban places requiring supplements of food and timber. The urbanization was the result not only of growing population but also of expanding external trade. Regional specializations began to develop, such as whaling in the areas along the southeastern coast of Massachusetts. Whale oil and spermaceti candles were among America's principal domestic products and most valuable exports, which made whaling an integral feature of the national economy. As Stuart M. Frank, chief curator of the Kendall Whaling Museum, explains: "Whaling was a major employer and a major source of revenue in New England. It was the first, and for decades almost the only, industry to offer parity employment to African Americans, Native Americans, Latinos, and Criollos, and the only venue where advancement was possible irrespective of race, creed, or color." It was the principal source of wealth for many of the nation's first capitalist entrepreneurs, and was largely responsible for establishing the nation's railroads and textile mills. Unlike most early Anglo American industries, its stage was the entire globe.

Ships' logs and journals kept by actual participants in the maritime industry are the intrinsic and fundamental documents of the seafaring experience. Typically the entries are terse, abbreviated, and further characterized by the specialized language and shorthand of the sea. Yet it is possible to glean from them a unique human experience. One early account relates to voyages of the brigantine Hope documented by the ship's captain, Joseph Ingraham.

PLATE 164 (OVERLEAF). Map of the Country Drained by the Mississippi. The misapprehension on this 1823 map led to one of the true horrors in U.S. history.

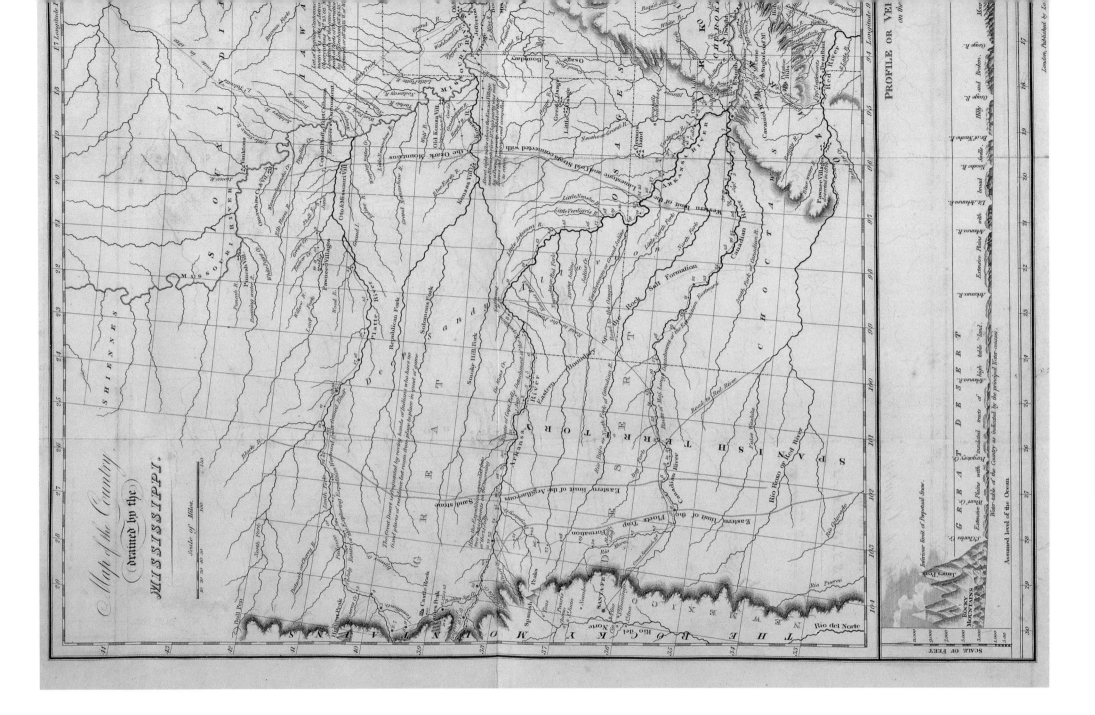

Map of the Country,
(drained by the)
MISSISSIPPI.

Scale of Miles.

PROFILE OR VE...
on the

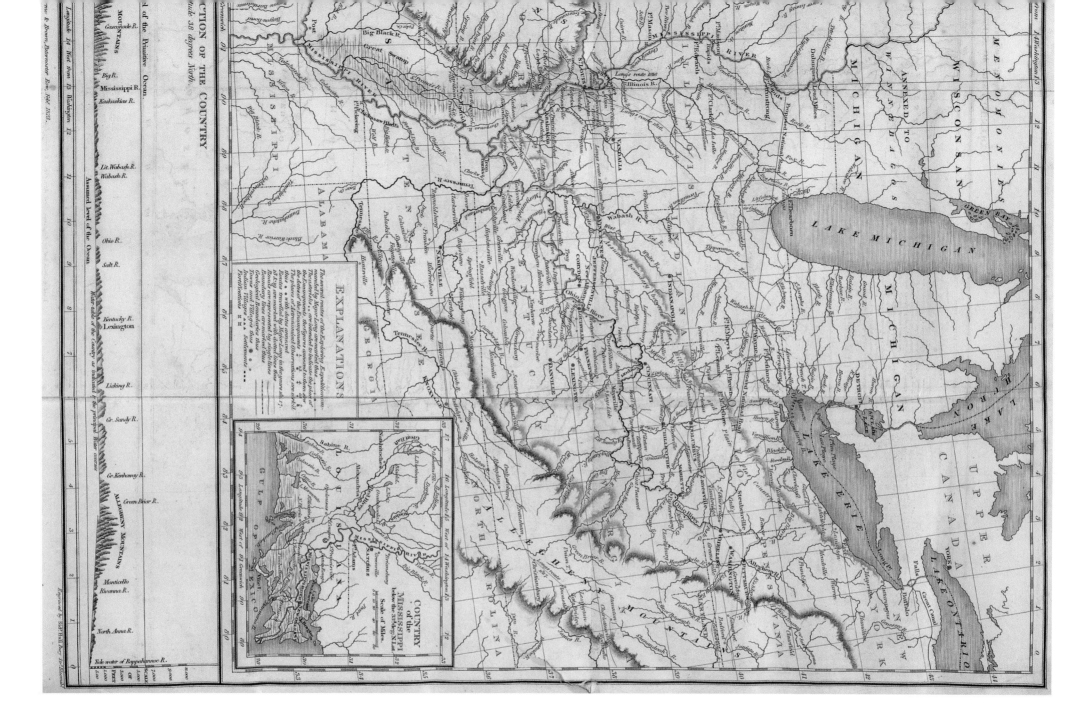

The *Hope* sailed from Boston for the Northwest Coast in 1790 to engage in the sea otter trade. Ingraham's four-volume journal of the expedition includes a number of references to whale sightings and to an encounter with the whaling ship *Necker* out of Dunkirk sailing under French colors, but with a master and crew from the United States. A sketch map (Plate 166) shows *Hope*'s "track round

Cape Horn," where "a very high & disagreeable Sea" was encountered, as well as "many whales spouting near us." The whaling industry offered adventure, excitement, honor, and glory to the hundreds of young men from the States who joined it every year. Ingraham's journal is Map as Path to Greatness.

At its worst, life on a typical whaler for a foremast hand was as nearly unendurable as a working life can be and not prove fatal. When Herman Melville (1819–91) jumped ship from a whaler in 1842, both the first and third mates, as well as thirteen members of

PLATE 165. *Map Showing Indian Reservations Within the Limits of the United States.* The solution to the problem facing white settlers was espoused by this 1892 map.

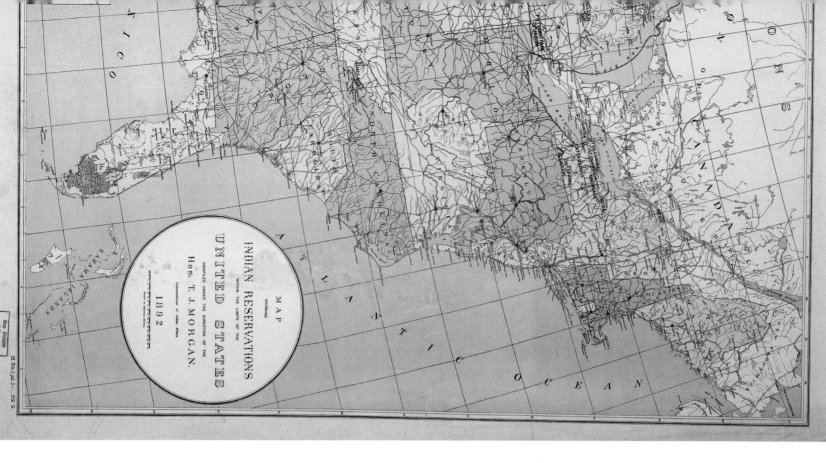

its crew of twenty-three, had escaped before him. Yet the image of the whale was vivid to the minds of Americans in the heyday of whaling. It filled the imagination as the tiger has for Asians and the wild boar for medieval Europeans. Melville might easily have read in the *Knickerbocker Magazine* a description of "an old bull whale, of prodigious size and strength...white as wool," named "Mocha Dick or White Whale of the Pacific." As he wrote of setting off on his first whaling voyage, "two and two there floated into my inmost soul, endless processions of the whale, and midmost of

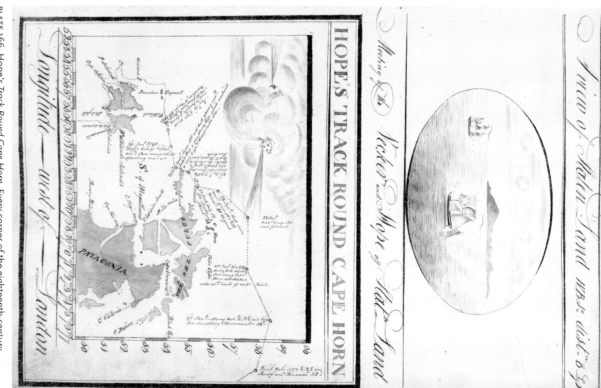

PLATE 166. Hope's *Track Round Cape Horn*. Every corner of the eighteenth-century terraqueous globe was visited by Yankee whalers.

them all, one grand hooded phantom, like a snow hill in the air." In a collection of essays by Matthew Arnold, Melville marked the following: "Our desire is not that nature may obey us, but, on the contrary, that we may obey nature."

While Melville was exploring the sea for what many consider the great Anglo American masterpiece of nature triumphant over mankind's willfulness, John Charles Frémont (1813–90) and his men were crossing and recrossing huge borderless areas of the American West. The goal of their epic odyssey was to help an interior-moving white-settlement frontier control both nature and natives by domesticating the environment to suit their European sensibility. (The approximately 143 indigenous languages spoken on the Pacific coast before the European invasion had evolved in historical environments alien to the experience of the white pioneers.) The U.S. federal government's desire to disperse the public lands into the private sector encouraged this geographical mobility, which became a trademark of life in the United States, and which initially manifested itself in the movement westward.

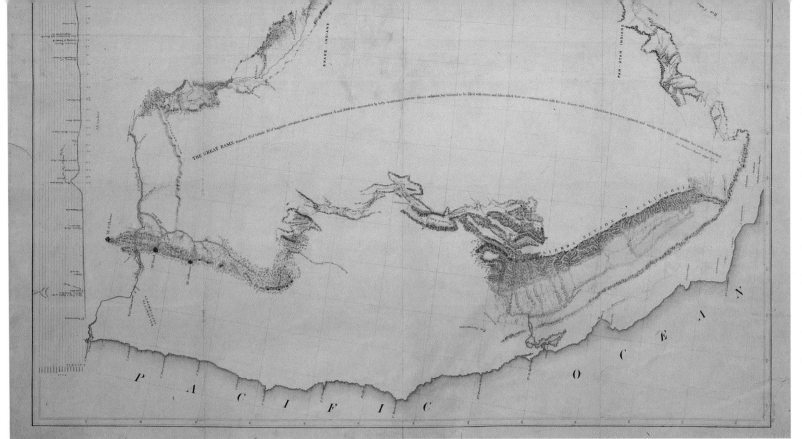

PLATE 167. *Map of an Exploring Expedition to the Rocky Mountains.* The size of Anglo America was transformed by this 1844 map.

The explorer and cartographer Frémont's long-term objective for the U.S. Topographical Bureau was to scientifically examine the Oregon Trail and to report on the rivers, the fertility of the country, the best positions for forts, and the nature of the mountains. In time he went on to Spain's California before returning home. On the completion of his assignments, he was the first white explorer to make a circuit of the entire West. His controversial audacity became a touchstone for his century. His maps helped transform the size of Anglo America.

His lasting fame was based on two trips. In 1842 he set out on a summer expedition to the Wind River chain of the Rockies. This produced the first map of the Oregon Trail, which was little more than a worn path to the Oregon Country and Spain's California when this vast land was known only to Indians, mountain men, and a few parties of hardy emigrants. However, a second expedition in 1843–44 had him back on the Oregon Trail where, thanks to his map, he met the great emigration of 1843. Moving through Oregon, he turned south into Nevada in January 1844, then crossed the snowy Sierra Nevada into California. By March he was in the Sacramento Valley, where he saw the weak hold New Spain had on California. Moving south on the "Spanish Trail," from Los Angeles to Santa Fe, he reached St. Louis in August. The detailed reports and the maps produced by Charles Preuss from Frémont's drawings (Plate 167) had a massive impact on the settling of the West by demystifying the Oregon Trail, as well as by showing that the Northwest was fertile and desirable. It is Map as Ticket to a Two-Ocean Nation. His famous reports fleshed out the routes with advice on when to travel, how to travel, where to rest, and how to behave respectfully with the various Indian tribes of differing customs inhabiting the journey's way. In the words of his wife, Jesse Benton Frémont, "From the ashes of his campfires have sprung cities."

At the start of the nineteenth century, Spain, Britain, Russia, and the United States had claims to part of the Far West; most claims were eliminated by treaties. Only Britain stubbornly remained in the Oregon Country, which Congress aimed to acquire by populating it. In 1826 a small British ship, the *Blossom*, was exploring the coast of Alaska. Its captain, Frederick Beechey, went ashore to meet the local people, the Inuit, who were standing on the beach. Speaking in sign language, Beechey asked for geographical information, a scene he later described: "The coastline was first marked out with a stick, and the distances regulated by the day's journeys. The hills and ranges of mountains were next shown by elevations of sand or stone, and the islands represented by heaps of stones, their proportions being duly attended to. The villages and fishing stations were marked by a number of sticks placed upright. In time, we had a complete topographical plan of the coast from Point Darby to Cape Kruzenstern." The Inuit map was a picture of the coast as if seen from above.

Nearly one hundred years later, in 1926, Silas Sandgreen, an Inuit hunter, produced a similar three-dimensional map of the Crown Prince Islands in Disco Bay, on the other side of the continent, on the west coast of Greenland (see Plate 168). Never having seen another map, and without any assistance, Sandgreen relied wholly on his own observations, as had his ancestors for centuries. Using only sledge and kayak, he plotted 83 islands and 10 reefs, covering 70 square miles. The best Danish chart of the period showed only 38 islands. The representations of the islands on the map are made of driftwood; reefs are indicated by pencil marks on the base of sealskin; a yellow pigment is applied to areas of swamp and grass; blue pigment covers the lake features, with black applied to areas covered by black lichens. Natural wood indicates the

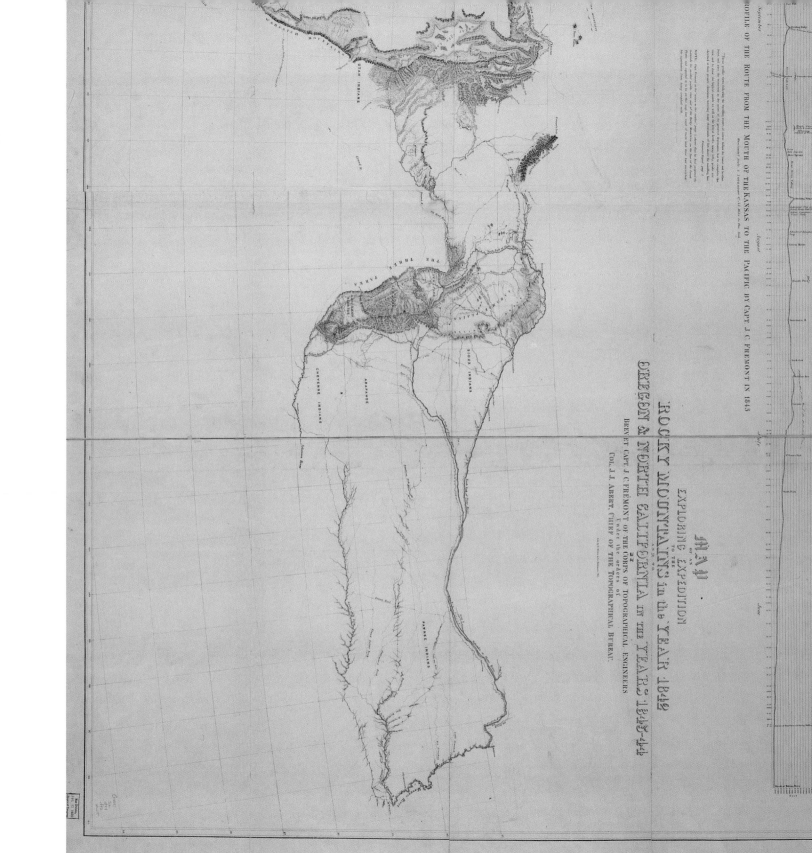

areas covered by tides; the bits of wood were sewn with gut to the skin, which was nailed to a wooden board. It is Map as Cultural Heritage.

Religion played a major role in the U.S. acquisition of the Oregon Country. As early as 1834, missionaries were busy converting the Indians to Christianity there, openly and sometimes violently suppressing traditional Indian religion and ceremonies. The same could be said of the natives of the Hawaiian, or Sandwich, Islands, though much of their indigenous culture survived. When Captain

Ingraham's sea otter population was hunted to the point of extinction, New England merchants discovered that the Hawaiian Islands were rich in sandalwood, which was prized by the Chinese. In less than a decade, this product was going the way of the sea otter, but in 1820 the first company of missionaries from New England arrived and Hawaii's relationship with the United States was solidified. Fourteen more missionary groups followed. They introduced traditional European education, Christianity, and the printing press to a complex and sophisticated society where enlightened

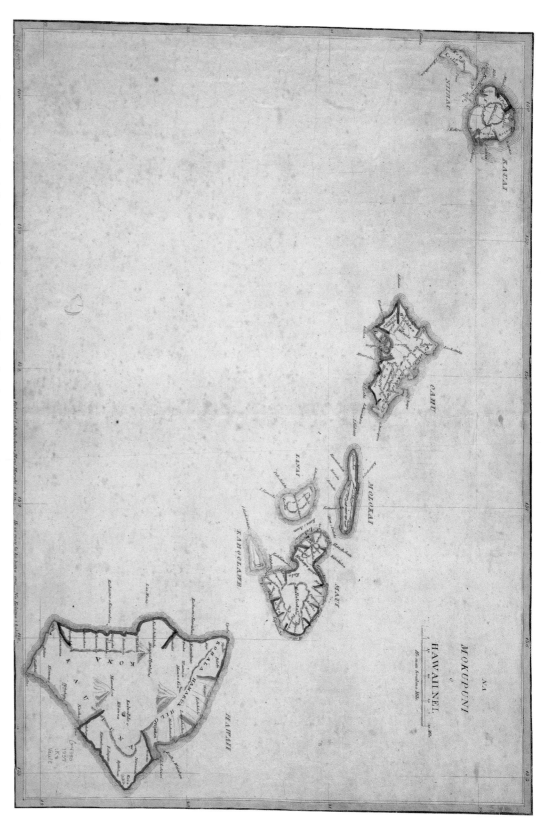

rulers in fruitful isolation had institutions of statehood in place. The fact that their architecture, fish farms, and agricultural methods were equal to anything engineered elsewhere gained the respect of all the European and American visitors. Two years after an 1837 map was made of the island chain in the Luhainaluna Seminary, the first printing press on the Pacific coast of Anglo America was sent from Hawaii to Oregon. The map (Plate 169) was made by an islander, Simona P. Kalama, and is written in the native language, which the missionaries had learned, and, having devised an alphabet, wrote, then printed in textbooks. It is Map as End of Isolation. In 1854, with the annexation of the Oregon Territory by the United States and the "manifest destiny" sentiment in full swing, the first, unsuccessful negotiations to annex Hawaii began.

Christianity was regarded as the national religion in Hawaii, but the great European migration to New England (1630–42) had also been saturated with religious ideas. The Puritans had expressed fears of the American wilderness; to them, it seemed out of control, like unredeemed man. (The historian Mary Beth Norton suggests this fear of the "wild" Indians on the Maine frontier was

a root cause of the 1692 Salem witch trials; the Puritans believed they were living "in the devil's snare.") Their goal was to establish a redemptive community of God's chosen people in the New World, a Christian commonwealth, as opposed to the more secular English communities along the Chesapeake Bay, where the Virginia legislature and Thomas Jefferson were central to formulating the thoughts behind the Constitution's First Amendment, guaranteeing religious freedom, along with church-state separation in the republic.

The United States was planned by its Founding Fathers to be a new experiment in religious freedom, for as John Adams argued, every civil society must countenance a plurality of forms of religious exercise and association. However, as historian Jon Butler believes, "the capacity of all these religions to uplift and inspire was tempered by an often equally strong propensity to divide, anger, and demean." Thus, to protect the civil peace and spiritual renewal simultaneously, the First Amendment was crafted. Nevertheless, Jefferson's hope that religion's potential to encourage men and women to treat each other well was not always justified in day-to-day U.S. life. The experiences of the Native and African Americans are two examples of this. Another was the trek of the Mormons, 1,500 of whom emigrated along the Oregon Trail into Mexican

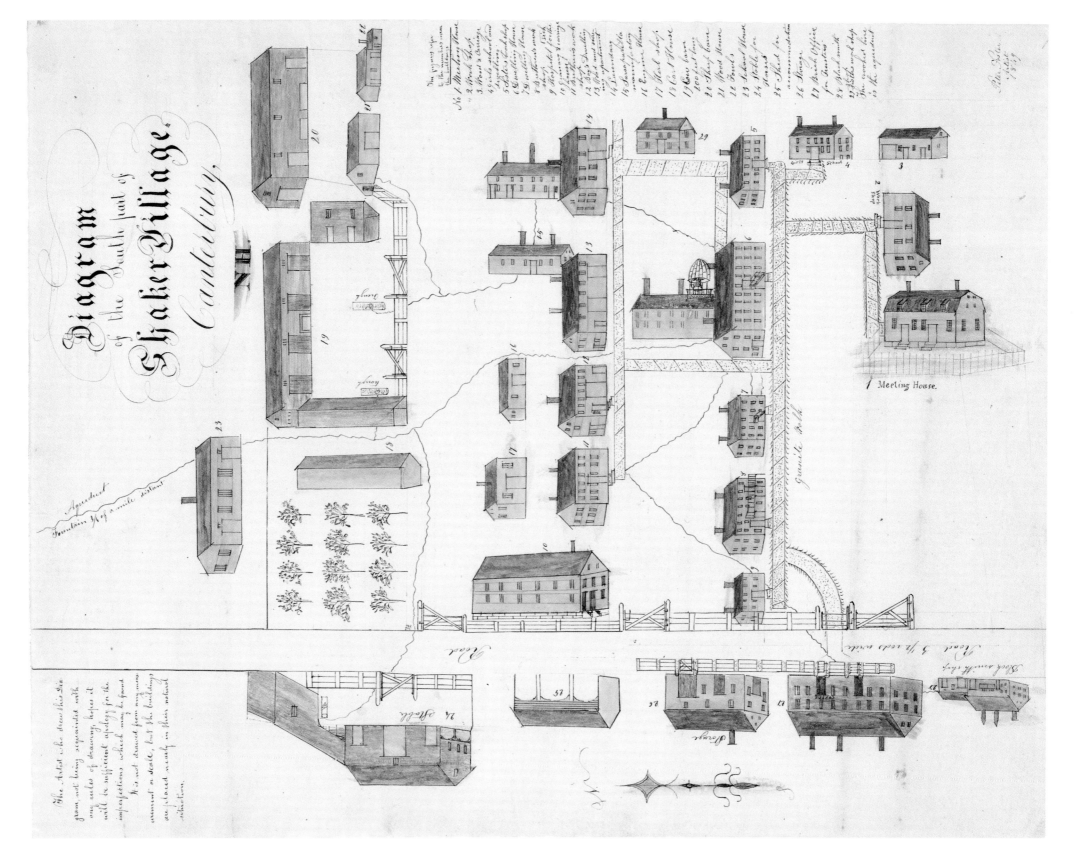

Diagram of the South part of Shaker Village, Canterbury.

1 Meeting House.

territory in 1847 (the Great Salt Lake area), to avoid the religious persecution they had experienced in the Middle West.

The first English Shakers arrived in New York in 1744. They predated the first reform era in the early nineteenth century, a utopian movement in which people removed themselves from the tumult of the burgeoning U.S. industrial society to establish Jeffersonian agrarian communities. Emphasizing the importance of inner spiritual "vision," and striving to redefine traditional gender roles, the Shakers tried to create a society protected from the chaos and disorder that they, like all future utopians, believed had come to characterize life in the United States as a whole. They derived their name from a unique religious ritual, a sort of dance in which members of the congregation would "shake" themselves free of sin while chanting loudly. Despite their of vows of celibacy, they eventually attracted a large following, establishing more than twenty communities similar to the one mapped by its trustee, Peter Foster, in 1849 at Canterbury, New Hampshire (Plate 170). Though their buildings were colorful, their communal society did not encourage individualistic decorative art. If a map was created, it was to serve as a visual documentation of the environment. Foster's map demonstrates the order and neatness that were part of the religion and the abundance the Shakers achieved when they were most successful. It is Map as Public Diary Entry.

Foster confesses in the upper left-hand corner of his plan "of the Church family" that he, "the artist who drew this diagram, not being acquainted with any rules of drawing, hopes it will be sufficient apology for the imperfections which may be found." The map is in a definite Shaker tradition of drawing, a tradition Foster clearly knew. All of the maps have the immediate impact of folk art. When studied, they have a simplicity and a purity that nicely reflects the stated goals of the Shakers. The exact identification of the community in the title suggests the plan was prepared for another community, perhaps to show the man-made "Aquaduct" to the left of the map's title, and the network of lines connecting the different structures, representing the underground lead pipes laid to carry the water to them. The legend on the right identifies the buildings on the map. Foster's labeling himself an artist in a community that prized strict conformity would not have amused Nathaniel Hawthorne, who, in 1851, visited the "foolish" Shakers in Hancock, Massachusetts, with his young son, Julian, and Herman Melville. A former utopian at Brook Farm, Hawthorne found the Shakers' "systematic lack of privacy...and supervision of one man over another...hateful and disgusting to think of." Further, "Everything [was] so neat that it was a pain and constraint to look at it; especially as it did not imply any real delicacy or moral purity in the occupants in the house." The author of the great Anglo-American novel on human frailty and religious hypocrisy, *The Scarlet Letter*, which he set in Puritan New England, concluded, "The sooner the sect is extinct the better." Imbued with the First Amendment creed, however, he never questioned their right to exist.

"It's incredible to see the infinite number of subdivisions into which the [religious] sects in America have split," French cultural critic Alexis de Tocqueville observed during his 1831 travels through the United States. Although there was a greater religious diversity in the northern states, a variety of religious practices were found throughout the country. During the Civil War different opinions on slavery within many religious denominations existed. Increasingly, Northern Protestant ministers condemned slavery, while their Southern counterparts sought to justify or condone it. Disagreements led to geographical splits within several denominations, such as the Presbyterians, the Methodists, and the Baptists. The Catholics, following Pope Gregory XVI's 1839 letter, condemned the slave trade but not the slaveholder, and stayed clear of the abolitionist crusade. The Jewish community was divided; some opposed it, some believed it biblically sanctioned. Just as such differences of opinion sundered the religious communities, so was the country divided and drawn into the horrors of a long, fratricidal war in which at least 620,000 soldiers lost their lives, along with an unknown number of civilian casualties. Civil War deaths surpass those in all other U.S. wars combined.

The demand for news during the Civil War dramatically increased overall newspaper circulation. Each day people wanted the latest information. The *New York Herald*, in particular, distinguished itself by its thorough, evenhanded, wide-ranging war coverage, unprecedented acumen, and accuracy, and its toning down of the flowery or bombastic language that characterized much of nineteenth-century newswriting. Its proprietor, James Gordon Bennett, inspired by Benjamin Franklin's *Autobiography*, had emigrated from Scotland in 1819, and successfully founded his penny daily to cross class lines and "exhilarate the breakfast table." It became the first U.S. newspaper to offer systematic foreign coverage, and within four years of its founding it assumed first place in the global circulation sweepstakes.

In the New England states, 95 percent of adults could read and write, while 75 percent of the children were in school; 80 percent of Southern whites were literate, with 39.7 percent of their children in school studying half the time of Northern children. More than two hundred full-time correspondents reported on the war, and since the camera lens was too slow to capture motion, "special artists" drew action pictures on the spot and sent them to their papers to be "transcribed" into woodcuts, which was how images were handled at the time. Heavy reliance on telegraph dispatches also kept the papers up-to-the-minute.

In the beginning, the North expected the war to be a short one. As commander of the Union force, General Winfield Scott conceived a strategy early in the war to crush the Confederacy with a blockade of its shipping combined with a major offensive down the Mississippi. The strategy was sometimes referred to as the Anaconda Plan. A cartoon map by J. B. Eliott, *Scott's Great Snake* (see Plate 171), expressed the Northern optimism about the prospects for a rapid victory, soon to be dashed by the debacle at Bull Run.

PLATE 170. *Diagram of the South Part of Shaker Village, Canterbury, N.H.* The stated goals and abundance of a religious community are depicted in this map.

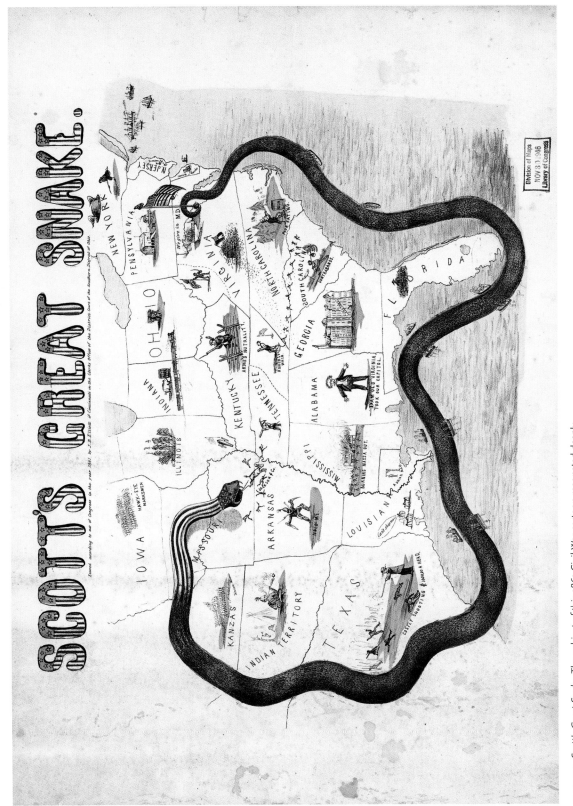

PLATE 171. *Scott's Great Snake.* The subject of this 1861 Civil War cartoon resonated deeply with contemporary viewers.

Scott was unprepared for the magnitude of the conflict; he retired in 1861 and was replaced by proud, arrogant George B. McClellan, who was a great general for training an army but a poor general for employing an army in battle. Scott's plan was never wholly abandoned. For viewers of Eliott's map there was a great deal of history attached to that snake. It was Map as Historical Reminder. Benjamin Franklin's famous woodcut from the *Pennsylvania Gazette* of May 8, 1754, *Join or Die* is considered the first American cartoon. It showed a snake in eight segments; each piece represented a colony. The snake later became the symbol of colonial union with the motto *Don't Tread on Me*. Eliott's cartoon jogged the communal memory of the value inherent in maintaining a union.

With huge armies maneuvering over vast areas during the Civil War, accurate topographical information was of crucial importance, both to the armies fighting the war and to the civilians desperate to follow the action at a time when nearly everyone in the United States knew someone in the war. Yet of the few maps readily available in 1861, most were out of date or lacked the data strategists needed. As McClellan reported, "Correct local maps were not to be found." The same story was told in the South. Federal authorities, however, were able to build on existing, fully equipped

mapping organizations, such as the army's Corps of Topographical Engineers and Corps of Engineers, the Treasury Department's Coast Survey, and the navy's Hydrographic Office. Union occupancy of key positions in northern Virginia in 1861 enabled federal officials to begin the first major mapping project of the war there as a cooperative undertaking involving both U.S. Coast Survey and army personnel—the pattern followed throughout the war. Losing no time, the front page of the *New York Herald's* June 17, 1861, morning edition featured one of the resulting maps, billed as "The Seat of War in Virginia. Positions of the Rebel Forces, Batteries, Intrenchments and Encampments in Virginia—The Fortifications for the Protection of Richmond" (Plate 172). It is Map as Here They Are. It presents newspaper publishers as true entrepreneurs. Soon Confederate generals were known to be reading Northern newspapers for scoops on the Union Army.

In August of 1861, the U.S. War Department issued an antileak order: nothing of the army's movements was to be telegraphed from Washington, D.C., until "after actual hostilities." Given the erratic nature of military censorship and the enterprising activities of some reporters, military plans still found their way into print. Political and editorial lines blurred throughout the country as

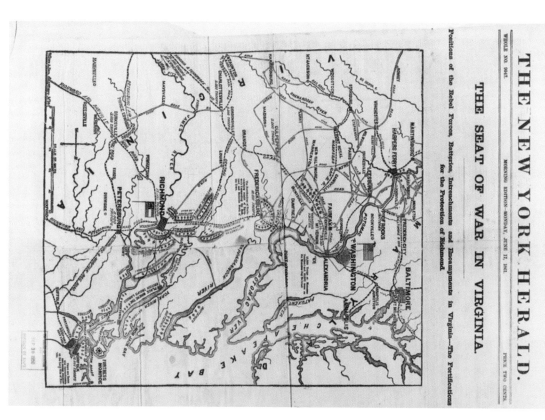

THE NEW YORK HERALD.

WHOLE NO. 9042.   MORNING EDITION—MONDAY, JUNE 17, 1861.   PRICE TWO CENTS.

THE SEAT OF WAR IN VIRGINIA.

Positions of the Rebel Forces, Batteries, Intrenchments and Encampments in Virginia—The Fortifications for the Protection of Richmond.

PLATE 172. *The Seat of War in Virginia.* Civil War maps were a key revolutionary player in the transformation of U.S. newspapers.

editors turned into politicians and politicians turned into publishers. General Ambrose Burnside shut down the *Chicago Times* for "repeated expression of disloyal and incendiary statements." Lincoln rescinded the order three days later. All in all, before defeating the South, his administration refrained from shutting down newspapers for political purposes, and the president simply tolerated an unprecedented amount of editorial abuse in the name of the First Amendment.

Before the Civil War, the number of emigrants from Europe averaged about 110,000 a year. Since most new arrivals gravitated to cities, urban areas grew dramatically, especially in the innovative northeastern states, the first to experience the impact of industrialization. When war broke out, the U.S. population was spread equally among the Northeast, South, and Middle West, though two-thirds of manufacturing employment was found in the Northeast. After the opening of the Erie Canal in 1825, New York City had become the leading port of entry for 70 percent of the European immigrants. By 1860, it was the largest U.S. city. "No migration...has occurred in the world at all similar to that which is now pouring itself upon the shores of the United States," proclaimed the *New York Tribune* in 1873. (Between 1820 and 1925, the influx

brought 36,307,892 people to the United States.) According to the 1890 census, the most densely populated spot in the world was a tenement house district: Sanitary District A of the Eleventh Ward in Manhattan (see Plate 173), with 986 inhabitants per acre. A map based on that census was made under the direction of the 1894 Tenement House Committee expressly for *Harper's Weekly* and shows the distribution of the principal nationalities by sanitary districts. It is Map as Melting Pot. It shows a crazy quilt of Germans, Irish, "Natives," Italians, Russians and Poles, Hungarians, Negroes, French, "Other Foreign Nations" (presumably Asians and Latin Americans), Bohemians, and "Unclassified."

They were depicted by proportion, which means those making up two-thirds of a district were given "control" of the district on the map to bring out in clearer contrast the "feel" of the district. Since the Scotch, English, Welsh, Scandinavians, and Canadians had not collected in colonies, they comprised the "unclassified" and were not charted, a fact that made the mix even greater than the map shows. The nationality of the residents was determined by descent from the mother. Over 76 percent of the white population in the city had foreign-born mothers, and over 40 percent were foreign-born themselves. New York had two times more Irish than Dublin, half the Italian population of Naples, the number of Germans to equal Hamburg, and two and a half times more Jewish people than Warsaw. After 1886, all who sailed into New York Harbor yearning to breathe free were greeted by the Statue of Liberty.

Surveying and mapping activities flourished in the United States as the people began moving inland beyond the crest of the Appalachians and over the inadequately mapped continent. The settlement of the frontier, the development of agriculture, and the exploitation of natural resources generated a demand for new ways to move people and goods with speed in all weather, something better than the reliable six-horse Conestoga wagon. Privately owned toll or turnpike roads and 1,875 miles of Post Road maintained for the mails by the Treasury Department from Maine to Florida were open to the wagons. The roads were supplemented first by steamships on the navigable rivers and by the construction of canals, and then in the 1830s by the introduction of railroads for imported steam-powered trains. The first U.S. railroad, or "gravity road," had been created by a British engineer in 1764 for military purposes in Lewiston, New York. After limping along for decades, the expansively funded federal National Road project stalled 50 miles east of St. Louis in 1852; but by then the thriving business community was imagining a coast-to-coast railroad and demanding serious support from the federal government, which in the early years of the republic had been quite beneficent due to lack of private financing available. By 1857, over 35,000 miles of track had been laid in a number of eastern states, using various means of financing, yet with some 4-5 million people living west of the Mississippi, little more than 3,000 miles had been laid there due to congressional battles between northern and southern delegates over the location of the transcontinental geographical route.

Suddenly, with the contentious South out of the picture during the Civil War, Lincoln and the Republican-controlled Congress

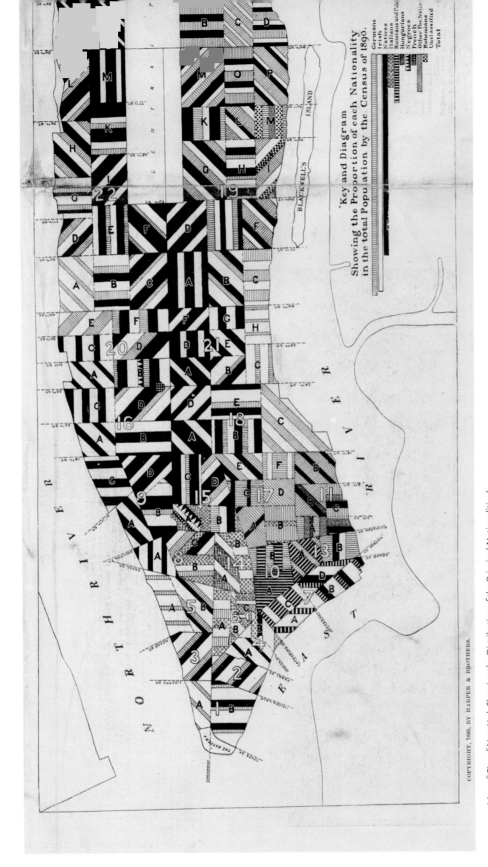

PLATE 173. *Map of City of New York Showing the Distribution of the Principal Nationalities by Sanitary Districts.* This 1895 map of New York City is the quintessential "melting pot" image.

COPYRIGHT, 1895, BY HARPER & BROTHERS.

PLATE 174. *How the Public Domain Has Been Squandered.* A railroad map is used to take on big business in this 1884 political poster.

passed the 1862 Pacific Railway Act and created the central route for the transcontinental railroad. Strapped by the war, Lincoln could not authorize complete funding. It was to be built by two private companies—the Central Pacific, working westward from Council Bluffs, Iowa (later shifted to Omaha, Nebraska), and the Union Pacific, working eastward from Sacramento, California. The two would join at Promontory Point, Utah. The financing was based upon the sale of government bonds to help create thirty-year loans for the construction companies and upon land grants to them. Besides putting their own stocks and bonds on the market, the two railroad companies were given alternating one-square-mile tracts on each side of the track, like a checkerboard, to sell, though the land had very little value at the time, especially in the desert. In 1864, the railroad being deemed critical to the nation's well-being, the act was amended to double the land grants and to give to the railroads all the timber on, and all the minerals underneath, the land.

All told, 33 million acres of land went to the investors in what became the Union Pacific Railroad, completed in 1869. To encourage further railroad building, an additional 103 million acres had been given as land grants by 1884, when the financing system and the resulting "railroad barons" became a political issue in the presidential election. Plate 174, a campaign poster for the Democratic

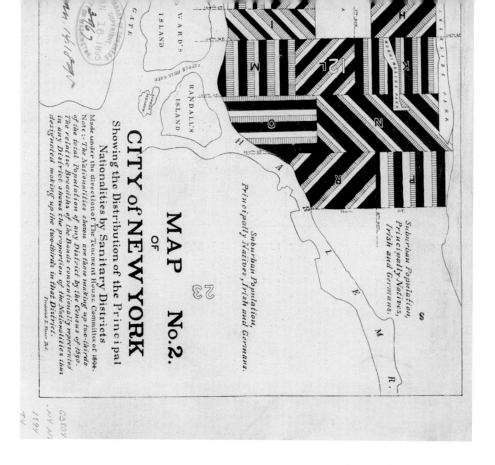

Party, explains "How the Public Domain Has Been Squandered" and gives the pertinent facts. It is Map as Political Platform. It proved a potent weapon when the Democrats successfully ran Grover Cleveland, a noted reformer, against the Republican nominee, James Blaine, whose reputation had been tarnished in 1869 by a railroad land grant scandal.

After the Civil War, the urban scene expanded into a national network of cities, spurred on by the Industrial Revolution, which was triumphant, especially in the northeastern states, aided and abetted by the immigrants in search of better wages and by the local steam railroads. No other continent, except perhaps Australia, has undergone such a complete cultural transformation as quickly as Anglo America. A fragile harmony between nature and technology was achieved during the first decades of the Industrial Revolution. But transcontinental colonization produced a rampaging industrialization, especially in the already developed Northeast, and in the national system of cities that evolved after the Civil War under the prodding of the Union Pacific Railroad. Before the war, four out of five people lived in rural communities with populations under 2,500; by 1920 city dwellers outnumbered country people. From the beginning, the cities had transatlantic connections, which vanished in the nineteenth century as the cities began to depend upon each other, which led to some manufacturing specializations, such as shoemaking in Haverhill, Massachusetts.

Settled by Puritans of the Massachusetts Bay Colony in 1640 on land purchased from the local Indians, who called it Pentucket,

Haverhill is in the state's northeast corner on the Merrimack River, thirty-three miles from Boston by rail and eighty-three miles from Portland, Maine. The Merrimack Valley was the richest industrial section in all Massachusetts. The waters of the river turned more spindles than any other stream on earth when the 1893 bird's-eye view of Haverhill by Boston's O. H. Bailey and Co. (see Plate 175) was made. It is Map as Capitalist's Dream. It was a time when Haverhill ranked among the chief industrial cities in the country, and was the shoe capital of the world—an occupation its 1899 Board of Trade explained the city "fell into." In no other U.S. occupation was there such a total transition from a winter handicraft by farmers to a finely organized and coordinated industry with every stage of production done by machinery. (There were 140 distinct operations in the making of some shoes.)

In 1804 there had been two carts to transport manufactured goods, mostly hats, from the town; but Haverhill's positioning on the most noted water-power stream in the world, its having a ferry and a bridge and being a railroad stop, led to the mass-marketing wonder depicted on the map. There was no U.S. drainage basin of comparable size so heavily occupied by industry. Few map images elucidate more clearly the results of the U.S. industrial community's legendary strength, demonstrated by the plethora of identified mills and factories, each having paid a premium for its star billing on the map. In reality, the map trumpets the all-powerful business establishments surrounding the city plan, as if the businesses were concrete emblems of the paternalistic "snake" constraining its labor force in spite of the powerful labor unions. This visual constraint on labor's power would have given comfort to possible investors. It also dramatizes what Thorstein Veblen labeled in 1899 "conspicuous consumption"—all those shoes!—or extravagant personal display as a motivating force within all social classes in any capitalist society.

After World War II, the shoe industry moved to the Midwest in search of cheaper labor costs, but the expansive, all-encompassing (in theory) economic and social success that created the Haverhill of the bird's-eye view laid the foundation for the urban-based pursuit of prosperity, which defined much more than the nation's economy. It also became a basic component of citizenship in the United States. The embrace of mass consumption during the three decades following World War II and the deprivations of the Great Depression was heralded as the "Golden Age" of American affluence, resulting in what the historian Lizabeth Cohen calls "the Consumers' Republic." With it came sprawl and suburbia, "the landscape of mass consumption," shopping malls, credit purchasing, sharpened divisions along gender, class, and ethnic lines, new forms of political activism through the civil rights and consumer movements, targeted marketing, and politicians who applied the latest marketing strategies to their political campaigns. Though the Industrial Revolution was not a uniquely American experience, the Haverhill map is a definitive U.S. cultural landscape. It made

PLATE 175 (OVERLEAF). *Haverhill, Massachusetts.* The U.S. Industrial Revolution is summed up by this 1893 bird's-eye view.

PLATE 176. *Panoramic Perspective of the Area Adjacent to Boulder Dam.* Boulder Dam offers a direct link to Babylonia and the Fertile Crescent.

many nostalgic for a more rural and pastoral era, when in their memories the pace of life seemed slower and the passage of time was measured by the four seasons rather than in a manner as relentlessly linear as railroad tracks.

Produced to promote tourism in southern Nevada, northwestern Arizona, and southwestern Utah, a 1934 perspective rendering of the Union Pacific System's service in the area focuses on the 725-foot-high Boulder Dam and the 115-mile-long Lake Mead, the largest man-made lake in the Western Hemisphere (Plate 176). The original site of the dam was to be at Boulder Canyon, about ten miles upstream of the present site on the Colorado River. The dam was eventually built at Black Canyon because the rock in its canyon

walls was denser and it would be able to capture more water. Wherever it was built, the dam's historical roots are found in the Fertile Crescent and the genius of Babylonia.

At the turn of the twentieth century, a portion of the Colorado Desert was renamed Imperial Valley, and an irrigation canal was cut in 1901 from the mighty river into the heart of the valley. By 1904 there were 7,000 people in residence, but the canal was clogged with river silt and the unwatered crops died. A second canal was dug, but floods drowned the crops and created the Salton Sea, while erosion was changing the course of the Colorado River and creating a new Grand Canyon. It took two years and $3 million to get the river back on its track to the Gulf of California. The results of

irrigation were now evident, but a serious method of controlling the river was needed to make the dream of a fecund Imperial Valley come true. This is where Boulder Dam came in. The money was allocated by the federal government and the work was two years away from completion in 1934 when the map was made. It is Map as Dream Realized. President Hoover had wanted to have the dam named after him when he was running for reelection in 1932; he was battling the Great Depression by putting more than 5,000 people to work on the dam, twenty-four hours a day, seven days a week, and he wanted credit for the project. Harold Ickes, the secretary of the interior for Franklin Roosevelt, who defeated Hoover, named it Boulder Dam, a decision overturned in 1947 when Congress, with Harry Truman's signature, renamed it Hoover Dam. This human achievement was tremendous no matter the name on the dam. It is the principal source of flood control, irrigation, and electric power for the entire Southwest.

The map places the Anglo American reputation for thinking big center stage. The site became a favorite tourist attraction, just as the 1934 map intended. In the public-spirited 1930s, funds were also available for roads, and in this arena something unknown in any other culture was happening in the United States. Anglo America was always a mobile society, starting with crossing the ocean in ships and followed by crossing the country in the Conestoga wagon, the canal boat, and the railroad, so the country's obsession with the engine-powered automobile seemed natural. Unlike in France, where good roads had existed since the reign of Louis XIV, in 1900 there were only 150 miles of well-surfaced roads in the United States. By the late 1930s, the miles of constructed highways surpassed 3 million, and the Big Three car manufacturers—Ford, Chrysler, General Motors—were major players, the industrial heart of the economy. In 1929, when there were more than 23 million cars on the roads, the sociologists Robert and Helen Lynd had summed up the central element of the nascent materialistic and increasingly secular "American way of life": "Ownership of an automobile has now reached the point of being an accepted, essential part of normal living." A resident of Muncie, Indiana, had told them, "We'd rather do without clothes than give up the car." New York City's Chrysler Building, embellished with hubcap friezes and radiator-cap gargoyles, was a stylish modern temple to the automobile, the evocative symbol for speed, movement, and excitement—i.e., the New World.

A Gulf gasoline *Florida Info-Map* from the 1930s (see Plate 177) advises, "Perhaps you have traveled many miles to get here, so here's a thought to keep in mind. A few more miles of driving now will add immeasurably to your storehouse of pleasurable memories... may mean the difference between just a trip and a glorious adventure.... Ten thousand miles of good highways invite you... get into your car and go!" And, as if Florida is not enough, because there are never enough glorious adventures, Cuba is included on the road map of Florida's main cities. Billed as available by ferry, true, Cuba nevertheless offers the mapmaker the opportunity to suggest the next great gasoline engine–powered travel machine for the go-go Anglo American—the airplane. Such images prove the advertising theory that "man has been called the reasoning animal, but he could with greater truthfulness be called the creature of suggestion." It is Map as Beyond the Blue Horizon. Road maps helped create needs and desires in even the poorest imaginations.

The machines that helped create the modern U.S. nation and bring about social cohesion also commercialized the Anglo American collective (if selective) memory in the form of movies. Motion pictures helped create a national identity, one nearing Olympian stature due to the ideals of the immigrants in charge of running the studios. Photographs, like maps, had placed the image on par with the word in human communication. Since the first U.S. movie companies were founded in the large cities, early movies usually

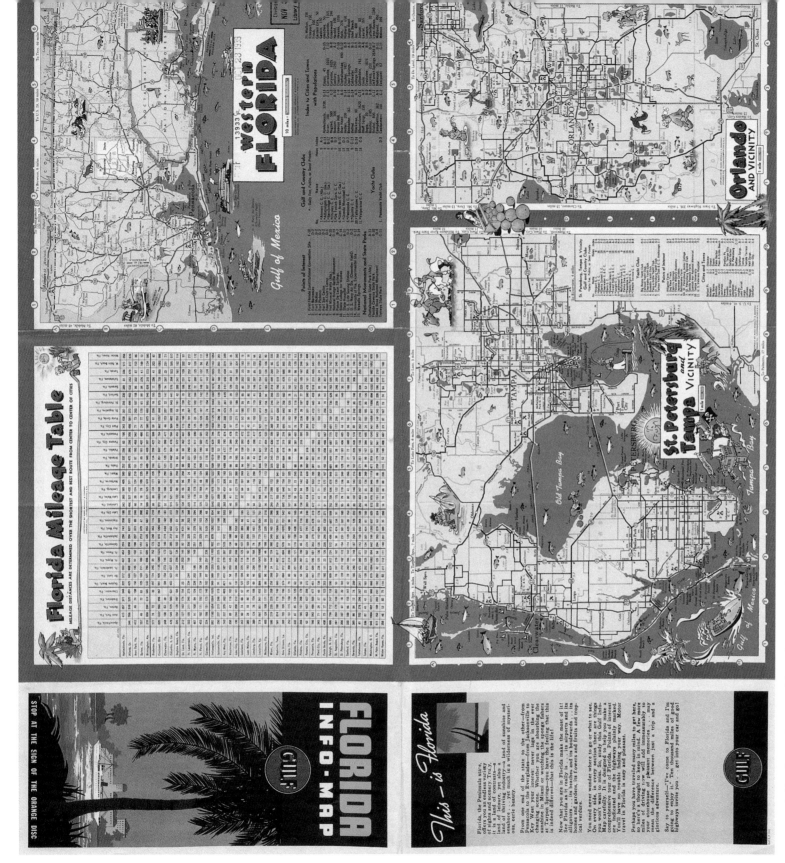

PLATE 177. *Florida Info-Map.* An automobile road map is uniquely iconic of the Anglo American civilization.

reflected the urban landscape, introducing it to the inhabitants of the rural landscape who were living the agrarian lives envisioned by Jefferson. Movies played a huge role in drawing people from the hard life of the farm to, often, an even harder life in the city.

Maps, like movies, are time capsules. Fire insurance maps, in particular, encapsulate the look and feel of another place and time, bringing urban history to life. They are a visual record of land use, a graphic inventory of the built environment, or cultural landscape. A 1929 fire insurance map made by the Sanborn Map Company shows a section of the MGM Studio, which was formed in

1924 in Culver City, California (see Plate 178). (One of the founding partners, Louis B. Mayer, entered the movie business as a theater owner in Haverhill, Massachusetts.) The map illustrates the transition the movies made from Edison Studio toy to major U.S. industry, two years after the "talkies" made their debut with *The Jazz Singer.* It is Map as Graphic Inventory of a Unifying Force. Mayer, more than anyone, was instrumental in creating, through his classy pictures, the accepted notion of the American Dream.

During the first half of the nineteenth century, most fire insurance companies were small and based in a single city. Consequently the underwriters could themselves examine properties they were about to insure. However, as insurance companies became larger and expanded their coverage to numerous cities, a mapping industry developed to support this need. D. A. Sanborn was a young surveyor from Somerville, Massachusetts, when he was engaged in 1866 by the Aetna Insurance Company to prepare insurance maps for several cities in Tennessee. Eventually, his Sanborn Map Company of New York monopolized the insurance mapping industry. The outline, or footprint, of each building was indicated and color coded to show its construction material—pink for brick, yellow

for wood, brown for adobe. Numbers inside the lower right corner of each building indicate how many stories the building had, while the numbers outside the building on a city street front would refer to the street address, allowing researchers to correlate these locations with census records and city directories. Buildings were identified by name. By the early 1930s, when 90 million people went to the movies weekly, the Sanborn Company claimed to have maps describing the man-made buildings on every street in more than 13,000 U.S. towns and cities. It was an inventory of the nation's cultural environment.

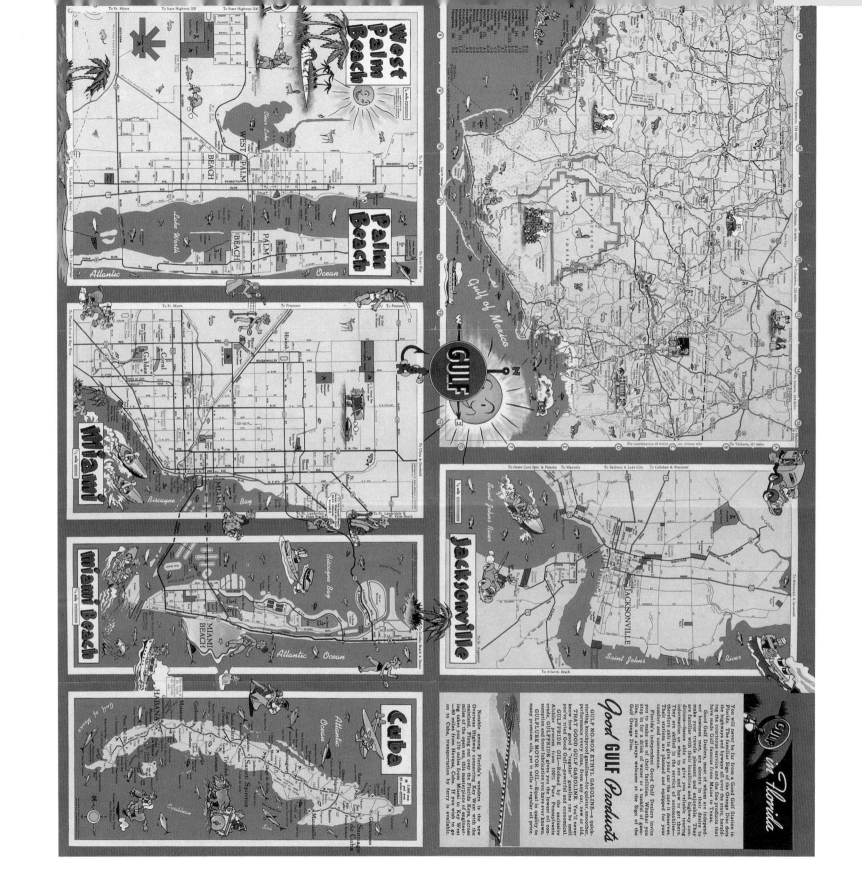

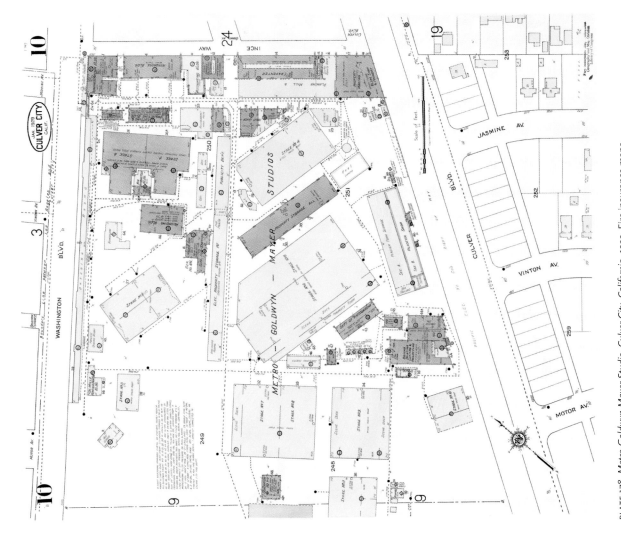

PLATE 178. *Metro-Goldwyn-Mayer Studio, Culver City, California, 1929.* Fire insurance maps are the perfect record of the cultural landscape.

One of the great subjects of the early movies, finding the balance between the urban and the rural, led to environmental decisions with predictable dire consequences. In the 1930s, when Sanborn was mapping cities, great concrete levees were being strengthened to control the flooding Mississippi; unwisely, marsh-building sediments were flushed into the Gulf of Mexico. Twenty years later, oil company engineers sliced up its marsh with more than 8,000 miles of canals for exploration, and the U.S. Army Corps of Engineers dredged fourteen major ship channels to inland ports, all of which introduced annihilating salt water to brackish and freshwater marshes; and the dumping of chemical waste into the Mississippi filled the region with destructive, toxic substances. The lifesaving wetlands are vanishing into the Gulf of Mexico at the rate of 21 square miles each year.

Bisected by the Mississippi, New Orleans was built in a bowl of reclaimed marshland, with Lake Pontchartrain to the north. In the eighteenth century the French created the extensive series of concrete levees, constantly in need of expensive repair. The city's surrounding wetlands and delta provided natural defenses against

hurricanes. Their destruction for commercial reasons and urban expansion led to the city's sinking farther and farther below sea level, increasing its vulnerability to hurricane damage. A major hurricane in the area was listed by the federal government as one of the three most likely catastrophic events it might face, along with a major West Coast earthquake and another terrorist attack on New York City. In 2002 the Red Cross refused to open hurricane shelters in New Orleans, citing the potential risk to its workers. On September 1, 2005, the city of New Orleans was devastated by Hurricane Katrina when the levee at the Seventeenth Street Canal was breached as water forced through the concrete.

The wetlands are some of the most diverse and fertile habitats in the world, and no other place on earth is disappearing so quickly. The struggle to stem this loss has become emblematic of the struggle to save the U.S. environment from natural and man-made factors. The goal is to restore healthy, natural processes. In 2004, however, a panel of experts convened by the National Academy of Sciences concluded that re-creating or maintaining what remains of Louisiana's wetlands is impossible. The panel suggested a "man-

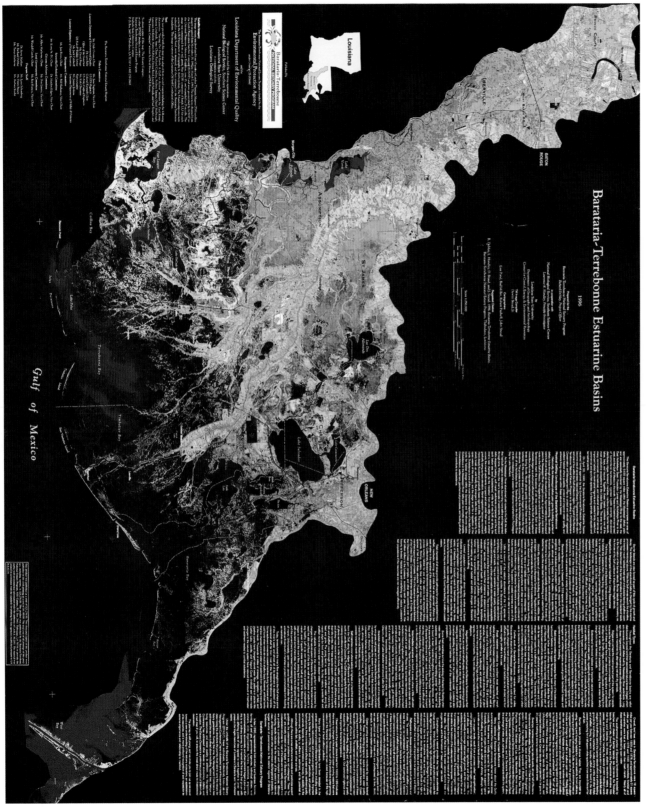

Barataria-Terrebonne Estuarine Basins

1996

Gulf of Mexico

Louisiana

BATON ROUGE

NEW ORLEANS

aged retreat," focusing state and local government resources on what realistically can be preserved in order for coastal Louisiana to survive. "If we don't draw this map," Dan Walker, a geologist who directed the study for the academy, warned, "nature will."

Historically, the Mississippi has changed its course approximately every thousand years in search of the shortest route to the Gulf of Mexico. The ridges that run north to south in Louisiana's Barataria-Terrebonne estuarine basins, located between the Mississippi and the Atchafalaya Rivers, mark the sites of the old river channels. In 1990 the 4.1-million-acre system received formal approval by the Environmental Protection Agency (EPA) and became part of the National Estuary Program. Its stated goal is "to develop a Comprehensive Conservation and Management Plan to protect and rebuild vegetated wetland habitat where possible, protect and improve water supply quality, and enhance living resources within these estuarine basins."

The living resources of the Barataria-Terrebonne have a direct tie to the habitat that sustains them. The accompanying text to a 1996 map of the awe-inspiring estuary system (Plate 179), created by Louisiana State University's Department of Geography and Anthropology and the Center for Coastal, Energy, and Environmental Resources, explains in detail the physical setting of the basins, the vegetation, and the great variety of its living creatures—about fifty species of mammals—and the water quality issues, including the human influences. (A community of 602,000 people live and work in the estuary.) It is Map as Act of Renewal. People from diverse groups have come together to protect and preserve the basins' fragile resources for future generations. They are striving for a new understanding of the estuary system, an appreciation of its resources, and a more profound recognition of and respect for its extreme importance to humankind. The map makes visible the generosity of nature. It seems an act of hope, as it depends upon the generosity of nature to forgive and forget human ignorance and neglect. It seems an act of faith in Walt Whitman's belief: "The earth never tires...." We can only hope this is true.

PLATE 179. *Barataria-Terrebonne Estuarine Basins.* Hope for a future after Hurricane Katrina is offered by this map of Louisiana's wetlands.

MAR DEL S

TERRA INCOGNITA

MERIDIONALE DISCO PERTO DA NOVO

Aguada
Culuen
Bahal
Gilolo
Mendana
Tuda
180
Bacca
Ambon

PONE
rdionale
NTE

Clima·1
Clima·1
Clima·2

170 165 160 155 150 145 140 175

Clima·12
5
Clima·7
10
Clima·4
15
Clima·5
20
Clima·4·
25
Clima·5·
30
Clima·6·
35
Clima·7
70
Clima·8·
40
75
Clima·9
45
Clima·10
50

Il modo di
trouare la di
stanza delle m

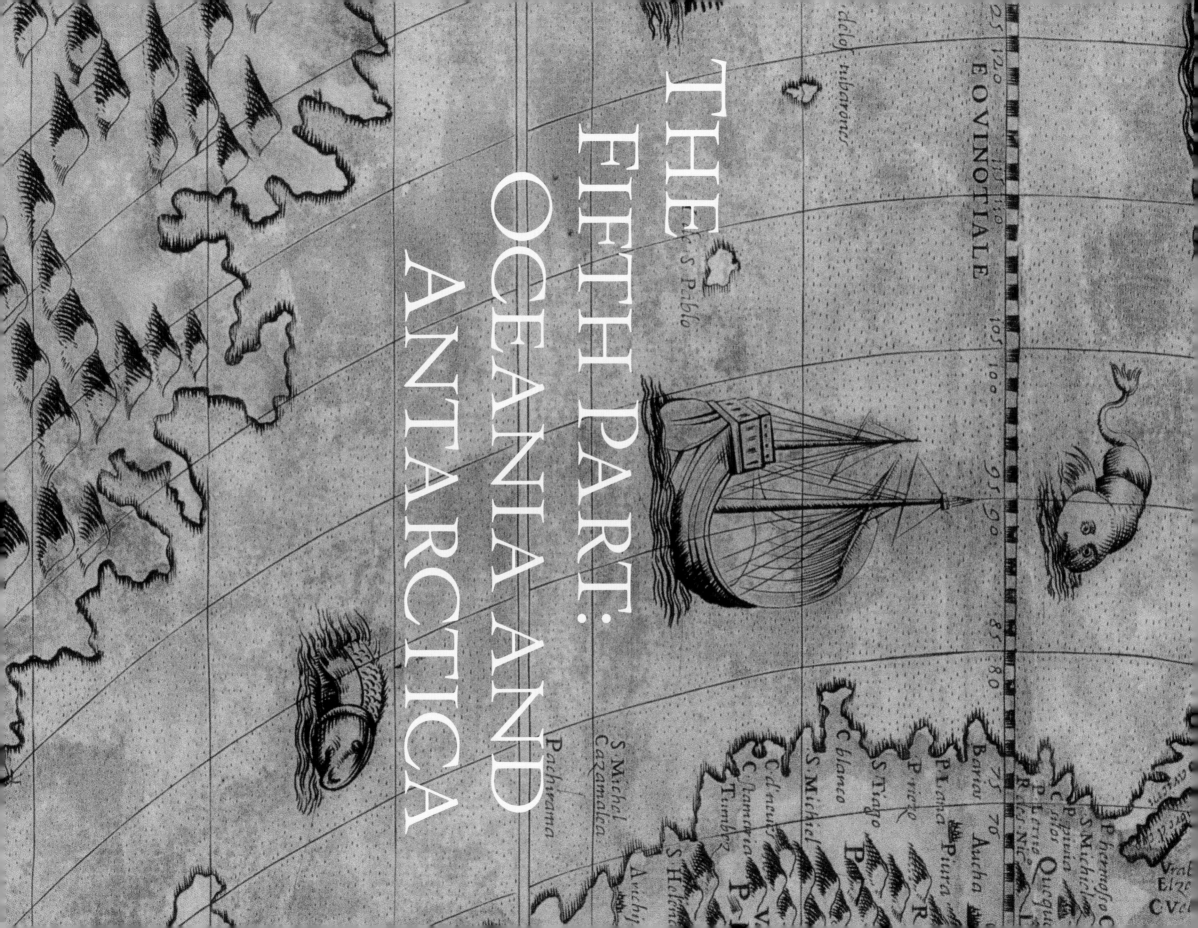

THE FIFTH PART: OCEANIA AND ANTARCTICA

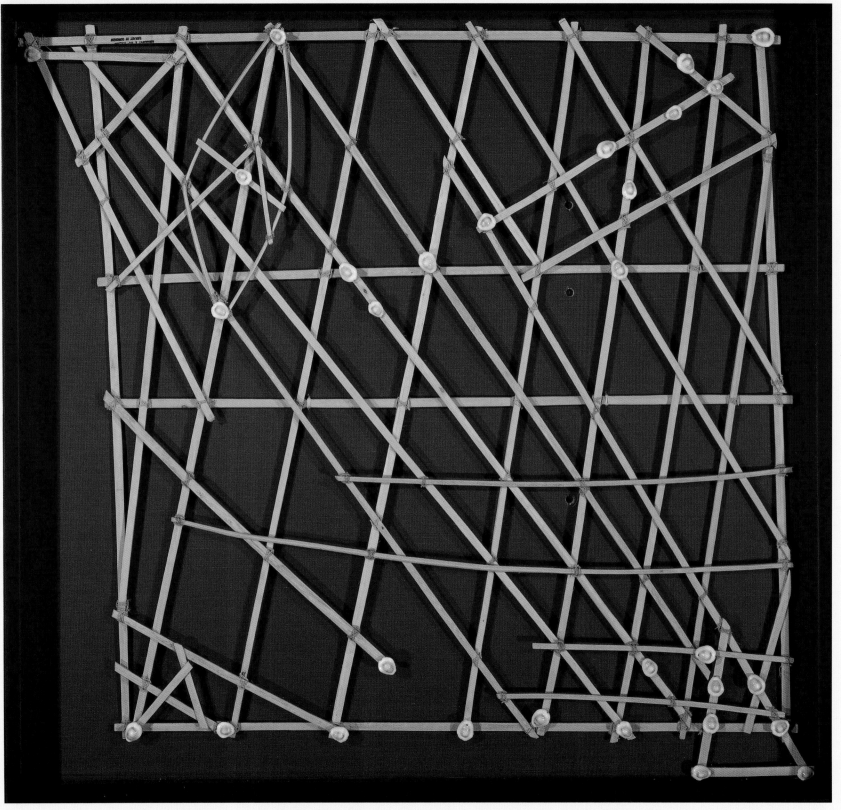

PLATE 180. *Marshall Island Stick Chart.* A Micronesian stick chart bears witness to one of the most profound relationships between man and nature.

OVERLEAF: Detail from p. 236.

Hroughout the sixteenth and seventeenth centuries, even well-educated Europeans remained largely indifferent to the discoveries in the New World. Most people were still held in thrall by the threatening Orient—Asia, Africa, and the Middle East—frighteningly present in the person of the "Turks," a derogatory term then applied to Muslims everywhere. Well into the eighteenth century, the Ottoman Empire controlled the southern realm of the Mediterranean world. Between 1670 and 1730, more than 5,000 Britons were sold in North African slave markets thanks to effective predatory measures both on sea and land by Muslim powers against European traders.

From the twelfth century, Christians feared Islam as a rival religious revelation, as well as fearing its successful expansion into Europe. It was this fear, aided by the Muslim monopoly of the overland spice trade routes, that had sent the fifteenth-century Portuguese on their mission to enter the Indian Ocean by circumnavigating Africa. Once this water route to the East was established, other cultural encounters were made by sailors from the Mediterranean world, such as Ferdinand Magellan, who circumnavigated the earth for Spain (1519–22) and added details of the Pacific Ocean to the European world map. He and others were continuing the cartographic journey eastward beyond the Asian frontier first described for them by Marco Polo.

OCEANIA

Though Oceania is the smallest "continent"—5.3 percent of the earth's land—it is one of the most diverse areas on the planet. Embracing the northern and southern edges of the equator, it comprises thousands of coral atolls and volcanic islands of the South Pacific Ocean, including the Melanesia and Polynesia groups; Papua New Guinea, New Zealand, and Australia.

The natives of Oceania were masters of observation and, by extension, of mapmaking. For millennia, the island people of Oceania journeyed along the coasts and from one island to another for trading and for visiting extended family members in their various clan groupings, often scattered across many small islands. The native people became especially distinguished in travel geography, as they observed minute details of coasts, atolls, reefs, currents, winds, and stars in order to navigate safely. They learned to read the ocean's surface, along with the stars in the sky. In particular, the great seafaring people of the Marshall Islands, named for the English explorer John Marshall in 1788, had a sailing vocation and

devised a uniquely beautiful method of recording in shorthand the memories of their journeys in outrigged canoes by using sticks and shells (Plate 180). It is Map as Mind's Eye. To most modern viewers, it is map as eye candy.

The Marshall Islands form two roughly parallel archepelagic chains known as Radak and Ralak. They are situated just north of the equator in the Pacific Ocean, about halfway between Hawaii and Australia. Comprising thirty atolls and reefs, they include 1,152 islands. With the Gilberts, Carolines, Marianas, and many scattered islands, they form Micronesia. They lie directly in the strong westerly set of the equatorial current, which is deflected by numerous atolls and reefs into local streams running north, south, and east. Equatorial doldrums complicate navigation among the islands. Being off the main trade-wind routes, the Marshall Islands received little attention from early European explorers, which allowed the inhabitants to go about their business with little interference until the beginning of the nineteenth century. Thus, their highly individual maps continued to be used as teaching tools and recording devices until about 1880, when they were supplanted by British Admiralty charts. Today no native seems able to use the indigenous stick maps.

Although the charts were constructed following a similar plan, each was the result of personal observation and could only be fully interpreted by its creator, who seems to have had a supernatural eye. (There were various religious rituals performed before each long journey.) The sticks were fashioned from the shoots of native trees; the midribs of coconut leaves produced the finer lines, while the coconut's fibers tied the clusters. Shells or seeds of proportionate sizes, tied on at their proper locations, indicated the islands. One stick map uses a large shell in the center to identify Kwajalein. It is believed there were three distinct types of stick maps. The first, *mattang*, embraced the entire world known to the Marshall Islanders, who with other ancient Polynesians and Melanesians crossed thousands of open-sea miles for many reasons—adventure, pilgrimage, and exile. (The natives of Madagascar, 250 miles off the coast of Africa, are of Indonesian and African origin, with a language that has the same roots as that spoken in Hawaii.) The second type of stick map, *rebbelib*, embraced one island group; and the third, *medo*, embraced only a few islands.

Generally the straight horizontal and vertical sticks form the framework of the map or portray the direction of the swells. The diagonal and curved sticks represent the swells aroused by the winds traveling at right angles toward each stick's concave side. Between neighboring islands, all the other prevailing winds, and

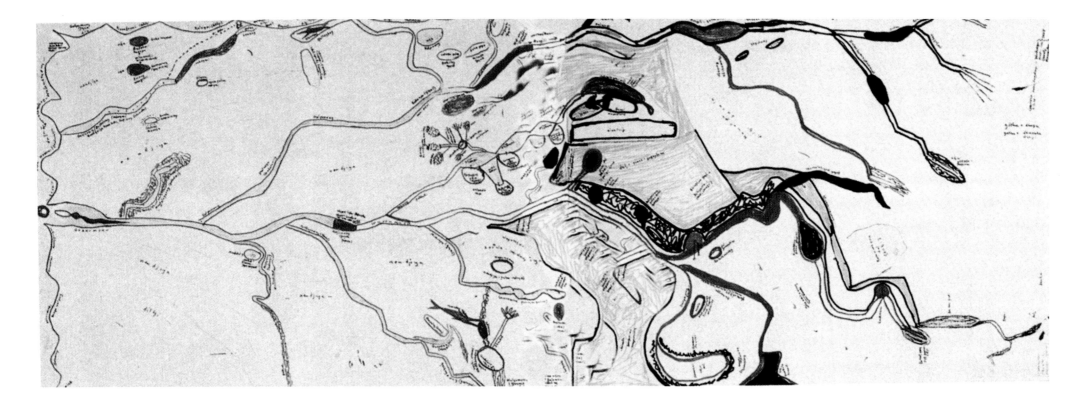

the various surfaces of the sea produced by the refracting cross-swells, had specific names. Their companionable presences indicated to the knowledgeable voyager his whereabouts. The stick maps bear witness to one of history's most profound relationships between man and nature. They document awesome navigational achievements as surely as the surviving epics about the heroic voyages made by these inhabitants of the Marshall Islands. The loss of this art ruptured an ancient cartographic tradition mediated between mankind and nature at a time when Europe and America were experiencing similar ruptures with nature owing to the Industrial Revolution. These maps are relics of the past, traces of the process of people making their own history. They also remind us that when memory ceases to be necessary or desirable, the continuities of meaning and judgment are also lost to us.

Like the inhabitants of the Marshall Islands, Australian Aboriginal people made maps to communicate practical knowledge to others in a manner unique to themselves. Unlike the Marshallese, however, the Australians created maps for short-term usage, most notably for ceremonies, and are still constructing and using their traditional images today. Their concern was to capture the sacred designs of the world around them. As the cartographic scholar Peter Sutton explains, "Aboriginal icons with topographic content depict something that is itself not so much a representation as a transformation." He asserts that the maps are not about siting locations. They are "in general highly formalized, abstracted, and frequently very symmetrical." They indicate in a figurative way.

One example from Australia's Arnhem Land Region, the northeastern corner of the Northern Territory, is a form of estate map. Drawn in pencil and felt-tip pen on paper by Djimbun and Mattjudi, the map (Plate 181) was made to delineate the land owned by the group or clan. The estate mapmakers, almost always men, depict space they traditionally inherit, or space where succession is being claimed, or space over which they have custodial-managerial responsibilities. The map shown was explained to the anthropologist Nancy M. Williams, an expert in land tenure, as it was being drawn; the pencil notes by her include details of geographical features, mythic and historical themes, and aboriginal place names discovered in response to her questions. Djimbun was a senior man of the Gurrumuru Dhalwangu clan, whose principal estate is focused on the Goromuru (Gurrumuru) River flowing into Arnhem Bay. Mattjudi was head of the Marrakulu clan, which has a long-term relationship with the Gurrumuru Dhalwangu. Stylized and simplified, the image is an iconic representation of the river's drainage system. Even though the map does not rest on a topographic base, the parallels with Western topographic maps would make subscribers to Jung's theory of the collective unconscious very happy. It is Map as Iconographic Tradition.

Meanwhile, the Yolngu mapmaking men of the eastern Arnhem Land Region use maps to create a system of knowledge to

PLATE 181. *Map of the Goromuru (Gurrumuru) River Area.* The focus of this aboriginal Australian map is the two artists' iconographic relationship with their river.

connect them with their ancestors. The knowledge exists in two forms: inside knowledge, which is restricted to initiated men, and outside knowledge, which may be shared with women and children. One map (Plate 182), a painting—ochers on bark—contains both forms of knowledge; it was made for sale by David Malangi. Called *Sacred Places at Milmindjarr*, the piece was documented by Peter Sutton with the artist. The map shows a portion of Malangi's clan country in the area of Ramingining. It is Map as Mythic Geography. It narrates the story (Dreamings) of the Djan'kawu sisters, founding ancestral figures of the region. Following the morning star from east to west, the sisters stopped on their way to give birth to the clans (landowning groups) and to create freshwater springs and wells—dark circles on the map—by plunging their digging sticks into the ground. Looking for fish, they caught a small catfish, shown on the map entering the river with the rising tide. Garangala Island, the Malangis' country, is depicted top left on the map. When asked about the map's significance by Sutton, the artist replied, "I know. You don't know." And several points on the map, such as the stripes in the upper right, were labeled secret, or inside, knowledge. Sutton concludes, "Although the mythology behind the painting specifies the particular places and clan countries involved, this particular interpretation collapsed the geography, the travels of the Dreamings, and the passage of time into a single image and provided a generalized account of the journey as a whole." Such maps open realms of spiritual experience as exciting to explore as the entire earth was in the Age of Discovery.

Marco Polo confirmed the longstanding European assumption of a southern continent by writing of a land called "Beach" 1,790 miles below Java. Along with Ptolemy, he inspired the great sixteenth-century European mapmakers to continue hypothesizing, though they knew from its circumnavigation that Africa was not connected to a southern continent. Published in Venice, a beautifully engraved and lightly colored 1565 map of the world by Paolo Forlani (see Plate 183) is a superb example of Italian printing from copper plates, as well as of the power myth held in the European cartographic world during the Age of Discovery.

Forlani's work of art presents a vast, southern Terra Incognita decorated with a camel, lion, leopard, bear, ape, rhinoceros, horse, griffin, goat, unicorn, and elephant. There are European ships sailing everywhere on the map, and the Greek concerns about being upside down were finally dismissed by the voyagers on those ships. Few maps convey the sense of adventure in exploration as does this Italian masterpiece with those ships literally caught between the modern and the ancient world. It is Map as Act Five in the Theater of the World. Even after Francis Drake sailed around the southern tip of America on his 1577–80 voyage and proved the phantom Terra Australis was not its southern extension as Forlani claimed, the myth persisted. It would take almost three centuries for European explorers and cartographers to fill in the map of the Pacific Ocean with the world of Oceania and Australia.

It was the Dutch who provided the first major clues for the Western world to the mystery of what actually existed in the great Southern Ocean. (The Chinese had knowledge of Australia in the

thirteenth century.) In 1616 the Dutch landed on an uncharted, rough coast with naked, murderous inhabitants; they named the place Eendrachtsland and considered this "New Holland" a worthless place. Was it the southern extension of New Guinea, or was it Polo's "Beach," or Forlani's great southern continent extending to the south pole?

The European idea of a land "down under" the equator in the Southern Hemisphere can be traced back to the Greeks. They believed the order and the balance inherent in the cosmos demanded such a place on planet Earth, though to their minds—lacking an understanding of the laws of gravity—a Southern Hemisphere would have been uninhabitable, not to mention too hot to sustain life. Ptolemy visually introduced the concept of Terra Australis Incognita (the unknown southern land) by enclosing the Indian Ocean with a massive landmass attached to Africa, an assumption that was carried into the late Middle Ages when his *Geographia* was rediscovered by Europeans via Islamic scholars.

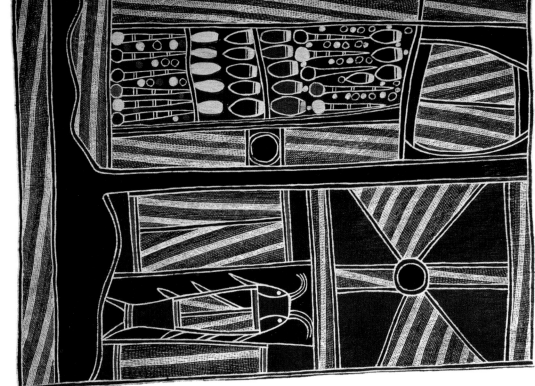

PLATE 182. *Map of the Murrinh-Patha Countryside.* A traditional homeland area has been transformed into a totemic landscape by this aboriginal Australian artist.

PLATE 183 (OVERLEAF). *Forlani Map of the Known World.* The enduring myth of the great land "down under" was fueled by this 1565 Italian map.

LA TERRA CONOSCIVTA FIN QVI

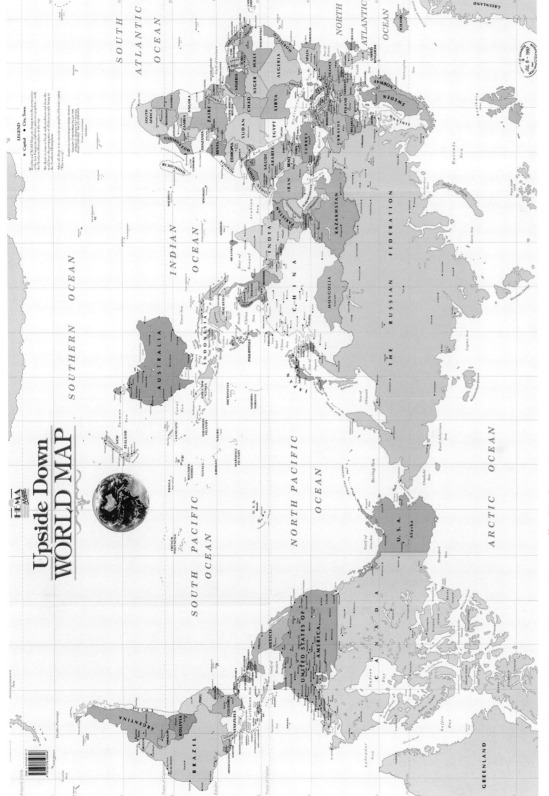

PLATE 184. *Upside Down World Map.* A distinct worldview is offered by this 1996 Australian map.

By the early eighteenth century, the British had moved into the Pacific. Captain Cook's three voyages between 1768 and 1779 were initiated by the British Admiralty to solve the mystery of Forlani's Terra Australis. Unlike the Dutch, who landed on the barren western and northern coasts of New Holland, Cook found the eastern coast fertile, though the natives were still hostile. He also proved it was not an extension of New Guinea. Then, by charting the accurate longitude of many islands in the Southern Pacific Ocean with the help of the new chronometer, he discovered it was a very large island unto itself, in fact a continent. Crisscrossing the sea, Cook set the land firmly in place on the map. By breaking up the legendary Terra Australis into identified pieces in a vast ocean, he pushed the mythical landmass below the Arctic Circle into the unattractively dangerous, frozen realm of the South Pole.

In 1788 a British penal colony was founded near Botany Bay, where Cook landed in 1770. He had raised the Union Jack and claimed the land for Great Britain. New Holland was soon "Australia." Though its political institutions and culture are derived from Europe, Australia exists geographically on the margins of Asia in Oceania. As a member of the British Commonwealth, and with close ties militarily to the United States, but with 60 percent of its export market in economically prospering East Asia, politically stable

Australia's role on the world stage could assume greater significance in the twenty-first century. A 1996 map produced in Brisbane called *Upside Down World Map* (Plate 184) is oriented south in the time-honored tradition of Eastern cartography. But, unlike its ancient predecessors, it was based on an act of social and political protest, albeit tongue in cheek. It is Map as Self-Esteem Booster.

Australia's history parallels that of the United States. Similar in size, the two countries were founded at roughly the same time by social outcasts from England, and both societies have a troubled past with their indigenous peoples and nonwhite immigrants, a gold rush, and a "wild west." While citizens of the powerful United States have no discernible self-esteem problem on the world's stage, Australians have suffered from merciless "down under" jokes, which led one student at Melbourne University, Stuart McArthur, to devise the prototype for the modern "South Up" map in order to properly celebrate Australia Day in 1979. "At last," he wrote with over-the-top good humor, "the first move has been made — the first step in the long overdue crusade to elevate our glorious, but neglected nation from the gloomy depths of anonymity in the world power struggle to its rightful position — towering over its northern neighbors, reigning splendidly at the helm of the universe.... Long live Australia — Ruler of the Universe!!"

It is ironic that the "flipping" of the traditional Western map makes it more obvious how much "stuff" is in the so-called Northern Hemisphere. It brings to mind the traditional front page of a newspaper where the "big stories" are always placed "above the fold." (In the case of a map, the fold would be the equator.) Even calling a map "upside down" seems an admission of existing below the fold. On the *Upside Down World Map*, Australia floats as a place apart in the Western imagination, no matter the orientation of the map and no matter what culture stocks the map shop.

Another Australian bond with the United States was forged in 1912, when Walter B. Griffin of Chicago won the international design contest for the capital city of Australia, Canberra. As Griffin told the *New York Times*, "It is the first time such a thing has been attempted on any large scale. The plan I have prepared for the Australian Capital will cover an area of 25 square miles and will provide for an immediate population of 75,000 with ample provision for the growth of the city. The plan is of the radial or gyratory

PLATE 185, *Canberra, the Federal Capital of the Commonwealth*. Australia's invented capital city is a symbol of political authority.

PLAN OF
CANBERRA
THE
FEDERAL CAPITAL
OF THE
COMMONWEALTH
OF
AUSTRALIA

NOTES

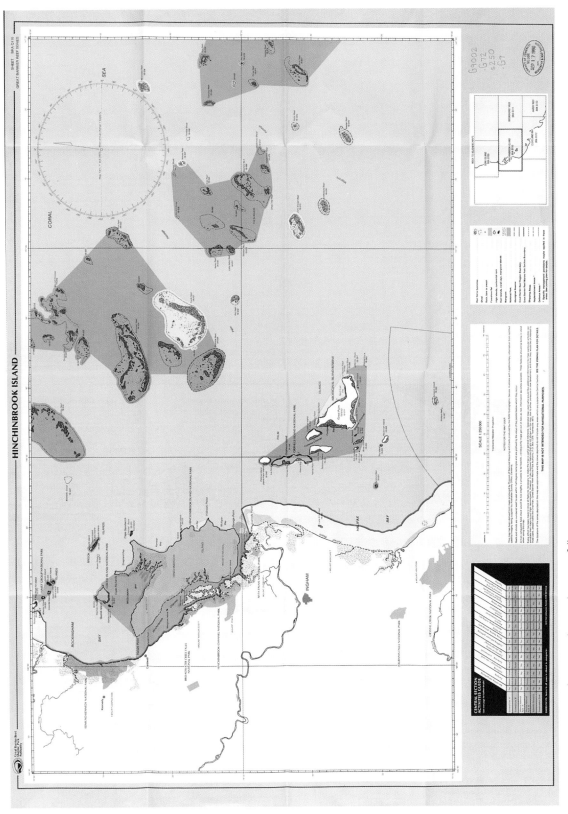

PLATE 186. *Great Barrier Reef Marine Park*. Australia successfully uses maps as a persuasive ecological tool.

type. There is one principal center from which streets and boulevards radiate to other centers, from which in turn thoroughfares radiate to subordinate centers." The next day, the newspaper's editorial reminded Griffin that Major L'Enfant had, in fact, carried out a similar plan in Washington, DC.

While the U.S. capital's southern site was the result of a political deal, an appeasement to get the southern states to pay the soldiers who fought in the American Revolution, Australia's site was the result of a decision to avoid Melbourne and Sydney's vying to provide a focus for national pride. But, unlike Paris, London, and Buenos Aires, neither of Australia's two major cities was the original nucleus of its nation, and like the United States, with more or less equal states, Australia needed a neutral capital city to serve as its administrative center. A 1927 map of Canberra (see Plate 185) shows how the plan was implemented with residential, retail, and minor industrial sites, along with the National Library and the requisite government buildings. It is characterized by what J. B. Harley calls symbolic realism, for what appears to be simply cartographic fact is also cartographic symbol. It is Map as Symbolic Treatment of Power. Its duality works to make it a political statement by offering a complex weave of nationalist ideas. Here the

cartographic image defines a social world and makes plain its visionary goals for an implied great nation of the future.

Another goal enhanced by the Australian government's maps was to save the Great Barrier Reef from destruction. Pollution generated by coastal development, sewage, agricultural runoff, global warming, overfishing, and improper marine recreation have had devastating effects on coral reefs, which are a vital component of ocean ecosystems, providing shelter for nearly one-quarter of all marine life. Since creation of the Great Barrier Reef Marine Park in 1975, the Park Authority has used maps as powerful tools of science and public affairs with a remarkable effect on the health of the famous coral reef, which evolved over hundreds of thousands of years and extends over 1,429 miles on the northeast continental shelf of Australia. It is the largest natural feature on earth, bigger than the entire area of Italy, and the world's largest World Heritage Site. Composed of the living organism coral polyps and the limestone skeletons they leave behind, coral reefs are among the world's most fragile and endangered ecosystems.

The reef is not a continuous barrier. It is a broken maze of coral reefs, including 2,800 individual reefs. This is what makes it the largest and most complex marine park system in the world. To preserve biodiversity while providing for reasonable use, a spectrum of zones was created by the Park Authority with the participation of the public, ranging from General Use Zones to Preservation Zones. To minimize human impact, most reasonable activities such as tourism, fishing, boating, diving, and research are permitted but controlled through zoning and management planning. The map for the Hinchinbrook Island area (Plate 186), like all the maps in the series, uses color coding to show what is acceptable behavior in the zones and where permits are required to undertake some activities.

Though the creation of zones was supported by both state (Queensland) and federal laws, the success of the program is aided by the unscripted message of this map, whose beauty and emotional plea transcend serviceability. Its authority as an official document, its power to carry the Park Authority's environmental message visually, provokes unquestioning acceptance of the rules from most people. Information in the form of a map seems factual and objective to a general public that is very often suspicious of a written text. The direct communication offered by maps can actually convince people to obey the laws, a critical objective with such fragile areas as Hinchinbrook Island. It is Map as Public Affairs Tool. Its clarity and the accessibility it offers to complex geographical data also allow the map to impress the affected community with the legitimacy of the Marine Park's scientific studies. Instead of seeming to prohibit access, which a book of zoning restrictions might do, the map is part of a "Guide for Users" produced by the park. Even the term "users" helps contain land-use controversies in a democratic state. Within the boundaries set by the Park Authority, safe and healthy fun is offered to one and all. The Park Authority's caring for the environment translates into its caring for the users.

Another type of zoning map that has *not* quieted controversies concerns itself with the maritime boundaries of nations. Based on the Law of the Sea conventions involving over 150 countries held under the auspices of the United Nations, New Zealand, for example, has since 1977 a Territorial Sea, which encircles the country for 12 nautical miles measured from the low-water mark of its coast, and an Exclusive Economic Zone (EEZ), which extends for 200 nautical miles from the same low-water mark. A map from the New Zealand Department of Lands and Survey (Plate 187) illustrates the country's territorial claims and its conflict with potential economic zones of neighboring states. The economic rights exist not only on the surface of the earth but also to the earth's core (mining, drilling) and to the sky above (airspace). It is Map as Three-Dimensional Territorial Claim.

The conventions were held to deal with unrestricted extension of jurisdiction and the proliferating territorial disputes over claims to maritime space and resources. The treaty allowed for the establishment of sovereign rights within the EEZ for the countries and their territories. (One of the reasons Britain fought for the Falkland Islands in 1982 was the attached sea area three times its own size.) Beyond the EEZ is the High Seas, outside any national jurisdiction. The Law of the Sea Treaty was closely integrated with, among others, the World Heritage Treaty, the Convention on Ozone Depleting Substances, and the Convention on Climate Change.

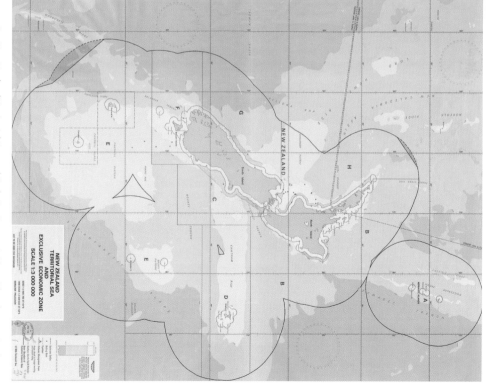

PLATE 187. *New Zealand Territorial Sea and Exclusive Economic Zone.* The changes in the modern world's attachment to the sea are reflected by this 1983 map.

Though the United States has resolved Atlantic Ocean boundary issues with Canada after years of bitter dispute, and is engaged in more than thirty other maritime boundary negotiations—some involving single tiny islands in Oceania chains that straddle trade routes or possibly sit atop large reserves of oil and gas—opponents in the United States argue that the Law of the Sea Treaty takes away rights of free movement and interferes with private industry's right to profit at the expense of biodiversity. The convention is so widely accepted, however, that the map of New Zealand is now viewed as interpreting international law.

ANTARCTICA

An Antarctic iceberg was drawn in 1700 by Edmond Halley on his voyage to gather magnetic variation data to solve the mystery of true north vs. the North Pole. Seventy-five years later, James Cook circumvented the ice-surround of Antarctica, ending speculation on the existence of Terra Australis Incognita. He wrote in his journal, "That there may be a Continent or large tract of land near the Pole, I will not deny; on the contrary, I am of the opinion there is, and it is probable that we have seen part of it."

In 1838 Lieutenant Charles Wilkes was sent by the U.S. government to explore the entire Pacific Ocean and find new lands in the Southern Hemisphere. The contents of his brief in what the sailors called the South

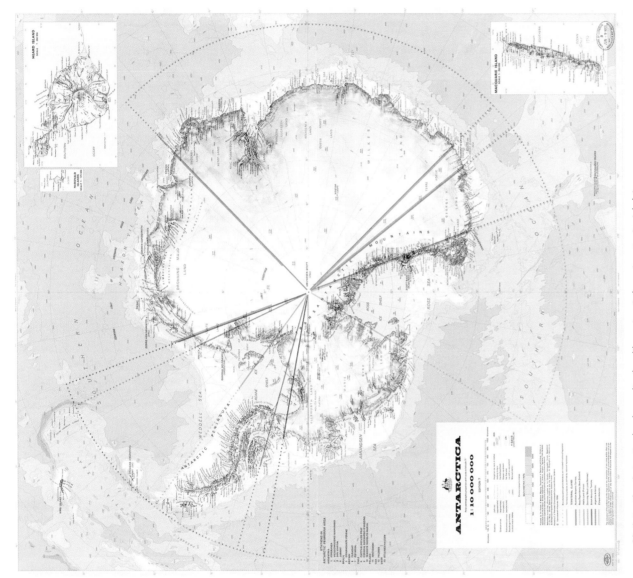

PLATE 188. *Antarctica*. Antarctica has been sliced up like an ice pie by various territorial claims.

Sea. Already, by 1820, an American ship on a sealing expedition under John Davis had entered in his log a landing on the Antarctic continent, though it was barricaded by ice. The next year, a Russian admiral, Thaddeus von Bellingshausen, had circumnavigated the ice-covered sea of Antarctica and had met an American skipper, Nathaniel Palmer, who was working among the uncharted islands. Yet, following orders heroically, Wilkes and his crew located and charted for the first time 1,500 miles of what was still thought of as Terra Australis Incognita during his voyage of discovery below Australia; his examined Antarctic coast is known today as Wilkes Land. It has been suggested that Herman Melville, having read Wilkes's narrative, based Captain Ahab's mythic pursuit of the white whale on Wilkes's famous search for the white continent.

Australia, Chile, and Argentina claim EEZ rights over Antarctica, rights that are not acknowledged by the forty-five member nations of the Antarctic Treaty (1959), twenty-seven of whom are consultive (decision-making) members. Of those twenty-seven members, Argentina, Australia, Chile, France, New Zealand, Norway, and the U.K. claim portions of Antarctica as national territory—and

some claims overlap. The United States does not recognize the claims, and along with Russia, reserves the right to make future claims. Antarctica is slightly less than 1.5 times the size of the United States, but it has no arable land and is covered with 98 percent thick continental ice sheet and 2 percent barren rock. It is administered through meetings of the consultative member nations. A 1986 map of Antarctica was produced in Canberra with the help of Tasmanian scientists (Plate 188). There is an index to the stations operated as research centers by twenty-six national governments party to the Antarctic Treaty, which prohibits any measures of a military nature. Military personnel and equipment may be used only for scientific research. The map has insets of McDonald Islands, Heard Island, and Macquairie Island.

With international rivalries spearheading the penetration of the Arctic and the Antarctic on the race to the Poles, the need for conquest was married to the need for knowledge. The map of the Antarctic continent offers a sense of closure to the Western imagination's relationship with the blank spaces on the world map. It is Map as Historic Quest Completed.

Because maps are social, concerning people in groups, some cultural realities of civilizations need cartographic assistance to make them visible. In many of these cases, maps share the hidden component of ideas, and they can exert the psychological power attributed to books, movies, and other works of art that stimulate the imagination and record the living elements in societies.

Using a stereographic projection, which is one centered on a point of the earth's surface, Adrien Bérubé at Canada's University of Moncton, created a map for the 1999 international summit meeting of French-speaking communities sponsored by L'Agence de la Francophonie and held in the city of Moncton, Canada (see Plate 189). As the map's notes make plain, the city hosting the summit became, for several days, the center of the universe for the world's French-speaking people. Thus radial distances are shown from Moncton, set dead center on the map. The notes justify the map's structure by reminding the viewer that most maps distort the face of the earth in any case, and most people's vision of the world, their reality, conforms to those distortions. Mapping cultural geography, such as places where a particular language is spoken, naturally creates a partial and biased view of the world, but its legitimacy cannot be questioned rationally. It is Map as Alternate Face of Reality. It is also a tribute to French-speaking people everywhere at a time when 90 percent of the world's 6,800 living languages are expected to disappear with the current generation. Since the prime motivation in language choices made by communities and societies is comparative status, or the perception of a language by members of a society as an important means to achieving life goals, this map becomes a celebration of the universal power of French. Languages are more threatened than are earth's remaining stock of birds or mammals. This map is an act of intervention.

DNA has been called the universal language of life. In 1865, when the genetic pioneer Gregor Mendel evolved his working hypothesis relating to inherited character traits in order to interpret certain realities observed in the orderliness and regularity of consecutive generations of culinary peas, he could not guess what their mode of transport might be within the plant's genetic structure. In 1944 Oswald T. Avery, Maclyn McCarty, and Colin McLeod demonstrated that the six-foot-long, twisted strand of DNA found in virtually every human cell contained the inherited genetic blueprint. As was later discovered, however, the human genome—the twenty-three pairs of chromosomes in which the DNA is tangled—is an active and diverse biological ecosystem not entirely concerned with fashioning individual human beings. Approximately only 1 percent of the encyclopedic human genome houses the mechanically pertinent genes. As Francis Collins, director of the National Human Genome Research Institute, explains, "We've called the human genome the book of life, but it's really three books. It's a history book. It's a shop manual and parts list. And it's a textbook of medicine more profoundly detailed than ever."

The publicly funded human genome project involved thousands of international researchers, and was led in the United States by the National Institutes of Health, the Department of Energy, and by Celera Genomics of Rockville, Maryland, a private company, which produced a map (see Plate 190). This consortium claimed in 2001 to have determined the order of almost all the 3 billion "letters" of biochemical code in the human genome. Strung together, these letters arguably spell out the directions for making and maintaining human life. The map is a true map because it shows spatial relationships in a designated space. It is Map as Historical Anthology of Self. It raises the question of how such a complex proposition as a human being can be coded with little more than 30,000 scattered genes—only five times more than baker's yeast. (Previous estimates had ranged from 80,000 to 120,000 scripting genes.) Most interestingly, the map has shown how individuals

ABOVE: Detail from p. 251.

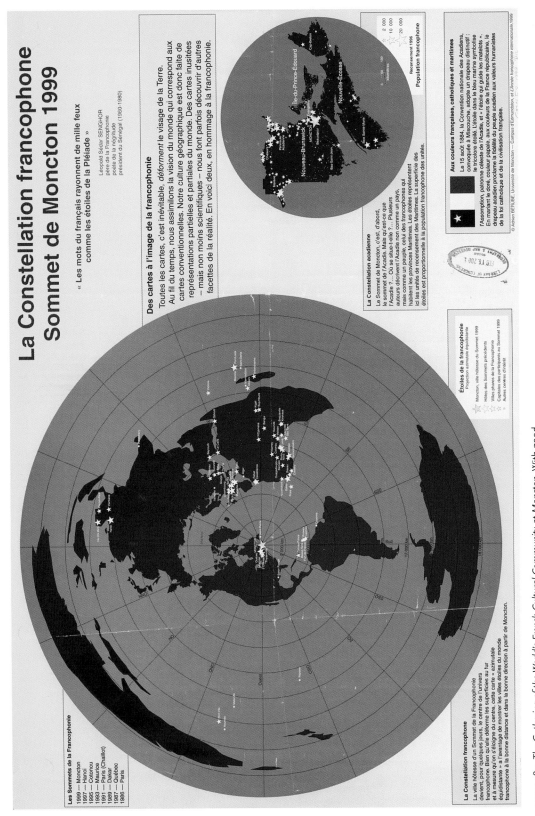

PLATE 189. *The Gathering of the World's French Cultural Community at Moncton.* With good reason, Moncton, Canada, is the center of the world on this 1999 map.

around the world are about 99.9 percent genetically identical, proving how recently the human species appeared and how little time it has had to diversify.

There is no gene for race. The individual human characteristics assigned to the various races, such as skin color and design of features, are inherited individually from each parent, along with everything else. Another major genetics controversy is homosexuality, and as Brian Sykes, professor of genetics at Oxford University, observes, "The scientific literature on the biological basis for sexual orientation is a battleground of claim and counterclaim." A map by geographer Tim Davis (see Plate 191) shows the gay and lesbian communities in 1990s Boston. It is Map as Subversive Urban Utopia. It depicts a public space—the antithesis of the coffin world of the closet—where homosexuals, growing up in constant danger of physical violence and insult, can be themselves and openly express affection, tenderness, friendship, fidelity, camaraderie, and companionship—can hold hands—while reconstructing what the philosopher Michel Foucault called "the aesthetic of the self." Thus a visible "ghetto" offers a means of escaping an invisible one, a mental one ruled by shame and secrecy.

The map locates a place where the sense of being inferior imposed by a homophobic society is neutralized. It depicts a communal support system that exists in full view of the dominant heterosexual world, which is oblivious to the daily psychological and spiritual transformations occurring in its midst there. As gay historian Didier Eribon explains, "Geographic distance, the search for different locations, the effort to inscribe oneself in a new space, are all conditions for reconstructing oneself." The escape route from the abusive past is visibility, which is made relatively safe in the urban phenomenon of homosexual communities like the one in Boston. The resulting "gay politics" have shifted the balance of power in the international cultural landscape and questioned the traditional apparatus of power while devising new possibilities outside the established systems for everyone.

While gay and lesbian adolescents must come to terms with the world's image of them, Thomas F. Saarinen used Environment-Behavior-Design research (E-B-D) and sketch mapping to explore the image of the world held by various adolescents. In the 1950s, Saarinen combined psychology and geography in a new field called environmental perception. The same type of research was just getting started in urban planning, sociology, and architecture to form the broad interdisciplinary field described as E-B-D. He studied the role of perceptions and behavior in decisions related to the environment at all levels. Sketch mapping greatly influenced this burgeoning field of mental or cognitive mapping. When Saarinen extended the technique to a world scale in the early 1970s, he col-

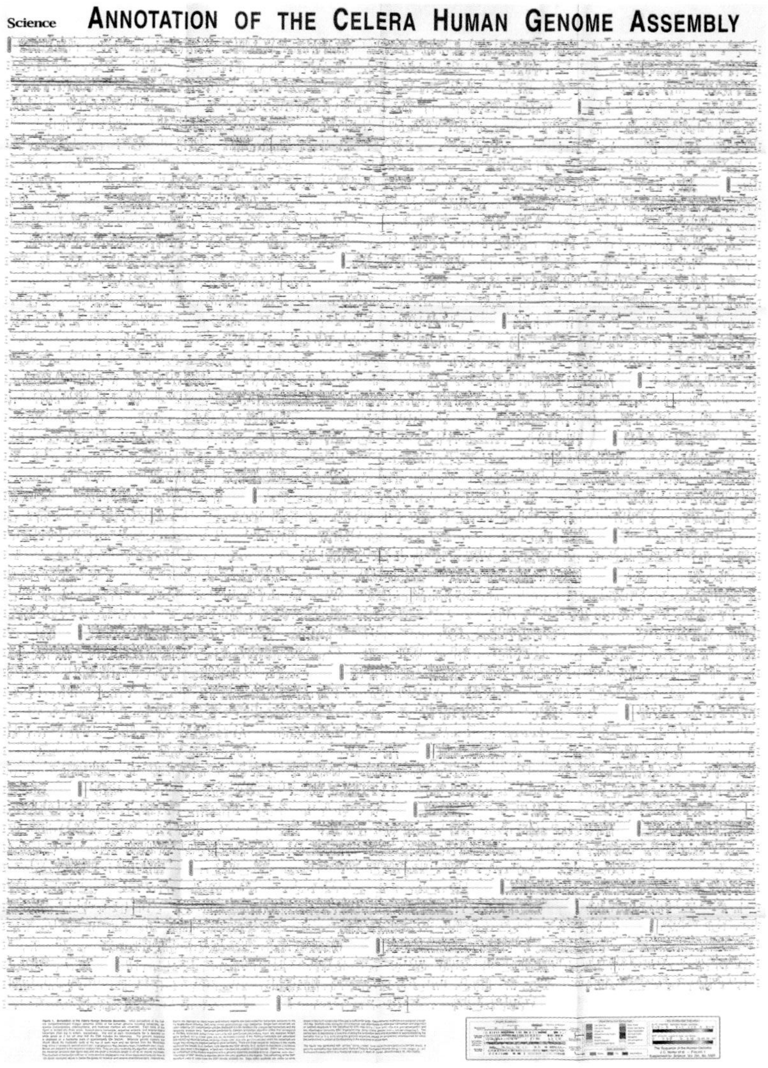

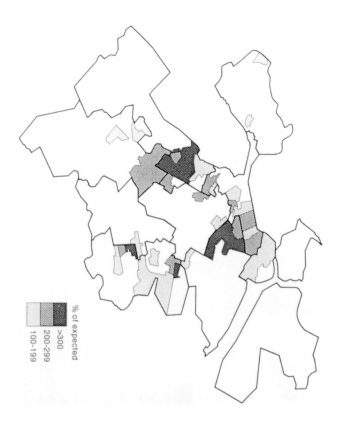

Science

% of expected
>300
200-299
100-199

PLATE 190. *Map of the Human Genome.* The human genetic blueprint is annotated on this 2001 map.

PLATE 191. *Boston: Gay and Lesbian Residential Concentrations.* An escape route from an abusive past via social visibility is charted on this map.

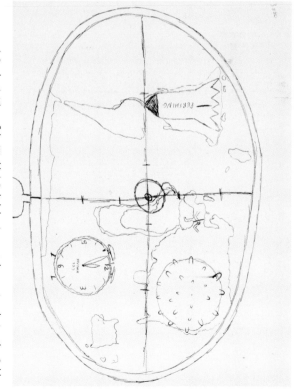

PLATE 192. A Student's *View of the World.* A Polish boy's mental mapping during the Cold War combined psychology with geography.

lected maps from youngsters everywhere for a specific project about student views of the world.

One remarkable map (Plate 192) was drawn by a thirteen-year-old Polish boy from Lodz. It captured the fear of the Cold War festering in the informed youth of his day. The mapmaker clearly saw himself in great danger, literally living in the sights of a gun with time running out. It is Map as Cold War Anxiety. It is hard not to feel compassion for a young person living in such an environment. The map communicates his exact state of being at the time, and he was certainly not alone in a dilemma not of his own making. Through the map, he shares the emotional experience of an entire generation.

The actual realm created by the Cold War was of limited duration. Maps of imaginary realms have long been a part of the cartographic world, and will be created as long as books are read. One of the most enthralling literary realms is a gift from William Faulkner (1897–1962), Nobel laureate (1950), and among the world's greatest literary innovators. His chronicle of a southern society and its history is set in mythical Yoknapatawpha County, Mississippi. His map (see Plate 193) expresses his belief that freedom can only be achieved in the context of community. In *The Town* (1957), he has his character Gavin Stevens describe Yoknapatawpha at dusk: "First is Jefferson, the center, radiating weakly its puny glow into space; beyond it, enclosing it, spreads the County, tied by the diverging roads to that center as is the rim to the hub by its spokes, yourself detached as God Himself for this moment above the cradle of your nativity and of the men and women who made you, the record and chronicle of your native land proffered for your perusal in ring by concentric ring, like the ripples on living water above the dreamless slumber of your past; you to preside unanguished and immune above this miniature of man's passions and hopes and disasters...."

Faulkner's map blended Lafayette County, where he had been born and reared, with his imaginary hill country of north Mississippi. "I discovered that my own little postage stamp of native soil was worth writing about and that I would never live long enough to exhaust it, and that by sublimating the actual into the apocryphal

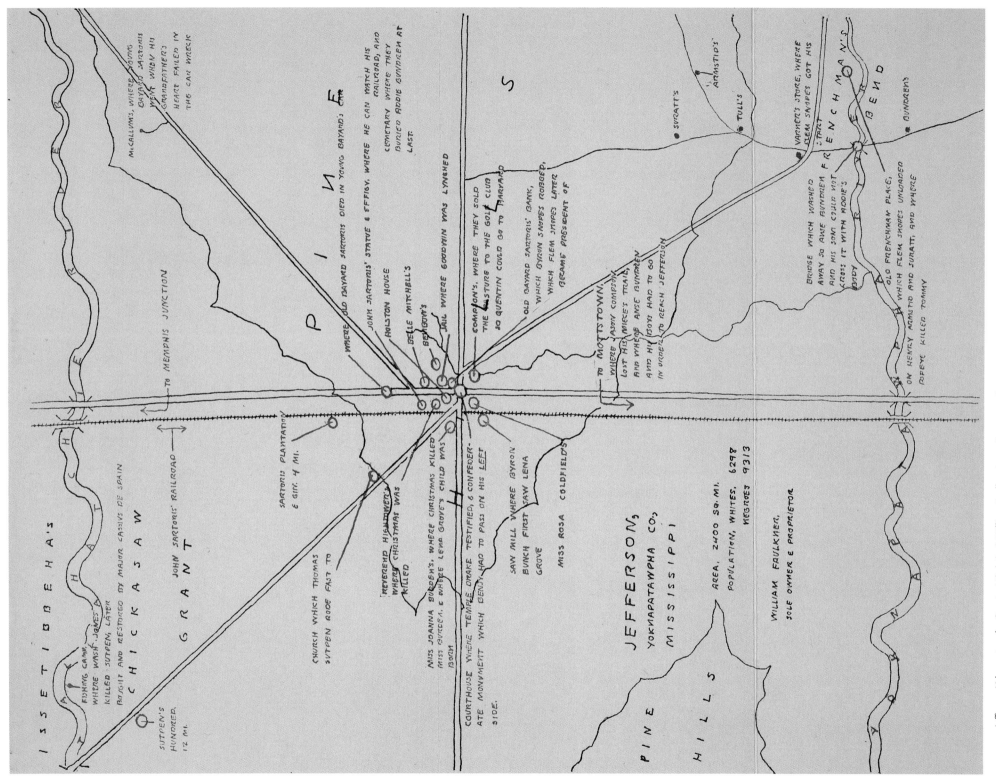

PLATE 193. *Jefferson, Yoknapatawpha County, Mississippi.* William Faulkner's 1936 annotated map of his created universe is spiritual geography.

I would have complete liberty to use whatever talent I might have to its absolute top. It opened up a gold mine of other people, so I created a cosmos of my own." He stocked his fictional cosmos full of contemporary issues and ideas. It is Map as Keystone of a Universe. For a writer with an all-embracing historical view of the land's exploitation and of the destruction resulting from the greed for material possessions, Faulkner was a natural to map his rural Yoknapatawphan earth, which he covers from its Creation to about 1950. The fiction set there embraces his entire writing career—from *Sartoris* (1929) to *The Reivers* (1962). His map has been called a historical map of the Christian tradition and its concomitant culture—"No Western man today can know where he stands if he has not gone through Yoknapatawpha County at least once," wrote the critic Gabriel Vahanian, placing the map in the realm of spiritual geography.

It is believed Faulkner had his map from the beginning and may have kept a copy on his writing table, though he published it for the first time in *Absalom, Absalom!* (1936). The placement of each locale and some events on the map suggests a spatial design controlled from the start by Faulkner's creative imagination and dictated by imaginative truth. And what he removed, such as the university at Oxford—his Jefferson—is also heavy with intent: the university was one of the chief sources of liberal opinion in the state. His chronology of Yoknapatawpha County begins in the map's northwest section and moves clockwise; most of the planters who enter the region before 1840 obtain their land from the Indians. If Faulkner's goal was to evoke a symbolic whole uniting distinct experiences, his map formally evokes the unity of his vision. He eminently succeeded in living up to theorist Willard Huntington Wright's description of an artist's nature—"an omnipotent god who moulds and fashions the destiny of a new world, and leads it to an inevitable completion where it can stand alone."

Another form of imaginary map is one that reveals an attitude about a particular place. Possibly the most famous is by Saul Steinberg (Plate 194). It appeared on the cover of the *New Yorker* magazine for March 29, 1976. It is Map as Cultural Egotism. It has become a symbol of the *New Yorker's* point of view. It shows the city as the one fixed point of reference in the universe. However charmingly satirical the image, the art historian Simon Schama suggests that it, and others in a similar vein by Steinberg, are "something close to a valedictory caution." The map "has a pessimistically sardonic edge...an impatience with a culture that compresses continental and intercontinental distance into so many Heres and Theres divided only by delays at La Guardia." It is a bird's-eye view with a difference, though it is a cultural text taking possession of the land. It magnificently captures a localized perception of reality.

Like all serious works of art, Steinberg's map has taken on layers of meaning over the decades. When New York State's Senator Hillary Clinton said, "I've recently learned that more people from the state of New York have given their lives on behalf of our country than any other state. That's not what a lot of people think about the state. They don't think of us as being such a critical part of our nation's defense," the map suddenly took on aspects of New York as Fortress America, guarding our nation from sea to shining sea."

And, after the 2004 presidential election, when the polarity between "blue" states and "red" states became a national issue, New York City became a symbol of the "liberal" or blue bastion, and many voters in the United States would have seen the Steinberg image as a political statement depicting the abyss between the two political parties. However, a map of the contiguous forty-eight states (see Plate 195) indicating whether a majority of their votes chose the Republican (red) candidate, George W. Bush, over the Democratic (blue) one, John Kerry, gave the superficial impression that the "red states" dominated the country, since they covered far more area than the blue ones. The fact that maps tend to be believed until they are discredited has graced cartography with an undeserved trust, which propagandists have used to their advantage. The red-state/blue-state dichotomy map was used to declare a "landslide" in 2004. It offers an example of map prejudice. It is Map as Pure Mapism. It fails to take into account the fact that states are composed of counties, and some red states had many blue counties. Thus the amount of red on the map is skewed because there are a lot of counties in which only a slim majority voted Republican.

One possible way to allow for this, suggested by Robert Vanderbei at Princeton University, was to use not just two colors on the map—red and blue—but shades of purple to indicate percentages of voters by county (see Plate 196). This approach shows what unbiased news reports revealed after the election: the country was

PLATE 194. *View of the World from Ninth Avenue.* Saul Steinberg's imaginary map reveals a particular attitude shared by many New Yorkers.

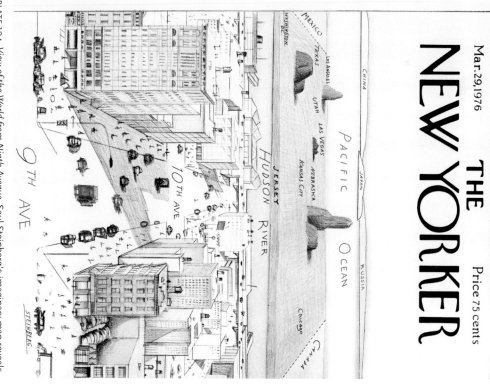

Mar. 29, 1976   Price 75 cents

THE NEW YORKER

actually very evenly divided between Republicans and Democrats. Yet another way to correct the red-and-blue cartographic sleight of hand was by use of a cartogram, a map in which the sizes of the states were rescaled according to their population and then colored by means of county-level election results (Plate 197). When this was done, the blue areas were much magnified, and amounts of blue and red became nearly equal, reflecting with greater accuracy the actual voting results of the 2004 election. Thus the landslide claimed by many Republicans via one cartographic form was discounted by the use of another form. And when shades of purple were used to indicate percentages of voters, a very small portion was taken up by true red counties—the rest being mostly shades of purple with patches of blue in the urban areas. Thus Republi-

cans and Democrats did not live in segregated states but were neighbors in nearly every U.S. community. Difference of opinion, a tenet of the Bill of Rights, was alive and well in the nation.

In 1884 Washington, DC, was the focus of another kind of election, one to select the zero degree (0°) meridian to be used as a reference line from which all other longitudes were measured. Until the forty-one delegates from twenty-four countries met at the 1884 International Meridian Conference in Washington, convened by President Chester A. Arthur, there were many prime meridians at play around the world. The conference was one of the first dialogues about international standards of communication. The extension of railroads east to west and the telegraph had been major instigators for a coordinated U.S. and English time zone system based on Greenwich time. Before 1883, when the telegraph lines began transmitting time signals to all major U.S. cities, there had been more than three hundred local times in the United States.

PLATES 195, 196, AND 197. *2004 Election Results*. These maps offer a perfect visual definition of "mapism."

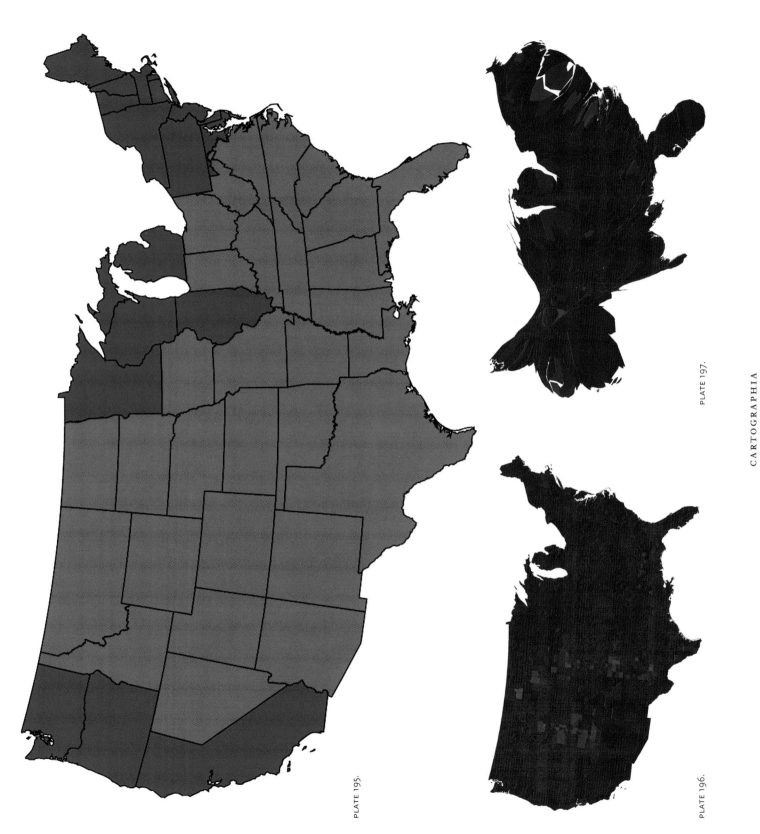

PLATE 195.

PLATE 196.

PLATE 197.

Creating an international time system, along with one prime meridian, required unprecedented cooperation to overcome obstacles emerging from nationalism. It was the powerful shipping industry and its advances in science, especially astronomical innovations in reckoning longitude, that forced the issues. The selection of the Greenwich observatory, as opposed to the Paris observatory, was in part due to the power and sprawl of the British Empire, as well as an acknowledgment of Greenwich as a true scientific center with global interests already affiliated with the United States. (In 1848 Great Britain had become the first country to adopt a time standard, made law in 1880.) A map from Thailand created right after the Meridian Conference celebrates the new prime meridian (Plate 198). It is Map as Act of Union. It practically shimmers with the message that time was now a shared commodity. The human community had been brought closer together.

Little did people imagine in 1884 just how closely the globe's peoples would eventually be connected via mass communication.

Using cartography's symbols to contextualize the disembodied realm of cyberspace is a well-established discipline. And similarly, each contextualization implies a narrative, a story, an interpretation. A 1999 map (Plate 199) created by the pioneering visualization researchers at Lucent Technologies Bell Labs led by Stephen Eick represents Internet traffic flow around the world by using a

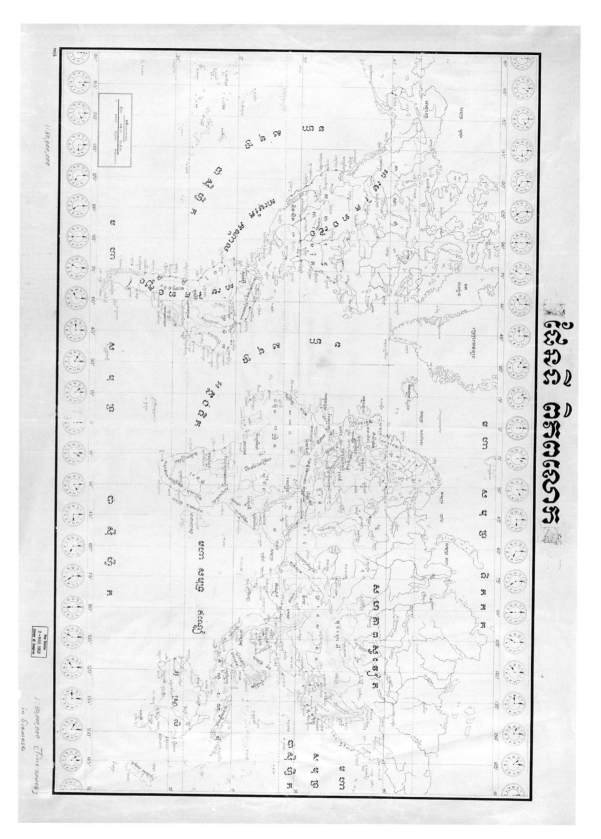

PLATE 198. *Time Zones in Siamese*. Global cooperation is exemplified by this map from Thailand.

PLATE 199. *Arc Map*. The Internet is visualized by the creators of this 1999 map.

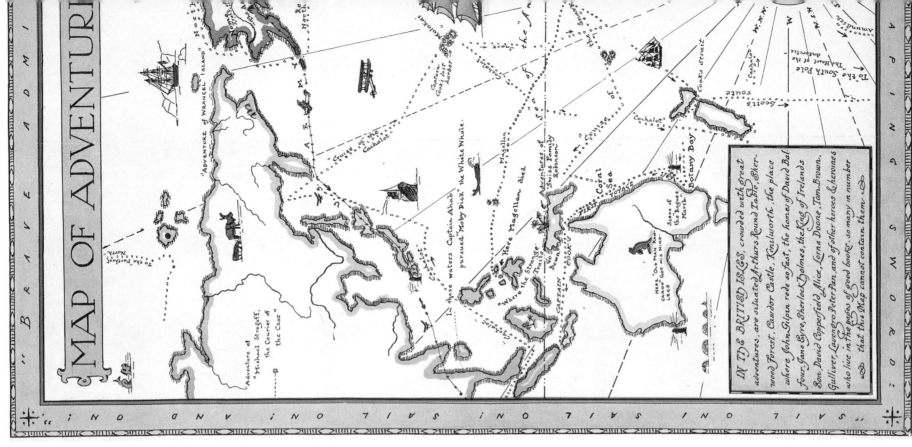

ters in the British Isles and in the thirteen original states. Geography plays a huge part in fiction, just as it does in the lives of explorers. But literary maps are usually not about discovery. They tend to give delight by locating place for people familiar with the imaginary characters, who often have more "reality" than even the greatest

three-dimensional network structure applied to a flat map. The color, thickness, and height of the arcs encode the traffic statistics for fifty intercountry links in 1993; the highest are the busiest. It is Map as New Economic Geography. (Online, the user of the map can rotate and view it from any angle.) Creating novel 3-D spatial metaphors to give a sense of the structure of information requires a wide range of analytical techniques and disciplines, which have evolved a new breed of cartographer—masters of charting virtual places. They deal with the issue of the "common mental geography" that exists beyond the computer screen. Some of these maps, like the one by the Lucent Technologies researchers, depict the physical structure and information traffic patterns of global networks, while some address the content and social spaces of the electronic world. All are gracing cartography with high-tech data visualization, expanding the artistic possibilities of interactive environments and their sensory presences. Though often more useful as symbols than as maps, these beautiful images are nonetheless charting the new economic geography that is transforming the way the earth's communities go about their business. Cyberspace is a theater of operations, yet another theater of the world, but one with a landscape dominated by change and by transformation. It offers a new Age of Discovery for cartographers.

Most of the younger generations envision the computer as a thrilling extension of human powers. They see the future of cyberspace as a long, thoughtful walk down an endless shelf of e-books with a new precision of reference. Though direction is remarkably linear in cyberspace, there are many arrows of direction in the mind's quiver. The computer's adherents can easily separate the activity of research from the particular form it has historically assumed, i.e., the book. But as Janet Murray of MIT insists, "The computer is not the enemy of the book. It is the child of print culture, a result of the five centuries of organized, collective inquiry and invention that the printing press made possible." She does not fear the imminent demise of the book even as she sees the computer's promise to "reshape knowledge in ways that sometimes complement and sometimes supercede the work of the book and the lecture hall." She would agree with Stéphane Mallarmé, who wrote, "Everything in the world exists to end up in a book."

Or on a map. One map of the world (Plate 200), compiled in 1925 by Paul M. Paine (1869–1955), mixes fiction and true stories of exploration and adventure. The map's continents have the titles of books and the locations of places associated with them, while dotted lines denote historic journeys. So Marco Polo, Columbus, and Magellan share space with Melville's *Pequod* from *Moby Dick*, just as they do in many people's minds. All exist in "the past." It is Map as History of the Imagination. Its full name is *Map of Adventures for Boys and Girls: Stories, Trails, Voyages, Discoveries, Explorations & Places to Read About.* Paine was head of the Syracuse Public Library from 1915 to 1942. His map has insets on the bottom corners listing important literary places and characters as well as historical charac-

PLATE 200. *Map of Adventures for Boys and Girls.* The joyful life of the imagination is posited by this map for children.

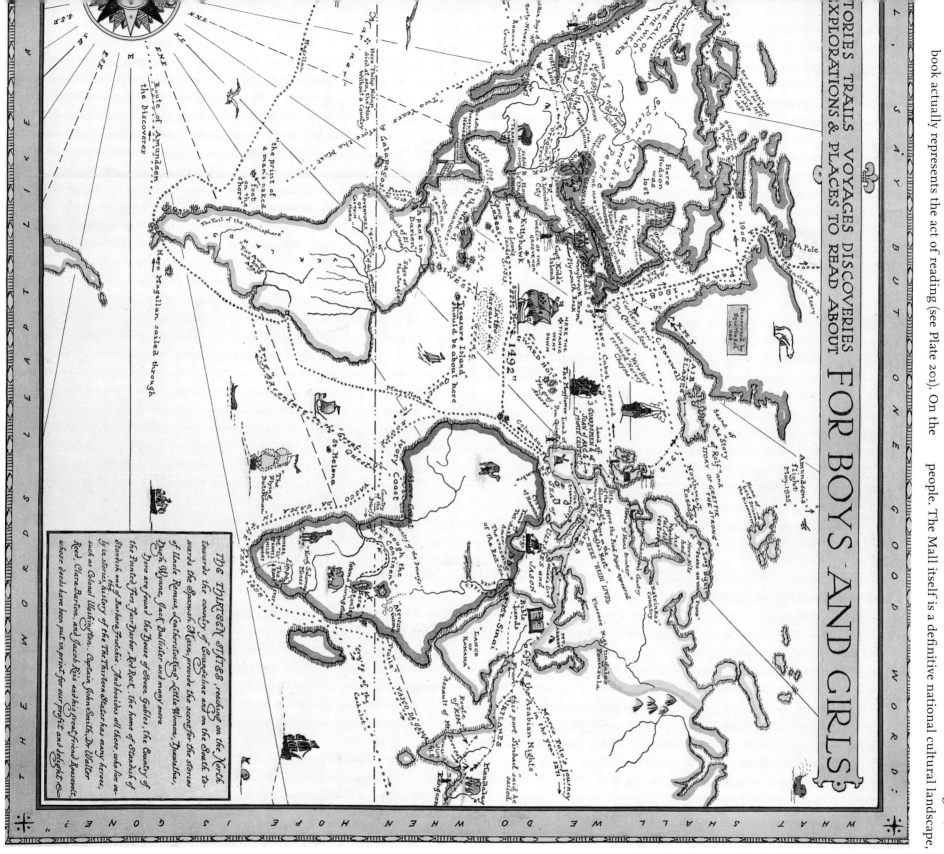

real figures of time past. This map celebrates setting forth on a voyage of discovery. It promotes reading as one of the great adventures.

Another map that celebrates the joy of reading and promotes the book actually represents the act of reading (see Plate 201). On the

the two major ways of map, the Mall in Washington, DC, surrounded by the buildings that house artifacts from all of the world's civilizations, is the site of the annual Library of Congress National Book Festival. More than seventy authors read from their books to crowds reaching 60,000 people. The Mall itself is a definitive national cultural landscape,

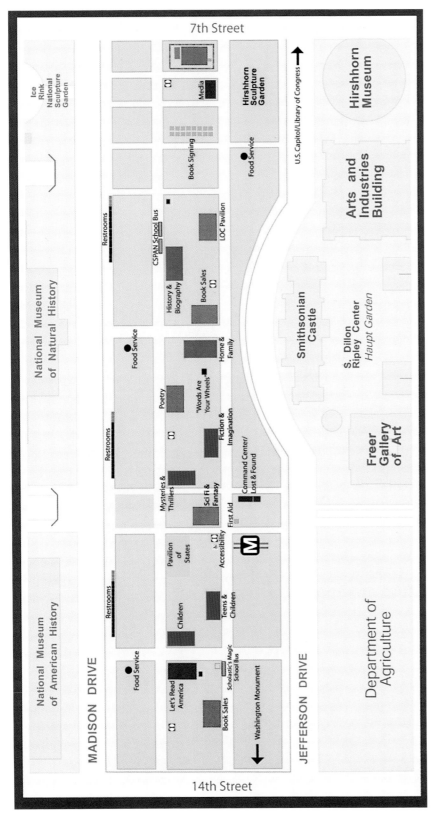

PLATE 201. *Book Festival Site Map*. Cultural interests merge with historical facts on this 2004 map.

THOMAS JEFFERSON BUILDING (LJ)

South	Southeast	Northeast	North
		Deck 37	
	Deck A	Deck 38 MLC'S 95-98	Deck 38 B - E B-F, F1200 P-PN6799 *Folios*
	Deck B	Deck 39 B	Deck 1 B
Deck 10 P	Deck C P	Deck 40 B	Deck 2 F
Deck 11 P	Deck D P	Deck 41 B	Deck 3 F
Deck 12 P	Deck 28 P, PY(Folios) F1260-3790 (Folios)	Deck 42 Directories	Deck 4 Directories Soc. Reg.
Deck 13 Eur Div Stacks	Deck 29 P, F(Folios)	Deck 43 C	Deck 5 D
Deck 14 N	Deck 30 P	Deck 44 E	Deck 6 D
Deck 15 N	Deck 31 N	Deck 45 D	Deck 7 Ref Coll
Deck 16 Asian Div. Stacks	Deck 32 N Folio (Caged)	Deck 46 D	Deck 8 D
Deck 17 P	Deck 33 P	Deck 47 Microfilm	Deck 9 D
Deck 18 P	Deck 34 P	Deck 48 D	NORTH
SOUTH	Deck 35 P	Deck 49	
	Deck 36 P	Deck 50	

JOHN ADAMS BUILDING (LA)

North		South	
READING ROOMS		Deck 12 R,V	
Deck 12 U,S		Deck 11 T	
Deck 11 T,G		Deck 10 Q,T	
Deck 10 T		Deck 9 Q	
Deck 9 Q		Deck 8 Z	
Deck 8 A		Deck 7 J	
Deck 7 J,TS300.M25-TS945.5.C54P86 (Folios) A92L84-A93.L.6 1955 (Folios)		Deck 6 Asian Div. Stacks	
Deck 6 Asian Div. Stacks		Deck 5 AfME Div. Stacks	
Deck 5 Asian Div. Stacks		Deck 4 H	
Deck 4 Asian Div. Stacks		Deck 3 H	
Deck 3 H		Deck 2 H	
Deck 2 H		Deck 1 Overflow Area	
Deck 1 L,G			

Rev. 08-29-02

PLATE 202. *Book Collection Locations*. The book stacks at the Library of Congress are mapped to provide the means for mapping civilizations.

and the festival is designed to enchant anyone who has ever picked up a book and entered a new world as thrilling as one of the national museums. On this map, one culture (literary) is literally superimposed upon another (historical). As at all major book festivals everywhere, many worlds collide. In Los Angeles, the annual Los Angeles Times Festival of Books is organized in association with UCLA. Being on one of the nation's major university campuses offers visitors stimulation and encouragement to enjoy the life of the mind.

For all the wonders of cyberspace, it is doubtful that the work of the Collections Management Division of the Library of Congress in Washington, DC, the world's largest library, will be superseded in the near future. "I cannot live without books," Thomas Jefferson wrote to John Adams in 1815. His words, and all the words in the 30 million books found in the Library of Congress, the nation's library, are the lifeblood of the world's great civilizations. (If Jefferson were alive today, he probably would not be able to live without his laptop either.) The map of the Library's stacks (Plate 202) shows the locations of the vast general collection, occupying 257 miles of bookshelves. (The rest of the Library's 532 miles of shelves are occupied by the collections of the individual Library divisions, such as the Asian, European, and Geography and Map Divisions, to name a few.) The map belies the mazelike mysteries of the stacks. It declines to show which decks are discrete realms and which ones have connecting hallways. For this fortunate user, it offered an endless journey of discovery into a serendipitous paradise, full of nonlinear discoveries. It was Map as The Way In to Mapping Civilizations. Though the stacks are closed to the general public, the stupendous contents housed there are available to

every adult in the Reading Room with a Library of Congress photo identification reader's card, even if the visitor is not writing a book with the Library. After all, the Library of Congress, America's Memory, is the nation's library. Unlike all other national libraries, it is the only one still open to everyone on a quest for knowledge, specialists and nonspecialists alike, no questions asked. In fact, it exists to answer questions, questions such as: "What is a map?"

AFTERWORD

In 1800 a ship called *The American* sailed from London to Baltimore carrying 740 books, an unknown quantity of charts, three maps, and an atlas. In time, the book and map collections grew from these humble beginnings to establish a Congressional Library to help provide the United States with the information required to make laws for an expanding nation. Today the Library of Congress is home to 130 million items on approximately 530 miles of bookshelves. The Library's Geography and Map Division houses 4.8 million maps, 60,000 atlases, 700,000 microfilm images, 300 globes, and 2,000 terrain models, making it one of the world's largest and most comprehensive cartographic collections.

In the pages of *Cartographia* are some of the great treasures of the Library of Congress's cartographic collection, among them the Waldseemüller world map, Ortelius's *Theatrum Orbis Terrarum*, and Champlain's map of New France. But the maps in *Cartographia* move beyond the treasures of Western cartography and delve into the Library's vast international collections of materials from Asia, Africa, and the Middle East. It is these international collections that bear witness to the civilizations from around the world from which Americans have come, and out of which the civilization of the United States has been created.

Most other national libraries are primarily collections in the official language or languages of their nation. Our diverse national character, however, requires that the Library of Congress collect materials from around the world and in numerous languages. If this collecting principle has its roots in a person, it would be in Thomas Jefferson. "There is in fact," Jefferson explained, "no subject

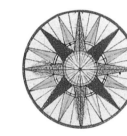

to which a member of congress may not have occasion to refer." Jefferson also noted, "Enlighten the people generally and tyranny and oppressions of body and mind will vanish like evil spirits at the dawn of day." Hence a national library that draws on all the cultures of the world will enlighten and expand the access its citizenry has to the world's knowledge.

Your journey through time and around the world via the maps in *Cartographia* provides only a small window into the Library's collections. The very heart of the Library of Congress is found in its vast collection of written, visual, recorded, and electronic materials that chronicle the development of the United States as well as the cultural antecedents upon which our culture is built. The incredible, wide-ranging collections include books, maps, prints, newspapers, broadsides, diaries, letters, posters, musical scores, motion pictures, photographs, audio and video recordings, and documents available only in digital formats. The Library serves first-time users and the most experienced researchers alike.

I hope that you, the reader, have found in the pages of this book information that furthered your understanding of maps as cultural documents, the art and science of mapping, and world history as expressed in maps. In addition, I hope you will continue to explore the topic of this book in a library near you, in person at the Library of Congress, or by visiting us on the World Wide Web at http://www.loc.gov.

James H. Billington
The Librarian of Congress

ACKNOWLEDGMENTS

The acorn for this oak of a book was sown in the fall of 1994 at my initial meeting with curators and specialists at the Library of Congress to plot our first project together, *Eyes of the Nation: A Visual History of the United States*, which was published in 1997. After I introduced myself, we went around the conference table for each of them to say a few words about their area of curatorial interest. Ron Grim, then cartographic historian in the Geography and Map Division, introduced himself and I unhappily confessed I didn't "get" maps. Ron sighed, looked up to heaven, and, lowering his head to the table, muttered, "That is the story of my life!" I immediately began my self-justification: "Oh, they're always too small and unreadable and beyond confusing." Slowly, Ron raised his head and gave me the look of a dedicated scholar determined to set the record straight. A great teacher, he showed me the profoundly moving 1507 Ruysch map (page 172) and said, "This map shows us how they tried to make sense of the news from Columbus. See how Ruysch neatly tucked the immense fragment of the New World beneath Asia? And Ruysch says, 'This map is left incomplete for the present.'" Having grown up in the movies, I wanted to see how the story ended, even though it lacked the element of suspense. Guiding me through a series of maps, Ron then revealed how America grew into itself cartographically, each new map a surprise for the mapmaker working with dispatches from the front. That was when I "got" maps. I've never been the same since.

A year after the release of *Eyes of the Nation*, I began working on the idea that became this book. My agent, Martha Kaplan, helped to shape the initial proposal, and Ron helped devise the outline for the book. By the time I wrote the proposal, I understood maps to be primary historical and cultural documents. This is a relatively new approach in the cartographic world and in the world of historians, accustomed as they are to working with old maps as things to be placed in a fixed historical context. In addition to the historical context, I wanted to examine the maps in *Cartographia* as revelatory works offering contemporary states of mind that have a story to tell about the culture from which the maps arose. Needless to say, this new approach to looking at maps took longer to capture on the page than I originally anticipated, since I was venturing almost literally into uncharted territory.

But soon the secret stories lurking in maps began to reveal themselves in the most peculiar ways. I remember viewing the Library's map of Kashmir (pages 86–87) in a vault full of scholars who were busily comparing it with aerial photos for geographic accuracy. Out of the blue, an Indian cataloger standing by my side remarked, "Our apples came from Kashmir." I asked if that might explain the temperate colors of the huge map. "Yes, it might, and also why all four seasons are represented on this map." Together, we began to explore the cultural story woven into this gorgeous map.

Along with this cataloger, an army of smart, inquisitive people made this book possible, both in person and in their books lodged in the Library's capacious stacks. I want to thank them all, but space limits me to those I hounded in the flesh most mercilessly. I must start with John Hébert, chief of the Geography and Map Division, who gave me total access to the 4 million maps in his care and to Dr. Grim, then one of the busiest members of his hardworking staff (and now curator of maps at the Boston Public Library); and I offer particular thanks to everyone in the Geography and Map Division, who made me feel like an unofficial member of their team, in particular Ed Redmond, Jim Flatness, and Diane Schug-O'Neill. In the African, Middle Eastern, and Hebraic Division: Mary Jane Deeb, Lee Avdoyan, Michael Grunberger, and Chris Murphy. In the Asian Division, the late Yoko Akiba, who read the history of an age in a single Japanese map—she really got maps! In the Rare Book and Special Collections Division: Clark Evans and Daniel De Simone. And Cordell Lee, not of the Library's staff, but in whose wonderful books and radiant presence I began the journey into the Chinese mindscape. Also, Susannah Lessard, John Paradiso, and Kathleen Howard kept me focused on the trees when I got lost in the forest of maps.

Without the gifted maestro of the Library's Publishing Office, Ralph Eubanks—negotiator and mentor—this book would literally not exist. And I would now be residing in a leafy bin if it weren't for his talented staff, my beloved colleagues—Margaret Wagner (supreme editor and loving friend), Susan Reyburn (teacher and wise medic), Evelyn Sinclair (supreme reader and prose stylist), Aimee Hess (splendid hunter and gatherer), Clarke Allen (gifted technician), Jesse Rhodes (intern extraordinaire), Colin Wambsgans, Anji Keating, Blaine Marshall, Wilson McBee (our newest staff member), and Linda Osborne (always present in times of need). At Little, Brown and Company, there is the incomparable Peggy Leith Anderson, who went way beyond copyediting to create a support system of her own for me, Julia Novitch, who read my handwriting and helped pick up the pieces, and Michael Sand, who dared to go where angels feared to tread and gave this massive enterprise a spectacular home. My thanks to Laura Lindgren for a beautifully designed book and to Pamela Schechter for ensuring the finest production possible.

Finally, I want to thank James McCourt for accompanying me through this and all my journeys.

—V.V.

CARTOBIBLIOGRAPHY

Note to Readers

The first part of each entry in italics is the link to the book's captions. If it is not the actual title of the map, the title follows as part of the bibliographic description.

Unless otherwise noted, each piece is from the Library of Congress.

Rare Book = Rare Book and Special Collections Division

G&M = Geography and Map Division

INTRODUTION: THEATER OF THE WORLD

PLATE 1. *Seutter's Atlas Novus.* In Mattheus Seutter, *Atlas Novus,* Augsburg, 1745. G&M, G1015 1745 S62 Vault, frontispiece.

PLATE 2. *Frontis-portrait from Theatrum Orbis Terrarum.* In Abraham Ortelius, *Theatrum Orbis Terrarum* (Theater of the Whole World), London, 1606. G&M, G1006 T53 1606 Vault, frontispiece.

PLATE 3. *Theatrum Orbis Terrarum Title Page.* In Abraham Ortelius, *Theatrum Orbis Terrarum* (Theater of the Whole World). Antwerp, 1570. G&M, G1006 T53 1574 Vault, title page.

THE MEDITERRANEAN WORLD

PLATE 4. *Cuneiform Tablet Showing Plan of Fields at Nippur.* University of Pennsylvania Museum (neg. S4-142017).

PLATE 5. *The Whole World in a Cloverleaf:* "Die ganze Welt in ein Kleberblat." In Heinrich Bunting, *Itinerarium Sacrae Scripturae,* Magdeburg, 1581. Courtesy the Norman B. Leventhal Map Center at the Boston Public Library.

PLATE 6. *Positioned Remains of the General Plan of the City of Rome.* "Posizione dei complessi e monumenti localizzati." In Gianfilippo Caretoni et al., *La Pianta marmorea di Roma antica: Forma urbis Romae.* Rome, [1960]. G&M, G1989 R7P5 1960 folio, p. 4.

PLATE 7. *Babylonian World Map.* The British Museum © The Trustees of the British Museum (Object no. 92687).

PLATE 8. *Egyptian Writing Board with an Architectural Drawing.* The Metropolitan Museum of Art, Gift of Norman de Garis Davies 1914 (14.108). Photograph © The Metropolitan Museum of Art.

PLATE 9. *Pyramids at Memphis.* "Pyramides de Memphis." In Commission des Sciences et Arts d'Egypte, *Description de l'Egypt.* Paris, 1809–22. G&M, G2490.F8 1809–1828, vol. 5, pl. 6.

PLATE 10. *Map of the Route to Paradise.* "Carte de la route du paradis." In Youssouf Kamal, *Monumenta cartographica Africae et Aegypti.* Cairo, 1926–51. G&M, G2445.Y8 Vault, Tome 1, folio 6.

PLATE 11. *The Thera Fresco from the West Room.* Wall paintings from the "Miniature Frieze." The Archeological Society at Athens. Excavations at Akrotiri, Thera.

PLATE 12. *The World According to Hecataeus.* In E. H. Bunbury, *History of Ancient Geography.* London, 1879. General Collections, G84.B94, vol.1, p. 148.

PLATE 13. *Ionian Coin.* The British Museum (BMC Ionia, 323 no. 1).

PLATE 14. *The Comet of 1742.* "Cometa qui anno Christi 1742." In Mattheus Seutter, *Atlas Novus.* Augsburg, 1745. G&M, G1015 S62 1745 Vault, vol. 1, map 4.

PLATES 15 AND 16. *The Bronze Liver of Piacenza.* Etruscan, c. third century BCE. Museo Civico, Piacenza.

PLATE 17. *Surveyed Fields.* In *Corpus Agrimensorum Romanor um, Codex Arcerianus A: der Herzog-August-Bibliothek zu Wolfenbüttel.* Leiden, 1970. General Collections, Z114.C67 t.22 folio, 21r/T6.6–16. Courtesy of Duke August Library, Wolfenbüttel.

PLATE 18. *Map of the City of New York.* William Bridges, *Map of the City of New York and Island of Manhattan as Laid Out by the Commissioners Appointed by the Legislature April 3, 1807.* New York, 1811. G&M, G3804.N4 1811.B7, frontispiece.

PLATE 19. *Map of Europe, Africa, the Mediterranean, and Asia According to Ptolemy,* by Nicolaus Germanus. In Claudius Ptolemy, *Geographia.* Latin manuscript, c. 1460. Renaissance and Medieval Manuscripts Collection, Manuscripts and Archives Division, The New York Public Library, Astor, Lenox and Tilden Foundations.

PLATE 20. *Map from Anonymous Astrological Miscellany.* Undated, mid-sixteenth century. Berlin, Staatsbibliothek, Handschriftenabteilung, MS Phill, 1479, fol. 28v.

PLATE 21. *The Peutinger Table.* Konrad Miller, *Die Peutingersche Tafel,* Stuttgart, 1962. G&M, G1026, P4 M5 1962.

PLATE 22. *The Universe After Cosmas, 550.* Manuscript copy by Johann Georg Kohl, c. 1850. G&M, Kohl Collection, no. 3.

PLATE 23. *Medieval Islamic Map of the World.* In Uman bin Muzaffar Ibn al-Wardi, *Kharidat al-'Aja 'ib wa Faridat al-Gharā'ib* (The Pearl of Wonders and the Uniqueness of Things Strange). Late seventeenth century. Near East Section, African and Middle Eastern Division.

PLATE 24. *Tenth-Century Persian Earthenware Bowl, Nishapur, Iran.* Los Angeles County Museum of Art, The Nasli M. Heeramaneck Collection, gift of Joan Palevsky. Photograph © 2005 Museum Associates/LACMA. (M-73-5-330).

PLATE 25. *The Second Safavid World Map.* Photograph courtesy Christie's of London.

PLATE 26. *The Sundering Sea of the East.* In Zakariya (Muhammad al-Qazwini), *Accib-ül Mahlokat* (The Wonders of Creation). Istanbul, c. 1553. Near East Section, African and Middle Eastern Division.

PLATE 27. *Schematic Map of the Land of Israel.* In Elijah Mizrahi, *Commentary on Rashi.* Venice, 1574. Hebraic Section, African and Middle Eastern Division, BS 1225.S6 M48 1574.

PLATE 28. *Map of the Holy Land,* c. 1252. In Matthew Paris, *Historia Anglorum.* England, St. Albans, 1250–59. Copyright © The British Library, Royal 14C. VII, ff.4v–5.

PLATE 29. *The City of Jerusalem.* Erhard Reuwich, "Civitas Iherusalem." In Bernhard von Breydenbach, *Peregrinatio in Terram Sanctam.* Mainz, 1486. Rare Book, Rosenwald Collection, no. 116.

PLATE 30. *The Life and Wanderings of Patriarch Abraham.* "Abrahami Patriarchae Peregrinatio et Vita." In Abraham Ortelius, *Parergon,* supplement of historical maps to *Theatrum Orbis Terrarum.* London, 1606. G&M, G1006 T53 1606, Vault, Parergon, folio 5.

PLATE 31. *Hebrew Map of the Holy Land.* In Abraham ben Jacob, *Seder Haggadah shel Pesah* (Passover Haggadah). Amsterdam, 1695. Hebraic Section, African and Middle Eastern Division.

PLATE 32. *Chart of the Mediterranean and Western Europe.* Mateo Prunes, [Chart of the Mediterranean, the Black Sea, the Coasts of Western Europe and Northwest Africa] 1559. G&M, Vellum Chart Collection, no. 7.

PLATE 33. *Taqi al-Din and Other Astronomers at Work in His Istanbul Observatory.* In Alaaddin Mansur, *Shahinshah-nama* (History of the King of Kings), sixteenth century. University Library, Istanbul, Turkey, MS No. FY404.

THE THREE-PART WORLD

PLATE 34. *Han Cosmic Mirror,* Freer Gallery of Art, Smithsonian Institution, Washington, DC: Purchase F1937.30.

PLATE 35. *A Map of the Countries Between Constantinople and Calcutta.* London, 1912. G&M, Title Collection—Asia—Southwest—1912.

PLATE 36. *Map of the April Tragedy.* Zadig Khanzadian, *Aprilian Egherni k'artes.* Beirut, 1965. G&M, G7151.S7 1965.K5.

PLATE 37. *Letts's Bird's Eye View of the Approaches to India.* Letts, Son and Co. London, 19—. G&M, Title Collection—Afghanistan—Pictorial—19—.

PLATE 38. *Mongolian Style of Cartography.* In *Yuan jing shido Dian tu dili kuo cheng* (History of Institutions of the Yuan Dynasty) 1329. Asian Division, B108.T51, no. 24.

PLATE 39. *Map of China and Foreign Lands, Hua yi tu.* 1136. Stone rubbing from original stone. G&M, G7820.L5 1136.H81 Vault Oversize.

PLATE 40. *Map of the Tracks of Yu. Yu ji tu.* 1136. Stone rubbing from original stone. G&M, 7820.L51 1136.Y81 Vault Oversize.

PLATE 41. *General Map of Territories from the Ancient to Present, of China and Foreign Countries.* In Su Shih, *Lidai dili zhichang.* c. 1573–1620. Asian Division, VB182.051.S11, vol. 2.

PLATE 42. *Bronze Incense Burner of P'eng Lai.* Freer Gallery of Art, Smithsonian Institution, Washington, DC: Purchase F1947.15.

PLATE 43. *The Map of the Place Coiled by a Dragon and Crouched by a Tiger.* In Ma Guang-zu and Zhou Ying-he, *Jing ding jian kang zhi* (The Gazetteer of Jian Kang Prefecture of Jing Ding Reign). Compiled 1261; wood block edition 1801. Asian Division, vol. 5.

PLATE 44. *Chinese Characters di tu* (Map of the Land). Yinxiang Yuan, Note and cover image for History of Cartography Project, University of Wisconsin, Madison, 1997.

PLATE 45. *Measuring the Yellow River. Huang he wan li tu.* Facsimile of 1368–78 original. Asian Division, Chinese Rare Book Collection.

PLATE 46. *Atlas of Guangdong Province.* Jiang Yi and Han Zuodong, *Guang dong yu tu.* 1685. G&M, G2308.G8 J5 1685 Vault Shelf, vol. 5, image 2, from Chinese front of book.

PLATE 47. *Military Map of Xinping County. Xin xi ying yu tu.* 1820. G&M, G7823.X63A5 1820.X5 Vault.

PLATE 48. *Detail of Macau Region from Coastal Map of China. Qi sheng yan hai tu* or *Wang li hai fang tu.* 1787–1820. G&M, G7822.C6A5 1820.Q5 Vault Shelf.

PLATE 49. *Hainan Island. Hainan dao tu shuo.* c. 1820–75. G&M, G7823.H25 E62 1875 H3 Vault.

PLATE 50. *Urban Map of Tianjin.* Qihuang Feng, *Tianjin cheng xiang bao jia quan tu.* 1899. G&M, G7824.T5A3 1899.F4 Vault.

PLATE 51. *Kangnido: Map of Historical Emperors and Kings and of Integrated Borders and Terrain.* Yi Hoe and Kwon Kun, *Yoktae chewang honil kannido* OR *Honil kangni yoktae kukto chi to* (1402). c. 1470. Ryukoku University Library, Kyoto, Japan.

PLATE 52. *Korean Traditional World Map.* "Chonhado." In *Tae Choson chido.* 1874. G&M, G330.T35.1874 Vault Shelf.

PLATE 53. *Shōen (Estate) Map of Minase Manor in Settsu Province.* In Hugh Cortazzi, *Isles of Gold.* New York, 1983. G&M, GA 1241 C67 1983, p. 67.

PLATE 54. *Evening Faces.* "Yūgao." In Murasaki Shikibu, *Genji monogatari* (The Tale of Genji) 1654. Asian Division, Japanese Section CLC PL755.35 76-1, vol. 9. Vault location 123.

PLATE 55. *Kyoto and the Region of Yamashiro. Yamashiro no Kuni ezu.* 18—. G&M, G7962 Y35.18 — . Y3 Vault Shelf.

PLATE 56. *Porcelain Plate with Gyōki-type Map.* G&M Vault Cabinet.

PLATE 57. *Map Showing Corporate Ownership of Agriculture and Forest Property Around Numazu. Numazuhon-machi, Higashimakado-mura, Minamimura obayashiōzahai ezu.* 1786. G&M, G7964.N9K2. N8 Vault Shelf.

PLATE 58. *Map Showing Land Ownership in Manohara Rice Field Area. Manohara shindan koshimborishita.* 18—. G&M, G9980 18—. M3 Vault Shelf.

PLATE 59. *Hokkaido (Ezo).* Tonsai Fujita, *Ezo kōkyō yochi zenzu.* Edo, 1854. G&M, G7962.H5 1854.F8 Vault Shelf.

PLATE 60. *Scenes of Life in and Around the Capital. Rakuchū rakugai-zu* (Pair of Folding Screens). Edo period, second half seventeenth century. Seattle Art Museum. Purchased with funds donated by Mildred and Bryant Dunn, supplemented by the Floyd A. Naramore Memorial Purchase fund. Photo by Paul Macapia.

PLATE 61. *Abe River Region.* Ichiryū tei Shoraku Dōjin, *Abekawa-dōri sanchū ichien ezu.* 1862. G&M, G7962.A32 1862 .I3 Vault Shelf.

PLATE 62. *Suruga Province/Shizuoka Prefecture.* Kōzaburō Kikuya, *Suruga no Kuni zenzu.* [Edo], 1828–59? G&M, G7963.S5 182- K5 Vault Shelf.

PLATE 63. *Tokyo Bay Coast Defenses. Shinkoku fukui butoku anmin, Okatame taihei kagami: Izu, Sagami, Mussashi, Awa, Kazusa, Shimōsa,* 1852. G&M, G7962. T66R4 1852.S5 Vault.

PLATE 64. *Isometric Map of the Ginza in Detailed Axonometric Projection.* H. Suzaki, *A Bird's Eye View of Ginza.* Tokyo, 1987. G&M, G7964.T7:2G 5A3.1987.

PLATE 65. *Wheel of Life. Srid pa 'i lo.* Painting on cloth, twentieth century. Asian Division, Tibetan Collection.

PLATE 66. *RVN and VC Provincial, CTZ, and Military Region Boundaries.* Compiled by 12 MACV, CICV, August 1966. 569th Engr. Co. (TOPO) (Corps). G&M, Title Collection — Indochina — Vietnam — Military —1966.

PLATE 67. *Land Use in Vietnam.* The National Geographical Society of Vietnam, *Ban đồ Việtnam Kinh-tế.* [Dalat], 1969. G&M, G8021.G4.1969.V5.

PLATE 68. *Seasonal Rainfall June to October.* In John Eliot, *Climatological Atlas of India.* Edinburgh, 1906. G&M, G2281.C8A5.1906, pl. 117.

PLATE 69. *Jain Pilgrimage.* Jodhpur, Rajasthan, India, c. 1760. Brooklyn Museum of Art Collection.

PLATE 70. *Map of Hindoostan.* James Rennell, *Hindoostan.* London, 1782. G&M, G7650.1782.R4.

PLATE 71. *Pictorial Map on Cloth of the Vale of Kashmir Showing Srinagar in Detail.* c. 1836. G&M, G7652.K4A5.1836.M2 Vault Rolled.

PLATE 72. *Index Chart to the Great Trigonometrical Survey of India.* From James T. Walker, *General Report on the Operations of the Survey of India, 1880–81.* Calcutta, 1882. G&M, QB396.I38 G&M Vault.

PLATE 73. *Map of India in Urdu and Hindi.* I. R. Khan, *Map of India.* 1932. G&M, Title Collection — India —19—.

PLATE 74. *World War II Poster in Arabic.* Alexandria, Egypt, 1942. G&M, Title Collection — World War — WWII —1942.

PLATE 75. *Sea Bottom Sediments Map Bordering Umm Said Area.* In Muhammad Adil Ahmad Yahyá, *Atlas al-suwar al-fadā'iyah li Dawat Qatar min al-qamar al-sinā'i "Landsat"* (Atlas of Qatar from Landsat Images) Al-Dawhah, 1983. G&M, G2249.81.C2.Y2.1983, p. 88.

PLATES 76 AND 77. *The Rawda District of Kuwait City.* "Rawda" and "Key to Symbols." In 'Abd Allah Hammadi, *Atlas jarā'im al-harb al-'Iraq īyah fī Dawlat al-Kuwayt* (Atlas of Iraqi War Crimes in the State of Kuwait). Kuwait, 1995. G&M, G2249.91 S8 H3 1995, pp. 344-45.

PLATE 78. *Land of Israel.* Jewish National Fund, *Erets Yisrael.* Jerusalem, 1936. G&M, Title Collection — Israel — 1936 — Jewish Settlement.

PLATE 79. *Mideast as Seen from Israel.* Russell Lenz. Wellesley, Mass., c. 1987. G&M, G7420 1987.L4 MLC.

PLATE 80. *Fra Mauro's Map of the World.* 1459. By permission of the Biblioteca Nazionale Marciana, Venice.

PLATE 81. *Female Figure in Manda Style.* Congo (Zaire). Tabwa Congolese (Zairean). University of Michigan Museum of Art, Ann Arbor. Museum purchase made possible by a gift of Helmut Stern 1987/1.157-1.

PLATE 82. *Lukala Wall Map.* Royal Museum for Central Africa, Tervuren, Belgium (E.PH.583).

PLATE 83. *Congo Cosmogram.* In Robert Farris Thompson and Joseph Cornet, *The Four Moments of the Sun: Kongo Art in Two Worlds.* Washington, DC: National Gallery of Art, 1981. General Collections, NB1099.C6 T5, p. 84.

PLATE 84. *West Africa from Gabon in the South to Niger, Mali, and Mauritania in the North.* Homann Erben (Firm), *Guinea propria, nec non Nigritiae vel Terrae Nigrorum maxima pars.* Nuremberg, 1743. G&M, G3735 1743 .H6 Vault.

PLATE 85. *Turkish Africa.* In Tab'hane-yi Humayunda, *Cedid atlas tecumesi* (Turkish General Atlas), [Istanbul], 1803. G&M, G1019 .T2 1803 Vault, pl.14.

PLATE 86. *Sultan Bello's Map of the Niger River's Course.* "A Reduction of Bello's Map of Central Africa." In Dixon Denham, Hugh Clapperton, and Walter Oudney, *Narrative of Travels and Discoveries in Northern and Central Africa in the Years 1822, 1823, and 1824.* London, 1826. General Collections, DT351. D392, p. 109.

PLATE 87. *A Rough Sketch of Equatorial Africa with Dispatch 177 from U.S. Minister to Berlin.* Institute National Geographique, *Croquis de L'Afrique Equatoriale.* Bruxelles, 1884. G&M, Title Collection —Zaire—1884.

PLATE 88. *Map of the Belgian Congo.* J. Lebegue & Co., *Carte de Congo Belge.* Bruxelles, 1896. G&M, Title Collection —Zaire—1896.

PLATE 89. *Map of the Great Forest Region.* Henry M. Stanley. New York, 1890. G&M, Title Collection —Zaire—1890.

PLATE 90. *Predominant Tribe in the Area.* Ghana Census Office. Accra, 1966. G&M, G8851.E1.1966 G5.

PLATE 91. *The Times Map of the Tribes, Peoples & Nations of Modern Africa.* Roy Lewis and Yvonne Foy. London, 1972. G&M, G8201.E1 1972.L4.

PLATE 92. *Royal Tapestry.* Bamum Kingdom, Cameroon Grassfields. Portland Art Museum, Oregon, Accession #70.10.8.

PLATE 93. *Northwest Part of Montserrado County, Liberia.* American Colonization Society. 18—. G&M, G8883.M6.18—.N6 ACS 21.

PLATE 94. *World Map by Martellus.* Henricus Martellus. 1489. Copyright © The British Library. Add. 15760.

PLATES 95 AND 95A. *Homestead.* Kwazulu-Natal Rock Engraving (photograph and drawing), Natal Museum, Pietermaritzburg, South Africa (site no. 2829DD 19; acc. No. 1988/1/5).

PLATE 96. *Montalboddo's Africa.* In Fracanzano de Montalboddo, *Itinerarium Portugallesi um.* Milan, 1508. Rare Book, E101.F88, title page.

PLATE 97. *Southeast Africa.* "Vixesimo tercio mapa de las tierras de la dha costa la India oriental." In João Teixeira, *Taboas geraes de toda a navegação.* 1630. G&M, 1015.T4 1630 Vault, map 23.

PLATE 98. *South Africa Black Homelands Consolidation Proposals.* Department of Bantu Administration and Development. R. S. A. *Swart tuislande konsolidasievoorstelle.* Pretoria, c. 1973. G&M, G8501.G6 1973-A3.

PLATE 99. *Africa.* U.S. Central Intelligence Agency. Washington, DC, 2003. G&M, G8200 2003.U51.

PLATE 100. *Battle of Adwa.* Anonymous oil painting. [Addis Ababa], c. 1970. African and Middle Eastern Division.

PLATE 101. Map of Kingdom of Ethiopia. Anonymous court geographer to Emperor Haile Selassie I. Addis Ababa, 1923. G&M, Vault Oversize.

PLATE 102. Earth's City Lights. Craig Mayhew and Robert Simmon. Created by data from Defense Meteorological Satellite Program Digital Archive. NASA. http://visibleearth.nasa.gov.

PLATE 103. Map of the Medieval World. Isidore of Seville, Etymologiae. Augsburg, 1472. Rare Book, Incu 1472.I81.

PLATE 104. The City of the Soul. Attributed to Thomas de Leu. In Bartolomeo Delbene (Del Bene), Civitatis veri, sive morum. Paris, 1609. The Folger Shakespeare Library, Washington, DC.

PLATE 105. A Knight on Horseback. In Giovanni Boccaccio, Des nobles maleureux. Paris, 1494. Rare Book. Rosenwald Collection, no. 427, folio FI(t).

PLATE 106. Île de la Cité, Paris. In Louis Bretez, Plan de Paris. Paris, 1739.

PLATE 107. The Hand as a Cognitive Map. In Richard Saunders, Physiognomie and Chiromancie. London, 1671. Rare Book. BF911.S2, p. 51.

PLATE 108 AND 108A. Hereford Mappa Mundi. Copyright © The Dean and Chapter of Hereford and the Hereford Mappa Mundi Trust.

PLATE 109. St.-Denis Floor Plan. In Werner Gross, Gotik und Spätgotik. Frankfurt, 1960. General Collections. NA440.G7, p. 26.

PLATE 110. West Rose Window of Strasbourg Cathedral. Strasbourg Cathedral.

PLATE 111. A Fifteenth-Century Guide to Weights and Measures for European and Mediterranean Cities. Arnaldo Domenech. [Siena], 1484. G&M, Vellum Chart, no. 4.

PLATE 112. A Complete and Perfect Map Describing the Whole World. Hadji Ahmed. Venice, 1559/1795. G&M, Vault Oversize.

PLATE 113. Du Pinet's Europe. In Antoine du Pinet, Plantz, pourtraitz et descriptions de plusieures villes. Lyon, 1564. G&M, G1028.D8 1564 Vault, folio I verso.

PLATE 114. Bordone's Ireland. In Benedetto Bordone, Libro di Benedetto Bordone. Venice, 1528. G&M, G1029.B6 1528 Vault, folio I verso (map 5).

PLATE 115. Spanish Armada: The Battle off Portland Bill. In Robert Adams, Expeditionis Hispanorum in Angliam vera descriptio. London, 1590. Rare Book, G1816.S45 1588.A3, image 5.

PLATE 116. The Low Countries Depicted in the Shape of a Lion. "Leo Belgicus." In Pieter van den Keere, La Germanie inférieure. Amsterdam, 1622 Vault, G&M, G185.K42.1622, p. 19 verso.

PLATE 117. The City of Cologne. "Colonia Agrippina." In Georg Braun and Frans Hogenberg, Théâtre des cités du monde. Bruxelles, 1576?-1620? G&M, G1028.B72 Vault, part 1, map 39.

PLATE 118. Christian Celestial. "Coeli Stellati Christiani Haemisphaerium Prius." In Andreas Cellarius, Harmonia Macrocosmica. Amsterdam, 1708. G&M, G1015. C4 1708 Vault, p. 22.

PLATE 119. A Map of the Arctic Circle. "Regiones sub polo arctico." In Joan Blaeu, Atlas mayor (Spanish edition). Amsterdam, 1662. G&M, G1015. B485.1659 Vault, vol. 1, folio A.

PLATE 120 AND 120A. Index to Atlas of Polder Maps. In Nicolas Kruikius, T'Hooge Heemraedschap van Delflant. Delft, 1712. G&M, G1863.D4C7 1712 Vault, plate 3.

PLATE 121. Plan of the Siege of Namur. Romanus de Hooge. "Namurcum." 1695. In Anna Beek et al., Collection of Plans of Fortification and Battles. 1684-1709. G&M, G1793-B4 1709 Vault, pl. 77.

PLATE 122. Fortification for Sar-Louis. Paris, 1708. In Anna Beek et al. Ibid., pl. 100.

PLATE 123. Trench Map of France and Belgium. Great Britain Ordnance Survey. Southampton, 1915. G&M, G5831.S65 s10 .G7, sheet 38c N.W. 1, La Bassée.

PLATE 124. General Map of France. Jean Joliveto, "Galliae regni potentiss nova descriptio." In Maurice Bouguereau, Le théâtre françoys. Tours, 1594. G&M, G1837 .B7 1594 Vault, pp. 20-21.

PLATE 125. Descartes's Mechanical Universe. In René Descartes, Principia Philosophiae. Amsterdam, 1644. Rare Book, B1860 1644, p. 114.

PLATE 126. Map of Tenderness. "La Carte de Tendre." In Madeleine de Scudéry, Clélie. Paris, 1654. Rare Books Division, Department of Rare Books and Special Collections, Princeton University Library.

PLATE 127. "Marine Chart of the Environs of the Isle of Oleron." In Le Neptune françois. Amsterdam, 1693-1700. G&M, G1059.N42 1693 Vault, vol. 2, leaf 6.

PLATE 128. Department of Paris. César-François Cassini, Carte de France... Premier feuille. Paris, 1757-89. G&M, Hauslab Collection, folio 30, sheet 1.

PLATE 129. A Geographical Board Game of the Republic of France. Jeu géographique de la République Française. Paris, 1795. G&M, G5831.F7 1795. M3 Vault.

THE FOURTH PART: THE AMERICAS

PLATE 130. The Kingdom of France Is Represented Under the Form of a Ship. London, 1796. G&M, G5831.A5 1795.K5 Vault.

PLATE 131. A Plan of the Mansion House, Land, Gardens, Etc., Belonging to the Right Hon. Robert, Earl Granvilles in Parish of Hawns of the County of Bedford. John Franklin. Hawns, 1767. G&M, G1818.B3G46 F7 1767 Vault, pl. A.

PLATE 132. The Military Survey of Ireland. Charles Vallancey. Dublin, 1776. G&M, G1830.V3 1776 Vault, pl. 7.

PLATE 133. A Basic Bilingual Route Map. Tim Robinson, "Iar-Chonnacht/West Galway." Book cover of Connemara, Part 2, a One-Inch Map. Roundstone, Ireland, c. 1990. G&M, G5782.C6G22 1990.R6 MLC.

PLATE 134. Geological Map of Southwestern England. In William Smith, A Delineation of the Strata of England and Wales with Part of Scotland. London, 1815. G&M, G1811.C5 S6 1815 Vault, sheet 11.

PLATE 135. Plant Geography. "Umrisse der Pflanzengeographie." In Heinrich Berghaus, Physikalischer Atlas. Gotha, 1845. G&M, G1046.C1 B35 1845 Vault, vol. 1, fifth abteilung, map 1.

PLATE 136. Ethnographic Map of the Balkan Peninsula. Jovan Cvijić. New York, 1918. G&M, Title Collection—Balkans—Ethnology—1918.

PLATE 137. Mine Contamination Map. Area: Sarajevo. BH MAC Sarajevo. Sarajevo, 2004. G&M, G6864.S2R4 2004.B4.

PLATE 138. Moscow. In Bol'shoi Sovetskii Atlas Mira. Moscow, 1937-39. G&M, G2019.B66 1937, vol. 2, pp. 18-19.

PLATE 139 AND 140. Europe and Asia Minor in 1914, and Europe and Asia Minor in 1924. In Lawrence Martin, International Conciliation, May 1924. G&M, G1046.F2M3 1924, figs. 1 and 2.

PLATE 141. The European Union. Lovell Johns. Bruxelles, 2003. G&M, G5701.F7 2003.L6.

PLATE 142. Ruysch Map of the Known World. Johann Ruysch. "Universalior Cogniti Orbis Tabula." In Claudius Ptolemeus, Geographia. Rome, 1507. G&M, G1005.1507 Vault, map 1.

PLATES 143 AND 143A. Waldseemüller Map of the World. Martin Waldseemüller, Universalis Cosmographia Secundum Ptholomaei Traditionem et Americi Vespucii Aliorunque Lustrationes. [St. Dié, France], 1507. G&M, G3200 1507.W3 Vault Oversize.

PLATES 144 AND 145. World and South Atlantic. "Primero de demarcaciones entre Castilla y Portugal" and "Quinto mapa de la verdadera demarcacion...." In João Teixeira, Taboas geraes de toda a navegação. 1630. G&M, G1015.T4 1630 Vault, maps 1 and 5.

PLATE 146. Map of Mexico City and the Gulf of Mexico. In Hernando Cortés, Praeclara Ferdinandi Cortesii de nova maris oceani Hyspania narratio. [Nuremburg, 1524.] Rare Book, Rosenwald Collection no. 654.

PLATE 147. The Oztoticpac Lands Map. C. 1540. G&M, G4414.T54:2O9 1540.O9 Vault.

PLATES 148 AND 148A. Gutiérrez Map of America. Diego Gutiérrez, Americae sive Quartae Orbis Partis Nova et Exactissima Descriptio. [Antwerp] 1562. G&M, G3290 1562.G7 Vault Oversize.

PLATE 149. Isthmus of Panama from Cartagena to Nicaragua Showing Both Coasts. c. 1700. G&M, G4870 18— .P Vault.

PLATE 150. Map of New Spain's Frontier. José de Urrútia and Nicolas de la Fora. Mapa, que comprende la Frontera, de los Dominios del Rey, en la America Septentrional. 1769. G&M, G4410 1769.U7 TII Vault.

PLATE 151. Map Based on the Joint Spanish-Portuguese Boundary Commission's Work in New Spain. Francisco Requena, Mapa de parte de los virreynatos de Buenos Aires, Lima, S[an]ta Fe y capitania g[ene]ral de Caracas en la America. 1796. G&M, G5200 1796.R4 Vault.

PLATE 152. Map of Dagua River Region, Colombia. 1764. G&M, G5292.D2 1764. M2 Vault.

PLATE 153. Map of Boundaries of Purchased Land in Region of Honda West of Magdalena River, Colombia. F. Roulin, Mapa de las tierras compradas al gobierno y particulares par el Cor[onel] Desmenard. Bogotá, 1825. G&M, G5294. H6G46 1825.R6 Vault.

PLATE 154. Land Use of the Trio Peoples in Southwestern Suriname. ACT: Center for the Support of Native Lands, Landgebruik van de Trio's in zuid-west Suriname. Arlington, Va., [2001]. G&M, G5261.G4 2001.G5 Copyright © Stichting Meu/Foundation Meu, Kwamalasamutu.

PLATE 155. Colorado River Basin. NASA.

PLATE 156. North East Coast of North America. Samuel de Champlain, Description des costs, pts., rades, illes de la nouvelle france faict selon son vray méridien. 1607. G&M, Vellum Chart, no. 15.

PLATE 157. *Manhattan Island.* Joan Vinckeboons, *Manatus gelegen op de Noo[r]t Rivier.* 1639. G&M, G3291.S12 Coll.H3 Vault.

PLATE 158. *A Map of the British and French Dominions in North America.* John Mitchell. [London], 1755. G&M, G3300 1755.M51 Vault.

PLATE 159. *Powder Horn.* Powder horn showing the Hudson and Mohawk River Valleys, Lake Ontario and Lake Champlain. 1757–60. G&M, Vault Cabinet, Powder Horn, no. 1.

PLATE 160. *Plan of Princeton, Dec. 31, 1776.* John Cadwalader. 1776. G&M, G3814.P9S3 1776.C3 Vault.

PLATE 161. *Norman's Chart of the Lower Mississippi River.* Marie Adrien Persac. New Orleans, 1858. G&M, G4042.M5G46 1858.P4.

PLATE 162. *Map of Knox County, Illinois.* M. H. Thompson. 1861. G&M, G4103.K6 1861.T4 TIL.

PLATE 163. *The Gerry-mander.* Elkanah Tisdale. Salem, Mass., 1812. Rare Book, JK 1347.G47 1812.

PLATE 164. *Map of the Country Drained by the Mississippi.* Stephen H. Long. In Edwin James, *Account of an Expedition from Pittsburgh to the Rocky Mountains....* Philadelphia, 1822. G&M, F592.J3 Vault.

PLATE 165. *Map Showing Indian Reservations Within the Limits of the United States.* T. J. Morgan. Washington, DC, 1892. G&M, Title Collection—US—Indians—1892.

PLATE 166. *Hope's Track Round Cape Horn.* Joseph Ingraham, *Journal.* 1791. Manuscript Division.

PLATE 167. *Map of an Exploring Expedition to the Rocky Mountains.* John C. Frémont, *Map of an Exploring Expedition to the Rocky Mountains in the Year 1842 and to Oregon & North California in the Years 1843–44.* [Washington, D.C., 1845.] G&M, G4051.S12 1844.F7 Vault.

PLATE 168. *Crown Prince Islands in Disco Bay, Greenland.* Silas Sandgreen. 1925. G&M, Vault Oversize.

PLATE 169. *Map of Hawaii.* Simona P. Kalama. *Na mokupuni o Hawaii nei he mau la ka ana, na Kalama ikakau.* Maui, Kulanui Lahainaluna, 1837. G&M, G4380.1837.K3 Vault.

PLATE 170. *Diagram of the South Part of Shaker Village, Canterbury, N.H.* Peter Foster. 1849. G&M, G3744.S5 1849.F6 TIL Vault.

PLATE 171. *Scott's Great Snake.* J. B. Eliott. Cincinnati, Ohio, 1861. G&M, Civil War, no. 11.

PLATE 172. *The Seat of War in Virginia.* From the *New York Herald,* morning edition, June 17, 1861, front page. New York, 1861. G&M, Civil War, no. 451-3.

PLATE 173. *Map of City of New York Showing the Distribution of the Principal Nationalities by Sanitary Districts.* Tenement House Committee. New York City, c. 1895. G&M, G3804.N4N46 1894.T4.

PLATE 174. *How the Public Domain Has Been Squandered.* Chicago, 1884. G&M, Title Collection—Land Grants—US—1884—Rand, McNally.

PLATE 175. *Haverhill, Massachusetts.* O. H. Bailey. Boston, c. 1893. G&M, G3764.H5A3 1893.B3.

PLATE 176. *Panoramic Perspective of the Area Adjacent to Boulder Dam.* A. V. Kipp. Union Pacific System, 1934. G&M, Title Collection—Arizona—Grand Canyon.

PLATE 177. *Florida Info-Map.* Rand McNally. Chicago, 1939. G&M, Title Collection—Florida Roads—Gas Ads—1931–39.

PLATE 178. *Metro-Goldwyn-Mayer Studio, Culver City, California, 1929.* Sanborn Map Company, 1929. G&M, Sanborn Collection, Culver City, CA, 1929, sheet 10.

PLATE 179. *Barataria-Terrebonne Estuarine Basins.* Barataria-Terrebonne National Estuary Program et al. Thibodaux, Louisiana, 1996. G&M, G4012.B2A4 1996.L6.

THE FIFTH PART: OCEANIA AND ANTARCTICA

PLATE 180. *Marshall Island Stick Chart.* G&M, Vault Oversize.

PLATE 181. *Map of Coromuru (Gurrumuru) River Area.* Djimbun and Mattjudi. 1970. Copyright © courtesy Anthony Wallis, Aboriginal Artists Agency, Sydney, Australia.

PLATE 182. *Map of the Murrinh-Patha Countryside.* Nym Pandak. 1959. Photograph courtesy of South Australian Museum, Adelaide. Copyright © courtesy Anthony Wallis, Aboriginal Artists Agency, Sydney, Australia.

PLATE 183. *Forlani Map of the Known World.* Paolo Forlani, *Universale descrittione di tutta la terra conosciuta fin qui.* Venice, 1565. G&M, G3200 1565.F6 Vault.

PLATE 184. *Upside Down World Map.* Hema Maps. Brisbane, Australia, c. 1996. G&M, G3200 1996.14 MLC.

PLATE 185. *Canberra, the Federal Capital of the Commonwealth.* Federal Capital Commission. 1927. G&M, Title Collection—Australia—Canberra—1927.

PLATE 186. *Great Barrier Reef Marine Park.* Great Barrier Reef Marine Park Authority. Townsville, Queensland, c. 1990. G&M, G9002.G72 s250.G7, sheet BRA Q110.

PLATE 187. *New Zealand Territorial Sea and Exclusive Economic Zone.* New Zealand Department of Lands and Survey. Wellington, NZ, 1983. G&M, G9081.F3 1983.N4.

PLATE 188. *Antarctica.* Australia Division of National Mapping. Canberra, 1986. G&M, G9800 1986.A9.

EPILOGUE

PLATE 189. *The Gathering of the World's French Cultural Community at Moncton.* Adrien Bérubé, *La Constellation francophone, Sommet de Moncton 1999.* Moncton, N.B., 1999. G&M, G3201.E3 1999.B4. Copyright © Adrien Bérubé.

PLATE 190. *Map of the Human Genome.* Celera Genomics, *Annotation of the Celera Human Genome Assembly.* Rockville, Md., 2001. Author's Collection.

PLATE 191. *Boston: Gay and Lesbian Residential Concentrations.* Tim Davis, "The Diversity of Queer Politics and the Redefinition of Sexual Identity and Community in Urban Spaces." In David Bell and Gill Valentine, eds., *Mapping Desire: Geographies of Sexualities.* London and New York, 1995. General Collections, HQ76.25. M36 1994, p. 292. Copyright © Tim Davis.

PLATE 192. *A Student's View of the World.* Piotz Puchowski. Lutz, Poland. From Thomas F. Saarinen, "Student Views of the World," in Downs and Stea, eds., *Image and Environment.* Chicago: Aldine, 1973. G&M, Saarinen Collection—Poland, Lutz.

PLATE 193. *Jefferson, Yoknapatawpha County, Mississippi.* From *Absalom, Absalom!* by William Faulkner, copyright © 1936 by William Faulkner and renewed 1964 by Estelle Faulkner and Jill Faulkner Summers. Used by permission of Random House, Inc. Rare Book, PS3511.A86.A65 1936.

PLATE 194. *View of the World from Ninth Avenue.* Saul Steinberg. Cover, *New Yorker* magazine, March 29, 1976. General Collections, AP2.N6763. Copyright © The Saul Steinberg Foundation/Artists Rights Society (ARS), New York.

PLATE 195, 196, AND 197. *2004 Election Results.* Michael Gastner, Cosma Shalizi, and Mark Newman. 2004. University of Michigan. Creative Common License http://www.personel.umich.edu/#mejn/election.

PLATE 198. *Time Zones in Siamese.* 19——. G&M, Title Collection—World—Time—19——.

PLATE 199. *Arc Map.* Stephen Eick, Bell Labs/Visual Insight. Naperville, Ill., 1999. Reprinted with permission of Lucent Technologies Inc./Bell Labs.

PLATE 200. *Map of Adventures for Boys and Girls.* Paul M. Paine, *Map of Adventures for Boys and Girls: Stories, Trails, Voyages, Discoveries, Explorations & Places to Read About.* New York, 1925. G&M, G3201.E65 1925.P3 MLC.

PLATE 201. *Book Festival Site Map.* 2004 National Book Festival, Library of Congress. Washington, DC, 2004.

PLATE 202. *Book Collection Locations.* Collections Management Division, Library of Congress. Washington, DC, 2002.

INDEX